CONFRONTATION ZONE

The Story of the 1989 U.S. Intervention Into Panama

Operation *Just Cause*

A Military Journal 1986-1990

by Rod Lenahan, Colonel USAF (Ret.)

NARWHAL PRESS
Charleston, South Carolina

ISBN: 1-886391-39-4 (paperback)
ISBN: 1-886391-38-6 (hardcover)

Library of Congress Catalog Card Number: 99-70127

LIBRARY CARD CATALOG CLASSIFICATIONS (suggested by the publisher): Air Force, U.S.A.; Army, U.S.A.; *Blind Logic* (code name, U.S. reconstitution of civil authority in post-Noriega Panama); *Blue Spoon* (code name, U.S. military operation in Panama); Bush, George, President, Foreign relations; Canal Zone, Panama; Central America, U.S. Military Intervention; Covert Operations, U.S.A.; Drugs, War on; *Elder Statesman* (code name, pre-intervention U.S. troop build-up in Panama); *Elaborate Maze* (code name, U.S. secret operation in Panama); Foreign Relations (U.S.A./Panama); JSOTF (U.S. Joint Special Operations Task Force); *Just Cause* (code name for U.S. military intervention in Panama); *Krystal Ball* (code name, U.S. reconstitution of civil authority in post-Noriega Panama); Lenahan, Rod, Col. USAF, Ret.; Marines, U.S.A.; Military Intervention, U.S. into Panama; Navy, U.S.A.; *Nimrod Dancer* (code name, U.S. troop deployment in Panama); Noriega, Manuel Antonio, General (military dictator, commander Panama Defense Force); Panama; Panama Canal Zone; Panama Defense Force (PDF); PDF (Panama Defense Force); *Post Time* (code name, pre-intervention U.S. troop build-up in Panama); *Operation Just Cause*, (code name for U.S. military intervention in Panama); U.S.A.; SEAL; Special Operations, U.S.; Special Forces, U.S.A.; U.S. Air Force; U.S. Army; U.S. Marines; U.S. Military; U.S. Military Intervention; U.S. Navy; U.S. SEALs; U.S. Special Forces; War on Drugs

COVER DESIGN: by E. Lee Spence and Bill Smith, photo of a civilian vehicle used and damaged in one of the running gunbattles with Marine armored combat vehicles in the background. Photo courtesy U.S. Southern Command Public Information Office. Back panel photo provides imagery of the H-hour attack on La Comandancia. Photo courtesy U.S. Army Institute of Military History.

TITLE PAGE: Close-up view of General Noriega's executive jet after the SEALs rendered it unflyable. Photo courtesy U.S. Southern Command Public Information Office.

Printed in the United States of America.

DEDICATION

To the soldiers, sailors, marines and airmen of Operation *Just Cause*, whose many sacrifices and often courageous deeds made them heroes, and to their families who endured hardships and in some cases the supreme loss for the sake of American ideals and commitments. Special dedication goes to the families of the twenty-three U.S. military personnel killed in Panama while participating in Operation *Just Cause* and the families of the nearly 300 Panamanians who lost their lives in the confrontation. The following is a list of the American military personnel who risked all and paid the ultimate price.

MARINE CORPS	**Military Unit**	**Hometown**
Cpl. Garreth C. Isaak	2nd Marine Div.	Greenville, SC
NAVY		
LTJG John Connors	Spec Warfare Gp.	Arlington, MA
BM1 Chris Tilghman	Spec Warfare Gp.	Kailua, HI
ENC Donald McFaul	Spec Warfare Gp.	Deschutes, OR
TM2 Issac G. Rodriguez III	Spec Warfare Gp	Missouri City, TX
ARMY		
Staff Sgt. Larry Banard	3/75th Rangers	Hallstead, PA
Pfc. Roy D. Brown Jr.	3/75th Rangers	Buena Park, CA
Pvt. Vance T. Coats	82nd Abn. Div.	Great Falls, MT
Spec. Jerry S. Daves	82nd Abn. Div.	North Carolina
Sgt. Michael A. Deblois	82nd Abn. Div.	Dubach, LA
Pfc. Martin D. Denson	82nd Abn. Div.	Abilene, TX
Pfc. William D. Gibbs	7th Inf. Div.	Marina, CA
Spec. Phillip S. Lear	2/75TH Rangers	Westminster, SC
Spec. Alejandro Manriquelozano	82nd Abn. Div.	Lauderhill, FL
Pfc. James W. Markwell	1/75th Rangers	Cincinnati, OH
Cpl. Ivan M. Perez	5th Inf. Div.	Pawtucket, RI
Pfc. John M. Price	2/75th Rangers	Conover, WI
Pfc. Scott L. Roth	89th MP Brigade	Killeen, TX
Pvt. Kenneth D. Scott	5th Inf. Div.	Princeton, WV
lst Lt. John R. Hunter	160th Aviation	Victor, MT
CWO2 Wilson B. Owens	160th Aviation	Myrtle Beach, SC
CWO2 Andrew P. Porter	7th Inf. Div.	Saint Clair, MI
Pvt. James A. Taber Jr.	82nd Abn. Div	Montrose, CO

ACKNOWLEDGMENTS

The author is deeply indebted to a score of people without whose help and assistance this effort could not have been accomplished. Among these is William Ormsby. My thanks for his unstinting help in providing a complete panorama of events in Panama as they were documented in the SOUTHCOM newspaper *Tropic Times* from 1986 through 1990.

Similar gratitude is expressed to Dolores De Mena, U.S. Army South Historian for her unending support. Also to my brother, Lawrence Lenahan who spent countless hours in the archives of the U.S. Army Military History Institute at Carlisle Barracks, PA, researching information and impressions captured in the institute's Oral History collection.

An equal amount of appreciation goes to another dozen officers and NCOs from all services who participated in Operation *Just Cause* and reviewed and commented on different sections of the manuscript.

Special thanks to three retired officers, Colonel Scott Crerar, U.S. Army, Captain R.A. Dalla Mura, U.S. Navy, and Colonel "Bob" of the Panama Canal Society, who gave of their time and talents in reviewing, commenting and refining the final drafts.

Thanks also go to the Isthmian Collectors Club (ICC) and the Society of Panamanian Memorabilia and Stamp Collectors for their courtesy in permiting the use of postcards from their collections.

Enduring gratitude to editor and publisher Dr. E. Lee Spence, the original finder of the *CSS Hunley.*

I apologize for any omissions or errors; they are mine. I regret that this manuscript does not give credit to all the Americans and Panamanians that contributed to the success of Operation *Just Cause*.

The Story of the 1989 U.S. Intervention into Panama

REVIEWS AND COMMENTS

U.S. Army Magazine

"Overshadowed in short order by the end of the Cold War and the massive incursion into the Persian Gulf, Operation *Just Cause* passed into history almost unnoticed. And yet, it was a real war, a demonstration of American military professionalism that portended the performance of Desert Storm and should furnish a paradigm for the future and an important study for any military historian. (*Confrontation Zone*) provides detailed and thorough coverage of the background, the prelude, the complex and comprehensive planning, the operations and the results achieved. If one wants a squad's, helicopter crew's or platoon leader's view of the action or a high-level discussion of the personalities, objectives and concerns associated with planning the mission, it is all here."

Frederick J. Kroesen, General, U.S. Army (Ret)
Association of the United States Army's Institute of Land Warfare

***NDIA- Special Operations Division* (newsletter)**

"*Confrontation Zone* breaks new ground by setting comprehensively covering all aspects of the operation from its inception to its successful conclusion. In the first two parts of the book, the reader is reminded that events didn't boil over suddenly as previous books have suggested, but rather percolated slowly and deliberately. Part Three/Four – Combat Operations – provides the multi-service elements both in planning and execution. You can follow all these operational events on maps and graphics that are provided, in addition to a glossary of terms and definitions that make a good Military History book a classic."

Dr. David Silbergeld, Commander, U.S. Navy (SEALS) (Ret)
Professor of History at the University of Pennsylvania

Former Commander U.S. Special Operations Command

"Operation *Just Cause* demonstrated to the world that the U.S. Military's efforts to revitalize its Special Operations Force was had been a smashing success. And of equal, if not greater significance was the total integration of conventional and unconventional forces in a swift and hard-hitting coup de main. Now for the first time we have a complete and well-balanced account of this short, but extraordinarily complex operation. In researching and writing *Confrontation Zone*, Rod Lenahan has produced the definitive work on Operation Just Cause."

James J. Lindsay, General, U.S. Army (Ret)

Former Director of Intelligence Strategic Air Command

"A great read. The story is put together and told well. The best accounting yet. Should be used at all Service Schools."

William Doyle, Major General, USAF (Ret)

CONFRONTATION ZONE

Former Chairman of the Joint Chiefs of Staff

"Once again, an outstanding job in telling a most interesting and accurate story of a complicated operation."

David C. Jones, General USAF (Ret)

***Officers Review,* Military Order of World Wars**

"Rod Lenahan follows his study of the Iran rescue raid, *Crippled Eagle*, with an exceptional in-depth study of the political and military events of Operation *Just Cause*. ...Tracing both the background and the decisions leading up to Operation Just Cause, *Confrontation Zone* describes in detail the joint contingency plan and how it evolved to meet a worsening political situation. ... this book should be mandatory reading in our staff and war colleges."

COMMENT ABOUT
CRIPPLED EAGLE
(*Crippled Eagle: A Historical Perspective of U.S. Special Operations, 1976-1996*, by Col. Rod Lenahan, Narwhal Press, 1998,)

***National Military Intelligence Association*, (quarterly, July 1998)**

"The *Eagle* tells the story from a perspective rarely seen, the actions of the 'hands-on-planners' and the JTF mission staff. Virtually all of its contents is derived from first hand accounts and active involvement in the events it portrays. ... (It) is unique and historically important because it tells the story as it happened. It does so without the use of political, military or academic hindsight designed to recast events or second guess the rationale for the decisions and actions of the players as they moved back and forth on the stage. The reader draws the conclusions and establishes the merit of the players from the circumstances and events of the time and their actions."

The Story of the 1989 U.S. Intervention into Panama

TABLE OF CONTENTS

PANAMA IN POSTCARDS

This set of pictures has been selected and adapted from post cards in the collections of the Isthmian Collectors Club (ICC, the society of Panamanian memorabilia and stamp collectors), as illustrative of how much of the world came to know Panama, and are used by their courtesy and permision. For purposes of clarity and to meet the requirements of this book, they have all have been converted to graytones, photo edited for clarity, cropped, reduced in size and reformatted.

USS Missouri cautiously approaching the first step of the Pedro Miguel Locks as seen from the Control House. – Photo by Leon Greene.

Panama: The Land Divided – The World United.

Thatcher Ferry Bridge, Miraflores Locks, Panama Canal.

Beautiful young ladies, dressed in Polleras and Montunas, colorful national costumes of Panama.

The Thatcher Ferry Bridge across the Panama Canal has a length of 6200 feet and is 200 feet above sea level. It allows an uninterrupted traffic between Panama City and the Interior of Panama, and is a vital link in the Inter-American Highway.

Macaw Parrot – Since the days of the pirates the colorful Macaw has been one of the most sought after parrots of the tropics. Native of several Central and South American countries, the various species are still found in abundance. Among the largest of parrots, they have a very long tail, a naked space around the eyes and a strong hooked bill sufficiently powerful to crack hard nuts.

Gaillard Cut through Continental Divide allowing waterway passage at 85 feet above sea level.

Night scene – Miraflores Locks, Panama Canal.

Goethals Memorial, Balboa, Canal Zone. Dedicated to the memory of Col. George W. Goethals, the symbolic 56-foot marble shaft represents the Continental Divide. Water pouring from basins on either side representing the locks, joins symbolically the waters of Gatun Lake with the Atlantic and Pacific Oceans. Facing the Prado, the Administration Building forms an impressive background.

Partial view of the City and the Bay of Panama.

National Sanctuary of Corazon de Maria, Panama City.

The Golden Altar, made of pure gold leaf over carved mahogany, was saved from destruction by Morgan's pirates in Old Panama in 1671 and transferred in 1677 by the Augustinian Fathers to its present site, the Church of San José in Panama City.

Marriott Caesar Park Hotel, Panama. Modern hotel facing the Pacific Ocean.

Pacific Entrance, Panama Canal, Rodman Naval Base, opposite Panama City.

Ruins of the Cathedral in Old Panama (Panama Viejo), surrounded by a beautiful park.

The famous "King's Bridge" – located near Old Panama (Panama Viejo) – on the trail to Cruces, over which the conquerors crossed, bearing their gold and treasures from the South, en route to Spain.

National Monument -- Panama – The Flat Arch of Santo Domingo built by the Spaniards in the year 1678 and destroyed by fire in 1761. It resists the inclemencies of the weather as proof of the faith of an Isthmus without volcanoes, which history and its geographical position have destined to be the Crossroads of the World.

The City of Panama, looking at Justice Promenade.

Aerial view of the Commandancia Complex.

2nd F. A. Ready to Fire. WWI style uniforms, circa 1941.

Fort Amador Parade Grounds and Barracks nestled at Pacific approach to the Canal. Circa 1941.

International Airport Omar Torrijos H., located outside of Panama City.

Madden Dam stores water supply for the efficient operation of the Panama Canal throughout the year.

Super Constellation at National Airport, Tocumen, Panama, 1st Pan Am flight into Panama.

VIP reception party held at National Airport, Tocumen, Panama, honoring arrival of the 1st Pan Am flight into Panama.

Duty Free Liquor Mart, Custom Gate.

CONFRONTATION ZONE

INTRODUCTION

Beginning in 1986, rumors of corruption within the Panamanian Defense Forces (PDF), its dominance over the life of Panamanians and the ruthlessness of its Commander, General Manuel Antonio Noriega, were among the first messages communicated to American military and civilian personnel when they arrived in Panama.

Most often repeated was the rumor, almost an allegation, that General Noriega was responsible for the murder of a political rival and former indirect associate, Dr. Hugo Spadafora. Spadafora was the only serious, charismatic Panamanian to openly challenge Noriega. Spadafora's decapitated body was found in 1984 stuffed in a U.S. mail sack in a roadside ditch near the Costa Rican border. The second "revelation" was that the Panamanian national elections of 1984 had been manipulated to ensure the Noriega/PDF candidate was elected. The third was that it would probably be necessary to bribe some PDF personnel during the process of getting your car inspected.

You were also told that the Traffic Police were quick to stop you for a driving infraction, and just as quick to settle the matter of the "fine" on the spot without issuing a traffic citation. This forewarning often became a first-hand experience within a few days or weeks, and was frequently experienced several times in a two or three year tour. The reality of this petty graft and the many visual indicators of a police presence tended to reinforce the acceptance of the larger allegations and rumors.

A walk around Panama City in the mid to late 1980's also quickly convinced the newcomer that the PDF, in all its various functions, was everywhere and was certainly the most singularly visible presence in Panamanian society. This was the environment in June 1986, when I reported for duty at U.S. Southern Command (USSOUTHCOM) Headquarters, Quarry Heights, Panama.

I was to be Director of Operational Intelligence, which translated to involvement in virtually every aspect of the command's intelligence structure, except long-term plans, programs and budgeting actions.

The SOUTHCOM Commander at the time was General Jack Galvin, a fluent Spanish speaker, very well-versed in Latin American affairs and very much the Statesman-Soldier. During my inbrief with General Galvin, he said the command was very busy, somewhat under strength for its growing responsibilities, and that the next few years were likely to hold some interesting challenges for the United States and its relations with the nations of Latin America. General Galvin was proven to be correct.

The American military operation that began on December 19, 1989 in the Republic of Panama had as its purposes the capture and extradition of General Manuel Noriega to the United States and the neutralization of the Panama Defense Force (PDF) as a dominant force in Panamanian society. The roots of this military action stretched back into a political quagmire that began more than three years earlier.

This reconstruction is an attempt to capture the interplay between political rhetoric and the evolution of military preparations for the inevitable collision. The document has been compiled from a wide range of open sources, both media and official material. Most of the material came from the participants, not from third-hand observations, speculation or hindsight.

An additional thread of continuity has been aided by my experience in Panama on the U.S. Southern Command staff in 1986 and 1987 but later in 1988 when I served as the J-2 for the initial Special Operations Joint Task Force. This task force was created in March 1988 when the Department of Defense (DOD) began planning for the possibility of a confrontational contingency in Panama.

The many cases of joint planning that preceded the operation, together with cooperation and teamwork that was demonstrated during the execution phase of *Just Cause,* set a bench mark. Hopefully, these efforts, once documented, will aid in the further development of the spirit of teamwork that always has been needed on the battlefield, but often has been lacking in planning, where it really can make a difference.

Operation *Just Cause*, like most military operations, was neither an impetuous act, nor a knee jerk response to a series of isolated precursor events. Virtually every major military operation has been a product of the months, years and decades of history that preceded it. Often times it is important to understand that history before one can understand the logic of the military actions and begin to judge their immediate effect and aftermath.

This is a story compiled from many viewpoints, each essentially correct, yet often incomplete in some way. When taken together they provide a mosaic of competing national wills and the stories of the soldiers, sailors, airmen, marines and civilians that were called upon to act above and beyond.

CONFRONTATION ZONE

PRELUDE

The first time I crossed paths with Manuel Noriega was in Nicaragua in the spring of 1985. It was early in the morning and I had just landed at Sandino Airport on the outskirts of Managua after a short flight from Costa Rica. Upon deplaning, I noticed a red carpet was being unrolled, and a military honor guard and band were being mustered, awaiting the arrival of an unknown dignitary. We were directed into the terminal through a side door and quickly passed through customs, immigration and luggage screening. I surmised the arrival was at least an hour away if the Nicaragua military were anything like their counterparts around the world. Better to be early and wait than be late. Although my curiosity was aroused, I made the judgment that my time could be better spent. Anyway, with this much visibility attending the arrival, I would probably learn who it was within a few hours. I picked up my rental car, a beat-up Russian Lada, and headed into downtown Managua, passing many of the landmarks I had studied before leaving the States.

This was my first, but not last, visit to Nicaragua or Central America. I was to come to know portions of the region quite well during the next five years. I had been assigned to 12th Air Force as the Director of Intelligence a few months earlier, and during my inbrief with the commander he showed me a message designating Twelfth Air Force as the air contingency planning element for the United States Southern Command.

SOUTHCOM, as it was referred to informally, had the responsibility for DOD contingency planning throughout Central and South America, which included Nicaragua with its Marxist-oriented revolutionary government. Nicaragua had been of concern to the United States since 1978 when Eden Pastora, also known as Commander Zero, took control of the National Palace and held it, and more than a hundred people, captive for 24 hours. The concern heightened when the Sandinista revolutionary movement toppled the Somoza regime in the spring and summer of 1979. The level of U.S. concern increased again under the Reagan administration because of the Marxist revolutionary nature of the new Nicaraguan leadership and its continued active support of the Marxist guerrilla movements in neighboring El Salvador.

The Reagan administration began supporting the 1980 home grown Nicaraguan Counter-Revolutionary movement (the Contras) philosophically and economically shortly after taking office in 1981. However, by the summer and fall of 1984, Nicaragua had risen higher on the list of countries of concern to the White House, the State Department, DOD and SOUTHCOM. This change in its status was prompted by its stated intent to add fighter aircraft and radar guided surface to air missile defense systems to its already substantial and growing inventory of ground weapons.

It was this possibility, and the confirmation that preparatory work for the air influx had been ongoing since 1982, that initiated a U.S. political campaign to dissuade the Soviet Union, Cuba, and Nicaragua from fulfilling this aspect of Nicaragua's 1980 military development plan. Simultaneously, U.S. military contingency planning was undertaken should the weapons systems be introduced. The political campaign succeeded. The delivery of surface to air missile (SAM) systems was cancelled and the Nicaraguan Air Force received Soviet attack and troop transport helicopters in lieu of fighter aircraft.

Given the increasing size of the resistance (Contra) forces, now in the thousands, up from a few hundred in 1980, the change in the aircraft type was militarily sound as well as politically astute. The helicopter fleet provided the Nicaraguan high command a more lethal, flexible and potent military instrument with greater mobility and firepower than a squadron of MIG-21 fighters would have. Thus, American military contingency planning continued and had to be modified. Revisions in contingency planning are normal and are accomplished in tandem and tempo with the change in the situation or military balance.

During my first trip to Nicaragua, I visited the American Embassy and given a quick area orientation around Managua by the assistant U.S. Defense Attaché. We spent that day touring the countryside and visiting the numerous Nicaguaran military installations in the area. That evening as we returned to the Embassy compound and were gravitating toward the Marine House for a cold beer, the marines were notified that an unidentified male was reported to be moving along the perimeter fence in the back of the compound, carrying a bag of some sort. The attaché and I immediately became part of the reaction element. We drew the duty of climbing to the top of the very steep hill that dominated the back of the compound. Meanwhile, the marines headed out in two teams along the base of the hill to check the fence line.

Since the attaché knew the real estate and the various landmarks, he was carrying the binoculars while I was relegated to toting an athletic bag which contained an UZI sub-machine gun and six ammo magazines. When we reached the top, we could see most of vegetation-encroached fence line and could not detect any movement other than the marines. After a thirty-minute patrol, the marines failed to find the alleged intruder or any signs that the fence had been scaled or penetrated and they retired to the Marine House to attack the Budweisers they had left standing on the bar.

The attaché and I remained on top of the hill. He showed me a series of overlook points from which he could observe many of the nearby military installations. Our visual tour was interrupted by the sound of approaching helicopters.

Within seconds, two Soviet-made whirly birds, an Mi-8 and an Mi-24, came into sight from behind the hill mass to the north heading south on a sweeping arc. One was the lead, the other in trail and slightly above, providing cover for the lead. As they passed abreast of the Embassy hill only three hundred feet away, it was possible with the binoculars to see the flight crew and some of the occupants. This was the second time my path and General Noriega's had crossed within the past thirty-six hours. We surmised the choppers were coming back from a VIP visit to the artillery garrison a few miles north and were enroute back to Sandino airport. The following day the Managua newspapers headlined the Panamanian leader's reception, visit and departure, and included a center spread confirming the helicopter's occupants and at least part of the itinerary.

I departed Nicaragua two days later and arrived at Torrijos International Airport in Panama about noon, processed through the chaos and jostling of Panamanian customs which made the paper stamping and hidden camera routine at Sandino seem highly efficient. During this brief eight-hour stay, I had a meeting with the new Commander of the 24th Composite Wing at Howard AFB, a sub-element of 12th Air Force. The commander was a professional counterpart and friend from our previous assignments. He had been the Deputy Wing Commander at the Tactical Fighter Weapons Center at Nellis AFB, while I was the commander of the supporting Intelligence Group. After a three hour whirlwind tour of the key U.S. military installations, we headed for his government quarters.

Like most of the family quarters at Howard, the unit was built on concrete supports that raised the house seven to eight feet above the ground. This unit was one of several located on one of the green covered hills that surrounded the flat main base and runway area on three sides. From the dining room window you could see the Bridge of the Americas and slightly to the left, the top of Ancon Hill, and to the right a few of the skyscrapers that pinpointed the invisible location of Panama City. Little did I know at the time, that in a year, I would be living on Ancon Hill and be in a position to observe the twists and turns of U.S.-Panamanian relations. This would include meeting General Noriega on several occasions, interpreting for him on another, and in participating in orienting him and members of his staff in crisis management procedures. Neither did I anticipate at the time that I would also be participating in some of the contingency planning that preceded Operation *Just Cause* and his ultimate demise.

FOREWORD

OPERATION *JUST CAUSE*
D-DAY / H-HOUR PLUS 6:30

Shortly after 7:30 AM on D-Day, six and a half hours into Operation *Just Cause*, a USAF C-141 from Fort Bragg landed at Howard Air Force Base in Panama. Its personnel manifest included the XVIII Airborne Corps Judge Advocate General (JAG) and additional G-3 Operations staff to assist in manning the JTF SOUTH/XVIII Corps Operations Center. As the tail ramp opened, the new arrivals looked out to see the Joint Casualty Collection Point. To most of the viewers the sight reminded them of a MASH (Mobile Army Surgical Hospital). They could see immediately that the medics were already treating soldiers. This was a new experience to most of the group. Only a few were Vietnam-era veterans exposed to similar sights. The reality of the mission and Operation *Just Cause* was quickly brought home. As they unloaded and waited for their ground transportation, they saw helicopters and C-130s transports landing, and young men in uniforms similar to theirs carefully being carried off in stretchers and quickly taken into the medical classification area. Looking in the direction of Panama City, they could see smoke rising into the sky from the remnants of the Comandancia and the burned-out remains of Barrio Chorrillo. Some wondered what had prompted this violent confrontation between the soldiers of two nations that at one time had been allies. Others wondered what awaited them, and a few wondered where was the man that was the focus of this effort. Some knew part of the story. CONFRONTATION ZONE tells the rest of the story.

One of the civilian vehicles used by the PDF and damaged in a running gunbattle. Marine armored combat vehicles can be seen in the background. Photo courtesy US Southern Command Public Information Office.

The Story of the 1989 U.S. Intervention into Panama

OPERATION *JUST CAUSE*

THE U.S. INTERVENTION IN PANAMA

PART ONE:
HISTORY AND BACKGROUND

Part One includes four chapters that set the stage and provide the backdrop for the balance of the *Just Cause* story. These chapters are presented from the perspective of an American living in Panama during the turbulent years of 1986 through 1989. The first two chapters provide a geographic and historic review of Panama and its evolving independent nationalistic relationship with the United States. Chapter Three provides a profile of the primary reason for the planning and execution of *Just Cause* – Manuel Antonio Noriega – while Chapter Four reviews the rhetoric drumbeat and political bombast that laid the emotional foundation for the evolution and escalation of the inevitable confrontation that followed in the "Zone." A selection of maps is provided at pages 310-331.

CHAPTER ONE
SETTING THE STAGE

Panama City, with a population of more than 600,000, was and is a bustling commercial environment with dense vehicle and foot traffic.The narrow downtown streets and major arteries are very congested during the morning and evening rush hours. The most colorful symbol of Panama traffic is the fleet of "Chivas" that dash up and down the main streets with their horns honking and Salsa music blaring. A Chiva is a privately owned and ornately painted bus that careens around the main streets of downtown Panama City racing from bus stop to bus stop in an effort to beat a competitor to the next cluster of potential passengers.

The city is composed of a collection of neighborhoods strung out in an ever-widening band from the edge of the old Canal Zone eastward for a distance of six miles along the Pacific shoreline. The metropolitan commercial sector gradually fades into a string of small suburban clusters along the main roads that eventually lead to the international airport complex located ten miles to the east.

Although the Canal is advertised as the major national attraction and a key source of revenue, it was the commercial possibilities, including the "easy" banking laws and the freedom of international trade and export, that attracted the real money. The number and the size of the banks in Panama is a surprise to the newcomer and the visitor alike. More than eighty international banks had offices in the city and more than a dozen had their own tall modern skyscrapers. In addition, many foreign and U.S. ships carried Panamanian registration as a matter of economic advantage because the lower safety standards and crew wages reduced the operating cost.

The Panamanian monetary structure is similar to the United States in that the U.S. dollar is the principal means of exchange. Panamanians of all social and economic levels are alert and eager to earn a dollar. This may mean cleaning your windshield while you are stopped at a traffic light, or salvaging, repairing and reselling a discarded air conditioning unit, or being an honest and earnest worker or business person.

The varied neighborhoods of Panama City begin at the foot of Ancon Hill near the no longer existing Canal Zone demarcation line. Their line of march begins with one of the oldest neighborhoods, Barrio Chorrillo. Largely composed of old wooden buildings, their style is reminiscent of the New Orleans French quarter. These ancient relics of the French presence and the French attempt to build the Canal housed the poorest of the poor. The Panamanian government was the landlord and, due to the dilapidated condition of the structures and the economic status of the inhabitants, no rent was charged.

The dominant structures that marked this neighborhood were the headquarters compound of the Panama Defense Force (La Comandancia), and an adjacent sixteen-story high-rise apartment building where many married lower and middle grade Panama Defense Force personnel and government employee's families lived. The Comandancia was built in 1935 as the central police headquarters. Originally, it was a single building, looking somewhat like a beached paddle wheeler with its curved ends and balcony overhangs running its total circumference. Beginning in the late sixties, its appearance and function began to change. The original low knee-high-exterior walls were heightened and extended, and other buildings added until the complex encompassed several city blocks and nearly a dozen buildings ringed and joined by a wall grown to seven feet in height. During the intervening years, it changed names and significance from a benign police structure, to the headquarters of the La Guardia National, and eventually to the headquarters of Panamanian Defense Forces.

The national prison, called the Carcel Modelo, was located less than two blocks from the Comandancia. This multi-storied building with cells ranging from the basement to the third floor was also set within its own walled compound. The streets in this part of Panama City were among the narrowest, and many were "Una Via - One Way" out of necessity.

Only a few short blocks north of Chorrillo and neighboring Barrio San Felipe lay Avenida Central and Avenida 4 de Julio. These two bustling thoroughfares are the "main streets" of downtown and the retail centers of this end of town. They also are major feeder arteries to the Plaza Cinco de Mayo area where political rallies were often held.

Immediately abutting Chorrillo to the east is an upgraded working class neighborhood, San Felipe. It consists of stone two- and three-story buildings with a mix of family businesses and a scattering of small iron balconies. If it were not for the tropical setting, San Felipe might pass as an old world middle class neighborhood. San Felipe includes the old colonial Spanish area, a raised sea wall and the dungeons of the old fort. The architecture of this neighborhood presents the look of a sedate European village to include the presence of a gourmet French restaurant and a broad promenade atop the old sea wall, which juts out into the Pacific waters of the Bay of Panama.

A small plaza dedicated to the many people of various nationalities who have contributed to the Republic of Panama is set protectively within the raised promenade. The Justice Palace, with a modest but new small-sized law center is adjacent to the plaza. A set of old interlocking three-story masonry structures, which appear to be one, rise above the promenade on the land side and house a collection of law offices and private apartments. At the end of this labyrinth of white stucco is an old, and at one time exclusive, swimming club taken over as a PDF Recreation Center some years back. Within a two-block walk is the National Opera House, and two blocks further, facing the bay, lies the low, unpretentious, gray, masonry Presidential Palace, encompassing a full city block.

From here the Bay curves inward, forming a crescent shoreline. Balboa Avenue, a divided boulevard, originates a few blocks east of the Presidential Palace and carries traffic from the old sections of the city to the newer and much more affluent neighborhoods of the upper class Panamanians, international professionals, and Americans who could afford to pay the high rent.

The American Embassy complex sits at a mid-point along the boulevard facing the bay. A monument to Vasco de Balboa, the first Spanish explorer who set foot on the isthmus, and succeeded in crossing it is perched on the bay side of the boulevard. The prestigious Panama City Yacht Club is a few blocks further on.

Three blocks inland a patchwork quilt of pleasant residential neighborhoods with a combination of apartment buildings and private homes merges with the bay side affluence and houses a major segment of the working middle class. The main arteries that support this corridor are Via España and Simon Bolivar, which parallel each other through overlapping residential neighborhoods. Further inland, Tumba Muerto, a third major artery that skirts the edge of the build-up area provided the best and fastest traffic route from the American military complexes west of the city to the international airport twelve miles to the east.

Less than a mile east of the Yacht Club is the very affluent neighborhood of Paitilla. Its cluster of thirty or so modern and fashionable high-rise buildings dominate the skyline of the hilly promontory. The contemporary and very upscale Union Club anchors the east end, echoing the affluence of the area. A small general aviation airfield, originally called

Marcos Gelabert, but now referred to as Paitilla airfield, sits just beyond the Union Club.

The towering Caesar Marriott hotel, known for its great food, fabulous Sunday buffet and overflowing dessert table, is located about two miles farther eastward, to the left of the shore road. Adjacent to the Marriott is the massive ATLAPA National Convention Center, which derives its name from the acronym for Atlantic and Pacific. A short distance beyond is Jimmy's, a Panamanian restaurant with an outdoor patio that is a favorite eating place for both Panamanians and Americans. Continuing another two miles, one finds the ruins of Panama Viejo (Old Panama). This is the site of the original Spanish settlement established in 1519.

The walls of the old cathedral bell tower rise over the ruins. In addition to the tower, most of the walls of the nunnery remain standing, as do some of the walls of the main government building and market. Less than a hundred yards away, a stone bridge built around 1600 still stands. An area adjacent to the site of the ruins was later chosen to be the home of a Panamanian cavalry unit, and a garrison was built beside the old ruins backing up to the bay.

The ruins are all that is left of the original settlement that was put to the torch when Henry Morgan, the English pirate, attacked it more than three hundred years ago. When Morgan began his attack, the people of Panama Viejo fought a delaying and diversionary action while relocating to the area now called San Felipe. In addition to their worldly goods, they moved a gold altar. Once at San Felipe, everything of value, such as the altar, was hidden and covered with mud. When Morgan finally reached San Felipe, he found nothing of value and left. Subsequently, the Spanish built a fort around the new location, a portion of which includes the still standing sea wall. Although rebuilt several times in the intervening 300 years, the last time in the early 1900s, it retains an Old World charm and provides a gentle breeze.

From Panama Viejo, the shore road, alternately called Via or Paseo Del Cincuestenario, turns inland and runs north through several scattered residential areas for four miles. It dead-ends into the last of the three east/west roads that lead to the international airport eight miles to the east. For more than forty years, the intersection had been marked by a tall statue of President Roosevelt. The statue was pulled down in 1987 as part of a demonstration of anti-American feelings and unceremoniously hauled away in the back of a municipal dump truck.

Without traffic, the trip from Quarry Heights, the SOUTHCOM Headquarters on Ancon Hill, to the airport can be made in twenty-five minutes. However, during the morning and evening rush hour, it routinely takes more than an hour, particularly if one is trapped in the flood of pedestrians, bicyclists, honking taxis and crowded buses as one passes through the congested suburb of San Miguelito midway along the route. A PDF barracks, known as Tinajitas, sat on one of the higher hills of the San Miguelito area.

The International Airport is essentially two complexes in one. The "new" civilian terminal, named after Omar Torrijos, is the closer to the city and the shoreline, and sits between a large parking lot and the "new" international runway, capable of handling virtually any passenger or transport aircraft. The old runway and its support complex, known by its original name, Tocumen, was the home of the small Panamanian Air Force. The old runway lies parallel to, but is offset a half a mile inland from, the newer civilian runway. The military complex included hangars, barracks, dining hall, an officer's club and maintenance facilities.

Approximately twelve miles beyond the airfield complex lay the sprawling PDF Army complex known as Fort Cimarron. The camp was the home of the fighting core of the PDF Army, Battalion 2000. The Battalion was the only "large" unit in the PDF, numbering in excess of 600 soldiers. Most other PDF army elements were company-sized units with a strength of approximately 200. Battalion 2000 took its name from its purpose; the assumption of the defense of the Canal on January 1, 2000, the day after the United States was to turn over total management of the Canal to the Republic of Panama. One of the battalion mottos, and of the PDF as a whole, that was often publicly displayed was "Control in 2000 and not a step backwards."

The weather in Panama is similar in many respects to central Florida, with mild temperatures in the winter, although it is still easy to perspire during midday with any kind of exertion. Rarely does the temperature drop below 75 degrees, except high in the mountains. Although it rains throughout the year, the heaviest rain occurs from May through July. Regardless of the time of year, the tides in Panama Bay and the Pacific approaches to the Canal are phenomenal in their rate of change. The level of the water can change as much as fifteen feet in some locales, and the distance between the high water mark and the lowest ebb of the tide can be more than a quarter of a mile. This is particularly noticeable along the Panama Bay where miles of mud flats lie exposed and appear deceptively solid to the eye at low tide, only to be completely covered with several feet of surging ocean water in less than ninety minutes.

Vegetation grows extremely quickly during the rainy season. The underbrush is at its thickest early in the year. The jungle can be found only a few feet from any built up area. And if not cut back regularly it can quickly encroach on an unattended area. Most trees are very tall and block views that were originally unobstructed during the days of the Canal building. The best example is the restricted view from the headquarters of the U.S. Southern Command at Quarry Heights which sat halfway up Ancon Hill and facing the Canal. The surrounding trees have grown to a height of 60 to 80 feet. They have reduced the previous unobstructed panoramic view of the Pacific approach, the Bridge of the Americas, Balboa Harbor, and the Miraflores Lock to a narrow vista of the Bridge of the Americas and this visible from only one point. In the other, landward direction, the surrounding vegetation severely restricts any view of Panama City to the tops of the taller buildings and a limited view of parts of Chorillo.

"Ancon," which means anchorage or roadstead, dates back to 1545 when a Peruvian explorer, Gonzalo Pizarro, who, seeking to gain control of the isthmus, sent two military expeditions to the area. One landed at the original city site, Panama Viejo (Old Panama), and pillaged it. The second landed at the base of the tallest hill in a sheltered cove and established a small presence, referred to simply as Ancon.

One hundred and thirty years later, in the wake of the destruction of Panama Viejo, by Morgan the pirate, the "new" city of Panama was laid out along the ocean front bay beginning at the base of Ancon Hill. Two hundred years later, the French Canal Company selected the Ancon hillside overlooking the anchorage as the site for its hospital. When the Americans came to build the Canal, they began calling the cove Port Ancon, which eventually gave way to Balboa Port, the Pacific entrance to the Panama Canal. A giant Panamanian flag flies 24 hours a day from the crown of the Ancon Hill at a dominating height of 654 feet.

Ancon Hill is one of two hills that sit between Panama City and the port of Balboa. The other hill is the smaller Sosa Hill that was used as a communications relay site. Balboa sits at the base of these two natural high points along the Canal breakwater.

Balboa is a quiet, picturesque bedroom community of white stucco buildings with red tile roofs and palm lined streets. The township was planned and built as a self-contained American community with churches, banks, theaters, commissary, a swimming club and schools. It was the de facto "capital" of the Canal Zone until the Torrijos-Carter Treaties were ratified in 1978. In the early eighties, Balboa became a mixed Panamanian-American community, however, most of its inhabitants continued to be Panama Canal Commission (PCC) employees and their families. The PCC, a joint American-Panamanian civil institution, replaced the American-owned Panama Canal Company with the implementation of the Torrijos-Carter Treaties.

The PCC was created to operate and maintain the Canal as a non-political entity. The PCC was governed by a nine-person board composed of five Americans and four Panamanians. The day-to-day executive who reported to the PCC Board of Commissioners held the title of "Administrator". An American citizen had held this position since the Commission was created. However, this was due to change on January 1, 1990 when a Panamanian citizen would assume the position while the numerical composition of the board would remain the same.(Five Am,ericans and four Panamanians). Next to the American military presence, the PCC constituted the single largest American population in Panama. PCC employees were long-term dedicated professionals. A majority of the American PCC employees had become de facto Panamanians. They constituted a separate faction and different mind set from the American military presence. Many had worked for the PCC for 16-20 years and raised their families in "the Zone" and resented the dissolution of their world caused by the Torrijos-Carter Treaties.

Quarry Heights acquired its name during the building of the Canal. Originally, the site was known as the Ancon Hill Quarry. The original quarry was carved out of the hill beginning in February 1909. The site yielded more than three million cubic yards of rock for use in the construction of the Canal. The quarry operation was closed down in October 1914, and the remaining plateau, with its then unobstructed view of the Canal, became a favorite recreation and picnic area for the American community.

In mid-1915 a unified U.S. Military Headquarters was organized and originally located in the village of Ancon. In early 1916, the headquarters known as "Provost Guard Camp," Balboa Heights, Panama Canal Zone was relocated to the former quarry location. In November of the same year, the new compound was named Quarry Heights and designated as the site for the new Joint Command headquarters (one of the first U.S. joint commands).

It was assumed at the time that the site was not large enough for a permanent headquarters and consequently all construction was to be of a temporary nature. This "temporary outlook" involved the dismantling (and movement) of some two dozen large wooden frame houses from the Canal construction sites where they were originally built (as temporary quarters to house senior officials for the length of the job) and their reassembly piece by numbered piece at the new, albeit temporary, command site.

The first and largest house to be moved had been the quarters of George Goethals, the first Governor of the Canal Zone. This house was located slightly lower than the military compound and overlooked Panama City. Its size dwarfed all others, and it is still the residence of the Administrator of the Panama Canal Commission. In 1986, sixteen of the original "run of the job" houses were still in use as family quarters for members of the SOUTHCOM staff. It turned out that because the Canadian pine used in their construction is a very hard and termite-resistant strain, most of the houses endured largely untouched for more than 80 years.

The SOUTHCOM compound, less than seven acres in size, shares the hill with the Panama Canal Commission (PCC), the Gorgas Army Hospital, and a large PCC housing area. The compact compound sat on the backside of the hill facing south toward the Bridge of the Americas and the Canal approach. The massive stone Panama Canal Commission building is lower on the hill and overlooks Balboa Harbor and the entrance to the Miraflores Locks. The Gorgas Hospital, a large, rambling, multilevel complex completes the list of the major tenants of Ancon Hill. The hospital sits at the lowest point and merges with a former Canal housing area and the outskirts of Panama City.

Balboa Harbor lays on the opposite side of Ancon hill and is the site of several large piers and docks where ships from around the world unload their cargo, and where shipboard tourists passing through the Canal on gleaming cruise liners disembark to visit Panama City for a few hours. Several PDF patrol boats were normally berthed at Pier Eight. In addition to housing PCC operations, Balboa is home to the American High School, several American churches, and a large YMCA facility which sat less than 200 feet from a PDF police station and the Headquarters of the Department of National Investigations (DENI), the Panamanian equivalent of the FBI. A large Esso fuel storage complex sits at the far end of Balboa, nestled very near (almost underneath) the city approach to the Bridge of the Americas. The Bridge of Americas can be pictured as the cross tie in the letter "H" arching over the Canal and linking the two continents with American military facilities strung out along both banks of the Canal forming the two vertical lines.

Aside from Gorgas Hospital and Quarry Heights, Albrook Air Force Station is the closest U.S. military facility to Panama City. The Albrook fence line began less than a half mile from Balboa High School which sat at the base of Ancon Hill. The front gate of Albrook faced Gaillard highway across which lay Diablo Heights, a mixed American-Panamanian housing area largely, but not exclusively, populated by PCC employees. Albrook's 6,000-foot runway has been closed for years, and in fact lies on the Panamanian side of a cyclone fence which delineates the American-Panamanian areas of control. The Panamanian Defense Force (PDF) maintained a small military-police presence and a flight of helicopters on their side. One of the former hangars on the PDF side was used as a holding warehouse for incoming and outgoing American family household shipments. In 1986, the American side of the runway area included a handful of transport aircraft, F-5 jet trainers and helicopters that were used to train Latin American aviation technicians and mechanics attending the Inter-American Air Forces Academy located at Albrook. The other principal function of the Air Station was to serve as a giant housing area and community support center for American Air Force personnel and their families. A magnificent view of the Panama City skyline could be seen from the high ground overlooking the old runway.

The former Albrook runway provided an open area and buffer zone between the American community of Curundu and the working class *barrios* of Panama City. The rear perimeter of Albrook mates with the boundary of Fort Clayton and provides easy access between the two complexes and the nearby Curundi housing area, home to a large number of army families.

American military bases and a series of small specialty facilities, such as the U.S. Army Tropical Disease Center, the Veterinary Clinic, and the Army Commissary complex are located to the north between Albrook and Clayton. These facilities constituted a series of isolated pockets along the two-lane Gaillard Highway that paralleled the Canal on the east side. Before the Torrijos-Carter Treaties, these facilities were within the Canal Zone in what used to be a contiguous chain of American control. The fence that delineated the former Canal Zone boundary was taken down in 1979 as a provision in the treaties. By 1986 these facilities were separate entities connected by the Panamanian-policed Gaillard Highway.

Ft. Clayton was the largest and most heavily populated U.S. Army Post in Panama. It housed the Army component headquarters, U.S. Army South and the 193rd Infantry Brigade, plus a host of other units. The 193rd Infantry Brigade was the principal American combat force in Panama. Although the post has several large family housing areas, a good percentage of Fort Clayton's married personnel live off post in Panama City or in nearby, but unprotected housing areas, such as Diablo Heights and Curundu.

The main gate of Fort Clayton is located about three and a half miles north of Quarry Heights/Balboa along Gaillard Highway, and faces the Miraflores Locks and a swing bridge over the Canal. The bridge, a combination road and rail bridge, remains closed to traffic most of the time. However, it is occasionally used by military convoys from Clayton to cross the Canal enroute to training areas and firing ranges on the west side, thus avoiding the congestion of both Balboa and the fringes of Panama City. The swing bridge is the only alternate way of crossing the Canal on the Pacific side of the isthmus (other than the Bridge of the Americas) with the notable exception of swimming or taking a boat across.

Less than a half a mile south of the Bridge of the Americas (in the opposite direction of Albrook and Clayton) lies Fort Amador. The Amador complex sits at the base of a peninsula that defines the east side of the Pacific approach to the Canal. Amador was the site of the headquarters of the U.S. Navy Forces in Panama, and the Panamanian Military Headquarters for the Joint Committee for Cooperation and Defense of the Canal.

Technically, this Panamanian headquarters commanded the military units of the PDF while the Panamanian national headquarters, the Comandancia, located in downtown Panama City, controlled all other elements of the PDF. In reality, General Noriega, who maintained offices in both complexes, was the commander of the total PDF structure. The PDF was a colloquia of interrelated functions managed by a core of classmates and professional year groups within the PDF officer corps. This included the Police, Customs, Treasury, and Forestry forces as well as the Army, Navy, and Air Force contingents.

Although Amador did not house any U.S. Army combat units, it was simultaneously home to more than 260 American families and 300 military members of the PDF. The PDF personnel included a military police platoon and four platoons of Army infantry, plus a Navy honor guard unit. These six units were billeted in a row of two-story masonry barracks adjacent to the Committee headquarters. The barracks lay directly opposite a row of the American family housing buildings separated by an open parade ground less than 100 yards wide. The memorial mausoleum housing the remains of General Omar Torrijos, the modern-day hero of Panamanian nationalism, sits on the Panamanian side near the end of the PDF barracks.

The U.S. Navy headquarters was set at a 45-degree angle to the north, less than 300 feet from the heavily-fenced Combined Headquarters building and within 700 feet of the PDF barracks. An unguarded American housing area was just outside and to the left of the jointly manned Amador front gate, with its Panamanian counterpart housing area across the street.

A narrow man-made causeway links Fort Amador to a series of small islands. This causeway extends more than a mile into Panama Bay. Until the late seventies, the causeway and the three islands were known as Fort Grant, and were under U.S. military authority. Control was transferred to the PDF Navy in the early 1980's as a result of the Torrijos-Carter treaties. The narrow causeway and the islands combine to separate the Pacific Ocean approach to the Canal from the open expanses of Panama Bay.

The first of the islands (Naos) was used by the Smithsonian Institute as a research site; however, the far end of the island houses a World War II bunker and an old coastal defense site, which is limited to PDF access exclusively. The second island (Perico) was the site of a World War II observation post and a 1940's style clubhouse. The last and largest of the three is Flamenco Island. This steep and rocky hill mass was the location of a major WW I and WW II coastal artillery battery and a large munitions magazine storage. After the PDF gained control, Flamenco became the garrison home of the PDF Special Operations and Antiterrorist Unit (UESAT). Personnel of this unit were highly trained and capable of both SEAL and Special Forces direct action type missions.

Traveling back along the causeway toward Amador, the full profile of the Bridge of the Americas fills the skyline. This high-arched steel bridge spans the Canal and links North and South America. The bridge has a unique roadway pattern, with each approach having two lanes dedicated for traffic climbing its span and one lane for those descending. The roadway is part of the Pan-American Highway network. Normally, several PDF police sedans or motorcycles could be seen parked on the "American" side at a scenic overlook watching for speeders or taking a rest break. The Panama City side did not have such a vantage point. These same PDF police units normally patrolled the next several miles of the "Inter-America," which included turnoffs to several U.S. military complexes.

Rodman Naval Station is the first complex. In addition to administration, maintenance and housing facilities, the station included three deep water piers and a small special boat unit and was home to the U.S. staffed Inter-American Naval School for small boat training and engine overhaul. The station also included a large, underground, munitions storage complex built into the side of a 300 foot hill which bears the name San Juan Hill.

Immediately adjoining Rodman is the USMC Barracks which housed Marine families and a company-sized guard force to provide guards for the naval station itself, the adjoining Arraijan Navy Fuel Storage Complex, as well as a radio intelligence facility at Galeta Island across the isthmus near Colon.

Just a hundred yards short of the second (i.e., Marine) entrance to Rodman, a sign identifies the turnoff to Howard Air Force Base, Fort Kobbe (an Army installation), and a Navy Housing area called Farfan. These three installations are contiguous and with the Arraijan fuel storage area essentially constitute one giant U.S. military reservation. The focal point of much of the Air Force and Army activity is the Howard runway and its adjacent parking and aircraft maintenance facilities. The single runway is capable of landing virtually any U.S. military aircraft; however, the small parking area severely curtails the number of aircraft normally accommodated at any one time. The typical Air Force contingent was six National Guard fighter aircraft (on a rotational tour for gunnery and bombing practice at the nearby ranges), a small detachment of rescue helicopters, and a small collection of transient USAF transports.

The Army combat presence at Fort Kobbe included a helicopter battalion, an artillery battery, a battalion of airborne infantry, plus a detachment of fixed wing Army C-12 Utility turboprop aircraft. All of these Army forces were elements of the 193rd Infantry Brigade headquartered at Fort Clayton. The back gate of the Howard-Kobbe complex opens onto a back-country road. In 1986, the road wound through a combination of tall palm grass and vine-covered jungle and after about 15 minutes of slow driving on the rutted road, dead-ended in the small seaside fishing village of Vera Cruz. The village boasted a seafood restaurant sitting at the water's edge. The restaurant was a favorite of both Panamanians and Americans, and was usually quite busy most evenings. In 1986, any further travel westward was only made by returning through Howard to the Pan-American Highway.

The Pan-American Highway continues west past the American complexes, the American Naval fuel storage area, the village of arraijan and a PDF Highway Police Station. It gradually climbs through the coastal hill country with the Pacific Ocean on the left and an ever-rising mass of patchy jungle on the right, which eventually yields to the 3,888-foot high mountain of Cerro Gaital, about forty five miles from Panama City. At one point, the highway crosses the runway of the PDF training complex at Rio Hato some ninety miles from Panama City. Originally built as a long range patrol base in WW II, the site has a respectable runway. The road continues to twist and turn, and gradually turns west and then back north as it wends its way 200 miles, through the western provinces of Panama. The provinces include Cocle, Hererra, Los Santos, Veraguas and Chiriqui. Each has a provincial capital, and in 1986 most had a PDF Army garrison of about 200 personnel. Some of these towns have lyrical names such as Penonome, Santiago, Chitre, Las Tablas, and David (pronounced Dah-veed).

David is the farthest west and sits about 25 miles short of the Costa Rican border. The two-lane Pan-American highway continues north through Costa Rica, Nicaragua, Honduras, El Salvador, Guatemala and Mexico all the way to the U.S. border, eventually joining U.S. 101 at the Mexico-California border.

CONFRONTATION ZONE

However, reversing your direction of travel at Howard, and recrossing the Bridge of the Americas (and the Canal), and then turning north at Balboa, you are travelling on Gaillard Highway. This two-lane road was named after one of the principal US Army engineers involved in the construction of the Canal. The road starts out paralleling the Canal, but then takes its own route to the Atlantic terminus at Colon more than fifty miles away on the other side of the Panama Isthmus.

The first few landmarks on this route are Albrook Air Station, Fort Clayton, Miraflores and Pedro Miguel Locks. Once beyond this cluster of American facilities, the road winds through miles of dense jungle, part of it a tropical rain forest. Offshoot landmarks are signs to the village of Gamboa and Madden Dam, which provides the millions of gallons of water required to operate the Canal locks. The tracks of the only active railroad in Panama run parallel to the road for the first ten miles then take their own course to Colon. Built in the 1850's, the railroad was originally a safe, efficient way of crossing the isthmus. After the Canal was completed, it became a charming and inexpensive means of tracing the path of the Canal through the locks and the lakes between Panama City and Colon. In the mid-eighties, less than six years after the railroad had been turned over to the Panamanian authorities to manage and maintain, it was declared unsafe by the U.S. Embassy, the Southern Command and the PCC, and Americans were advised not to use it. The reason was the poor condition of the roadbed, deteriorating rolling stock, a series of mishaps, and almost no maintenance on the trestle that carried the tracks over Lake Gatun at the Colon end.

About ten miles west of Panama City, Gaillard Highway turns away from the Canal and joins National Transisthmus Highway 3 which links the eastern end of Panama City and Torrijos Airport with the city of Colon on the Atlantic side. Colon is very much an international trade city and boasted the largest tax-free zone in the world. It is situated at the Atlantic approaches to the Canal. The population of Colon is much smaller than Panama City and the PDF presence was correspondingly lower, as was the American military population.

Several American military facilities in the area had been closed or severely reduced in scope as various provisions of the 1977 Torrijos-Carter Treaties took effect in 1979. Fort Sherman, which had housed the School of the Americas and a small Navy detachment housing area, were the principal U.S. facilities operating in the mid to late '80s. The U.S. military presence was found primarily in a military police detachment and an Army Training Unit which operated the nearby U.S. Army Jungle Operations Training Center (JOTC). The only combat presence was a permanent Special Forces training battalion and a rotational light infantry or ranger battalion that was undergoing a six-week jungle warfare training program run by the JOTC cadre and the SF unit.

CHAPTER TWO
HISTORICAL PERSPECTIVES

Beginning in mid-1985, reports, rumors, speculation, and concerns about Manuel Noriega's possible involvement in rigging the 1984 national elections, the laundering of drug money, and corruption in the PDF began to circulate in Washington. This was coupled with the perception that the longer the PDF and Noriega occupied the seat of power, the slower progress would be toward a stable and democratic government in Panama.

These concerns grew as the clock kept ticking towards the transfer of the Canal from U.S. to Panamanian control. The continued safe and effective operation of the Canal was, and continues to be, a concern to U.S. political, economic, and strategic interest. Ships from all nations of the world ply its waters seven days a week, twenty-four hours a day. Disruption of the Canal operation for any period of time beyond a few days would have worldwide impact.

Typically, more than 13,000 ships pass through the Canal each year, an average of 32 ships per day or one about every forty-five minutes in a never-ending stream. About 65 percent of these ships are coming from or going to a U.S. port. Although only about 100 U.S. military ships use the Canal in a normal year this number can increase sharply during international crises. The volume of oil carried through the Canal by ship began to decline in 1983. This was due in part to the construction of super tankers that are too large for the Canal locks; however, this decrease was offset by the same amount of oil and more which now flows through a pipeline that parallels the Canal.

The protection and continued operation of both of these highly critical and physically vulnerable economic lifelines is of continuing interest to the United States. In addition, Panama is the only U.S. stepping stone to Latin America. Although a commercial jet flight from Miami to Panama takes only about two and half hours (flying directly over Cuba), a flight from Los Angeles to Panama is nearly five hours, and it is another three to four hours from Panama to the nearest capital city in South America. Without the opportunity of a Panamanian refueling stop, the United States' ability to support (much less sustain) any major operation (military, civil, or humanitarian) into South America is dependent on the good will and cooperation of Colombia or Venezuela granting overflight and landing rights.

Many U.S. political personalities, Congressman, Senators, government officials, and congressional staffers, have visited Panama over the years for short, whirlwind updates. Some of these visits have been as short as two hours. In these cases, typically, the visitors met with the U.S. Ambassador and the Commanding General of the U.S. Southern Command at Howard Air Force Base for a plane side chat. Other visits included an overnight stay, discussions at the Embassy, a visit to the massive Panama Canal Commission (PCC) administration building and the nearby Miraflores Locks, and possibly private discussions with the Ambassador or the Commander of the U.S. Southern Command.

During the mid-to-late 1980's, depending on the visitor's timetable and itinerary, a wide variety of issues were discussed. The insurgency in El Salvador, the situation in Nicaragua, U.S. military exercises in Honduras and, occasionally, the drug and political situation in Latin America were regularly addressed. However, as the media picked up on the possibility of a Noriega drug connection, interest in Panama itself rose.

In the aftermath of *Just Cause,* several Washington Post analysts claimed U.S. decision-making concerning Panama had been affected by the diverse opinions and interest of the American policy community. The White House, Congress, the Department of State, the Department of Defense, and the Central Intelligence Agency each viewed the situation and evolving developments from different and perceptually opposing perspectives.

According to a the same Washington Post article, entitled the "Long Road to the Invasion of Panama" (January 14, 1990), National Security Advisor John Poindexter had flown to Panama along with Elliott Abrams, the Assistant Secretary of State, in December of 1985. The purpose of the visit was to inform General Noriega officially of U.S. concerns and urge him to take corrective actions. This may have been the first such "Washington" meeting with this purpose, but it was not to be the last. According to the same article, a sterner version of the same message was delivered to General Noriega in December 1987. This time the message was delivered by Assistant Secretary of Defense Richard Armitage.

Visits by one or two congressmen or an occasional senator, to include a meeting with the Commander in Chief of U.S. Southern Command, were not unusual in the mid-to-late eighties. If the topic of Noriega came up, it was usually within the context of a question from the visitor: "What is your assessment of this Noriega fellow?"

Many times this was an honest expression of interest. However, as the calendar moved farther into 1987-88, the questioner was often looking for a reaffirmation of an opinion already held. During the dialogue, questions concerning whom might succeed Noriega and how this succession might be accomplished were brought up by the visitor. There were no easy answers. There was no apparent replacement candidate on or off stage. There was no organized opposition inside or outside the PDF. Panamanian political parties, with the exception of the Democratic Revolutionary Party (PRD), which supported the PDF and Noriega, were fragmented and bickered among themselves.

An image that had evolved over the years and had been nurtured by the PRD, cast the local Panamanian opposition as opportunist and capitalist, composed of the wealthiest segment of the population. This group included the editors and publishers of the newspapers, bankers, many of the professionals, and the more well-to-do merchant community. This group, although wealthy, was a small minority of the population with very little political influence outside of its own private circles.

The "poor" people, the day workers, laborers, and the unions were "represented" by the PRD party. It had been the PRD and the PDF that had managed to wrestle the "Yankee" to the ground and wring the promise of Panamanian control of the Canal from the "Norte Americanos."

Although the local Catholic Church was influential in most segments of Panamanian society, it was no match for the PDF's governmental and police infrastructure. The PDF influence included a neighborhood network of informants, two newspapers, and radio and television stations.

Up until mid-1987, U.S. TV news was broadcast on the single American military channel, and did not, by U.S. choice, include any commentary on Panamanian affairs. Nor did the weekly American military newspaper carry any Panamanian news. Throughout 1987-1988 it was not unusual for the Latin American edition of the Miami Herald to be confiscated by the PDF as the master proofs arrived at the airport. This successfully prevented the papers from being printed and distributed in Panama. Eventually, faced with continued harassment, American papers stopped shipping altogether.

A rhetorical question occasionally asked by the American military host of the political visitor (particularly those who were urging action) was, "What are your suggestions for filling the political vacuum that will be created by the departure (voluntary or involuntary) of Noriega?" Normally, the visitor's response was something to the effect of, "Well, we will discuss that when he is gone!" Likewise, the larger question, "How do you convert or dismantle an institution that has been running a country for more than twenty years without creating civil and economic chaos?" also went unanswered.

The option preferred by most senior U.S. military officers serving in Panama in the pre-1988 time frame was to work to change the PDF from within, through positive contact with its junior and mid-level officers. The most objective senior officers saw this as a way change could evolve rather than being the product of a revolt or foreign imposition. However, the reality of the "how" aspects of this approach remained problematic in the face of the dictatorial structure of the PDF and the large base of popular support the PRD could muster.

It was also recognized by both senior and junior American officers and Non-Commissioned Officers (NCOs) in Panama that influencing the PDF through military-to-military channels in and of itself, even if moderately successful, could not solve the basic issue of corruption in the police, judicial, commercial, and other governmental functions. These areas of concern were decidedly outside the purview and responsibility of the U.S. military structure in both Panama and Washington.

Another question that was raised occasionally by visitors was, "What type of arrangements are being made for a U.S. military presence after the year 2000?" The immediate answer was that all draw down and turnover actions that were called for by the Torrijos-Carter Treaties of 1977 were being and would continue to be implemented in accordance with the time table and provisions of the treaties.

Contrary to the general perception that total responsibility and authority for the safety, security, and operation of the Canal would rest solely with the Government of Panama after 1999, a major provision of one of the treaties vested both nations with the responsibility of insuring the Canal remained open and safe for the unimpeded use of international maritime shipping. The treaties did not forbid a U.S. military presence after 1999; however, neither specified what form such a presence might take. The framers of the treaties left the follow-on measures to be worked out between the responsible authorities of both nations, as the situation unfolded in the mid-to-late nineties. One decision to be made was where the U.S. Southern Command headquarters would be located. Should it be continued in Panama or should another location in Latin America be sought? It could be relocated to the United States mainland or disbanded all together.

Senior U.S. officers in Panama had wanted to tackle these issues, at least at the discussion level, in the early to mid-eighties. They were aware that if any construction were required at a new location, long political negotiations, congressional approval, budgeting actions, and actual construction time indicated decisions and commitments should be made in 1988-1990 period.

The other school of thought advocated waiting until the mid-to-late nineties to see what the political situation in Panama was and then initiate discussions with the Panamanian government in power at that time. This same theory held that expressing any interest in continuing a U.S. military presence (even if it were only a staff and logistics structure devoid of combat forces) would be seized by both Panamanian ultra-nationalist and leftist elements as a U.S. move to renege on the treaties.

Both sides of the coin had merit to varying degrees, but a clear middle ground was not evident, so the State Department philosophy of "Wait and See" prevailed, while the Department of Defense and the PCC continued to meet the provisions of the turn-over timetable. The U.S. Southern Command staff presumed the headquarters would be relocated to the United States sometime in the late nineties, so there was very little purpose in devoting energies or time to a question that was beyond their tenure and would essentially be a national-level political decision.

There were more pressing issues facing the command in the mid-to-late eighties. These included support to the government of El Salvador (the U.S. had a 55 person military training presence in country), monitoring the continued Sandinista military buildup in Nicaragua, and the progress of the burgeoning native resistance elements. These two actions alone involved managing a comprehensive reconnaissance and surveillance program. Coordinating a continuing series of field exercises and nation building projects in Honduras was another major task that required a semi-permanent logistics and command and control structure. Such a structure, i.e. designated JTF-*Bravo* was created at Palmerola, a Honduran Air Force Base in the central part of the country with the permission and cooperation of the Honduran government. The Honduran leadership was concerned about the Nicaraguan leadership goals of exporting their Socialist/Marxist revolutionary philosophy and creating and arming subversive movements. In addition, unprogrammed emergency relief operations throughout the theater, plus reconnaissance and communications support to counter-narcotic interdiction operations off the coast of South America, all combined to set the SOUTHCOM's day-to-day and mid-term priorities. The Panamanian domestic situation was viewed to some degree as a Department of State, i.e. political, problem.

These were the issues that most concerned the command, as well as the over arching "War of Information" vis-a-vis El Salvador and Nicaragua. This was a term coined by General Galvin who was the Commander in Chief of the Southern Command in the mid-eighties. It referred to the information and propaganda campaign waged by leftist movements in El Salvador and the United States to discredit U.S. activities by creating and circulating posters showing children allegedly injured in bombing raids in El Salvador and others demanding the U.S. "Stop the bombing." These posters could be purchased in Georgetown and could be found plastered on refuse containers in the District of Columbia. The impression conveyed by the posters was designed to invoke recollections of the Vietnam era, playing on familiar themes. It did not matter that the accusation was false.

There were no American combat aircraft of any type stationed in El Salvador and no American combat aircraft from any location ever conducted bombing or strafing operations in El Salvador. In fact, the little girl shown in the most graphic poster had lost her leg to a guerrilla land mine.

The "War of Information" also referred to the Nicaraguan government lobbyist and the public relations campaign they waged in Washington and New York. This included Sandinista sponsorship of "tours" to Nicaragua for academics from various Midwestern and "liberal" universities in the United States as well as journalists from the U.S. and Europe. The Nicaraguan "War of Information" also included, with the assistance of Fidel Castro, the creation of a parallel structure to the Catholic parish structure. This "new" church preached a "Liberation Theology" which supported and was supported by the Sandinistas in their effort to further influence the Nicaraguan populace and visiting foreign "Internationalistas," a generalized term applied to European liberals, socialists and idealists with a decidedly anti-western, anti-U.S. philosophy. Demonstrations by these groups were at times a weekly occurrence at the U.S. Embassy in Managua.

General Galvin's thrust in identifying this fourth "War" front was the fact that the adversaries of freedom and democracy had shown a marked affinity for taking advantage of the U.S. constitutional guarantees of free speech and an uncensored press to undermine and fragment our society. Some trace this movement to a Soviet (Socialist) worldwide political and propaganda effort begun in the 1963 time frame to undermine popular support for U.S. government policies.

The first major public effect of this type of effort was evident in the mid-sixties regarding American involvement in Vietnam. However, Vietnam was not the exclusive focus, nor the only "front" of this war of propaganda and misinformation. Panama in the mid-to-late sixties was the scene of planned agitation and demonstrations against the "Yankee Imperialist and Oppressors." In 1964, American control of the Canal and the physical separation of the Canal Zone and its better lifestyle from Panamanian Panama was made a theme and bedrock for cultivating unrest and anti-American sentiment.

The banner of Panamanian nationalism and calls for the "return" of the Canal were the seeds from which the treaties of the Carter era sprung. There never was an issue of "returning" the Canal; it never was Panamanian. It was an American creation with workers from as far away as Spain, Italy and the Caribbean islands contributing to its construction. However, the "return" theme played well on the streets of Panama and in the media. It was easy in those times of turbulence and discord for its message to be received regardless of its lack of factual substance. Lost in the rhetoric was the other fact that the Republic of Panama was itself a creation of a United States policy.

The idea of a trans-isthmus canal was conceived more than 450 years earlier, less than 20 years after Spanish explorers claimed the isthmus and most of Latin America for Spain. In 1534, the King of Spain ordered a survey be conducted to determine the feasibility of creating a waterway between the two oceans. Nothing more came of the idea until the nation of Colombia (which had broken away from Spanish rule in 1824, and included the territory of Panama) granted a construction concession to a French consortium in 1878. Known as the French Canal Company, and operating under the leadership of Ferdinand de Lesseps, the company began construction of what was planned to be a sea level canal in 1880. De Lesseps had directed the successful construction and completion of the Suez Canal eleven years earlier. However, Panama proved to be a different and more difficult challenge. After a mighty nine year struggle with nature in the form of torrential rains, landslides, and a host of tropical diseases, including malaria, work was stopped on this second great French effort.

The U.S. government had also been interested in the prospect of constructing a canal across the Darien Isthmus as early as 1870, eight years before the French initiative, and less than five years after the conclusion of the American Civil War. A series of surveys were conducted by American teams and a Presidential commission was established to evaluate the reports. The various expeditions took a heavy toll in lives, mostly U.S. military engineers from the Naval Coastal Survey Department and the Army Corps of Engineers. Another route that held some possibility was through Nicaragua. This route would have begun at the Atlantic junction of the Costa Rican and Nicaraguan borders, and run up the San Juan River to Lake Nicaragua, then into Lake Managua, and westward to the Pacific. The United States discarded this option when it was confirmed that the Lake Managua portion of the route was the site of ancient volcanoes, whose continued inactivity was suspect.

In 1902, twelve years after the termination of the French effort, the U.S. government sought to conclude a treaty with Colombia which would grant the United States the right to build a canal across the isthmus and operate it in perpetuity. Colombia refused because of the loss of Colombian sovereignty inherent in the perpetuity clause.

The United States was not dissuaded by the rebuff and quietly encouraged the local Panamanian authorities to declare their independence. (Panama had been attempting to break away from Colombia since 1821, and wanted to establish itself as a separate entity as had other regions of Central America.) This chain of events was prompted by American aspirations to create a water passage through Central America linking the Pacific and Atlantic Oceans. Such a passageway would substantially decrease the time, cost, and danger of a voyage around the very treacherous Cape Horn at the southern tip of South America.

President Roosevelt was highly supportive of American expansion as a world power and had been lobbying the U.S. Congress to buy out the French investment and complete the canal. On November 3, 1903, the Panamanian "imdepemdence seekers" who were in favor of the U.S. initiative (and their own national freedom) declared their independence from Colombia. The U.S. government immediately recognized the new nation, and supported this political action with a military show of force.

The United States had a modest, but timely, U.S. Navy and Marine presence in Panama which was ordered to provide protection to the new government. Its tactical mission was to protect the Panama railroad that was the first trans-isthmian link between the two oceans. The combination of immediate recognition and the military presence deterred the Colombian government from taking action to counter the Panamanian declaration.

Fifteen days later, on November 18th, after a series of negotiations, the Republic of Panama granted the U.S. government the right to build a canal across the isthmus and administer a stretch of land five miles either side of the canal as U.S. property. The U.S. government paid the new republic 10 million dollars for the land grant and agreed to an annual payment of $250,000 thereafter. (This amount was increased over the years due to changes in the economic situation.)

The U.S. government also paid the insolvent French Canal Company 40 million dollars for its investment, and the equipment that it had left on the site. The U.S. construction effort was begun within the year and completed 10 years later. The first official passage through the completed Panama

Canal occurred in August 1914.

In contrast to the French sea level approach, the U.S. project included construction of three sets of locks that allowed ships to be raised and lowered 85 feet during their transit. Each lock was 1,000 feet long and 110 feet wide and 40 feet deep. The locks were designed to be flooded by water from the massive Gatun dam and reservoir-lake that were built as part of the project.

From that era to the present, the history and prosperity of Panama has been tied to that of the United States. However, the nature of Panamanian governmental development has often been more a product of neglect rather then parental training. In 1939 and again in the mid-fifties the treaty was amended. The amendment eliminated the U.S. right to intervene in the internal affairs of the Republic, but did not change the U.S. control of the Canal Zone. Manuel Antonio Noriega was a precocious toddler at this point in Panamanian history.

One the hundreds of Chiva busses that are characteristic of Panama's public transportation system. Photo courtesy of the author.

CHAPTER THREE
MANUEL ANTONIO NORIEGA

"Tony" Noriega was born in the late 1930's in Panama City, but spent his first few years of his life in a country village in Darien province near the Colombian border. By his sixth birthday, he was back in the capital and grew up in the working class neighborhood of San Felipe, one of the older sections of Panama City, adjacent to the Canal Zone. He could easily see the exclusive and seemingly plush housing of Fort Amador and the forbidden causeway and fortified islands of Fort Grant and the fence separating the Canal Zone from Panama City. In 1958, when Manuel was a teenager, his older brother, a lawyer and member of the Panamanian diplomatic corps who was stationed in Peru, was able to get Manuel accepted into a first class Peruvian Military School in Lima. After spending almost five years in Peru, attending school during the week and weekends with his brother, Noriega returned to Panama in 1962 and took a job as a government surveyor. Subsequently, he met Omar Torrijos, a senior officer in the National Guard who encouraged him to join the Guard. Noriega was in his mid-twenties in 1964 when he joined the La Guardia Nacional, the forerunner of the PDF. There was a ripple of tension and nationalism in the air.

January 1964 witnessed major rioting and confrontation between American and Panamanian youths at the Canal Zone fence at the foot of Ancon Hill. The issue centered on the question of jointly flying the Panamanian and American flags in the Canal Zone. A mob of Panamanian teenagers assembled at the fence separating the Canal Zone from Panamanian territory. The verbal exchange between U.S. and Panamanian students quickly devolved into a fence climbing riot which ultimately claimed the lives of four U.S. soldiers and 21 Panamanians. The nearby 4th of July Avenue was soon renamed the Avenue of the Martyrs in permanent memory of the Panamanian dead.

The riots, demonstrations, and confrontational nature and martyrdom attached to the Panamanian deaths were deemed serious by U.S. authorities. In 1965, after a year of internal debate and political maneuvering, negotiations between the United States and the Republic of Panama on the future status of the Canal and American control of the Canal Zone began. Panamanian nationalism had been reborn and it became a major force in all future dealings with the United States. Lieutenant Manuel Antonio Noriega was involved from the beginning.

Noriega was a hard worker with a quick mind and a burning ambition to be a person of stature. He soon became a junior, but reliable associate of one Captain Omar Torrijos. Lieutenant Noriega attended several military training schools during the late sixties, including an U.S. Army course on military psychological operations at Fort Bragg, N.C. in 1966. In 1967 he attended the U.S. run Jungle Warfare (now Operations) Training Center in

Panama where he learned the prevailing U.S. Army philosophy on guerrilla and insurgency warfare.

In 1967, after two years of discussion and compromise, the U.S. and Panamanian negotiators reached an agreement on two new treaties. One outlined the procedures by which the U.S. would surrender sovereignty of the Canal Zone to Panama, and the other dealt with the protection of the Canal. Strong feelings were afoot in both government assemblies, and neither country ratified either treaty.

In 1968, Dr. Arnulfo Arias was elected President of Panama for the third time in almost 30 years, and for the third time was thrown out of the office within a few months by a coup organized by senior officers of the National Guard. The National Assembly was dissolved at the same time and constitutional guarantees were temporarily suspended. Colonel Jose M. Pinilla and Colonel Urrutia were the leaders of the coup. Within a few days, Pinilla was sworn in as the Provisional President. A short time later, Pinilla was replaced by a civilian official nominated and supported by Omar Torrijos, who had been instrumental in orchestrating the coup.

By early 1969, Brigadier General Torrijos had emerged as the nation's strongman and Caudillo, the proverbial "Man on Horseback." Latin American politics have been dominated by the presence of this strong man figure (quite often in military uniform) for more than 160 years.

Once the structure of the decades family dynasties, with their large land holdings, began to fall apart in Central America, the power vacuum caused by the fragmented civil political groupings often caused chaos and confusion. This turmoil and instability was generally abhorred by the military structure, and often was taken advantage of by a visionary on horseback. Omar Torrijos was such a man, and as such, cultivated a strong national image among the people and developed a dedicated cadre of supporters within the National Guard. Manuel Noriega was one of this inner circle.

By 1972, Omar Torrijos had acquired full civil and military powers as the Commander of the National Guard. A new constitution was created at the same time that identified the National Guard as the protector of the nation and the guardian of the Constitution.

In the mid-70's, at the rank of Major (soon-to-be Lieutenant Colonel), Noriega was appointed head of the Intelligence (G-2) section of the new Panamanian Defense Force. In 1975, under the tutelage of Torrijos, the Panamanian government moved to nationalize the banana industry which represented a major U.S. commercial investment. Shortly thereafter, representatives of the United States and Panama signed an agreement in principle to negotiate a new treaty arrangement. As the Chief of Intelligence and a Torrijos insider, Noriega had a front row, if not an inside seat, to these events and the political and public manipulations that accompanied them.

By loyal and dedicated service and competence, Manuel Noriega was now part of the career hierarchy of the PDF and soon to be part of its chain of succession. As with many Latin military structures, officers move upward through the structure and assume positions of varying degrees of authority and responsibility, in accordance with their standing among their peers and the measure of their competence and loyalty to the institution and the senior leadership. Manuel Noriega was also a family man with a wife of many years, Felicidad, and three daughters Sandra, Thais and Lorena.

Lieutenant Colonel Noriega knew the system and continued to develop a professional and supportive relationship with Omar Torrijos. Torrijos had raised the banner of Panamanian nationalism to new heights, and set as one of his foremost goals the dismantling of the Canal Zone structure and acquisition of control of all canal operations. Manuel Antonio Noriega agreed.

Torrijos, a tall, charismatic figure with sharp features, keen, alert eyes and a quick mind, had long been recognized as the key Panamanian leader. He formally acceded to that position on the international stage in Washington, D.C. in the fall of 1977. The event that heralded this recognition was the September 7 signing of the "new" canal (turnover) treaties by President Jimmy Carter, on behalf of the United States and Brigadier General Omar Torrijos signing for the Republic of Panama.

After years of turbulence, unrest and agitation, and periodic confrontations between young Panamanians and their American student counterparts, the issue was theoretically "solved" when the Torrijos-Carter Treaties were ratified by a national plebiscite in Panama in October 1977 and by the U.S. Senate the following spring. The debate in the U.S. Senate was long, vocal, and hard, and concluded with the Senate ratifying the treaties by a margin of only one vote.

On a sunny day in mid-June 1978, Brigadier General Omar Torrijos and President Carter again met, this time in Panama, and formally exchanged the instruments of ratification. The first dealt with the disestablishment of the Canal Zone, and the turnover of the operation of the Canal to the Republic of Panama as of December 31, 1999. The second treaty defined the international neutrality of the Canal and the obligation of Panama and the United States to guarantee that neutrality beyond the date of the turnover even if this meant unilateral U.S. action. Implementation of the two treaties was scheduled to begin a year later (in 1979).

In the latter half of 1978, Torrijos, with the backing and support of the PRD political party, named Aristides Royo, a lawyer and former Education Minister, as President. Royo had been heavily involved in negotiating the two treaties.

1978 was also a year of change and turmoil elsewhere in Central America, and included events of high interest to the U.S. SOUTHCOM Commander in Chief and his staff as well as a host of CONUS-based contingency forces. The most significant of these events was the leftist-oriented Nicaraguan Sandinista National Liberation Front (FSLN) campaign of political propaganda and military actions against the Nicaraguan National

Guard, the Somoza regime, and the landed oligarchy in Nicaragua.

The FSLN leadership had been waging the struggle without much success for nearly fifteen years. They began to make significant political gains in the mid-70's when they received support from Fidel Castro and cloaked their Marxist leanings in terms of Nicaraguan nationalism and social democracy. They also adopted the name of a legendary Nicaraguan revolutionary of the 1930's, Augusto Sandino, and began calling themselves "Sandinistas". Increased financial, training and material support came from Fidel Castro in the mid-70's and indirect moral support came from the United States in the late '70s when it began to withdraw support from Anastasio Somoza, the Nicaraguan President. The aftertaste of failed American political involvement in Southeast Asia prompted the American administration to exercise a "hands off" policy.

The Somoza family had held the Nicaraguan national leadership post and the reins of government for more than four decades. Annastasio Somoza was both the President and the commander of the National Guard, as had been his brother and father before him.

The tide of public opinion in Nicaragua had begun to change in January 1978. The benchmark was the murder of Pedro Joaquin Chamorro, the publisher of the leading opposition newspaper, who was gunned down by unknown assailants. Rumors and speculation quickly spread alleging that elements of the National Guard were responsible. The magnitude of popular support for change was most evident in the summer of 1978 when a FSLN nationalist revolutionary figure by the name of Eden Pastora led a small band of guerrilla combatants into the center of the capital city, Managua. Pastora, also known as Commander Zero at the time, seized control of the main government administrative building, the National Palace, controlled the building for 24 hours, and on the second day, surrendered it peacefully and left Managua to the cheers of the local citizenry.

The event was repeated in spirit the next year, beginning in May, when the FSLN launched a major military campaign against the National Guard with the aim of deposing the Somoza regime and seizing power. The U.S. under the leadership of President Carter, following its "hands off" policy, refused to provide either military or material support to Somoza or the National Guard. The FSLN was emboldened, and the National Guard began fighting defensively, gradually giving ground to the advancing and growing rebel force. Somoza fled Nicaragua for Miami on July 17, 1979.

Two days later, the victorious Sandinistas marched into Managua and took control of the city, the government and the country. Within days President Carter authorized a $1.8 million aid package to assist in the reconstruction of the country. In August, Somoza was granted political sanctuary in Paraguay and took up residence there. Within sixty days he was assassinated by unknown gunmen in a scenario similar to the demise of Trotsky after the Soviet Revolution of 1917. Both Torrijos and Manuel Antonio Noriega had watched the entire sequence of events with interest.

However, they were more concerned with the impending implementation of the first provisions of the Torrijos-Carter Treaties.

On the first of October 1979, the U.S. and Panamanian military institutions entered into a new arrangement for the "combined" defense of the Canal and created the Combined Board (Military) for the Defense of the Canal. The Board was the administrative vehicle for coordination between the U.S. Southern Command and the Panamanian command.

By the first of November 1979, the old Canal Zone boundaries were dismantled and some 65 percent of the former "Canal Zone" had been transferred to Panama and Panamanian control and upkeep. The U.S. maintained control of several facilities and areas, and operated others in conjunction with the PDF as areas of joint control.

By early 1980, it became apparent to the White House and the U.S. Southern Command, that Nicaragua (now under the open Marxist leadership of the Sandinista junta) was a staging, training, and political-military-economic support base for the leftist rebel movement in neighboring El Salvador. Nicaragua also held promise of being a springboard and training ground for further unrest in Central America. The beginnings of a native anti-Sandinista resistance movement was also evident in Nicaragua, as was the elimination of virtually all other Nicaraguan political factions except the FSLN.

In early 1981, the new Reagan administration cut off aid to the Nicaraguan-Sandinista government, and by early 1982 it had begun providing support to the internal Nicaraguan resistance groups now known as "Contras." (The term came from a contraction for Counter-revolutionaries, coined by the Sandinista leadership and propaganda machine in Managua.) The focus of U.S. governmental interest in Latin America became priority issues. These included Nicaragua with its growing military strength, the continued guerrilla war in El Salvador, and the political fragility of the governments of Honduras and Guatemala.

In Washington, Panama was not viewed with the same concern as these other situations, although the potential transfer of the operation, maintenance and security of the Canal was never far from the minds of the Commander, U.S. Southern Command and his staff in Panama.

By mid-1981, it was evident that the Sandinista master plan called for conversion of its military forces from a small, irregular, guerrilla militia to a conventional military force decidedly larger and better equipped than its neighbors. The planned force would be modest in comparison to U.S. and Cuban standards, but would dwarf all other Central American military structures, and serve as a shield behind which the Sandinistas could train subversives and export their revolution. The force model was to be a combination of the Soviet Combined Arms philosophy, Cuban-style implementation, and a stylized Warsaw Pact air defense system.

Mid-summer of 1981 also saw a major change of players on the Panama scene. Omar Torrijos the Commander of the PDF, the leader of modern day

Panamanian nationalism and the man who set the timetable for the U.S. relinquishment of the Canal in motion died when the small plane in which he was flying crashed in a rainstorm the night of July 31. A year later Panamanian President Royo resigned (two years short of his 5 year term, Oct.'79 – Oct.'84) in favor of Vice President Ricardo de La Espriella, who assumed the office of President by acclamation of the Panamanian National Assembly.

In 1983, the National Guard was redesignated the Panamanian Defense Force (PDF) and the creation of two Army combat units (Battalion 2000 and Battalion PAZ [Peace]), were begun along with a bolstering of the Panamanian Navy and Air Force elements.

At the same time, Colonel Noriega became the first Commander of the PDF and assumed the rank of Brigadier General. Manuel Antonio Noriega had moved from being the man behind the throne and the information keeper to being the man in the middle, a role he relished. Shortly thereafter, the office of the Panamanian Presidency again changed hands, this time through a national election, which some say was stained by fraudulent voting practices. The result was that Nicolas Ardito Barletta became the first directly elected President in 16 years. Barletta was inaugurated in October 1984 for a five-year term of office.

The 1983-1984 period had also witnessed a tremendous change in Nicaragua and a major expansion of its military forces and the construction of armor, artillery and infantry garrisons, airfields, and radar sites throughout the country. This growth was recognized by the Reagan administration and became a growing matter of concern, both politically and militarily.

The continuing Nicaraguan military growth and its periodic cross-border incursions into Honduras in the mid-1980's contributed to the evolution and development of additional U.S. military capabilities. These included extensive joint contingency planning and operational training. These efforts of 1984-1986 involved many of the U.S. military forces (and planners) who were later to participate in the development and execution of Operation *Just Cause*. Many of the planners were influenced by their experience as junior and mid-grade officers in Vietnam, and the growing recognition that joint planning and cooperation would be the basis of success in future military endeavors.

During the course of the preceding nine years (1975-84), Manuel Noriega had met many American officials, and had seen U.S. ambassadors come and go. He had also witnessed the almost biannual transfer of military command at Quarry Heights, Fort Clayton, and Howard Air Force Base. He attended social engagements at the invitation of senior Americans and returned the courtesy periodically throughout the years. On most of these occasions, he was the listener and observer, always aware and measuring these "big brothers" from north of the border. He was also a learner.

Typical of this aspect of his personality was the interest expressed and the questions he asked during a training session hosted by a team of SOUTHCOM officers where he and a half dozen PDF military staff officers were shown how a crisis management team was organized and functioned. He did not dominate the session, nor inhibit his staff from asking questions, nor attempt to intimidate the two American officers that conducted the orientation. His questions were always germane, practical, and typically aimed at clarifying a situation or option.

In the mixed American-Panamanian military social environment, he did not seek to be the center of attention but was quietly gracious. During one such event he was the senior guest at an American military Dining-In, and, as such, sat at the head table along with eight other officers, both American and Panamanian. During the course of the dinner, an adventurous young American officer managed to crawl unnoticed along the length of the head table depositing a pat of butter on the right shoe of all the officers seated there. Once the culprit was safely back in his seat, one of his co-conspirators requested permission of the President of the Mess to speak. Permission was granted. The speaker requested that all the officers seated at the head table be fined a bottle of wine for wearing unauthorized material, i.e., butter, on their uniforms. The senior American officer, an Army major general, was somewhat taken back by this “affront,” but Manuel Noriega took it in stride and later complimented the bold adventurer.

Manuel Antonio Noriega had the opportunity to observe American officials, both military and civilian, for most of his adult life. Beginning with his middle grade assignment to the intelligence section of the National Guard, he began to assess and formulate an opinion on the American character, political, military, and popular. He witnessed the passage of dozens of ambassadors and assessed the majority of these representatives as people of soft words and little action.

Over time he acquired a similar opinion of many American politicians, the difference being the words were sometimes harsher but the impact no more severe or sustained. He had witnessed the fall of Somoza, the rise of the Sandinistas, and the immediate naive largesse of President Carter. He had seen the yo-yo nature of American support to the Contras and the battle between the U.S. executive branch and the Congress. He had seen the near collapse of the government of El Salvador in 1983 until the U.S. government dug into its pockets and began equipping and training the El Salvadoran Armed Forces.

At the same time, he saw the United States, haunted by reflections of Vietnam and its divisive impact, limit its active military presence in El Salvador to 55 advisors who were not allowed to accompany the Salvadoran units on combat operations or, initially, to carry weapons. He had seen American and world rhetoric and economic pressure have no significant impact on the leaders of Iran, and the strident demands of Islamic fundamentalists virtually drive an American president from office. He had also seen the American people elect a movie actor to be their national leader.

He considered this leader to be part John Wayne and part cardboard cowboy.

During the early part of the decade, Manuel Antonio Noriega was allegedly involved in discussions with U.S. government non-military officials about possible support to the Contras. Coupled with his long-term relationship with elements of the U.S. policy and intelligence community, these relationships created in his mind the perception that he was essential to U.S. interests. This perception was periodically reinforced throughout the mid-eighties as the U.S. pursued counter-narcotics efforts in Latin America, often with Panamanian cooperation.

On the other side of the coin, General Noriega (the man in the middle) visited Nicaragua in early 1985 and was received with full military honors. He was flown on a tour of several major Nicaraguan military facilities in a Soviet transport helicopter with a Soviet Hind attack helicopter in trail as a security measure. He assessed the inner circle of the Sandinista hierarchy as people of action. They had succeeded in capturing a government, almost with the acquiescence of the United States, and then hold it in the face of openly hostile rhetoric and vacillating U.S. support to the native resistance movement (i.e., the Contras).

In the fall of 1985, the civil government of Panama again changed hands. On September 28, Nicholas Barletta who had assumed the office of the President in October of the previous year, resigned because he was unable to muster sufficient support within the National Assembly to initiate an economic stabilization program. Barletta was replaced immediately by his First Vice President, Eric Ardor Delvalle, who was seen by many to be a front man and puppet for Noriega.

During his tenure as commander of the PDF and de facto Head of State, Noriega had dialogues with many Latin American leaders, both political and military, ranging from the idealist Alan Garcia of Peru to the realist Fidel Castro of Cuba. Manuel Noriega was a man in the middle who had learned to move with the ebb and flow of the waters that swirled around him. Part of that tide was the changing interest, priorities, and concerns of the United States leadership. It was through an act of jovial congeniality that Brigadier Noriega became General Noriega. Just prior to the annual conference of the chiefs of the Latin American military services, General Paul Gorman, US Army, then Commander in Chief of SOUTHCOM (who had recently been promoted to full general with the upgrading of the Command) commented to Brigadier Noriega that now all of the heads of services attending the conference were four stars with the exception of Manuel. He continued that perhaps it was time to upgrade the rank of the PDF Commander from Brigadier to full General. With this thought expressed, the American General offered Noriega a brand new set of four star ephaulets to formalize the change in stature before the conference. Noriega accepted and attended the international meeting wearing his new rank.

Manuel Noriega was viewed by some U.S. political leaders, pundits and commentators as another Marcos, Somoza, or "Baby Doc" Duvalier, who, when pressured, would take a bagful of money and depart the scene. Manuel Antonio Noriega was made of different cloth. He could not be bought off. He had seen more than four American political administrations conduct relations with Panama and Latin American with varying degrees of attentiveness, limited consistency, and little long term planning. Tentativeness and lack of thoughtful planning and follow through seemed to mark most American political initiatives.

He saw differences of opinions and approaches in some areas when the issue or objective was the responsibility of the military, or in the case of narcotics, the Drug Enforcement Agency. He also knew these organizations and their ability to fully pursue an objective to a conclusion was restrained by diplomatic considerations, interagency squabbles, and differing political agendas in Washington.

Manuel Antonio Noriega had seen and known to varying degrees a succession of senior American military officers who were his counterparts and contemporaries. He had seen the post of Commander in Chief of the U.S. Southern Command change hands no less than six times. He had seen the role and the strength of the command expand, and he had seen the rank of the commander elevated from two star to three star and eventually to the grade of full general. Most importantly, he had seen, met and conversed with each of these men, several in his native tongue. In each case, they took his measure against their own backgrounds and he took theirs. He noted the tremendous difference in the personalities, intellect, and military bearing of each and formed a composite image to which he felt, in some cases, superior.

Although his assessment of the American political leaders and the senior military officers he had met may have been historically correct, there were other American personalities, political, military, and private that he had not known (and he judged these incorrectly). He may have met George Bush in 1976, and again in 1983, but in the late 1980's he underestimated the persistence, decisiveness, and commitment of this American president. He also underestimated the power and feeling of the American people when angered by events that they considered barbaric and unwarranted.

He also underestimated a cadre of other American officers who had been junior and middle grade troop leaders and staff officers in Vietnam and carried with them the hard lessons about commitment and the goal of winning. Many of these same officers had seen the results of the lack of material support cause a disaster in the Iranian desert in 1980, and the cost of last minute planning in Grenada in 1983. Many of them had seen the potential for a US-Sandinista military-political confrontation smoldering in the streets of Managua and the highlands of Nicaragua in 1984-1988 and had been involved in the planning and training of American forces for that possible contingency.

Manuel Antonio Noriega was only partially aware of this growth of the U.S. quick reaction capabilities and the professional resolve among the emerging generation of cross service "contingency" planners who had been learning and maturing from the experiences of the previous decade. Many of these same officers began to see the almost inevitable clash of interest, wills, and perceptions between the United States and the PDF, and were not taken aback or surprised when a series of potential boiling points were reached in the mid-eighties.

Lastly, General Noriega tended to view the American presidents in the mold of President Carter and failed to assess that the nature of the man behind the Presidential Seal changes with each new incumbent and each will react differently when the values he holds dear are threatened.

Birth and death of the Comandancia with 1935 photo as central Police Station above, afternoon of 20 December 1989, below. Photo courtesy US Southern Command Public Information Office.

CHAPTER FOUR
RHETORIC AND UNREST

1986 was the last year of calm in Panama. The friction and minor irritants that were to become openly evident in the following years were still largely hidden under the veneer of the bustling metropolis of Panama City and the active lifestyle that was enjoyed by Americans and Panamanians alike. However, the growing arrogance of the PDF police was particularly galling to Americans, and the sight of the poverty and squalor of the shantytowns and overcrowded high rise tenements was a strong reminder that the wealth of Panama was not distributed equitably. The contrast in the news content, viewpoints and visceral language of the opposing newspapers and tabloids were harbingers of greater internal conflict.

The last days of June 1986 ushered in the era of active U.S. military support in the "War on Drugs." After six months of State Department delays a January request from the President of Bolivia was honored. The request asked for U.S. support in the form of a helicopter task force to assist Bolivian counter-drug police units and field officers of the U.S. Drug Enforcement Agency in conducting a major cocaine disruption campaign. DOD was given the authority to support the Bolivian request and the mission was given to the U.S. Southern Command. A series of planning meetings were held on the Fourth of July weekend and within seventeen days a helicopter task force constituted from the resources of the 193rd Infantry Brigade was on the ground in the Bolivian back-country.

The Counter-Drug Task Force flew out of Howard Air Force Base in mid-July with six partially dismantled *Blackhawk* helicopters in the cargo bays of USAF C-5 transports. The force included food service, medical, communications, weather, intelligence, and military police as well as the aircrews and mechanics.

The operation was initially heralded with skepticism in the American media and suspicion in the South American press, but within ten days it had proven its effect on cocaine processing. The price of the coca leaf dropped below its "fair market value" and a large segment of the cocaine processing effort was suspended. The operation, nicknamed Operation *BLAST FURNACE*, accomplished this without sacrificing the national sovereignty or pride of the Bolivian nation as many leftist–leaning newspapers in South America had initially claimed. They labeled the U.S. support as an American military "invasion." The conduct and support of Operation *BLAST FURNACE* was a key focus of the Southern Command and its Army component throughout July and August and well into September. By the conclusion of the deployment the *Blackhawk* aircrews had airlifted the bi-national counter-drug forces to more than a hundred suspect drug processing sites in the Bolivian outback.

Fortunately, events in Panama were relatively quiet during this period, and the attention of the Southern Command was devoted to a range of other continuing issues in addition to Operation *BLAST FURNACE*. These included: the growing strength of the Nicaraguan Armed Forces, the periodic aggressiveness of the El Salvadoran guerrillas and the detection of arms movements from Nicaragua into El Salvador.

The arms movements were by both land and sea. The water route was of particular interest to the command because of the potential for volume transfers and ease of movement. AC-130 transport aircraft of the USAF 1st Special Operations Wing (1st SOW) had been pressed into service as a surveillance platform but this was a short term and expensive solution to a long-term problem.

Other surveillance options were being tested that summer in Panama. The purpose of one test was to determine the utility of using high resolution radars suspended from aerial balloons to detect the illegal waterborne movement. The concept was sound. The radar worked well, the image definition was exceptional and the data link to carry the image down the balloon tether to the mother ship worked with one major drawback. The tether apparently acted as a giant lighting rod and was struck by lighting several times during sudden summer storms while on sea trials off the Panamanian coast. The test was called off and the engineers sent back to the drawing boards to solve the problem.

Meanwhile, back in the United States, in mid-September, President Reagan declared a "National Crusade on Drugs." The next day an executive order was released which directed the Federal work force including the military to undergo drug testing. The tests were begun in Panama soon thereafter. The "War on Drugs" had begun and was a dominant media theme in Washington in the closing months of 1986; however, other events still held the forefront of interest in Central America and the U.S. Southern Command headquarters in Panama.

Events such as the continuing guerrilla war in El Salvador and the massive earthquake of October 10th that damaged much of the capital city, San Salvador, were more the focus of interest. The United States responded with emergency aid for the hundreds of thousands who were left homeless while the insurgents used the chaos to further infiltrate supporters and agitators into the city. In the words of the President of El Salvador the earthquake did more damage to the economy of the country in six seconds than the war had in the preceding six years.

One of the footnotes of October 1986, occurred in Nicaragua where Sandinista forces shot down an American owned civilian C-123 transport aircraft that was dropping supplies to Contra forces in southern Nicaragua. One crew member survived the crash and was captured. He was put on trial in Managua and found guilty but was released a short time later. One month later on November 6, 1986 the "Arms for hostages-Irangate" scandal hit the Washington papers and took over the headlines for the next several months and periodically thereafter well into 1987.

The Story of the 1989 U.S. Intervention into Panama

On March 11, 1987, a major earthquake and torrential rains devastated a remote northeast region of Ecuador, cutting off road access to the region. The area was the site of logging and oil drilling operations crucial to the Ecuador economy. The human loss included 100 dead and 1,000 missing or in need of assistance. The U.S. Southern Command was again the DOD agent for support in the recovery effort. This was the same role that it had performed in the wake of the El Salvadoran earthquake. However, the challenge was different and more demanding. The Ecuador effort included road construction assistance, emergency helicopter airlift of injured Ecuadorians and the resupply of isolated communities. The relief and construction effort went on for several months.

On March 31st, it was a guerrilla attack on an isolated El Salvadoran military garrison that resulted in the death of 43 El Salvadoran soldiers and one American advisor (a young Special Forces Sergeant) that became the focus of the headquarters. This occurred in the middle of a major combined Honduran-American exercise involving a range of U.S. contingency reaction forces that had been deployed from the United States to central Honduras. Palmerola Airbase was the center point for the joint force exercise which included field training and extensive "battle plan" reviews of the several contingency plans prepared to respond to Nicaraguan provocations.

A little later in the spring it was a Nicaraguan military excursion into Honduras that became the focal point of American military and executive concerns. American troops and logistic support were quickly dispatched to Honduras as a warning to the Sandinistas and as a sign of support to the Honduran government. This Nicaraguan probe was larger and better planned and executed than earlier moves against the border camps of the Democratic Resistance Forces, the formal title of the Contras. The Nicaraguan effort, however, was not successful and did not inflict any serious losses on the Contras, nor did the event involve any Nicaraguan-American confrontation although an American contingency force was deployed from the United States to Palmerola as a counterbalance.

One of the other footnotes of the period occurred on April 28th. A young American civilian, a self-proclaimed socialist and Sandinista supporter living in Nicaragua, was killed on that date when the Nicaraguan militia patrol he was with was ambushed by a Contra squad. The American was carrying a rifle and dressed in a Nicaraguan militia uniform as were the other members of the ambushed patrol.

By the spring of 1987, the rumors of Noriega's alleged involvement with the drug lords of South America had taken on a presumption of fact, particularly in the political environment of Washington. The subject of "drugs" was a surefire headliner for most American politicians and reports that Noriega was under investigation prompted some members of Congress to take special interest in publicly denouncing him.

As these rumors of Noriega's political, humanitarian and drug transgressions began to resurface, the U.S. Southern Command's interest began to take on a greater Panamanian hue. Long time Panamanian employees and friends of Americans in Panama quietly began to express disgust and dissatisfaction with Noriega and ask "When is the United States going to do something about him?" The answer most often given was, "It is up to the Panamanian people to change the Panamanian government, not the United States."

Within the American military community, small new obstacles to meaningful cooperation between the Panamanian military and the American forces began to assert themselves. Some were annoying, such as holding an American serviceman under police or military detention until formal release papers had been processed through the respective bureaucracies. This was a change from previous long standing practice of releasing the man to the American Liaison officer on duty within the eight hour limit per established treaty related agreements.

Another example of harassment was the detention of the officer in charge of a SOUTHCOM physical exercise group. The group routinely had been running on the Fort Amador causeway. The PDF claimed the group constituted a military formation and required formal permission from the PDF under the terms of the Torrijos-Carter Treaty to conduct the run. Similar Treaty provisions declared any group of three military vehicles constituted a convoy and not only required PDF permission to use the Panamanian roadways but could not move without a PDF escort. This particular provision was rarely imposed prior to 1987, but later became another harassment tactic.

On June 6, 1987, General Fred Woerner succeeded General John Galvin as Commander in Chief of the United States Southern Command in a formal military ceremony at Howard AFB. Admiral William Crowe, Chairman of the Joint Chiefs of Staff (CJCS) presided over the ceremony honoring General Galvin for his work in the theater and transferring the U.S. Southern Command flag to General Woerner. General Galvin commented in his remarks, "It is difficult to leave this command, but I have a great consolation. And that is the commander who follows me, General Fred F. Woerner, is the best prepared commander ever to take command of the United States Southern Command." General Woerner had only been away from Panama for fifteen months. From April 1982 through March 1986, he had served as commander of the SOUTHCOM Army component (the 193rd Infantry Brigade) and concurrently as commander of the U.S. Army Security Assistance Agency, Latin America. General Woerner, like his predecessor, was fluent in Spanish and knew the region well. He also knew Manuel Antonio Noriega, having watched the young G-2 move into higher positions of power within the PDF.

General Woerner and General Galvin before him, and Lt. General Dennis McAuliffe the American Director of the PCC, were attuned to the often arcane and complex personality and perspective driven nature of

Panamanian politics where the most frequently used weapons were half-truths and whispered accusations rather than violence. For the most part these "opinions" were recognized by McAuliffe, Galvin, Woerner and Marc Cisneros, the SOUTHCOM J-3 (Director of Operations) for what they were and understood the motivations behind them. All of these officers spoke Spanish, had studied the Latin American cultures of Central America, and had many years of experience and exposure to the vagaries and intrigue of the contesting forces.

Although the PDF was a strong institution it was not a monolith nor were all its members slaves to its commander. Several senior officers with much to lose had left the country for safer climates and denounced Noriega from afar. However, a month earlier in late May, Colonel Diaz Herrera, the PDF Chief of Staff, one of the most senior officers in the PDF was involuntarily retired. Herrera was very much annoyed and disturbed by his dismissal as he considered himself a candidate to replace Noriega. Herrera went public on Sunday, June 7, 1987 with a series of allegations. This was one day after General Galvin had turned over command to General Woerner.

Some of the Herrera allegations were old: the Spadafora murder, money laundering and drug shipments. Two were new: Herrera claimed that Noriega plotted the death of Torrijos and had rigged the 1984 national elections to put a more pliable candidate Nicolas Ardito Barletta, into the President's chair. These claims were implicitly believed by many. The story was instantly headline news and the war of rhetoric reached another plateau. The Panamanian opposition and American papers began blasting away at Noriega on the front pages, followed by a stream of editorials.

The Herrera claims evoked a major reaction within the Panamanian opposition who issued its first anti-Noriega statement on June 9th and took to the streets in a series of peaceful demonstrations during the day, while vandalism and tire burning took over in the evening. During the demonstrations there were several physical clashes between the protestors and the police. After two days of daylight political confrontations and nighttime vandalism, including the blocking of intersections and the burning of tires and cars, the Delvalle government, late Wednesday the 10th of June (subsequently called "Black Wednesday"), declared a "State of Emergency." This was accompanied by a formal decree that suspended basic constitutional guarantees for ten days.

The decree suspended Panamanian guarantees of freedom of movement, freedom of association and assembly, freedom of expression, and the inviolability of private property and correspondence. The decree also gave the police authority to make arrests without warrants, and detain individuals for longer than 24 hours without arraignment or benefit of legal counsel.

During the course of the next several days, the "State of Emergency" declaration allowed the government to curb the demonstrations, many of which had made the U.S. television and print circuit. The main streets in the downtown area and near the University were the principal scenes of the demonstrations, and included Via Espana, Via Argentina, Via Brazil and Calle 50 in the central banking district plus the Trans-isthmian Highway near the University. The government measures included deploying PDF military units to secure key intersections and bolster the police presence. This was the first use of military elements of the PDF to assist the police structure.

The continued unrest in the city caused a change of venue for the American Balboa High School graduation ceremony scheduled to be held on Thursday night, the 18th. Originally, the celebration was to be held in one of the large auditoriums in the Atlapa National Convention Center near the Marriott hotel. Much to the disappointment of the expectant graduates, but to the relief of concerned parents, the location was changed to one of the large hangars at Albrook that was normally an aircraft maintenance training facility for the Inter-American Air Forces Academy.

Meanwhile, prompted by the size of the demonstrations and the apparent show of popular discontent within the Panamanian society, a small group of U.S. Senators in Washington began an effort to formally comment on the situation in Panama with a Congressional Resolution. As a result of this Congressional effort, Senator Christopher Dodd, the Spanish speaking chairman of the Senate Sub-committee on Western Hemispheric Affairs, flew to Panama on the 19th to get "a sense of what is going on."

The Senator's avowed intent was to head off the adoption of a Congressional Resolution condemning Noriega for his alleged drug involvement. Dodd hoped that by advising Noriega of the impending event he could persuade him that it was time to gracefully step down from the post of Commander of the PDF and retire from Panamanian affairs. Dodd believed that if he could convince Noriega to do so, he in-turn could persuade his fellow law makers to kill the resolution. The day after Dodd's arrival, June 20th, the Panamanian National Assembly voted to extend the State of Emergency decree indefinitely.

During the course of his short visit, the Senator held discussions with the both U.S. and Panamanian officials and a cross section of the Panamanian opposition. The American officials included the U.S. Ambassador Arthur Davis and the new SOUTHCOM Commander, General Woerner.

Panamanian officials included President Delvalle, the Foreign Minister, and General Noriega. Non-government personalities included Archbishop Marcos McGrath, and a host of political, business, civic, professional and student leaders all of which included members of the opposition groups. Although the Senator met with General Noriega he was unsuccessful in persuading the General to step down. At a press conference on the 21st at Howard, just before departing for Washington, the Senator said he did not support sanctions against Panama and he felt "there is an opportunity here to resolve the differences peacefully in this country."

Five days later, on Friday June 26th, the U.S. Senate adopted a resolution, by a vote of 84 to 2, which urged the government of Panama to restore the constitutional guarantees, to take steps to help insure free and fair elections, to establish genuine autonomy for civilian authorities, and to seek the removal of the PDF from non-military activities and institutions. The U.S. action drew condemnation from Panamanian spokeman and was viewed by Noriega as the casting down of the gauntlet. He replied with a barrage of rhetoric suggesting the U.S. Congress would do well not to meddle in the affairs of another country and that the Congressional action was another indication that the United States was looking for reasons to renege on the Canal Treaties. This latter claim had come to be a favorite Noriega and PRD theme that gained acceptance in some circles in Panama.

However, three days later, on Monday the 29th, the State of Emergency was canceled and the constitutional guarantees restored. The American community relaxed somewhat, but the breather was short lived.

The next day, Tuesday the 30th, the U.S. Embassy complex in Panama City was the target of violent anti-American demonstrations orchestrated by a small core of well-known pro-government elements. The demonstrations began about 11:00 AM and continued until mid-afternoon. The Chancery, the Consulate and the U.S. Information Service buildings were the main targets of the rock and paint throwing crowd, some of whom used iron bars to break windows within reach of the perimeter fence. The demonstrators carried signs and placards and chanted anti-American slogans, but did not attempt to scale the fence or gain access to the grounds. None of the American personnel within the buildings were injured and the Embassy promptly filed a diplomatic protest along with a bill for damages with the government of Panama. The bill was paid shortly and was accompanied by a note inferring the demonstrators were just exercising justifiable outrage at the government of the United States.

As a result of the events of the preceding three weeks, the American military authorities changed the location of many of the upcoming Fourth of July celebrations from public sites open to both Panamanians and Americans to sites within the protective confines of U.S. military installations. Some of the more significant of these changes were publicized in the Southern Command news media on July 2nd. These included the move of an outdoor band concert from the Ancon Hill near the main PCC Administration building to a sports field on Fort Clayton, and the movement of the traditional night time fireworks display from Sosa Hill at Balboa to inside Fort Clayton. Similar measures were taken within the American community at the Atlantic (Colon) end of the Canal. The annual Fourth of July celebrations proceeded throughout the American communities but on a much subdued level and without fanfare or flair. This was in great contrast to previous years when the American national holiday had been an opportunity to welcome the Panamanian people to American installations for a day of food, games, carnival rides, bands and parades.

In previous years, it was not unusual for PDF military units to participate in the demonstrations, the music contest and the grand parade. Not so in July 1987. Not only were there no Panamanian units participating or marching but there were no American military units either. The patriotic American holiday traditionally noted for parades and flags was marked by a decided non-military signature. The only uniforms in the small parade belonged to Cub scouts and Brownie girl scouts. The single band that marched was a U.S. Army band wearing blue-jeans and white T-shirts. Three PCC fire department vehicles constituted the total display of equipment. Overall, it was a decidedly meek demonstration of American pride and capabilities.

Approximately three weeks after the Herrera revelations the Panamanian Court of Justice issued a public invitation for Colonel Herrera to come forward with his evidence and a promise that a trial would ensue. Herrera did not accept the offer and he gradually faded from media focus and center stage. Subsequently, the PDF police rushed his barricaded residence and arrested him. After a period of imprisonment, interrogation and alleged beatings, he was deported to Venezuela never to be heard from again.

The opposition crowds continued to periodically take to the streets and the heretofore fractured opposition began to show some organization and influence as the impact of a declining economy spread to more sectors of the population. Moderates, initially mostly professionals and eventually businessmen, formed a loose coalition united by their desire to see Noriega step down. The movement came to be called the National Civil Crusade, and its members, Civilistas. The Crusade, a coalition of more than 100 professional business groups began to orchestrate protests against Noriega and the PDF/PRD dominated government.

The tempo of demonstrations continued to build throughout the autumn. It began with peaceful motorcades through downtown by the opposition. The occupants typically wore white shirts or white blouses and waved white handkerchiefs while blowing their car horns. Often, pedestrians on the crowded sidewalks cheered the demonstrators and waved white handkerchiefs in support. These initial efforts quickly gave way to counter motorcades by Noriega supporters. Some of these led to confrontations and not a few Americans making U–turns and illegal left turns to avoid being caught in the middle of an advancing motorcade.

The Civilistas initiated several other non-violent techniques to express their displeasure with the regime and gain international and popular support. Two of these included the banging of pots and pans for five minutes at certain pre-designated times of the day. This technique was augmented at night by the flicking on and off of house and apartment lights at the same time. The noise of the pot banging was most effective and could be heard clearly at the Comandancia and on Quarry Heights where it was evident that the residents of the nearby poorer sections of Panama were part of this outburst.

The blinking lights could be best observed from the high ground on Albrook Air Station where a panoramic view of the downtown skyline could be had. The flickering lights were a noticeable, but certainly not an overwhelming, signal of unity or bravery. Estimates placed the light demonstration as indicating less than fifteen percent participation.

The American Military Police (MP) liaison section, which was authorized by the existing Panama Canal treaty to operate in Panama City, began monitoring the riots and demonstrations. The liaison team forwarded reports on the routes, nature and scope of the activity to the Provost Marshal's Office (PMO) which relayed the information to the USSOUTHCOM Watch Center. After looking at the complete picture and evaluating the situation, the command would put out a public notice on the American radio and television channels which identified the problem areas and advised Americans to avoid these areas.

Throughout all these events the opposition demonstrators remained nonviolent, but the same could not be said for PDF. One of the often frustrated plans of the Civilistas was to announce, through the network of local churches, that an "Assembly for Freedom" was going to be held at the main Cathedral in downtown Panama City at a specific time. Typically there were several announced routes of march starting from neighborhood churches, melding as they came closer to the Cathedral area. The early marches succeeded but the PDF police quickly developed a counter tactic of blocking the individual march routes and dispersing the marchers before they could fully assemble.

In several cases, the PDF Riot Police, self-nicknamed the Dobermans, took the offensive against the opposition in an effort to intimidate the demonstrators and onlookers. Americans had been advised to avoid any area where a demonstration was erupting, but in a few cases curiosity won out, often to the detriment of the American. In one case, on Friday, July 10, 1987, a young airman who lived downtown decided not only to watch a demonstration but also take pictures. He and several news photographers were attacked by the PDF police, roughed up and taken into custody and remained in the central jail, the Carcel Modelo overnight. Within twelve hours of the first detention, two American soldiers were arrested by the PDF police, and charged with destruction of private property for tearing down a political poster that had been hung on the Popeye's restaurant where the two Americans were getting some food. The two soldiers also spent the rest of the night in the Carcel and were released the next afternoon.

In other instances, PDF police units raided bank and newspaper offices, such as the anti-government La Prensa, pushing workers around and breaking windows and furniture. The target of these raids were members of the opposition and the institutions themselves. During one such raid on August 4th hundreds of angry opposition supporters stood in a driving rain storm and taunted officials from the Panamanian Attorney General's Office and plain clothes security agents with shouts of "murder" and "justice." This, as the agents conducted a three-hour search and carried away boxes of confiscated documents from the headquarters of the opposition, the National Civic Crusade, located in the Panamanian Chamber of Commerce building.

Two days later, the Crusade leaders vowed to defy a government ban on demonstrations and continue their protest activities. Throughout the many months of violent demonstrations the University of Panama, and in particular the two major thoroughfares that bounded it, were frequently the scene of spontaneous episodes of rock throwing and tire burning by "the students" which snarled up traffic very quickly. In late August, about 300 real and alleged students were involved in a nine-hour demonstration in the streets that involved burning trash and cars trapped on the downtown campus. The student demonstration ended about 5:00 PM with the arrival of the police. Although these demonstrations usually involved only a small number of instigators, the chaos they generated and the media publicity that their rampages garnered aided in the growing tensions, particularly when many of the demonstrations quickly took on an anti-American tenor. Often, as darkness closed in, more unruly elements would use the demonstrations to stage fires at intersections. One of their favorite fuels were automobile tires which generated considerable smoke, smell and consternation among both Panamanian and American families living in the vicinity.

In late 1987, a key difference in the nature of the environment was noticeable. During the previous year, the troubles were viewed by many Americans, particularly those living downtown, as being largely "Panamanian vs. Panamanian." Up until the fall of 1987, numerous U.S. service persons looked out their apartment windows and watched the Panamanians riot without feeling any threat to their security. But, as of October, things escalated to include a "Panama vs. U.S." tone.

In early October, the PDF arrested eight U.S. military personnel at 8:30 PM while the individuals were walking back to their hotel from a nearby local restaurant. The eight constituted two separate groups picked that night at different locations. All of the servicemen were taken to the Comandancia, the PDF general headquarters, where they were photographed, questioned and held for several hours until they were transported to the Balboa Police Station about 11:30 PM. They were detained at the police station until 4:00 AM then transferred to the PDF military police station on Fort Amador where they were further questioned and photographed again. Eventually, they were released to U.S. control at 7:00 AM. The manner in which this action was handled by the PDF violated a key provision of a 1980 military cooperation agreement which among other civilities requires that U.S. military forces representative be notified within two hours of the detention of any U.S. personnel.

On the same evening as the eight Americans were detained, and only hours after dozens of protesters distributed underground opposition, newspapers in the banking district and burned effigies of Delvalle, Noriega and cabinet members, Panamanian President Eric Ardor Delvalle went on National Television. He announced that the government "won't (would not) permit any more attempts against the fundamental base of the Republic or (tolerate) actions against the democratic government which I represent." He continued with, "Subversive acts of any kind will be sanctioned (met) with the total weight of the law." An extended period of sullen quiet followed.

In November 1987, the U.S. Senate passed a second resolution. This time the resolution was backed by actions. It cut off military and economic aid to Panama. This action added additional fuel to the verbal conflict and provided the PDF and the PRD with more "evidence" of the alleged U.S. intent to renege on the Treaties and to impose its will on Panama regardless of the cost to the Panamanian people. Anti-American rhetoric began anew.

Married American personnel who lived downtown, particularly those with small children (who rode bright yellow American school buses twice a day, some on routes that could take them close to areas of potential trouble) became more and more concerned as did their commanders. Surveys and preparations were made to bring all military personnel and their families who were living downtown onto the U.S. installations if the need arose. The demonstrations, street violence and interrupted traffic became such a daily occurrence that some units began asking their personnel living in the downtown areas or who had to transit the downtown to call in and report any indications of trouble in their neighborhoods. This became essential to control rumors and gain some appreciation of what actually was happening downtown.

While attempting to pinpoint the locations of Americans living in Panama City it was learned that the latest U.S. maps of the city were thirteen years old. This was not a new or unique problem. Contingency planners and the intelligence staff at the Southern Command headquarters and other American units had faced it repeatedly in the preceding years. The year before it was discovered that there were no U.S. tactical maps or charts available to support Operation *BLAST FURNACE.* A large scale Bolivia hydrographic chart became the mainstay. Three years before, the same problem of outdated U.S. tactical maps had faced U.S. contingency planners charged with monitoring Nicaragua. U.S. charts predated the Sandinista takeover and none of the widespread military or government construction projects that had taken place after the Sandinistas came to power were portrayed. Fortunately for U.S. planners, both the Nicaraguan and Panamanian mapping communities were more conscientious, and, through some quiet initiatives copies of the more current native charts were obtained.

Pinpointing the trouble spots in Panama City became a greater and more persistent challenge. The Army military intelligence unit that had human intelligence (HUMINT) as its mission was prohibited from operating in Panama as it was a "friendly" country. However, the unit was the recipient of numerous informant reports. Unfortunately, many of them were based on speculation and rumor rather than direct observation or reliable access. Concern that any one of the PDF or the Democratic Revolutionary Party sponsored counter protests or rallies could lead to a determined or unruly mob marching on some of the smaller and less well guarded U.S. facilities was real.

One such candidate was the tiny, isolated and highly political symbol of U.S. presence, the Southern Command headquarters compound at Quarry Heights, less than a twelve minute walk from the PDF Comandancia. The compound could be approached on three sides, one directly from the older section of Panama City, a second up Ancon hill through the PCC housing area, and a third, up a footpath from Balboa. The compound had no defenses and the guard force normally consisted of a six-to-eight man U.S. Military Police squad and a counterpart PDF MP detachment which shared joint responsibility for access control.

In the early phases of unrest, the possibility of positioning fire trucks with water cannon inside the compound, but placed out of sight from any of the approaches, was considered as a precautionary non-violent response measure. However, because the fire trucks were PCC units, not U.S. nor U.S. military, this option was not looked on favorably by the PCC or the American Embassy. The Embassy, as an extension of the Department of State, wanted Noriega out of power, but being on the scene (and in the line of fire) it desperately wanted to avoid antagonizing the PDF. The goal was to achieve the first two objectives (Noriega out and avoid confrontation) without increasing the risk to the American civilian community.

The number of incidents involving Americans and the PDF, normally the Police branches, continued at a persistent but fluctuating rate. These incidents included small but direct confrontations between U.S. Military Police patrols and PDF elements. These incidents most frequently occurred on the never-never land that was formerly Canal Zone territory, still used by the U.S. forces (housing areas, etc) but was open to PDF and Panamanian access. When the situation started to show potential signs of danger to the 7,000 U.S. families and transient American citizens living in unprotected areas, the U.S. Military Police strength was only two under strength MP companies, one at each end of the Canal (Panama and Colon). The MP responsibilities included security for fifteen installations and training areas. Typically less than ten patrols were employed in the installation security role. The normal patrol duty day ran twelve hours and there was no U.S. ready reaction-reinforcing force available except for the small Spanish-speaking liaison team that was on duty.

The physical security mission of the Army Military Police, the Naval duty guards and the Air Force Security Police essentially was discharged by manning guard posts at installation entry points and conducting vehicle patrols in the built-up or military critical segments of the installations. None of the day-to-day police-security forces were manned, or equipped to conduct sustained off-the-road security patrolling along the entire perimeter of the installations. In many cases, the fence line or perimeter was not accessible by vehicle and only with great difficulty on foot. The combination of thick and living jungle coupled with darkness made the detection of penetrators a major challenge.

By December 1987, the issue of installation and personnel security had become more difficult, totally outweighing the capability of American police-security detachments. This was particularly true for the Army, which had the longest "fence line" and the largest number of unfenced off-post housing areas. Recognizing the danger and persistency of the threat and the growing number of encroachments, criminal, political and military, the senior Army Commander, Major General Bernard Loeftke instituted a program of aggressive perimeter patrolling. The program involved an MP team operating with an infantry patrol to conduct day and nighttime patrols in the jungle around the U.S. installations. Particular attention was given to areas of known or suspected activity, and areas of special vulnerability (undefended, unfenced housing complexes) or sites such as communication facilities which were critical to the U.S. force posture.

It was in this environment, in December of 1987 that U.S. Assistant Secretary of Defense Richard Armitage delivered his message of official U.S. concern and displeasure to General Noriega. The combination of the message and the general nature of the Panamanian people to extend the Christmas-New Year holiday season added to the period of relative tranquility that prevailed during December 1987 and carried into January 1988, although reports of Cuban arms shipments to Panama persisted.

Back street dwellings in Barrio Chorrillo. Photo courtesy of the author.

Oblique overview of Comandancia Compound and immediate vicinity in the foreground during the clean-up and leveling of the compound shortly after the conclusion of Operation *Just Cause*. Avenue Fourth of July (Line of Departure) running left to right and approach to Bridge of Americas, Balboa village in mid-ground, Photo courtesy of the author.

This photo taken May 1990 shows the area where the Comandancia once stood after the compound had been completely leveled and the rubble cleared away. Photo courtesy US Southern Command Public Information Office.

PART TWO:
PRELUDE AND PRECAUTIONS

Tensions began to build significantly in early 1988 when several watersheds were reached as substantial Panamanian civil resistance to the Noriega regime grew. These watersheds were a basis for the beginning of U.S. military contingency planning in March 1988. The ebb and flow of confrontations and incidents in the balance of 1988 and into 1989 dictated a parallel fluctuation in the tempo and focus of the military planning and training effort. The next four chapters trace this political-military evolution. Chapter Five covers the political and propaganda war. Chapter Six provides a close look at the events as they effected Americans in Panama and reviews the security measures taken by SOUTHCOM and DOD. Chapter Seven reveals the development and flow of both the defensive and offensive-oriented contingency planning from which the final design for combat operations evolved. Chapter Eight summarizes the extent of military preparations for what to some was an inevitable confrontation of arms. In essence, these four chapters document several layers of history, the latter three previously being somewhat obscured by the more public nature of the political and propaganda war waged by both sides.

CHAPTER FIVE
THE WATERSHEDS OF 1988

The Panamanian civil opposition had fallen dormant a few weeks before Christmas 1987. The year end symbols of the holiday season quickly dominated the landscape both physically and psychologically, with colored lights adorning many homes and windows. Lampposts were turned into tinsel versions of Christmas trees. Nativity scenes popped up everywhere including in front of the PDF Police Investigation headquarters in Balboa. However, the holiday atmosphere faded away early in the New Year and reality again took hold.

By mid-January 1988, the possibility of conducting a Noncombatant Evacuation Operation (NEO) of American military dependents and civilians was clearly on the minds of the USSOUTHCOM staff and informed officials in Washington. Part of the preparation for this possibility involved the creation of 11 two- and three-man evacuation assistance teams from within the liaison and investigation elements of the in-country army military police contingent. The teams became intimately familiar with where Americans lived off-post. They identified primary and alternate evacuation routes to U.S. bases from these sites, surveyed possible helicopter landing sites in the vicinity of the living areas, and conducted day and night time reconnaissance of the evacuation routes. The teams also had a contingency mission to locate, assist, and recover Americans trapped in their off-post quarters, injured or stranded during demonstrations. The planning and training continued throughout January and February, and by March all the work had been done and both the NEO and the contingency recovery plans had been fully developed and quietly exercised.

On Sunday, January 31, the PDF requested SOUTHCOM assistance in a search for a Panamanian Air Force transport aircraft missing in the uncharted backcountry rain forest of Darien province. Initially the assistance was limited to providing a tactical refueling system to the forward PDF search base. The system, along with 1,000 gallons of aviation fuel, was immediately flown by two U.S. Army *Chinook* heavy transport helicopters to the search base. On Monday, a USAF reserve C-130 joined the effort and flew two area search missions. The crash site was found on Thursday. On Friday two U.S. Army UH-60 *Blackhawk* helicopters attempted to insert 30 PDF troopers into the area of the crash site, but bad weather and heavy low lying clouds prevented the insertion. When the PDF team finally reached the crash site the next day, they found no survivors among the ten passengers and the two-man aircrew. This was probably the last official act of friendly cooperation between Panamanian and American military forces.

Politics and protest had been set aside during the holidays, and the local civilian opposition (Civilistas) remained moribund until Friday, February 5, 1988, when the Miami and Tampa newspapers heralded the indictment of Manuel Noriega and 15 others on drug trafficking charges. The indictments were handed down by two U.S. Federal Grand Juries in Florida, one in Tampa and another in Miami. The charges claimed the defendants were involved in drug trafficking and money laundering on behalf of the Colombian Medellin drug cartel. According to some estimates, the cartel was responsible for processing and delivering 80 percent of the illegal cocaine that was being smuggled into the United States.

On Monday, the PDF launched its counterattack, sending a petition to President Delvalle asking him to expel the Southern Command and all American troops. On Wednesday, following the lead of the PDF petition, the Panamanian Foreign Ministry declared there was no provision in the Panama Canal Treaties which allowed for the presence of the U.S. Southern Command and its role as a regional headquarters. The Ministry contended the only legitimate role of the U.S. military presence in the Republic of Panama was the defense of the Canal and any other missions exceeded the existing protocols.

American television and Panamanian opposition radio and print media picked up the drumbeat caused by the indictments, and turmoil erupted again on the streets of Panama. On the 9th and 10th of February, Jose Blandon, a former associate of General Noriega who had left Panama earlier, testified before a U.S. Senate sub-committee that Noriega was active in drug transactions, and had allegedly received $5 million in payoffs from the Medellin cartel for his cooperation. The next day a Panamanian accountant testified that he had laundered $11 billion dollars of Cartel funds through

Panama with the help and knowledge of Noriega. The opposition newspapers renewed their barrages, calling for Noriega to step down.

Anti-government street demonstrations, including one staged by University students during the second week of February, involved the erection of barricades, and the burning of tires and three government vehicles. The government reacted to the continued unrest by closing three opposition radio stations and an opposition newspaper.

In another harassment action, this one aimed directly at American military, the PDF detained 30 U.S. service members while they were enroute to work at their duty stations. Twenty-three of the Americans were picked up for wearing their military uniforms while traveling on motorcycles and motor scooters. Four were detained in their cars and three on foot on the same grounds. This included one individual who was detained while walking from the Amador Golf Club parking lot to his nearby office, both located on Fort Amador. The Southern Command responded by citing a 1979 Letter of Agreement between U.S. and Panamanian military authorities which amplified a treaty provision and allowed U.S. personnel to wear their uniform when traveling between their residence and their duty station as well as when traveling between military installations. There was some speculation that this Monday morning action was in retaliation for the brief detention of one of General Noriega's daughters who was stopped for speeding on Albrook.

Popular opinion appeared to support the civilian opposition's call for Noriega to step down. Under mounting domestic political pressure and at the quiet suggestion of the U.S. State Department, Panama's heretofore figurehead President Arturo Delvalle, in a nationally televised broadcast on the 25th of February, "relieved" Manuel Noriega of his post as Commander of the PDF. Delvalle stated Colonel Marcos Justine, the PDF chief of staff, would replace Noriega. Within hours both Justine and Noriega rejected Delvalle's orders, claiming the President did not have the authority to relieve Noriega.

The next morning at 4:00 AM, in a ten minute emergency session of the legislature, the pro-Noriega PRD party which controlled the National Assembly backed Noriega in his claim and decertified Delvalle as President and installed Education Minister Manuel Solis Palma as "Minister in Charge of the Presidency." Delvalle immediately denounced the Assembly's action and called for a nationwide general strike to begin in two days as a show of universal protest. The pro-Noriega elements immediately and forcefully shut down the main opposition newspaper, *La Prensa*.

In the wake of these events, the State Department reaffirmed that the U.S. government recognized Delvalle as the legitimate head of state, but stated the United States had no plans to intervene militarily in the internal affairs of Panama. However, off-stage, as a precautionary measure, the U.S. Southern Command was directed by the Joint Chiefs of Staff to review the existing contingency plans and make recommendations as to the enhancement of the U.S. security posture in Panama. As part of US national decision process by General Woerner, CINCSOUTH, who had occasionally met with General Noriega privately to discuss specific situations, was told to cease all meetings with General Noriega. Another channel of communication was closed.

A few days later on February 29th, a national strike led by the Civilistas began with Panama City being its focus and the removal of Noriega the theme. However, the marchers were more representative of the small upper and economically better-off middle class than the typical street worker, day laborer, or rural farmer. This latter group was where the roots of the Democratic Revolutionary Party (PRD) and the PDF were anchored. The next day (the 1st of March), President Delvalle, now in hiding, (but still recognized as the Panamanian Head of State by the U.S. government), issued a Presidential Proclamation freezing all Panamanian assets outside of Panama.

Within 24 hours, on March 2, 1988, the U.S. Department of State reaffirmed U.S. recognition of Delvalle as the Panamanian Head of State and advised U.S. banks to honor the proclamation, and not disburse funds to the Government of Panama, the PDF, or Manuel Noriega. This request by the State Department was reinforced the next day when U.S. Federal District courts issued restraining orders to four U.S. banks, formally suspending any further transfer of funds or U.S. dollars to the Government of Panama. This move marked the official beginning of the economic sanctions. The next day, the 3rd, the "new" Palma government ordered Panama's 118 local and foreign banks closed until further notice because the government could not provide enough money to cover withdrawals.

Opposition leaders claimed Noriega was in the process of purging the PDF leadership of individuals suspected of being disloyal. The opposition spokesman said two colonels and two majors had been fired. Colonel Marcos Justine was listed as one of the Colonels that was relieved. By mid-day on the 4th, the national strike which had begun five days earlier and had paralyzed Panama City had run its course. The streets started to return to normal although at a much quieter tempo. On the economic front the situation was bad and likely to get worse. Thousands of Panamanian pensioners had taken to the streets when they could not cash their retirement checks in the wake of the U.S. freeze and the Panamanian bank closures. The Panamanian Foreign Minister announced the government was unsure whether it would be able to pay the 130,000 government and PDF personnel their pending mid-month paychecks.

During the course of the strike, government security agents raided and destroyed an opposition radio station, charging that it had broadcast an appeal for an anti-Noriega demonstration. The next day, unruly demonstrators gathered in front of the demolished radio station, set up barricades of burning trash and set fire to a minivan and a car. Anti-riot police responded in force and chased the demonstrators into side streets, firing tear-gas grenades as they moved. This was followed up by pumping massive amounts of tear gas from portable tanks into the surrounding buildings, eventually filling the entire neighborhood with the stinging fumes.

In a mid-week announcement, Archbishop Marcos McGrath, long known for his moderate stance and efforts to remain impartial, read a statement signed by 20 Catholic clerics calling for the full and effective subordination of the Panamanian military forces to civilian authority. The statement was taken by observers to be a major shift in Panamanian affairs, with the Church publicly coming out in support of a civilian government and constitutional rights and against the continued dominance of the PDF.

On March 11, a planned demonstration by the civil opposition in the central banking district was broken up by government riot police firing tear gas grenades and spraying the acid gas from portable canisters.

Four days later, on the 15th, PDF Riot Police, using tear gas, shotguns loaded with birdshot, and a water cannon, broke up a demonstration by 500 unpaid public employees from the Social Security Administration's main hospital in downtown Panama City. In Colon, the manager of a supermarket chain said two of their stores had been attacked by gangs of Noriega thugs, who demanded free food for government employees. A few days later, the government began selling sacks of food, called "dignity bags," to the unpaid workers.

The convergence of these events did not sit well with all members of the PDF. Some, concerned about the possibility of American military action, began planning a coup to depose Noriega. On the 16th, within forty-eight hours of the publicized arrival of additional American security elements, a group of PDF officers launched a coup intended to peacefully depose Noriega.

Rumors of the attempt reached Noriega beforehand from some of the junior officers and he initiated precautionary countermeasures. Shooting briefly erupted at the PDF headquarters early in the morning; however, the attempt collapsed quickly when the senior initiators were abruptly arrested and imprisoned.

A few hours later a PDF spokesman said nine army and police officers had led a coup attempt to seize the headquarters. The leader of the failed attempt was identified as Colonel Leonidas Macias, the Panama City police chief and a senior member of the PDF general staff. Other PDF senior officers supporting the attempt included the PDF Chief of Intelligence, Lt. Col. Wong, the former key point of contact with SOUTHCOM in his previous position on the Combined Board.

A young PDF captain by the name of Giroldi was instrumental in the Noriega counteraction at the Comandancia and was soon promoted to major by Noriega for his loyal and effective actions. The new major was also given command of the Comandancia security company.

Various reports indicated that a dozen officers linked to the coup attempt were imprisoned and another 20 forced into early retirement or exile. In one case, two Panamanian Air Force officers who successfully gained asylum at a U.S. airbase in Panama, were flown to the United States on Saturday the 19th, and in a TV interview stated that the PDF was stockpiling weapons around the country in anticipation of an American invasion.

Although unsuccessful, the coup attempt escalated local unrest and concurrently the threat to U.S. personnel throughout the Panama City area. Again anti-government demonstrations and street violence erupted throughout the downtown area. Cars were set on fire, barricades raised, and tires torched at intersections.

In other more peaceful demonstrations, Panamanian dock workers in Balboa blocked key roads in a protest against the government for not being paid. The demonstrating workers blocked the two main entrances to the port area by positioning three railroad cars across on the rail approach and two 40-foot Sea-Land shipping containers across the roadway entrance. In addition, the demonstrators placed two more Sea-Land containers across the nearby Gaillard Highway, the only immediate alternative to bypassing the roadblocks at the port. The dock workers did not man the roadblocks, and the PDF cleared the obstacles later in the day without incident.

The collective impression of these scenes and the chanting of vocal demonstrators and counter-demonstrators filled the eyes and ears of the Americans living in downtown Panama City and a vast number of American TV screens throughout the country, Miami, New York, and Washington.

Concerned for the immediate safety of U.S. citizens, and prompted by the violence associated with the strike along with increased harassment of Americans, President Reagan directed that additional security forces be dispatched to Panama. Air Force and Army military police and Marine infantry elements were sent to Panama to bolster security at the U.S. installations. The first units flew into Howard Air Force Base on March 18, 1988 and included a 44-man USAF Security Police flight trained in airbase defense, 6 dog teams, 100 Marines, and 212 Army military police.

The same day, in Washington, the U.S. Secretary of State George Shultz, during a televised appearance on *Meet The Press*, said in response to questions concerning Panama, "that Noriega must leave sooner or later—the sooner the better." Referring to the ongoing diplomatic dialogue between administration officials and the PDF Commander, Schultz said Noriega "should settle quickly before the opportunity that's there before him to go to Spain should disappear."

A few days later President Reagan said he still had hopes that General Noriega would relinquish power and leave Panama. Shortly thereafter Reagan formally revoked an estimated $2 million in trade privileges that Panama had enjoyed. The move was part of the U.S. plan to put economic pressure on Noriega to step down.

On Monday, March 28th, Panamanian plain-clothes agents and uniformed riot police invaded the Marriott Hotel, which had been the site of several opposition press conferences during the previous 30 days. Shortly after 6:00 PM, the plainclothes agents, brandishing pistols, burst into the hotel and began hauling opposition leaders outside. Within a few minutes uniformed PDF police arrived and sealed off the buildings. Eight journalist and some twenty opposition supporters were taken into custody. The journalists were released within hours, but the opposition activists were detained overnight.

As March 1988 drew to a close, and with it a month of political strikes and economic protest, physical destruction and vandalism, accompanied by a hardening of views and resolve on all sides, a spokesman for Archbishop McGrath announced the archbishop had talked with both opposition and the government leaders. The spokesman stated the Archbishop had a positive impression that a solution could be found to the paralyzing conflict of wills that had gripped the country. The spokesman said the Church was offering its services as a mediator, and saw the resignation of General Noriega as a key ingredient to any solution. The Church's offer of mediation was accepted by the opposition coalition in a formal letter on April 1st. Neither the PRD nor the PDF made any public comment.

The Comandancia photographed the day after the initiation of Operation *Just Cause*. Photo courtesy US Southern Command Public Information Office.

View representative of the older wood frame dwellings found in Barrio Chorrillo. The highrise adjacent to the location of the old Comandancia can be seen in the background. Photo courtesy of the author.

CHAPTER SIX
INCIDENTS AND PRECAUTIONS

In the wake of the March 16, 1988 coup attempt and the paralyzing series of national strikes, General Fred Woerner, the SOUTHCOM Commander, in addition to openly requesting the deployment of additional security forces, quietly requested JCS permission to create two joint task forces and begin contingency planning in earnest.

The U.S. national leadership was likewise very concerned by recent events and particularly concerned for the safety of the U.S. population living off post. The Secretary of Defense approved the SOUTHCOM request and authorized the deployment of an additional 1,300 security forces, and the low visibility formation of the two joint task forces.

Immediately following the approval, General Woerner initiated planning for the creation of an in-country Joint Task Force (JTF-Panama) drawn from within his existing theater resources. Simultaneously, he requested General Lindsay, the stateside Commander of the U.S. Special Operations Command, to create a joint special operations task force (JSOTF), to be referred to as JTF-South and to begin planning for offensive contingency operations to neutralize the PDF.

Meanwhile, the additional Army, Air Force, and Marine security elements were airlifted to Panama. The force included an Army military police battalion, an aviation task force, a specially trained Marine Corps counterterrorist unit, three Air Force air base ground defense flights, two additional dog squads, and command, control and support elements. The reinforcement raised the number of American security forces sent to Panama in the last two weeks of March to 1,900.

Almost in direct response to the increase in the U.S. security force posture and political rhetoric, the PDF began the creation of para-military groups of citizen volunteers to augment the PDF. These units were called Dignity Battalions, soon to be nicknamed DIGBATS by the American military.

The American aviation element, dubbed Task Force Hawk, was flown in via USAF Military Airlift Command (MAC) C-5 transports on the 5th of April, and included 26 helicopters: 15 UH-60 troop transport *Blackhawks*, four OH-58 *Kiowa* observation and seven AH-1 *Cobra* attack helicopters. The helicopters would provide rapid transportation and highly mobile firepower projection to the ground security force if needed.

By early April, there were eight MP companies in Panama, plus a Marine infantry company from Camp Lejeune, NC. Confrontations between U.S. forces and the PDF increased dramatically in the second week in April, the most volatile being a series of "skirmishes" and firefights between elements of the newly deployed Marines and unidentified intruders. The first incidents took place on April 11 and 12th at the U.S. naval petroleum storage area and were concentrated at a corner of the sprawling 800-acre restricted zone near the village of Arraijan to the north of the Howard AFB complex.

During the first incident, a Marine corporal was caught in a crossfire between two Marine patrols and accidentally shot. The second incident lasted more than two hours and included extensive shooting by the Marines, but no conclusive evidence of a PDF presence was found. A few days later, while attending a dedication ceremony at the Rio Hato Army base, General Noriega made a public comment about the incident. He suggested that the young Marines must have been very nervous, had fired at jungle sounds which were unfamiliar to them, and the human figures they claimed to have seen were figments of their imagination.

Noriega's comments ran counter to the description provided by a senior Marine NCO who had led one of the Marine patrols on the second night. The NCO said his patrol was on a small hill, overlooking one of the 36 underground fuel tanks, when he spotted 15 individuals about 500 feet away through his night vision equipment. The NCO said the intruders also were using night vision equipment, wearing black uniforms and carrying weapons. He recalled they were moving professionally and within a few minutes had moved to positions somewhat surrounding the Marine OP. The NCO assessed the motive of the group was two fold: self-training and probing of the Marine security posture.

Upon hearing gunshots and seeing muzzle flashes, he told his machine gunner to return the fire on the muzzle flashes. This portion of the engagement lasted about 15 minutes with the intruders withdrawing and the Marines suffering no casualties.

A third incident occurred a week later, around midnight April 19th, with unidentified intruders firing on an American sentry. The sentry returned fire and the intruders faded away. During a fourth incident, some 30 intruders were detected by a concealed U.S. Army Special Forces element. The Americans set off two claymore mines as the group approached the American position. The intruders quickly retreated and departed the area without firing a shot. The incidents stopped, and the intrusion situation remained quiet for an extended period. This time frame paralleled the political discussions and negotiations that were going on between senior officials of the U.S. Department of State and representatives of the PDF and General Noriega. The former were seeking the departure of General Noriega, the latter merely buying time and upping the ante.

American officials involved in this dialogue included Elliott Abrams, the Assistant Secretary of State for Latin American Affairs. While the Noriega-State Department dialogue was ongoing, civil unrest continued to expand in Panama City as more segments of the population took to the streets. One example included 300 members of a civilian women's group, who were assaulted by baton wielding PDF police women as the protestors were staging a march demanding the ouster of Noriega.

In late May, the U.S. administration sent another State Department official to Panama to pursue yet another round of negotiations with General Noriega. Michael Kozak, Deputy Assistant Secretary of State, was the envoy. The principal American bargaining chips were the drug indictments handed down by the federal grand juries in February. Although President Reagan authorized the trip and the continuation of the dialogue, Vice President Bush was opposed to any agreement that involved lifting the indictments. A few days later, on May 25th, George Shultz, the U.S. Secretary of State, announced that at the final moment of the negotiations, Noriega refused to accept the arrangements his representatives had made during the month-long negotiations. Secretary Schultz also stated that no further negotiations were being contemplated.

In June, three months later than usual, public schools throughout Panama finally opened. The schools normally opened in March, the beginning of the school year. However, the chaos of February, March, April and May had precluded this and many other normal activities.

In mid-June, the opposition coalition, the National Civic Crusade, marked its first year anniversary as an organization with a small protest outside the Cristo Rey Church in downtown Panama, the site of many anti-Noriega demonstrations. At a rival news conference, mid-level leaders of Noriega's ruling Democratic Revolutionary Party (PRD) called for a grass-roots party congress to replace the current Party leaders with a more progressive leadership group. However, no concrete action followed this brief call for some form of internal democracy. The PRD closed ranks and continued to align itself with the PDF and Noriega.

During the summer months, Noriega and the Democratic Revolutionary Party resumed attempts to mobilize the Panamanian population against the U.S. Noriega used his control of the PRD party newspapers and government radio and TV as conduits for the flow of yellow journalism, repeating the same claims and charges over and over. The themes again were Panamanian nationalism, Yankee imperialism, and the alleged intent of the U.S. to renege on the Canal Treaties and the turning over of the canal. Noriega and his propaganda machine tried to paint the Panamanian opposition as capitalist and puppets of U.S. business. The campaign was open and vocal, and a well-orchestrated, but a poorly disguised psychological operation.

In addition to increasing the size of security forces on the ground in Panama, one of the American military precautionary measures was to increase the availability of CONUS based combat units that could be moved quickly to Panama in the event contingency operations were required. One of these measures involved rotational deployments of three Ranger battalions. Beginning in mid-August, the battalions deployed to Panama on a back-to-back schedule to undergo jungle warfare training at the Army Jungle Operations Training Center (JOTC) at Fort Sherman, near Colon. The Rangers underwent a modified version of the normal JOTC curriculum that included more raiding operations and live-fire exercises than the normal instructionally oriented jungle operations and survival course.

Several other American precautionary actions served both a humanitarian and security purpose. One of these was the construction of a six mile road from the seaside village of Vera Cruz to the Pan-American Highway allowing access to and from the village without the residents or visitors having to traverse the main areas of the Howard/Kobbe complex. Initial clearing was begun on September 1, 1988, with completion projected for mid-1989. Further reinforcing the security screen around Howard, the USAF security police strength now numbered in excess of 500 personnel. Nearly 300 of these personnel were deployed nightly at 98 concealed observation and security outposts in the jungle on the hills surrounding the main base.

Meanwhile, civil unrest was still fermenting and spreading throughout the Panamanian civilian population. On the 15th of September, more than 50 civic associations demanded that the government annul an executive decree which infringed upon the right of free assembly.

The next day, PDF counter-intelligence agents detained the former Panamanian Ambassador to the United States for insisting that Delvalle was the legitimate President. Also in mid-month, the Balboa Port Employees Union called for a general strike and denounced the Noriega regime for not completing payment of employee salaries. According to the union leadership, there was enough money to finance PDF military parades and international communist meetings, such as a recent "Anti-imperialist Tribunal," which was sponsored by the Panamanian government and attended by delegates from "socialist and radical" governments around the world.

The union announcement drew a strong counteraction from the government. Within 38 hours, four of the union leaders were detained. The same day, the PDF took over the Electric Power Institute because its employees complained about the lack of pay, and also seized the National Institute (high school) because of student demonstrations. The 18th closed with an opposition communiqué circulating throughout the city announcing the formation of an "active movement" composed of "patriotic" Panamanian civilians and military personnel who planned to initiate armed activities against the Noriega regime. The recently created Panama's Workers Confederation issued a communiqué repudiating the government efforts to restrain the right of protest and demanding fair salaries.

The government countered with public rallies, most staged by the PRD, which in turn were used to feed the electronic and pulp media. Part of the effort called for the expansion of the voluntary people's militia units (Dignity Battalions) to augment the PDF, and prepare for the "inevitable clash of arms" with the Americans. It was said to be the right and the obligation of the population to join the Dignity Battalions and prepare to stand with the PDF against the "aggressors."

Battalion membership was largely drawn from the poorer sections of the city and often included petty criminals and thugs. Some joined for the additional money and the perceived special status. Membership also meant free cerveza (beer) at the recruiting and training sites. During the first three to four months, training was very rudimentary and irregular for these part time opportunists and zealots. Weapons familiarization was limited to weapons that did not have bolts or firing pins. Over time, this changed as a particular group progressed in their training. Eventually, some of the more qualified personnel were issued a set of military style fatigues.

Although not initially classified as a viable military force in the normal sense of the word, the "DIGBATS" did provide Manuel Noriega another instrument of intimidation as well as a ready-made core of vocal supporters at rallies.

In November 1988, SOUTHCOM filed a formal protest with the PDF regarding another unique and somewhat irregular harassment tactic. This involved low-level flights over several U.S. facilities and housing areas by PDF aircraft. The SOUTHCOM letter documented and reiterated earlier protest letters and addressed seven specific overflights (low altitude buzzing). The PDF aircraft involved were flights of two to five single engine propeller driven T-35 trainers, reminiscent of World War II P-51 fighters. The aircraft operated without prior coordination, flying below five hundred feet and, in some cases, as low as 50-100 feet over American housing areas, schools, Fort Amador, and Quarry Heights and 100-200 feet over Howard AFB. Also included in the SOUTHCOM letter was a protest concerning a September 29 uncoordinated PDF tactical parachute drop on the Panamanian section of Albrook runway.

In early December, the American Army headquarters at Fort Clayton took measures to restrict vehicle traffic and deter any vehicle-oriented terrorist incidents. The action involved closing off several unguarded access roads to unfenced family housing areas, such as the Curundu housing area. The security measures included installing a series of four-foot high concrete barriers on access roads, and inspecting the under-carriage of all vehicles entering for bombs. Similar inspection measures were also instituted at other installations including Rodman Naval Station, Howard AFB and Quarry Heights.

In mid-December, Admiral Crowe, the Chairman of the Joint Chiefs of Staff (CJCS) visited Panama and the U.S. Southern Command to get a firsthand update on events in the region and to discuss U.S. policies with General Woerner. During the same time, the U.S. Ambassador to Panama, Arthur Davis, speaking publicly for only the second time since his arrival in Panama nearly three years earlier, said human rights abuses in Panama were continuing to rise. Davis cited reports by the Panamanian Human Rights Committee that more than 60 Panamanians were being held "for political reasons without due process of law." The reports said 20 former PDF military officers suspected of involvement in the March coup attempt were still under arrest as well as 47 members of the political opposition parties.

Two weeks later, in a letter dated December 29, 1988, the PDF demanded that the Southern Command cease publication of its English language newspaper, the *Tropic Times*. The PDF claimed the newspaper opposed the Panamanian government and violated the principle of non-intervention, citing it published "slanted and ill-intended articles on General Noriega and the PDF." The command responded with the following public retort: "Unlike other local media sources, the U.S. forces do not fabricate information to mislead the public or censor international news accounts concerning their environment. The *Tropic Times* is designed to keep members of the U.S. forces community abreast of U.S. military, domestic, regional, and international news which impacts on them." The American response closed with the phrase: "This is even more significant since a free press has been denied (the people of Panama) and no U.S. papers have been allowed in Panama since last year."

As the calendar moved into 1989, and a new U.S. senior personality moved closer to center stage and the White House, President Elect George Bush made plans to celebrate his inauguration, the PRD and the PDF held sway in Panama while the political opposition, the Civil Crusade, remained fragmented.

One example of PDF actions occurred on Sunday night, January 8, 1989. In a replay of the events of March and April 1988, U.S. Marines on guard duty at the Arraijan petroleum tank farm detected unidentified individuals moving along the tree line near a Marine observation post (OP). The intruders fired on the Marine OP. The Marines, seeing two tracer rounds incoming, returned fire. No casualities were reported in this incident. About an hour and a half later, and a few kilometers away, another Marine OP spotted an intruder at the ammunition supply (and storage) point. The Marines verbally challenged the intruder, who responded by raising a weapon. The Marines opened fire and the intruder fled.

A month later, the PDF initiated another harassment tactic. On February 9th, the PDF detained seven U.S. military vehicles in separate incidents at the Chagres River Bridge near Gamboa. All of the vehicles were enroute to Panama City. Nine hours later, after a series of negotiations, three of the vehicles and their occupants were allowed to proceed while the other four vehicles were forced to return to their bases near Colon. The next day, a U.S. Army ambulance responding to an emergency request was delayed nearly an hour by the Policia de Transito (Traffic Police) who told the ambulance crew they were "tired of U.S. ambulances running around with sirens and red lights and were going to put a stop to it." The detention of the ambulance made the 39th recorded incident since the first of the year that violated the freedom of movement guarantees stipulated in the Canal Treaties.

In late February, the Panamanian government ordered the Electrical Power Company to cut the electricity to 78 residences that were under a lease-back agreement to DOD. Originally PCC quarters, the units had been turned over to the Panamanian government had then leased them to DOD. Although the cost of utilities, including the electricity, was being paid to the utility company, the rent proper had been routed into an escrow account since the previous April as part of the U.S. freeze on payments to the Government of Panama (GOP). In order to avoid a confrontation, the Southern Command relocated the residents to other quarters, and gave the required two-week notice of termination to the Panamanian government.

In the first 48 hours of March 1989, the Civilistas came alive, mustering more than 100,000 protestors to march in an anti-Noriega rally. The rally was timed to coincide with the visit of the OAS Human Rights Commission. The downtown streets were packed with Panamanians waving flags and banners, with shouts of "Justice." Thousands more cheered from balconies and threw confetti on the marchers below. A holiday mood prevailed, although the PDF had launched a surprise crackdown the day before designed to intimidate the population. The PDF tactic involved stopping thousands of cars, buses and taxis with outdated license plates (a normal occurrence in Panama), and handed out $25 fines on the spot. The action failed to deter the would-be marchers, and the presence of the OAS Commission forestalled any direct PDF/PRD counter-activity.

Early in the morning of March 3, 1989, the American community received a harsh reminder that peaceful coexistence was at the whim of the PDF. Shortly after 7:00 AM, the U.S. military police station at Fort Clayton was notified by a representative of the DOD school system that the PDF had commandeered a U.S. school bus loaded with children. The bus had been taken to the PDF Traffic Police Headquarters located at the base of Ancon Hill, a quarter of a mile from Albrook Air Force Station. The PDF claimed the buses were being operated illegally because the operating fees had not been paid. By 7:15 AM, seven buses had been detained and moved to the PDF site. An MP reaction force was alerted and held in readiness at Fort Clayton while a Spanish speaking American Military Police officer departed for the PDF traffic headquarters along with an MP liaison team.

By the time the officer and the team arrived at the detention site at 7:26, nine buses and 100 American children were being held in the station parking lot. The American MPs removed the ignition keys from the buses and directed the drivers and children to remain on the buses. The PDF responded with more police and vehicles, essentially forming a loose cordon around the buses. This was countered with the arrival of three MP vehicle patrols and eight plain-clothes MP personnel. An MP was immediately placed on each of the buses to prevent PDF personnel from boarding them.

At 7:45, the PDF attempted to tow one of the school buses; however, the MPs using an American vehicle blocked the tow truck from closing with the bus.

By 8:00 AM the PDF decided to negotiate. Teams of MP's evacuated all of the children and the DOD drivers without incident; however, the PDF wanted to retain the buses while the Americans wanted the vehicles released. The situation became tenser and the dialogue between the PDF traffic commander and the American MP officer became hostile. After an hour and fifteen minutes, and no progress, the Commander of the US Joint Task Force

Panama deployed the MP reaction force company to Albrook AFB in close proximity to the site of the incident. The MP company reached Albrook at 9:15. This company was reinforced within fifteen minutes by a second. Within five minutes (9:35) the PDF released the buses, and by 9:50 AM, all the Americans had departed the site, leaving the PDF with an empty parking lot.

Separately, 12 other American school buses were stopped and released that morning after the drivers were given tickets for operating "improperly" licensed vehicles. Subsequent investigation revealed that the American civilian who was operating the bus fleet under a contract with the U.S. Army South had chosen not to pay the required Panamanian operating fees under the pretext that since the buses were U.S. government vehicles, the law did not apply. This independent action provided the PDF with the legal rational for their action. U.S. Army South promptly cancelled the contract and reissued it to another party.

As the oppressive realities of the situation, and the proximity of the national elections (only nine weeks away - May 7) dawned on the Panamanian political opposition, the various leadership elements began to put their individual differences aside and pull together. Campaigning for the upcoming elections became the new battleground. Vigorous and open campaigning became the fare of the local newspapers, radio and television, marches, and rallies.

During March, the PDF set up checkpoints and roadblocks in an attempt to intimidate the population and control demonstrations. Part of this increased government presence included elements of Battalion 2000 manning checkpoints supported by armored vehicles equipped with a 90mm gun. This was the first time PDF military units were involved in a public display of force. Elements of the Dignity Battalions, now somewhat better trained, also became a street fixture.

On Wednesday night, April 5, 1989, the war of petty annoyance took on a new and potentially more menacing nature. Late that night, an American civilian, Kurt Muse, a long-term resident of Panama and a "Zonian" was arrested by the PDF at Torrijos International Airport as he returned to Panama after a visit to the United States. After receiving word of the arrest from waiting family members, the U.S. Military Police liaison immediately attempted to obtain custody of Muse, but the PDF failed to admit to knowledge of his whereabouts, or the fact that they had him in custody, until late the next day. The PDF finally admitted the detention, and said Muse had been involved in operating a clandestine radio station for the opposition; and he was being charged with "crimes against the security of the Panamanian State ... and promoting subversion."

It was not until noon on Friday that U.S. officials were able to gain access to Muse. A few days later the PDF reported confiscating more than $350,000 worth of transmitters, antennae, microphones, and video equipment in Muse's apartment. The PDF also claimed Muse had named five other Americans who were involved in the radio broadcast and had admitted receiving the equipment and taped programs from American contacts. The U.S. Department of State protested the arrest and the incarceration, and continued to do so throughout the following months to no avail. However, the Embassy was able to maintain contact with Muse through a series of frequent visits.

During early April 1989, the potential for a major, violent confrontation grew more likely because minor confrontations between U.S. personnel, including MPs, and PDF elements, were occurring more frequently. Although careful dialogue, patience, and diplomacy often diffused a situation before it reached an explosive point, sometimes the PDF came out on top. One such event occurred on April 6 when two American MPs attempted to stop the PDF from entering and searching an American civilian residence. The two MPs were surrounded by 10 heavily armed PDF soldiers while other PDF personnel entered the house and conducted the search.

Meanwhile, as the May election came within in sight, both sides of the Panamanian political equation heated up the tempo of campaigning, routinely taking to the streets in peaceful demonstrations. The events of April 20 and 21 were representative. On the 20th, the three opposition candidates from the Democratic Opposition Alliance (ADO) led a march of thousands through the downtown business district turning the major avenues into a sea of bodies and colorful opposition flags and banners. The PDF did not react, nor was there any harassment by groups of DIGBATS who watched. The next day, General Noriega led a march of tens of thousands of PRD/PDF supporters winding through the old section of the city. The government march included top PDF officers, the acting president, Manuel Solis Palma, and the three government-backed candidates.

Part of the Civilista's strategy was to make the May 7 election an international event and a validation of their protest movement. International observers were invited from the Organization of America States (OAS), the United Nations, and several independent political civil liberties groups. Notables such as former American Presidents Jimmy Carter and Gerald Ford were scheduled to be among the international observers.

Two days before the elections, at 9:00 PM on May 5, the PDF, claiming the imminence of a U.S. invasion, attempted to seal off the former Canal Zone by setting up a series of checkpoints and roadblocks. The tactic came as a surprise to the Americans.

The Military Police deployed reaction forces to 13 of the checkpoints to prevent any detention or harassment of Americans. However, some Americans were stopped at other checkpoints, harassed and detained by the PDF. At some checkpoints, the PDF pulled weapons and tried to search and confiscate cars. The MPs intervened, and pushing and shoving occurred between MPs and PDF. Despite the low boiling point, no shots were exchanged, no Americans were injured, and most were returned to American control quickly. The situation had eased substantially by dawn. The PDF dismantled the checkpoints later in the day.

When election day arrived, the lines at the voting sites were long but orderly. By midday, based on exit interviews, it seemed that the opposition candidates were winning despite reports of widespread voter fraud and ballot stuffing by Noriega supporters. Later in the day, and despite the presence of the international observer teams, the ballot boxes were confiscated by the PDF police. This action was followed, within hours, by General Noriega publicly declaring the voting to be null and void.

The confiscation and nullification did not sit well with the Panamanian people, the political opposition, the United States, or the world press. Emotions started to rise and the gaming of "what ifs" began. The following day, May 8th, a company of PDF infantry deployed into the jungle high ground behind Fort Clayton and set up overwatch positions. During the next two days (the 9th and the 10th), the PDF detained and tried to arrest several members of MP Liaison Evacuation teams.

By midday of the 10th, emotions and unrest were still running high. The civilian opposition alliance again joined together and conducted a protest march through downtown Panama City. As the number of marchers grew and the lead elements arrived at the Santa Anna section, stick and baton-wielding groups of thugs from the Dignity Battalions attacked the marchers. The Civilista Presidential and Vice Presidential candidates and political leadership were singled out for "special treatment".

The carnage was recorded live by several television teams and became media fodder on the evening news throughout the United States and the entire Latin American world, except Cuba and Nicaragua. The TV images included the Vice Presidential candidate, Billy Ford, covered with the blood of his slain bodyguard, being beaten by a pipe wielding DIGBAT while uniformed PDF police stood by and watched.

This unparalleled use of open and unbridled violence prompted President Bush to order the deployment of an additional 2,000 U.S. troops to Panama. The order was issued on May 11.

As the additional forces were alerted for movement, some service members living off-post in Panama made plans to send their families back to the United States while others were ordered to move onto the U.S. military facilities. The dislocation of families was received with mixed emotions.

Many of the families were both saddened by the impending separation, and happy to be leaving the turmoil and tension of Panama behind them. Others looked at the inconvenience of moving into lesser accommodations on the military installations as the best of the options available. The outbound movement of the American dependents was nicknamed *Blade Jewel*, while the inbound reinforcement of soldiers, marines, and airmen was known as Operation *Nimrod Dancer*. By May 18, 1989, all of the off-post dependents had been relocated to U.S. installations in Panama or evacuated to the United States. The American dependent pullout and consolidation further affected the already damaged and shrinking local Panamanian economy.

In the wake of the build-up of the security forces, which included additional Air Force security flights, two Army companies – a light infantry and a mechanized infantry – plus a mechanized Marine Light Armored Infantry (LAI) company, there was a temporary reduction in the number of incidents.

In mid-May, because of increased PDF boldness and the growth of the Dignity Battalions, General Woerner directed the Commander Joint Task Force-Panama (Major General Bernard Loeffke, the in-country contingency reaction planner) to initiate a series of training exercises. The purpose of the exercises was twofold: to maintain force proficiency and assert U.S. rights under the terms of the 1979 Torrijos-Carter Treaties. The exercises and drills fell into two broad categories. Individual unit movements and small unit training exercises were conducted under the title of *Sand Flea(s)* while larger company/battalion level and multi-service joint exercises were called *Purple Storm(s).*

The former developed and maintained individual combat and combat support skills while the latter provided a basis for the development and perfection of joint force inter-operability. The exercises were categorized and evaluated beforehand by their visibility to the PDF and the risk of possible confrontation. They ranged from relatively benign, low visibility-low risk to high visibility-high risk.

Logistic nicknames such as *Harvest Bear* and *Harvest Eagle*, which were very familiar to the USAF Tactical Air Forces, took on new meaning to hundreds of troops from all the services arriving in Panama. Throughout the middle of May, prefabricated and inflatable structures and tent cities drawn from *Harvest* contingency stocks sprouted on U.S. military facilities and training ranges on the "American" side of the Canal.

Most of the *Nimrod Dancer* security augmentation troops arrived in Panama via transports of the Military Airlift Command (MAC). Critical equipment was also delivered in C-141 strategic transports. Huge C-5 transports designed to carry large, outsized cargo regularly made deliveries to Howard. Heavier outsized equipment and large quantities of sustaining material was delivered by navy and commercial ships.

One of the larger American units to be marshaled and deployed was a mechanized infantry task force from Fort Polk, Louisiana. The task force was structured around a fleet of M-113 armored personnel carriers (APC) and two infantry companies, and key support elements drawn from throughout its parent the 5th Infantry Division (5th ID).

Within 36 hours of receipt of the deployment order, the lead elements of the task force were moving. The first contingent consisted of a full mechanized company, and its multi-ton M-113 APCs. They moved by highway from Fort Polk to England Air Force Base, Alexandria, Louisiana, where the entire unit was loaded on long-range MAC transports and flown directly into Howard AFB.

During the next 72 hours, the balance of the task force personnel were flown to Howard, while the remaining heavy equipment was moved overland to port facilities at Beaumont, Texas. There it was loaded on navy transport ships that immediately sailed for Panama.

Once the lead company was on the ground in Panama, it moved to a field camp set up within the Howard, Kobbe complex. The site was a hastily improvised camp near the Panama Canal consisting of a few permanent buildings, two inflatable buildings provided by the Air Force, plus a host of tents. The inflatable "bubbles" originally designed to house deployed Air Force tactical command and control and medical elements resembled large gymnasium-sized versions of World War II Quonset huts. Much of the site preparation and set up was accomplished in unison with Air Force "Red Horse" combat construction units also deployed from the United States.

Within a few weeks, the 5th ID Task Force was working (and living) out of three base camps. These were the original site which the unit called Camp Roadrunner, another site composed of Quonset huts at the Empire Training Range, and a third site on the back side of Albrook Air Force Station at the edge of Panama City.

The task force had arrived in Panama at the beginning of the rainy season and had to contend with the almost daily torrential downpours as it trained on the Southern Command field ranges, guarded U.S. facilities near Panama City, and maintained a quick reaction alert. For the next five months, the men and machines of the 5th ID served as mobile "firemen" for the Southern Command. They moved their formidable M-113s with their rapid-fire machine guns and assault squads to potential trouble spots when needed. At other times, working in conjunction with elements of the 193rd Infantry Brigade, they conducted exercises reaffirming the United States right of movement and presence under the terms of the Treaties.

In August, the PDF attempted to detain MP patrols at Fort Amador and the Curundu housing area. The Southern Command quickly responded with a reaction force of MP patrols, Army mechanized infantry in tracked M-113 APCs, and Marines in their imposing eight-wheeled armored assault vehicles. The American units sealed off the two areas and U.S. sniper teams took up visible overwatch positions. Initially, the PDF began to aim their weapons at the U.S. forces, but quickly reevaluated the situation, lowered their weapons, released the MPs, and quietly withdrew.

Throughout the summer and fall, the deployed American combat units as well as the MPs routinely conducted freedom-of-movement operations, patrolled the Galliard Highway (the main road along the Canal), with the armored personnel carriers and MP vehicles. These demonstrations, nicknamed "roadrunner missions" by the U.S. troops, were often provided air cover by Army helicopter gunships, Air Force A-7 or OA-37 attack aircraft.

In response to the increased tempo of U.S. political rhetoric and the military exercise activity, the Noriega press increased its anti-American diatribes and attempted to foment a new wave of war hysteria among the Panamanian populace and the Latin American community at large. The Organization of American States was one of the primary targets. The front page of the pro-government newspaper, *La Critica,* ran banner headlines protesting the U.S. military exercises, claiming they were evidence of, and a mask for, an imminent American invasion.

In September, the personnel of the initial 5th ID two company Task Force were replaced by a full battalion from Fort Polk. By the end of September the 5th ID Task Force numbered 725 personnel and included four fully equipped and urban warfare trained companies. During the previous 90 days, the soldiers of this CONUS-based battalion had undergone extensive training in urban warfare and maneuvers in the states, and had been in regular contact with the two companies that were already in Panama. The lessons learned by the initial "Roadrunner" contingent were regularly passed back to the CONUS based units.

In mid-October, the commander of the 3rd Brigade of the 7th Infantry Division (Light) arrived in Panama along with the full brigade and assumed tactical responsibility from the 1st Brigade which had been deployed to Panama earlier as part of the rotational contingency buildup. The 1st Brigade began its rotation back to Fort Ord on October 16th. Once settled in, the officers, NCOs, and men of the 3rd Brigade immediately became involved in mission planning, training, preparation, and rehearsals for their possible contingency role. Every three weeks, one of the brigade's battalions rotated into the JOTC, where the battalion leadership was briefed on their part of the operation and the companies, platoons, squads, and fire teams were drilled in the tactical aspects of their responsibilities. Most field training was conducted as part of the *Sand Flea* exercise program. In addition, freedom-of-movement convoys were conducted twice weekly from Fort Sherman, the brigade headquarters, near Colon to Fort Clayton near Panama City.

Throughout the months of October and November, and into December, the various forces continued their training and show of force presence with only a few minor confrontations with PDF forces. The training profile ranged from individual and squad-level drills to sharpen combat skills, to larger exercises to perfect unit coordination, and, eventually, to the joint force exercises called *Purple Storms*. During the period October 1 to December 20, 1989, JTF-Panama conducted 44 *Sand Flea* operations and five *Purple Storm* operations.

Although every operation did not result in a physical response from the PDF or the DIGBATS, many of the U.S. operations were exploited for anti-U.S. propaganda purposes in the local papers and on television. Most of the rhetoric published or broadcast stated that the U.S. Forces were violating the Panama Canal Treaties and the sovereignty of Panama. Unlike in August and September, uniformed PDF never directly confronted the U.S. Forces during this time frame. The only physical confrontation came from DIGBATS.

Some of these "civilians," however, were identified by intelligence sources as actually being PDF leaders and soldiers dressed in civilian clothes.

During every U.S. operation, a mobile Psychological Operations Handheld Broadcast (PSYOP HB) team accompanied the core unit. They would broadcast, in Spanish, the purpose of the operation and counter any protest the PDF would stage. Additionally, a Joint Audio-Visual Detachment Team (JAVDET) accompanied the unit. It photographed and video taped the operation. Many of the operations were shown on Southern Command News (SCN) Television to counter any PDF propaganda that may have been forthcoming. In fact, many times the videotape shown on the Panamanian government-controlled channels was edited from the earlier American broadcast.

The *Sand Flea* and *Purple Storm* operations proved invaluable to the units in JTF-Panama. All of the JTF-P units practiced both their offensive and defensive plans on numerous occasions. Command and control problems between services and higher headquarters were resolved and were continually reviewed. Support and coordination requirements and difficulties were discussed during the after-action review for each operation. Additionally, the intelligence community within USSOUTHCOM, Joint Task Force-South (JTF-SO) and JTF-Panama expanded their knowledge of the PDF order of battle, its command and control structure, force reaction time, and degree of commitment to General Noriega. As time elapsed, the PDF became more and more complacent about these activities.

In late May, President Bush advised the Secretary of Defense that he wanted the SOUTHCOM Commander General Woerner, replaced as soon as practical. This was a reflection of the hardening of the President's opinion and the American position vis-a-vis the situation in Panama. Upon learning of the impending action, the Army Chief of Staff, General Carl E. Vuono, a close friend of General Woerner made a trip to Panama to advise Woerner of the impending change and suggested it was time to retire. On June 20th, Admiral Crowe, the Chairman of the JCS, recommended a former Army Vice Chief of Staff, General Maxwell Thurman, a firebrand and action oriented officer, who himself was about to retire, as General Woerner's replacement. The general consensus at the time was General Woerner and his immediate predecessor, General Galvin, were the kind of commander-diplomat-soldier you have if you want to solve problems diplomatically. While on the other hand General Thurman, given his personality, was the commander you would want in charge if you had decided diplomacy was not going to work and you had to be fully prepared to fight.

On a separate Washington front, President Bush approved National Security Directive 17 on July 22nd which directed (authorized) American forces in Panama to assert U.S. Treaty Rights within certain restraints and controls. The NSD established four levels of actions. Category I (Low Risk/Low Visibility) included actions such as publicizing the evacuation of U.S. dependents and placing members of the PDF under U.S. escort whenever they entered U.S. installations. Category II (Low Risk/High Visibility) included increased U.S. Military Police patrols, battalion units would deploy from the states for intensive training, and troops would practice amphibious and night operations. Category III (Medium Risk/High Visibility) included increased reconnaissance and armed convoys in the vicinity of key PDF installations (less the Comandancia). Category IV (High Risk/High Visibility) included options for U.S. forces to take full control of several joint and limited use facilities such as Fort Amador, the Amador Causeway and Coco Solo.

In mid-August, after obtaining SECDEF and Presidential concurrence of General Thurman's nomination to replace General Woerner, Admiral Crowe asked General Thurman to review the SOUTHCOM contingency plans. In early August, acting on the CJCS request, General Thurman visited Fort Bragg and received a series of briefings that laid out the plans as they then stood. Later in August, General Thurman and the new SOUTHCOM J-3, Brigadier General William Hartzog, met with Lieutenant General Carl Stiner, the Commander of the XVIII Airborne Corps, to discuss the validity of the current plans in view of the increasingly more strident nature of the political situation. The SOUTHCOM J-3 directed his planners to revise plans accordingly. General Hartzog briefed the revised order to General Kelley, the JCS J3, on September 15th.

The Woerner-Thurman Change of Command ceremony took place two weeks later at Fort Clayton at 9:00 AM on Saturday, September 30, 1989 and was officiated by General Robert T. Herres, USAF, the Vice Chairman of the JCS. Admiral Crowe, the former Chairman, had retired only a few days earlier, passing the responsibilities of the office of Chairman to General Colin Powell. Both Powell and Thurman had been alerted to their respective transfers six weeks earlier and had begun separate intensive programs of study and self-education which included Panama. General Powell brought memories of the war in Vietnam and his recent (less than two years ago) experience as former assistant National Security advisor to President Reagan.

On the same day as the Woerner-Thurman change of command, the USAF held an official ceremony at Albrook closing the Inter-American Air Forces Academy (IAAFA) in Panama and transferring its cadre to Homestead AFB in Florida. The academy had been organized in 1943 to provide technical training and education in aeronautical support specialties to 14 Latin American countries. During its tenure in Panama, the school provided training to more than 26,000 students.

The longstanding tension and uneasiness that was the hallmark of the Panama scene in 1988 and 1989 was punctuated a few days later by a second coup attempt within the PDF. On the third of October, a young PDF Major, commander of the Urraca Battalion, which included the Security Force Company (the Dobermans), and with the support of the 4th Infantry (Reconnaissance/Cavalry) Company, both stationed at the Comandancia, seized the complex and took General Noriega quasi-prisoner. This October coup was led by Major Moise Giroldi. As a Captain, Giroldi had been instrumental in suppressing the March 1988 coup attempt. Giroldi was a believer in Panamanian nationalism and supporter of Noriega, but also believed it was time for the general to step down for the sake of the country and the PDF. Giroldi undertook this effort in an attempt to resolve the overall situation in a bloodless manner. Noriega had stood as godfather to one of Giroldi's children, and the young major believed he could reason with his "El Jefe." He hoped to convince Noriega to formally relinquish command of the PDF and gracefully retire.

Giroldi had communicated his intent through his wife to senior American officers on Sunday evening, October 1st. The coup was planned to begin the next morning, Monday the 2nd. Giroldi's plan called for seizing the Comandancia and announcing the intent of the coup on the national radio. He asked his American contacts to block two roads leading to the city. The new American commander, General Thurman, communicated the notice of a possible coup to Washington with a note of skepticism, but prepared plans to move U.S. units to the blocking areas as a precaution. However, he refrained from ordering any actual movement due to the potential that the "tip" and the "request" were part of a PDF scheme to further aggravate the situation and "catch" the Americans in a compromising position. A SOUTHCOM Crisis Action Team (CAT) was activated at Quarry Heights to monitor the situation. The standing JTF Panama CAT had been relocated to Fort Clayton, taken up residence in the US Army South Operations Center and was focused on military contingency operations. General Thurman wanted his information center immediately at hand.

The next day at the appointed hour, there was no indication of any unrest or disturbance at the Comandancia, and there was no radio announcement. General Thurman notified General Powell of the lack of action and again stated his skepticism. That evening, Giroldi's wife again contacted the Americans and said the coup had been delayed, and was now scheduled to begin the following morning. The request to block the roads was restated. General Thurman again advised Washington.

While General Thurman advised Washington, the U.S. Army South Commander, Major General Cisneros (as a precautionary measure), alerted and ordered Marine forces to move to off-road positions near the potential blocking points, but not block the roads or stop any traffic pending further orders. In addition, he positioned surveillance teams along the approach route to provide early warning of any PDF military movement. None occurred. The next morning at 8:00 AM, the sound of gunfire from the Comandancia signaled the initiation of the attempt, but there was no accompanying radio announcement.

General Noriega and his immediate staff arrived at the Comandancia earlier than expected. The surprised rebels did not challenge them, strip them of their weapons or detain them. The Noriega group, sensing the rebel hesitation, but choosing not to start a one-sided gunfight, quickly made their way up the stairwell to the general's office suite. They found the office telephones were still functional. Noriega promptly used them to call for help.

Elements of Battalion 2000 at Fort Cimarron were alerted, loaded into trucks, and began an hour plus race towards the Comandancia. At the same time, the 6th and 7th Infantry Companies (Macho de Monte) at Rio Hato (located ninety miles from Panama City) were also alerted and PDF aircraft dispatched from Tocumen to pick them up. Within three hours of the Giroldi initiative becoming known, these three PDF units were converging on Panama City and the Comandancia. Some troops from Rio Hato were airlifted into Paitilla Airport, which is less than two miles from the Comandancia. Together with the forces from Fort Cimarron, they stormed into the Comandancia and quickly overpowered the now outnumbered and outgunned rebels, most of whom surrendered on the spot. The enlisted troops were disarmed, searched, and then loaded onto trucks and taken away under guard. At least eighty were imprisoned. The officers were not so fortunate. Fourteen officers from the units involved in the attempt were executed. Major Giroldi was even less fortunate. Shortly after he had turned over his weapon and surrendered to Noriega, he was led away, interrogated and tortured for several hours, and then summarily executed.

The coup had lasted less than four hours. The PDF had reacted quickly and with greater ingenuity, as evidenced by the extemporaneous airlift operation, than either Major Giroldi or SOUTHCOM had envisioned.

In the aftermath of the attempted coup, the two rebel PDF units involved, the Public Security Company (the Dobermans), and the Cavalry/Reconnaissance Company were disbanded. In addition, the defenses, personnel, and weapons strength at the Comandancia were increased and several combat units of the PDF were repositioned to enhance their future reaction capability. One of these was the highly trained UESAT anti-terrorist unit which was relocated from its garrison on Flamenco Island, at the end of the Fort Amador causeway, to Panama Viejo moving into the barracks of the disbanded Cavalry unit.

At Quarry Heights, the quick suppression of the attempt gave rise to concerns of possible PDF orchestrated anti-American terrorist activity. The new American Commander, General Thurman, ordered an increase in the American security posture at all installations. He and other senior officers had reason to consider the possibility of pipe bomb and molotov cocktail attacks against U.S. installations, undefended housing areas, and American businesses. Stringent security checks were initiated at all U.S. military installations. No incidents occurred.

The "second coup attempt," coming immediately on the heels of General Thurman's assumption of command, made him, already one of the world's great workaholics, even more so. It also changed the environment from occasional frustration, and some verbal and physical jostling between

SOUTHCOM and the PDF, to one of almost unavoidable confrontation. Long after the coup crisis subsided, Thurman, a lifelong bachelor who worked 18 – 20 hours a day and thought everyone else should too, looked upon the Quarry Heights CAT as something that should be maintained. It worked well for him. It dovetailed with his work schedule, giving him a 24-hour-a-day staff. He was well supported. The Quarry Heights SOUTHCOM CAT was kept going, even though by the "standard" measure of a crisis it was not necessary. This was particularly true given the 24 hour operation of the Command Operations Center, the Intelligence Watch Center and the Joint Reconnaissance Center all collocated in the Tunnel less than fifty feet from the headquarters building. However, given the tension of that period and the distractions of their normal work, none of the existing centers fully satisfied the immediate information needs of General Thurman.

In one of his first staff meetings, General Thurman asked, "Where is my alternate CP (command post)?" When a negative answer came, he set as a top priority the creation of an alternate CP at Howard AFB, resulting in considerable building and reconstructing in the main operations building. He also halted a Tunnel remodeling program that had been funded and even, to some extent, begun because of the physical turbulence and security vulnerabilities that the construction work would create.

October also saw the establishment of the new Counter-Narcotics Directorate. Its operational plan was prepared over the four-day Columbus Day weekend by a team of planners working 18 hours a day. October also saw what was to be the last great guerrilla offensive in the Salvadoran War take place with many casualties suffered by both insurgent and government forces. In the long run, the government came out ahead and negotiations led to peace.

SOUTHCOM staff elements were working in overdrive during this period given all that was going on in Panama, El Salvador, and other areas. While the various contingency forces were gearing up for their respective roles, the staff workload increased tremendously. The tension and long days of 1988 paled in contrast to the last quarter of 1989. Seven-day work weeks, 11-13 hours a day, were the norm for the intelligence, communications, operations and planning staffs. The new Counter-Narcotics directorate was not excepted, working pretty much the same hours. They were specially chosen mostly young and mostly single, with a single mission focus and, without the distractions of family responsibilities, and were better able to manage the workload.

On October 27, SOUTHCOM announced that it had revised its Personnel Movement Limitation (PML) definitions and the structure of the notification system. The new definitions kept the basic framework but added a fifth, more restrictive level, PML *Echo*. Under PML *Alpha*, disturbances are nonexistent and no threat to U.S. lives was present, so personal travel was not restricted. PML *Bravo* indicated a slightly increased level of threat, and isolated disturbances were possible. Travel caution was required as well as avoidance of the potential areas of disturbances. PML *Charlie* was declared when there was a decided increased threat to U.S. personnel. Personnel movement was limited and selected areas, establishments, bars, discos, casinos, and nightclubs were off limits. PML *Delta* indicated there was a threat to U.S. personnel and all public areas in Panama should be avoided. Travel was restricted to designated routes between U.S. installations that were patrolled by U.S. forces. Only essential military travel was authorized in Panama City. All personal travel and outdoor activities outside U.S. installations was prohibited. PML *Echo*, the new addition to the structure, prohibited all personnel movement off U.S. installations because of the potential threat to U.S. lives. Only military personnel on essential missions were allowed to travel off U.S. military installations. Schools and installation support facilities were closed or operated on restricted schedules.

Two weeks later, on November 13th, the Inter-American Commission on Human Rights, an OAS sub-body, released a 61-page report accusing the Government of Panama (GOP) of widespread human rights abuses including murder, torture, and political repression. The report also stated the current Panamanian regime was "devoid of constitutional legitimacy." The report was delivered to the Foreign Ministers of the Western Hemisphere Nations at the annual General Assembly of the OAS in Washington. Almost simultaneously in Guatemala, the Conference of American Armies (an annual meeting of the senior military officers of the Latin American countries) was being held. A paper was unanimously adopted at the military conference. It asked General Noriega, as the military leader of Panama, "to comply with these principles (of the basic rights of the people) for the benefit of all American countries especially in their efforts to protect the continent's democratic process from any types of totalitarianism and subversion." Neither of these documents had any positive effect on the Noriega regime.

Despite the increasing tensions and concerns, an effort was made to maintain a level of normalcy within the American community. On Saturday, November 11th, a flight of *Dragon Fly* OA-37 close air support aircraft based at Howard provided a missing man fly over during the American Veterans Day Memorial Ceremony held at Corozal Military Cemetery near Fort Clayton. And on Tuesday, November 14, a mini-fleet of seven war ships, five U.S. and two from Colombia, docked at Rodman Naval Station. The contingent held an open house and band concert on Wednesday and remained until Saturday, the 18th when they departed via the Canal to participate in the annual UNITAS Inter-American Naval Exercises.

During the 4th week of November, Thanksgiving week, a number of seasonal events had to be postponed, cancelled, or relocated due to the ongoing tensions and potential for confrontation. The Amador Officers Club located near the PDF controlled causeway was temporarily closed. Thanksgiving dinner and Sunday brunch were held at the much smaller but safer Quarry Heights Officers Club. Additionally, the annual 193rd Infantry Brigade Formal Dinner Dance which was to be held at the Fort Amador Officers Club was relocated to the Albrook Club.

Tensions escalated sharply on Friday, December 15, when the Panamanian Legislative Assembly, which was controlled by the Noriega political machine, appointed General Noriega as the "Maximum Leader" and the official head of the Panamanian State. Within hours, and in front of a large crowd and a bank of television cameras, Manuel Antonio Noriega, brandishing a gleaming ceremonial machete, declared that a "state of war" existed between the United States and the Republic of Panama. Rhetorically at least, the battle had been joined.

The next evening, Saturday December 16, at approximately 9:00 PM, a carload of off-duty SOUTHCOM staff officers were challenged at a PDF roadblock a few blocks from the Comandancia. The roadblock was manned by a half dozen uniformed PDF. A group of some 40 civilians were also congregated near the roadblock. The American car was one of several in line at the roadblock. When the American vehicle reached the checkpoint, the PDF attempted to pull the occupants from the car. After not receiving a PDF response to their query as to why they were being singled out, the officer driving the American car accelerated away from the scene.

Several of the PDF troopers fired at the departing vehicle. Lt. Robert Paz, a Marine officer attached to the new Counter-narcotics Directorate who was riding in the back seat, was hit and critically wounded. Although the driver drove the injured officer to nearby Gorgas Army Hospital, the Marine lieutenant died shortly thereafter.

Major General Cisneros was notified of the incident during the U.S. Army South's Christmas Formal that was underway at the Fort Amador Officers Club. Cisneros calmly announced that shots had been fired near the Comandancia and that a US serviceman had been shot. He cancelled the event, sent spouses home, ordered a heightened readiness posture and placed personnel on a shortened recall status.

A similar scenario occurred throughout the collective SOUTHCOM community. A SOUTHCOM Operations Directorate Christmas Party hosted by Brigadier General. Hartzog at his Quarry Heights house was terminated abruptly about 10:00 PM when the Command Post notified General Hartzog of the shooting incident and death of Lt. Paz. Most of the officers attending the party reported to their duty stations after seeing to the safety of their wives and dates.

At General Cisneros's direction AH-64 and OH-58s helicopters were launched on reconnaissance missions to survey the highways between Panama City and the PDF bases at Rio Hato and Fort Cimarron. Other helicopters were alerted and prepared to transport the 1st Bn 508th Airborne from Fort Kobbe to Fort Amador if needed. While these missions were underway, General Cisneros went airborne in an UH-60 *Blackhawk* and conducted a visual reconnaissance of downtown Panama City; again, no significant PDF activity was observable. The Rio Hato and Fort Cimarron reconnaissance missions likewise detected no PDF activity. Although a major PDF initiated confrontation did not appear imminent, precautionary measures were warranted.

Within an hour of the death of Lt. Paz, the quiet of the barracks of the 534th Military Police Company was broken when the alert platoon was notified to load-up and move out to Fort Amador and secure it. The unit's HMMWVs were parked next to the barracks, fueled and armed. The standard configuration included a M203 grenade launcher with 6 HE rounds, two M16 A2s with eight hundred and forty 5.56 rounds, and one M-60 machine gun with three crates of 7.62 mm ammunition, every fifth round a red tracer. Also cached with the vehicles were three M9 pistols with 30 rounds per person, night vision goggles, and a night vision scope for the M-60 machine gun and all personal gear to include rucksack, protective mask, etc. All the equipment was positioned in a prearranged manner allowing it to be easily reached and employed.

All personnel donned their protective vest while the gunners slid their M-60s onto gun mounts on the top of the vehicles. The MPs were given the order to lock and load their weapons. Once all the teams were ready, the company headed out the front gate of Fort Clayton at a rapid pace, using horns and flashing lights to announce their movement and clear the road.

As the force approached the front gate of Fort Amador, they passed many civilians and dependents. Some of the civilians hollered at the convoy to "kick butt," while others wished the MPs good luck and shouted to them "be careful". The reaction teams moved to their pre-selected points within the sprawling complex, essentially cordoning off the American areas of the installation. Shortly after the American positions were established, the MPs spotted PDF personnel emerging from their barracks with weapons. In a few instances, small teams of PDF drove their private vehicles to within 15 feet of some American positions before veering away. The American order of the day was to hold fire unless fired upon. Apparently, the PDF were under a similar restraining order as there were no confrontations or exchanges of fire throughout the night.

Approximately 30 minutes prior to the time of the Paz shooting at the roadblock, another American officer and his wife, both of whom spoke Spanish, had been stopped and detained at the same checkpoint. The couple had been enroute back to Rodman Naval Station after having dinner at a downtown restaurant. Upon being stopped at the checkpoint, the PDF asked the couple for their identification cards and told them to pull over to the side of the street and wait until the cards were checked. The couple obliged.

Immediately after the Paz shooting incident, the PDF took the pair to a nearby PDF station and blindfolded them with masking tape. They were then put into the back of a pickup truck and were driven a few minutes to another location. The American couple was kept blindfolded and was interrogated for about four hours. During the interrogation, the officer was beaten and kicked in the groin and head, and threatened with death if he did not provide information on his work and unit. The wife was threatened with sexual abuse and slammed against the wall with such force that she collapsed. Some time after 1:00 AM, the couple was taken to a nearby main street, Fourth of July Avenue, and released. They arrived at Rodman at 2:15 AM, where they related the events of the previous six hours.

General Thurman, upon learning of the events, advised Washington immediately, increased local security measures, and imposed the most stringent category of the personnel movement, PML *Echo*. This action restricted virtually all U.S. military personnel and their families to American installations. In addition, he ordered additional elements of the armored task force, including several M-113 APCs, to be moved to the city side of the Canal that night.

The next day, Sunday the 17th, the overt American security presence was decreased, and the readiness posture generally reduced from an immediate reaction status to a one-hour recall. However, the air of concern and alertness did not subside to that which had passed for normal barely a week earlier. The members of the operations, intelligence, and communications segments of the SOUTHCOM, US Army South, Howard AFB and Rodman Naval Station either knew something was up or could feel it.

Sunday afternoon, General Powell invited the service chiefs to his quarters for a last minute discussion. During the meeting General Al Gray, the Commandant of the Marine Corps, reminded General Powell and the other service chiefs that a composite Marine Air–Ground Task Force, the 11th Marine Expeditionary Unit (MEU) which was Special Operations Capable (SOC), was available. It was already afloat two days short of California, had 30 days of sustaining supplies, could be easily diverted and be off Panama within a few days. However, the consensus among the Joint Chiefs was that the United States needed to react as soon as possible, and that the approximately 24,000 troops already earmarked and trained for specific missions under the Contingency Plan 90-2 would be more than enough to ensure quick success. With the Joint Chiefs in full agreement, General Powell departed to meet with the President.

That evening, President Bush, during the meeting with his national security advisors, which included the Secretary of Defense and the Chairman of the Joint Chiefs, General Powell (and after reviewing the most recent series of events), made the decision to execute the *Blue Spoon* (military intervention) Operation Order. Upon his return to the Pentagon, General Powell, with the concurrence of the Secretary of Defense, passed word of the President's decision to the service chiefs, General Thurman and several of the CONUS-based force Commanders.

Operation *Just Cause* was "on." The Execution Order (message) was issued at 18/2325Z December 89. The mission statement read:

"USCINCSO will conduct joint offensive operations to neutralize the

PDF and other combatants, as required, so as to protect U.S. lives, property, and interests in Panama, and to assume full exercise of rights accorded by international law and the U.S./Panama treaties."

Beginning on December 18th, some Panama-based American units conducted specialized training, brushing up, and reviewing their contingency plans and combat drills. By the 19th the flow of questions from dependents was unending: "What's happening? Why are you on duty? So and so is not. When are you coming home?" These and other queries and concerns began to multiply.

At 6:00 PM on the 19th General Hartzog held a meeting for all "ops" personnel in the Tunnel. At the meeting, he told everyone that Operation *Just Cause* has been approved for execution and parts of it are already underway or moving in place. All those on the CAT night shift are to stay. All those on the day shift could go home but must return by 10:00 PM, less than four hours away.

As the evening of December 19th progressed, the individual battalions, companies, platoons, aircrews and squads were given information in ever-greater detail. A sober sense of reality prevailed and began to show on the faces of the soldiers. As cover for their stress and fear, jokes were told and people laughed. Yet, when the first increment deployed, there was a definite sense of finality.

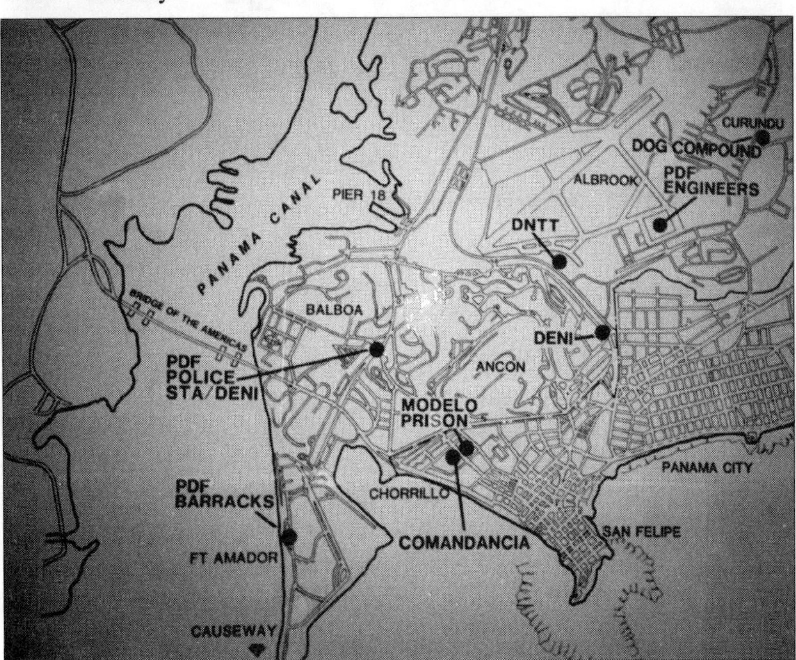

Graphic providing locations of key PDF facilities in Panama City. Photo courtesy of US Army South Office of History.

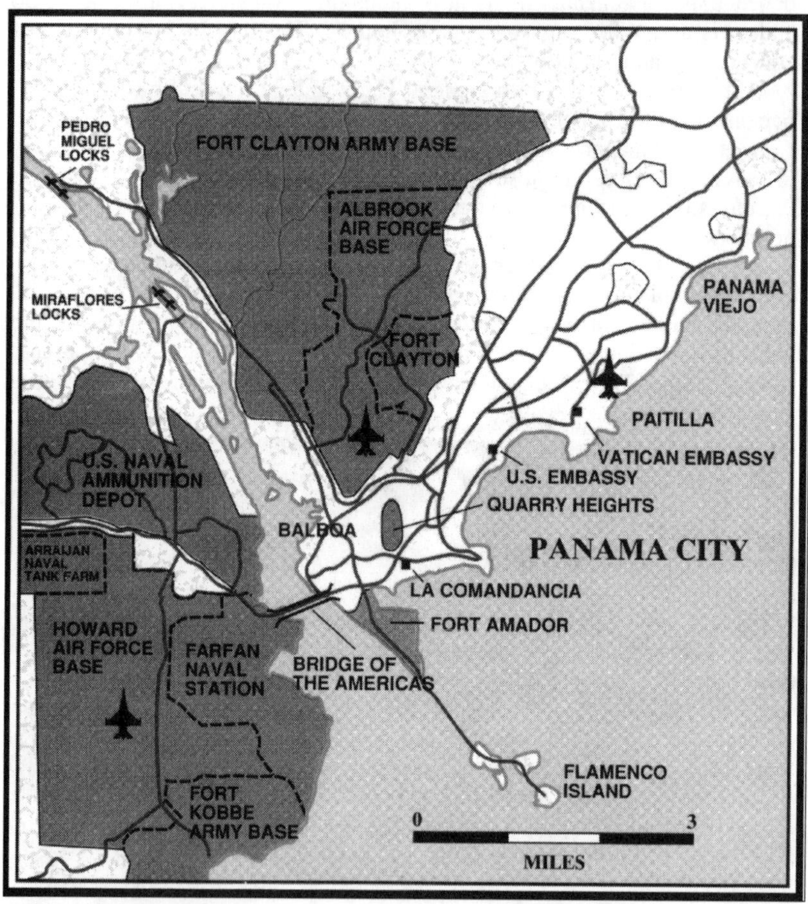

Map of Panama City and environments. Photo courtesy US Army Center for Military History.

CHAPTER SEVEN
THE PLANNING WAVE

OPERATION *JUST CAUSE* PLANNING OVERVIEW

While the events described in the preceding chapters were occurring on the public and political horizons, another set of military precautions and planning actions were occurring below the visible horizon. This chapter catalogs the evolution of these actions.

The defense of the Panama Canal has been a mission of U.S. military forces since the waterway was completed in 1914. Various defense plans had been created during the intervening 80 years as the nature of the potential threat to the Canal operations changed. These evolutions took on a more formal process in the mid-sixties when the U.S. Southern Command was created as the U.S. joint headquarters for the Latin American region. The normal JCS process calls for the typical plan to be reviewed every two years, unless some event or situation precipitates an out-of-cycle review or change.

As of mid-1987, CINCSO OPLAN 6000-86, the defense of the Canal and its several options were predicated on defending the Canal and insuring its uninterrupted operation against external threats. This was to be accomplished with the aid and cooperation of the slowly maturing PDF, which was scheduled to assume major responsibility for Canal security in 2000. Earlier versions of OPLAN 6000 and its sub-components did not anticipate a threat from the PDF itself; however, beginning in June 1987, the potential for a hostile PDF action began to emerge as a decided possibility. The SOUTHCOM commander, General Fred Woerner, who had completed a previous tour in Panama only two years earlier (as commander of the Army forces), sensed the difference and directed his planners to review the existing plans against the emerging situation.

That same month, June 1987, General Manuel Antonio Noriega, the commander of the PDF, initiated the forced retirement of the PDF Chief of Staff, Diaz Herrera, a senior colonel, who believed he was next in line to assume the position of commander of the PDF. Within a week, the ousted officer retaliated against Noriega by going public with accusations of election fraud, drug involvement, and political murder. In the succeeding weeks and months, various Panamanian civilian groups took to the streets and began to mobilize their resources. Demonstrations and marches became the norm, although the tempo ebbed and flowed.

During the summer and fall of 1987, dissension was simmering and periodically reaching a boiling point as Panamanians became more dissatisfied with the continued domination by the PDF and General Noriega. The degree of unrest and agitation was often influenced by external as well as internal events.

The potential for a U.S.-Noriega confrontation escalated in late

February 1988 when media headlines in Miami and Washington heralded the fact that two U.S. Federal Grand Juries in Florida, in separate actions, had indicted General Noriega and several of his PDF associates on various counts of drug-related crimes.

The turmoil created by the renewed civil protest, together with a continued campaign of minor PDF harassment directed against American military personnel, raised the level of concern among the SOUTHCOM leadership. This occurred at the same time that the basic contingency plan for the defense of the Canal OPLAN 6000-86 was scheduled for its mandatory two-year review. Under the normal process it would be months before the review would yield a new JCS-approved edition of the plan.

By 1988, the PDF was as much a social and political system as a military force. It was a conglomerate of police, military and paramilitary organizations with a total strength approximating 15,000 personnel. Of this number some 3,000 to 3,500 were combat troops. The PDF had two battalions and 10 independent company units scattered throughout 13 military zones in addition to a largely ceremonial cavalry squadron and a 100 man special forces unit. The PDF's air arm had roughly 50 aircraft while its navy numbered 12 patrol boats. Complementing Panamanian Defense Forces were the so-called "Dignity Battalions" which were little more than loose formations of laborers, many unemployed. There were 14 such battalions of varying size and capabilities.

After taking stock of the situation, his available forces, and planning options, General Woerner requested and received authorization on February 28, 1988 from the Chairman of the Joint Chiefs of Staff (CJCS), Admiral William Crowe, to undertake contingency planning in a low key, low visibility, compartmented mode. The SOUTHCOM staff planners and their counterparts from the operational components created an entirely new plan. The new plan recognized the PDF as a potentially hostile force and the primary threat to the security of the Canal and Americans living in Panama. SOUTHCOM provided the first draft of the revised plan to JCS on March 4, 1988.

It had been decided early in the planning process that one of the guiding principles of any major American military action would be the overwhelming and simultaneous application of firepower, shock, and force across the spectrum of PDF locations. It was believed that the swift and unexpected application of a force package with elements tailored to each location would greatly aid in the attainment of political, military, and humanitarian goals as well as limit the loss of life on both sides. American planners believed that this goal could be achieved if operational security could be maintained during the planning and rehearsal phases and if tactical surprise could be achieved during the initial combat actions.

The new plan, nicknamed *Elaborate Maze*, was created in the detail required of an operations order rather than in the generalized nature of a concept plan that was normal. Both General Woerner and his Deputy

Commander, Major General Eugene Fisher, USAF, and the U.S. Army Forces SOUTH Commander, Major General Bernard Loeffke, believed time was running out. They believed, along with the SOUTHCOM operations, intelligence, and plans staff, that the plan stood a high probability of being executed in the foreseeable future and without much warning.

The SOUTHCOM planners drew on the list of key U.S. and Canal facilities and the existing American in-country force structure to develop the defensive aspects of the plan. They also initiated a low profile intelligence collection effort to flesh out the incomplete picture of their former ally, the PDF. This effort required some innovative actions by a small segment of the planners, operators, and intelligence personnel. Some went fishing off Flamenco Island; others took family picnics to potential helicopter landing zones. Bachelors visited grandmothers and other relatives of Panamanian girl friends who lived in buildings overlooking the Comandancia. They conducted an extensive research of classified files, topographic maps, and unclassified historical material, and within a week had succeeded in assembling a basic information framework from which they could begin building an operational game plan.

Elaborate Maze had four options, or phases, which constituted the overall concept of operations (CONOPS). The phases ran from purely defensive measures to selected offensive (decapitating) actions. The first three phases involved the defense of American lives and property, continued operation and defense of the Canal, and the deployment of additional security forces from the United States. Forces already stationed in Panama were given the contingency mission to be prepared to conduct a Noncombatant Evacuation Operation (NEO) of U.S. civilians by a combination of air and sea, if the situation dictated.

The newly created fourth phase (option) outlined a plan for selected offensive operations against key elements of the PDF command and combat potential. This phase called for the use of American military power to quickly neutralize the PDF and its potential to threaten U.S. interests, property, and personnel.

SOUTHCOM had been involved in several other major contingency planning actions in the preceding four years. These ranged from national level contingency planning involving Nicaragua in the fall of 1984 and the subsequent two years to the impromptu deployment of an aviation task force to Bolivia in 1986 to support US-Bolivia counter-narcotic efforts. In addition, SOUTHCOM had coordinated several large scale, quick reaction, show of force deployments from the United States into Honduras to counter Nicaraguan offensive actions along the Nicaraguan-Honduras border. SOUTHCOM had also worked with the Atlantic Command (LANTCOM) several times during the previous two years in reaction to unrest and the potential threat to Americans living in the periodically unstable country of Surinam on the northern coast of South America.

The SOUTHCOM planners, as was the pattern in most situations, drew upon the service assets assigned to the command, rather then those generally earmarked as supporting the theater. However, in every case, the suitability of the force to the mission, and availability of the force to include its deployment/reaction capability were basic factors that went into the selection and sequencing of the forces within the planning and combat flow.

Working in tight coordination and unison with planners from its in-country sub-unified Joint Special Operations Command known as SOCSOUTH, and its conventional force components (U.S. Army SOUTH and the stateside air force component - 12th Air Force), the SOUTHCOM planning cell completed the revised and expanded "second edition" of the OPORD on March 18, 1988.

For *Elaborate Maze*, the SOUTHCOM planners drew first upon their in-country assets (Army, Navy, and Air Force) to fulfill the defensive and combat support services. The initial offensive actions were assigned to special operations forces (SOF), most of which were based in the States with the exception of Charlie Company, 3rd Battalion, 7th Special Forces Group which was based in Panama. The plan called for the in-country conventional forces to provide immediate protection of U.S. personnel and facilities and follow-on support to the SOF missions. The special operations forces tasked for the mission included Army Special Forces and Rangers, Navy Special Warfare (NSW) forces, including SEALs (Sea-Air-Land teams) and Special Boat Unit personnel, and Air Force Special Operations Forces.

In Panama, U.S. Army South (USARSO) would provide the majority of the conventional forces from units already stationed in Panama. The principal in-country force was the 193rd Infantry Brigade, which included a parachute battalion, an aviation battalion, a field artillery battery, and military police units. Twelfth Air Force (12th AF), which was headquartered at Bergstrom AFB, Texas, would provide air support through its Howard-based Southern Air Division and 24th Composite Air Wing that included A-7 fighters on rotational tours, and OA-37 Close Air Support (CAS) aircraft. A Panama-based helicopter detachment from the Military Airlift Command's 23rd Air Force (the USAF Special Operations Air Force) would provide immediate tactical airlift, while AC-130 gunship aircraft also from 23rd AF would provide surgical fire support. Long haul airlift would be provided from MAC's 21st and 22nd Air Forces with air refueling support provided by tankers from the Strategic Air Command. The long haul deployment airlift would bring in reinforcing CONUS-based army units, such as a light infantry brigade from the 7th Infantry Division (Light) out of Fort Ord, California.

There were only a few naval combat assets based in Panama. The naval force capability was limited to a detachment of Naval Special Warfare (NSW) personnel which included a small SEAL element, a few coastal patrol boats, and a reinforced, but still small, Marine security force, which included the reinforcing infantry company from Camp Lejeune. As in other earlier planning situations, the use of CONUS-based Navy and Marine assets to augment SOUTHCOM was examined. The long deployment time of a Navy/Marine Task Force (7-10 days) and the unpredictability as to the mix of forces invariably forced the SOUTHCOM staff to realistically consider these LANTCOM naval resources in only two scenarios. One was a situation with long lead-time, such as a deliberate show of force or major evacuation effort, and at the other end of the time line was a follow-on relieving or reinforcing force.

The value of large navy surface units, such as an aircraft carrier, was questionable in the context of the PDF, which had only a very limited air defense capability and the Panamanian Air Force did not pose an offensive air or strike threat. In addition, there was no large array of Panamanian military installations worthy of bombing strikes. For these operational reasons and the perennial debate of who would exercise operational control of naval forces, SOUTHCOM elected to build its quick reaction options around a combination of in-country forces and CONUS-based army and air force units. The selected units could be marshaled rapidly and consistently, and deployed directly into combat if necessary.

The JCS approved the first edition of *Elaborate Maze* for additional planning and refinement in late March 1988 and, at the request of General Woerner, directed that a fifth phase, reconstruction and restoration of Panamanian civil law and order, be added to the plan.

Elaborate Maze called for two joint task forces to be created, each with a specific but complementary mission. A conventional joint task force (JTF-Panama) was to be created in Panama to coordinate the actions of the in-country forces. However, due to security concerns and not wanting to give the PDF any additional pretext for claiming an imminent American invasion, or provide grounds for further harassment of American personnel, General Woerner elected to begin his combat planning within the special operations community.

Although *Elaborate Maze* provided strategic direction and theater-operational planning guidance, the responsibility for developing the more detailed supporting and tactical plans began with a set of planners from the SOUTHCOM Special Operations Command (SOCSOUTH) augmented by a joint Army/Air Force SOF planning cell deployed from the United States. On March 23, 1988, General Woerner, after conferring by secure phone with General Lindsay, the Commander in Chief of the U.S. Special Operations Command (CINCSOC) from whom the SOF CONUS resources would come formally activated the Joint Special Operations Task Force (JSOTF). It was identified insignificantly as JTF-SOUTH and tasked to further refine the tactical planning, deployment preparations, timetable execution, and force training.

The JSOTF was created at Hurlburt Field, Florida, the home of the Air Force Special Operations Command (AFSOC) from units already deployed on a special operations joint service field exercise that extended across the southeastern United States. The staff and forces included personnel from the

U.S. Army 1st Special Operations Command stationed at Fort Bragg, and 23rd Air Force (the Air Force Special Operations Command) at Hurlburt Field, Florida. The operational forces included Rangers, Special Forces, an Army helicopter unit, and the USAF 1st Special Operations Wing. A Navy SEAL planning element joined the JSOTF within 24 hours of the alert.

The focus of this initial planning effort was the Comandancia, (a Ranger mission), Flamenco Island and Paitilla Airport (SEAL missions), General Noriega's beach house at Rio Hato, and several Special Forces surveillance objectives including the Pacora River bridge leading to Fort Cimarron. This plan called for the special operations forces to accomplish their D-day missions in a matter of six to eight hours, after which they would turn over their positions or be reinforced by conventional units.

One of the follow-on actions that flowed from these early preparations was the formation of a Naval Special Warfare (NSW) headquarters in Panama. Located at Rodman Naval Base, the unit was created to coordinate and control the existing theater based Navy SPECWAR forces. These forces included a SEAL detachment and a Special Boat Unit that had been formed as part of the Navy support to the SOUTHCOM counter-narcotics effort.

During late March 1988 time frame, the SOUTHCOM Army component (USARSOUTH) under the command of Major General Bernard Loeffke (located at Fort Clayton, a fifteen minute drive from Quarry Heights) set up a planning cell to flesh out the tactical details of the conventional force (JTF Panama) aspects of *Elaborate Maze*. This particular effort continued quietly and unobtrusively throughout March and into April. General Woerner formally activated JTF-Panama on April 9, 1988 with General Loeffke dual-hatted as the Commanding General US ARMY SOUTH and as Commander, JTF Panama. Virtually every American unit in Panama was placed on the JTF rolls. The JTF Panama staff, although largely composed of personnel from U.S. Army South headquarters (60 to 65 percent), did include Air Force, Navy and Marine personnel from the service components. The JTF headquarters manning was slim. The approved document listed a total of 80-121 billets and was based on earlier JTF manning documents. Actual manning was on the lower end of the spectrum as planning needs dictated.

General Loeffke's main focus was to develop a "joint" approach within the staff and a combined arms philosophy within the available forces. He quickly called for a major joint training event to be conducted at two-week intervals, in concert with the evolution of the planning and the availability of forces. Over a period of time, as additional forces flowed into Panama as a security hedge, JTF Panama created three subordinate Task Forces based on organizational and geographic considerations. A brigade of the 7th Infantry Division became Task Force Atlantic, responsible for the Colon area. The Pacific side of the isthmus was divided into two areas separated by the Panama Canal. The 193rd Infantry inherited the east bank that included Fort Clayton, Albrook AFS, and Panama City and all its environs. The

Marine forces drew the west bank which included the American complexes of Howard, Rodman, Kobbe and the Arraijan Fuels Storage area.

As the two JTF planning staffs continued to refine the operational, support, and tactical details of both the special operations and conventional force aspects of the plan, President Reagan approved the deployment of additional security forces to provide increased protection of U.S. lives and property.

During the JCS review of the expanded plan, JCS staff officers recommended, and Admiral Crowe concurred with their recommendation, that *Elaborate Maze* be divided into a series of four complementary but distinct plans under the overall name of *Prayer Book*, dropping the name *Elaborate Maze* in the conversion process. This decision enhanced the overall security and simplified the dissemination of the appropriate plan or plans to the commands and organizations that were involved.

The security augmentation and defensive plans were grouped under the name *Elder Statesman*. The plan for a possible noncombatant evacuation operation was titled *Klondike Key*. *Blue Spoon* was the nickname given to the offensive operations which included both the Special Operations Task Force and conventional force elements such as the in-country 193rd Infantry Brigade and elements of the reinforcing 7th Infantry Division. The last plan, which dealt with the reconstitution of Panamanian civil law and order, was initially titled *Krystal Ball* and subsequently renamed *Blind Logic*.

On May 9, 1988, the JCS formally approved the new *Prayer Book* series "for further execution planning." Shortly after this approval, responsibility for special operations force planning was transferred from the initial JSOTF planning team to the Joint Special Operations Command (JSOC) at Fort Bragg.

Meanwhile, the SOUTHCOM J5 (Plans) staff element began work on the new plan (*Krystal Ball/Blind Logic*), dealing with preparations for the reconstitution of civil law and order. This involved bringing specialists from Stateside Army Reserve units (where most of the Civil Affairs skills resided) on active duty. Civil Affairs units include personnel with all the skills to run a civilian municipality from lawyers and judges to civil administrators, police, and fire personnel.

As the spring of 1988 rolled over Panama, the plans/OPORDs of the *Prayer Book* series matured and represented a controlled response to the situation as it was perceived at the time. General Woerner had envisioned that the measured buildup of U.S. forces planned for in the *Elder Statesman* option (subsequently renamed *Post Time*) would not go unnoticed by the PDF. Woerner hoped the build-up would influence some of the senior PDF "moderates" and possibly the rank and file of the PDF to separate themselves from General Noriega (and possibly depose him) rather than run the risk of a no-win military confrontation with American forces.

Although on the surface US/PDF tensions appeared to lessen in May and June of 1988, General Woerner and the SOUTHCOM staff still considered the situation extremely volatile. They recognized the initiative in any deliberately planned provocation would lay with the PDF. General Woerner, during discussions with Brigadier General Marc Cisneros, his Director of Operations (J-3), decided to raise the possibility of adding elements of the XVIII Airborne Corps to the CONUS based contingency force list.

Several months prior (in March 1988) to General Cisneros raising the possibility of formally adding elements of XVIII Corps to the contingency force list, Lt. General John W. Foss, then Commanding General of XVIII Airborne Corps, was appraised of the need for a quick reaction contingency plan to support SOUTHCOM. General Foss was advised of the requirement on a very close hold basis, similar to that occurring within the Special Operations community at the time.

This was not the first time that combat and combat support elements of the XVIII Airborne Corps had been earmarked as key players in SOUTHCOM quick reaction contingency plans, nor was it the first time the Corps staff had been involved in SOUTHCOM contingency planning. The history of this type of cooperative planning, which also involved the 12th Air Force as the air counterpart, had its contemporary roots four years earlier in 1984. The Corps had, as early as July 1984, been designated as the senior "ground forces" planner for a range of SOUTHCOM Central American contingency plans. The Corps Commander at the time was Lt. General James J. Lindsay, who took a very positive and deliberate approach. In partnership with his 12th Air Force general officer counterparts he readily took this tasking to heart. Jointly they developed and executed several large-scale joint Army-Air Force-SOF training maneuvers "off the reservation" i.e. at locations other than the normal Corps stomping grounds.

This earlier planning effort involved cadres from both the XVIII Corps and the 12th Air Force headquarters as well as representatives from MAC and SAC, and the Army and Air Force special operations communities coming together to support SOUTHCOM in contingency planning. These efforts included SOUTHCOM-Nicaraguan contingency planning, and plan driven joint operational contingency execution training exercises such as the *Sand Eagle* series. These live play exercises were conducted in the U.S. Working with a superior ground troop database on Nicaragua military installations and capabilities (largely collected and compiled by its own intelligence team), this composite XVIII/12AF/SOF planning team developed a time-phased plan that employed each of the force capabilities to its best advantage in a coordinated and complementary fashion. In essence, this contingency planning and the associated exercises to include numerous deployments to Honduras were an unintended precursor and training at the operational staff levels for *Just Cause*.

In addition, the staffs and forces worked together in numerous CONUS exercises and contingency reaction deployments into Central America. Such efforts included joint field exercises as the *Aharas Tara* series in 1985-1986.

Virtually all of these efforts were conducted under a joint or bilateral cooperative arrangement. Lt. General John W. Foss picked up the XVIII Corps mantle in October 1986 and carried it for the next two years including Operation *Golden Pheasant* in March 1988. *Golden Pheasant* was the nickname for a massive quick reaction deployment which involved airlifting a sizeable U.S. military force from the United States into Honduras. It was one of several quick reaction show-of-force operations launched to counter border incursion's into Honduras by the Nicaraguans in their efforts to neutralize the CONTRAS.

The March incursion and the reactionary Show-of-Force was accompanied by the activation of a SOUTHCOM Crisis Action Team (CAT) one of the many CATs to be called to duty during the next 18 months and the second that month. A CAT is a group of staff personnel specially identified and assembled to monitor a crisis situation and serve as a coordination focal point for information and actions. It also can serve as a commander's brain trust in evaluating potential situational changes and developing possible U.S. military options (Courses of Actions - COA) before the commander is faced with an adverse fait-accompli. In March, SOUTHCOM had two separate CATs active simultaneously. One was focused on the Nicaraguan-Honduran-Contra (*Golden Pheasant*) situation and was disbanded by the end of the month. The second CAT was focused on Panama. Its activation had been prompted by a coup attempt against General Noriega. Although the coup failed and its perpetrators removed from the PDF scene, the SOUTHCOM Panama CAT never really was disbanded, although it shrank and expanded as tensions and events in Panama unfolded. Eventually, it served as the nucleus of a Panama contingency planning group which evolved overtime into Joint Task Force Panama, the in-country contingency reaction force.

The initial SOUTHCOM-Panama-PDF contingency concept called for the XVIII Airborne Corps Headquarters (and the 82nd Airborne Division's Ready Brigade) to be prepared to support SOUTHCOM as an immediate reaction, second tier force should the situation in Panama deteriorate to a point that the U.S. was forced to take military action. The first tier elements would be Special Operations Forces and the existing in-country American forces primarily U.S. Army South's 193rd Brigade providing an immediate in-country reaction capability. However, it was not until the summer of 1989 and the pending change of SOUTHCOM Commanders that Panama contingency planning became a near full time planning effort for a small group of XVIII Airborne Corps staff officers.

Simultaneously, with the XVIII Corps being designated the "ground planner" in 1984, the Tactical Air Command's 12 Air Force, headquartered at Bergstrom AFB, Texas was designated as the SOUTHCOM "Air Planner." The 12th Air Force Commander at the time was Lt. General Jack I. Gregory. He was succeeded by Lt. General Chuck Cunningham in June 1985. Both of these gentlemen in partnership with their XVIII Airborne

Corps counterparts were driving forces in the development of an integrated approach to Army-Air Force-SOF contingency planning and force training on behalf of SOUTHCOM. In June 1987, Lt. General Merrilll A. Mc Peak became the 12th Air Force Commander. He was succeeded one year later in July 1988 by Lt. General Peter T. Kemp who registered renewed interest in the planning effort and continued in command throughout the preparation for and execution of *Just Cause*.

In June 1988, General Cisneros met with a small group of operations and plans representatives of the XVIII Airborne Corps to review the situation and discuss bringing the Corps into the planning process. One consideration discussed involved the Corps headquarters assuming the lead in the tactical planning as the senior Joint Task Force. SOUTHCOM knew that the Corps always had a brigade of the 82nd Airborne Division on a standby alert with an eighteen hour "wheels in the well" reaction capability. This "fire brigade" represented an immediate reinforcing capability that could quickly be added to the in-country and SOF force structure to rapidly add "mass" if needed.

Lacking a situational emergency, these discussions extended late into the fall of 1988. In November and at the request of General Woerner, the JCS J-3 Director of Operations, Lieutenant General Kelley, formally designated the XVIII Corps as the "executive agent for planning" and the core around which future joint tactical planning and command and control would evolve. However it was not until early 1989, that the Corps planners began to focus on this assigned responsibility. In February 1989, a joint planning meeting was held at Fort Bragg, North Carolina. The meeting was attended by planners from SOUTHCOM, JTF-Panama, Twelfth Air Force, the Joint Special Operations Command, 23rd Air Force, XVIII Airborne Corps and SOCSOUTH. A key outcome of the meeting was the active assumption by the Corps of its role as executive agent for future planning.

By the end of August 1989, the *Blind Logic* plans had achieved the form that the planners felt would accomplish the mission of beginning the restoration of Panamanian government and government services should the order to execute ever be given. *Blind Logic* could be executed independently, concurrently, or in sequence with *Blue Spoon* (augmentation of forces and NEO having been overtaken by events). The planners determined it could also be executed, with varying degrees of predicted effectiveness, in circumstances involving a Reserve unit call-up, the selective use of individual reservists or with only in-place forces.

By September, *Blind Logic* planning had been suspended. The 96th CA representatives had departed. The Reserve planners were debriefed and returned to the 361 CA Brigade while what remained of the planning cell prepared to brief the staff principals, then the CINC. These two briefings would complete the internal SOUTHCOM planning cycle. During the summer several of the SOUTHCOM principals had changed. Brigadier General Hartzog had replaced Brigadier General Marc Cisneros Director of

Operations (SCJ3). Similarly the SOUTHCOM Director of Plans changed. Brigadier General Bernard Gann, USAF, was now the plans chief. Although both officers (Hartzog and Gann) were generally aware of *Blind Logic*, neither had been briefed in detail since the summer revisions. After several delays, both generals were briefed simultaneously and approved the plan, leaving only General Woerner to be briefed and approve the CA plan.

By September 18, a new planning priority requirement had surfaced. The responsibility for the development of a Counternarcotics (CN) campaign plan was given to the SCJ5 staff on September 18 with a suspense date of October 15. *Blind Logic* went back on the shelf and efforts to brief General Woerner or his replacement, General Thurman, were suspended.

In October 1988, General Carl W. Stiner became Corps Commander after recently completing a tour as Commander of the Joint Special Operations Command (JSOC). Over time, and largely as a result of contingency planning and deployments, including those to Central America, the XVIII Abn Corps staff and the senior officers of the three Army units involved came to an operational conclusion. They came to appreciate that, once on the ground, the 82nd, the 7th and the 101st Divisions, although not the same, were similar type organizations and were, to a respectable degree, interchangeable and mutually supportive.

The designation of the Corps as the SOUTHCOM ground force planner created a philosophical conflict of interest among the Corps planners, including Lieutenant General Carl Stiner (former commander of the JSOC and the 82nd Airborne Division). The already approved SOUTHCOM/Woerner Concept of Operations envisioned a slower buildup and more measured commitment of forces than the Corps' doctrine of "strike quick, strike hard" dictated. The Corps' planners and General Stiner preferred a Concept of Operations that emphasized the rapid use of overwhelming force to quickly achieve the stated objectives. They believed the introduction of the 7th Infantry brigade, which would take six to ten hours of air-landing operations at Howard (the only U.S. controlled airfield in Panama), would give away any element of tactical surprise. They favored a rapid parachute insertion. However, at this point in time (February-March 1989), lacking a stimulus to support their view, the Corps' job was to develop a joint tactical plan to support the strategic and operational objectives of the JCS-approved plan–not seek a major revision of the SOUTHCOM concept. Another difference in philosophy was the timing of the assumption of command by the XVIII Abn Corps. In the Woerner-Cisneros-Loeffke concept, the Corps would assume command sometime after events had started and shortly after the Corps headquarters got in-country. The XVIIIth and JCS J-3 philosophy put the Corps in command from the start of the operation and relinquishing control to the in-country structure after the major mission actions had been accomplished. The two philosophies hung in the air for several months, from February through the late summer.

The lull in the political confrontation between the Civilistas and the

PDF/PRD ended with Noriega's preemptive seizure of ballot boxes in reaction to the impending defeat of his candidate during the May 1989 presidential election. This was followed within days by a brutal PDF/DIGBAT attack on the opposition party candidates as they participated in a march protesting General Noriega's highhanded declaration that the election was null and void. In reaction to this turn of events, President Bush ordered the deployment of an additional 1,900 U.S. troops to bolster security. The deployment was nicknamed Operation *Nimrod Dancer* and involved a range of troops and capabilities.

Although the troops were deployed as a combination of show of force and an added security measure, this increase (deployment) was also one of the force buildup options of the *Elder Statesman/Post Time* plan (i.e., defensive security force augmentation). Due to the increased tension, the XVIII Airborne Corps began rotating a planning cell to Panama to augment the Army headquarters (USARSOUTH) and the Corps began to develop an operational concept more along the lines of the Corps philosophy. Informal coordination with the Joint Special Operation Command (JSOC), also located at Fort Bragg, and planners from the Military Airlift Command, 12th Air Force, and the 23rd Air Force (the Air Force Special Operations Command) was also accomplished with the Corps' concept of operations in mind.

Similar concepts, involving essentially the same family of forces, had been developed several years earlier when General Jim Lindsay had been the XVIII Airborne Corps Commander and Lt. General Chuck Cunningham, the Commander of 12th AF, had been his Air Force counterpart. Many of these concepts had been developed and rehearsed in a series of joint assault operations in support of SOUTHCOM and Nicaragua related contingency plans.

The Corps essentially produced two plans concerning Panama that summer. The first was JTF SOUTH OPORD 90-1 (the one it was charged to develop). This was delivered to SOUTHCOM in mid-September for review and approval. The second plan, unnamed and unnumbered at the time, was the Corps preferred Concept of Operations and held in abeyance. OPORD 90-1 was quickly overtaken by two events.

The first event was a change of commanders in SOUTHCOM. The *Army Times* had announced in early August that General Woerner was retiring September 30 to be replaced by General Max Thurman. General Thurman was an action-oriented individual, and had served in the XVIII Airborne Corps earlier in his career. General Thurman was an Anglophile who did not know Latin America, but did know, after six weeks of intensive research, study, and intellectual preparation, that he did not like or trust Manuel Noriega.

Prior to his assumption of command in late September, General Thurman had visited Fort Bragg six weeks earlier, on August 18, 1989 where he was given two briefings on the Panama Contingency plans. The first, presented by a Plans Officer from US Army South, was an overview of *Blue Spoon* and the expected role of XVIII Airborne Corps. The second briefing discussed the execution of the Special Operations aspects of the planning which have been purposely kept as a separate planning compartment except for the JCS, SOUTHCOM, USARSO and JSOC leadership. This was normal for most special operating planning and in the case of Panama given the highly sensitive nature of two key aspects of the special operations mission - the capture of General Noriega and the rescue of Kurt Muse - security compartmentalization was the norm. At the conclusion of the USARSO presentation, MG Roosma, the Deputy Commander XVIII Corps and the senior XVIII Airborne Corps attendee, privately informed General Thurman that the USARSO plan as presented was not the "Corps plan." He continued the dialogue explaining that the Corps leadership including General Stiner did not agree with the role of the XVIII CORPS as presented by the USARSO Plans Officer and that they (the Corps) "would (given the option) fight the war differently." General Thurman responded, "I understand and tell General Stiner I want him to understand he is going to be my war fighter."

Less than three weeks later, in early September, General Roosma led a team of XVIII Abn Corps planners to Panama for a planning review. The review took place during a three-day period spanning the 4th through 6th. In addition to General Roosma, the Corps team included four staff officers, the Corps G-3 (Operations), the G-2 (Intelligence), the G-3 Plans officer and the G-3 plans officer for SOUTHCOM plans.

General Roosma was of the opinion that neither SOUTHCOM nor US Army South (USARSO), then commanded by Major General Bernard Loeffke (a former Chief of Staff at the XVIII Abn Corps), had the wherewithal to serve as a tactical Joint Task Force Headquarters. Specifically, he did not believe the USARSO staff had either the training or the experience to discharge the myriad of functional responsibilities attendant with being a full-up JTF headquarters. He believed this to be particularly true in a complex and fast moving operation as envisioned in Panama.

He was not alone in this opinion. He believed that General Thurman, after his "warfighter" comment and the JCS J-3 Lt. General Kelley, after private discussions about a JTF Panama during the recent Worldwide J-3 conference, were of the same opinion. Brigadier General Marc Cisneros, the SOUTHCOM J-3 at the time, attended the conference and listened to these informal discussions, but as the junior officer, refrained from expressing a strong opinion. Shortly thereafter he was promoted to Major General and was transferred from his staff position at SOUTHCOM to US Army South as its new Commander replacing General Loeffke. Brigadier General Hartzog, newly arrived from the States, replaced General Cisneros as the SOUTHCOM J-3. A few weeks later General Roosma discussed the subject of the JTF and when the XVIII CORPS should be brought into the combat equation with General Hartzog. In the same general time frame, General

Roosma held a similar discussion with the Commander of the Joint Special Operations Command (COMJSOC) during the same time frame. The focus of that discussion was how to bring in maximum combat power "early-on" and have it make the correct impact.

Essentially there were two schools of thought and two ways of approaching the problem. One advocated a controlled, relatively slow and overt introduction of U.S. military forces in an effort to preclude hostilities or hold them to a minimal level through reason and intimidation. This was the approach favored by General Woerner. The other school, the XVIII Corps,' envisioned the application of overwhelming military power in a direct assault role to terminate the conflict quickly. The primary objective of the XVIII Airborne Corp was focused on neutralizing the organized elements of the PDF structure - i.e. the forces that were identified and could pose a threat if not neutralized quickly.

The *Blue Spoon* plan that General Thurman inherited from Woerner was a very deliberate plan based on the principle of mass and force intimidation. It was based on General Woerner's assessment that a deliberate semi-overt build-up of U.S. military force, coupled with direct psychological pressure on the second and third tiers of the PDF hierarchy would produce a Panamanian solution. General Woerner believed a successful internal Panamanian action to depose General Noriega would preclude the need for an American initiated US-PDF military confrontation.

General Woerner believed the plan had a good chance to succeed without firing a shot and he reasoned that if the strategy failed, then he had sufficient force to overwhelm the PDF while protecting the American population at large. Moreover, he was convinced that the relatively small and scattered elements of the PDF outside Panama City would be too disorganized to pose much of a threat.

General Thurman, his J-3 (Brigadier General Hartzog), and Lieutenant General Carl Stiner, Commander of the XVIII Airborne Corps/JTF-South, came to the problem with a different perspective. This perspective was reinforced by the unsuccessful coup attempt of October 3rd and the prompt counteraction by the PDF. The new American team (Thurman and Stiner) perceived the PDF was capable of concentrating and or dispersing their forces rapidly which could cause a great deal of trouble for U.S. forces during a long build-up period envisioned under General Woerner's game plan. The playing field had changed significantly, warranting a cold review and recalculation of the American plan and other options. It was determined that tactical, if not strategic, surprise was to be sought coupled with the application of mass.

The Dignity Battalions were an unknown part of the equation and in the minds of some commanders and planners warranted greater concern. Far less was known of this para-military irregular force threat. What was known was largely speculative rather than factual. The precise number of Dignity Battalions was unknown, as was their individual force strength and their capabilities. A Dignity Battalion (DIGBAT) was not composed of the typical 400-600 persons found in a conventional force battalion. A battalion could range from a loose coalition of 60-80 poorly trained and equipped PRD supporters to a hard core group of a dozen dedicated and relatively well armed individuals out to inflict as much harm as possible on Americans, almost without regard to their own lives or safety. In the minds of some, the Dignity Battalions were groups of hoodlums with guns who, although unpredictable, were a lesser random threat to be addressed as they presented themselves, then the better trained and equipped, and geographically and institutionally identifiable military and police elements of the PDF.

The second event that killed 90-1, and essentially gave birth to 90-2 (the Corp's concept) occurred three days after General Thurman had assumed command. This was the unsuccessful military coup led by Major Giroldi, who attempted to remove General Noriega from his position of leadership without bloodshed. The coup failed within four hours of its initiation, with most of the enlisted participants imprisoned and the officer leadership killed. Political and media critics criticized SOUTHCOM, i.e., General Thurman, for not aiding the coup or taking advantage of the attempt. General Thurman responded that the coup was led by a questionable individual who had supported Noriega during an earlier attempted coup and this effort could very well have been a PDF (Noriega) trap to ensnare the United States in a political quagmire.

Two days after the coup, and five days after assuming command, General Thurman convened a meeting in Panama with the key planners to review the situation and make some judgments. During his opening remarks, General Thurman designated Lieutenant General Carl Stiner, as his overall joint operational commander, i.e., Commander Joint Task Force South (JTF-SOUTH) and called for a "new" plan to deal with the "new" situation which the attempted coup had precipitated. Although some cracks in the PDF solidarity existed, most personnel seemed loyal to the institution, if not to Noriega. As significant was the rapid response to Noriega's request/order for assistance and unexpected logistic flexibility exhibited by the PDF in rapidly moving elements from two of their major outlying combat units into Panama City.

The XVIII Airborne Corps planners flew back to Fort Bragg that night, and within days formalized their preferred concept of operations into a "new" plan. This was designated JTF-SOUTH OPORD 90-2. At the same time the Corps signal staff began creating one of the most important supporting documents, the Joint Communications Electronic Operating Instruction (JCEOI). One of the Signal Brigade's "Iron Majors" drew the preparation duty. This involved identifying each organization, regardless of service or function, that was to be involved in the plan (should it be executed), and contacting their communications planner. Once contact was made, detailed information on the unit's combat structure and force disposition had to be documented and verified. Once this data was assembled, each unit and subunit was assigned a call sign, call word, network identifier, and radio frequency. The first edition of the JCEOI was produced in early November. Subsequent changes and additions to the overall task force structure resulted in the publication of 600 copies of the second edition, and eventually 1,000 copies of a third edition.

As the "new" plan evolved, it was periodically briefed to General Thurman and his key staff, plus Major General Marc Cisneros, who recently assumed command of the Army component, U.S. Army South. As the former SOUTHCOM Director of Operations, Cisneros had witnessed the entire evolution of the U.S./PDF confrontation and had participated in virtually all the contingency planning that SOUTHCOM had been involved in during the previous three years. General Cisneros had joined the SOUTHCOM staff as a Colonel in 1986, was nominated for Brigadier General by General Galvin in 1987, and nominated for Major General by General Woerner in 1989. With the second promotion, Marc Cisneros went from being a senior SOUTHCOM staff officer to being the Commander of U.S. Army South (USARSOUTH) and simultaneously Commander of JTF Panama, replacing General Loeftke, on 23 June 1989, as the focal point for most of the in-country operational planning.

General Thurman requested an additional increase in security forces and within a few days additional military police forces were alerted for deployment to Panama. At the same time, the JCS J-3, working with the Director of the Defense Intelligence Agency (DIA), activated a joint operations/intelligence team to review all the targets and other operational areas of interest and insure that the very best intelligence was provided to JTF-SOUTH.

On Sunday, October 15, General Stiner flew to Washington to provide a planning update to General Powell, the new Chairman of the Joint Chiefs of Staff (CJCS). General Stiner was accompanied by Major General Gary Luck, the Commander of the Joint Special Operations Command (JSOC). General Luck, in his JSOC capacity, was the designated Commander of the Joint Special Operations Task Force (JSOTF), which was tasked with many of the early H-Hour missions. Sunday's planning discussion was followed on Monday by General Luck briefing General Powell on JSOC's quick reaction capability and a separate compartmented plan it had been tasked to develop to rescue Kurt Muse from the Carcel Modelo prison. Later that day, General Powell, accompanied by General Luck, met with the Secretary of Defense and subsequently the trio presented the two special operations briefings to President Bush for information purposes. No decisions were expected or forthcoming; however, the presentations and associated discussions laid the groundwork for the Muse rescue plan to be folded into the overall series of initial actions should OPORD 90-2, *Blue Spoon*, be executed.

A few days later, on Friday, October 20, the SECDEF approved the immediate deployment of an SOF quick reaction contingency package to

Panama. The package included a strike command element, an aviation unit, an intelligence surveillance team, and a command, control, and communication element. Once situated in Panama, the force was folded into the overall increased tempo of night training exercises.

General Thurman approved the XVIII Airborne Corps "quick strike" concept (JTF OPORD 90-2) on October 30, kindling the cycle of earlier operational and airlift planning that had occurred no less than three times in the previous 18 months. The force equation was weighted differently. The airlift challenge went from one with a small tactical lead and sustained strategic logistic flow to one requiring a major tactical lead with strategic implications, to be followed immediately by a larger second phase tactical air operation, then to a third phase massive sustained logistic flow.

In many respects, OPORD 90-2 bore a striking similarity to its two predecessors, the quick special operations version of March/April of 1988, and the more formal and comprehensive SOUTHCOM version of May/June-October/November 1988. The three iterations mirrored the evolutionary course of events. The original target list remained essentially unchanged, although some priorities were altered and a few additional targets were added. The biggest change was in the U.S. force structure and order of commitment. Essentially the revised plan reversed the role of the XVIII ABC's 82nd Airborne Division's ready brigade and the initial mission brigade of the 7th Infantry (Light) Division. The 82nd's brigade would constitute the second wave of tactically delivered forces, while the 7th ID follow-on units would be air-landed and serve as the major component of the third wave.

Another key change reflected in OPORD 90-2 was subordinating the Joint Special Operations Task Force (JSOTF) and melding the in-country JTF-Panama staff with the corps staff now designated as Joint Task Force South (JTF SOUTH). This placed all operational elements under a single operational commander, and on a single integrated execution timetable, although the missions and execution timetables of both the SOF and in-country forces remained essentially unchanged during Phase One operations.

The third change directed by General Thurman was that the entire operation be carried out as an integrated campaign. This included the final aspect of the plan, the follow-on military-political action to reconstitute the Panamanian government and civil order. This guidance was a reaffirmation of what Generals Galvin and Woerner had implied when they asked U.S. government and congressional visitors, "What do you want to do after Noriega is gone from the scene?" During the period of June 1986 through October 1989, neither the Department of State, under whose purview such matters fall, nor the executive political leadership, nor the congressional hawks had addressed the subject, built a plan, or prepared for the civil consequences of a military action. It fell to the military planners to accomplish.

CONFRONTATION ZONE

Although military planners had developed the entire series of plans, their primary focus was on the initial and follow-on combat actions as these phases held the greatest potential for the loss of American lives, both military and civilian, if not carried out quickly and successfully. *Blind Logic*, the plan to restore law and order in Panama and reconstitute the civil government, received little senior attention until early December, when all other major actions to neutralize the PDF had been planned and were being rehearsed.

The PDF was dispersed in a variety of locations throughout the country. However, not every military location or little police outpost could or needed to be attacked simultaneously. The majority of the critical PDF command and control nodes, key force elements, and the majority of U.S. citizens as well as political and property interests were located either in, or in proximity to, Panama City, Colon, or the former Canal Zone.

In the view of most American planners the Canal Zone and its key facilities and Panama City and its immediate environs were the critical areas of operations. In October the PDF had demonstrated its ability to react and rapidly reinforce the Comandancia from both Rio Hato in the west and Fort Cimarron in the east. In the wake of these actions, the two locations had gained greater significance in the concerns of the planners and could only be ignored at the peril of the rest of the operation. The balance of the country and its scattered PDF elements fell into a lower priority category.

The Panamanian Defense Force was organized geographically into thirteen regional Military Zones. Over the years its leadership had extended its influence and assumed unto itself control of numerous everyday facets of government. Although the PDF strength totaled nearly 15,000, less than 3,500 were members of military combat units. The bulk of the force consisted of several varieties of police units, each with a different function, organizational structure, and level of training. Some of these divergent elements included the Conservation Police, the Treasury Police, the Presidential Guard, the Traffic Police, the Customs Service, and the National Police. Each included administrative personnel, particularly the National Police who administered the entire vehicle control system from inspection and registration to transfer of titles.

The police and customs segments, in particular, represented an institution warped by graft and corruption which ran from individual traffic patrolman up to the heads of departments and divisions. Although these forces did not present a military threat in the conventional sense, they represented a potentially lethal threat to American civilians, dependents, or unarmed service personnel.

The threat posed by the Dignity Battalions had also grown since their creation 18 months earlier. Rudimentary para-military training had been conducted by various elements of the PDF and the police. By October 1989 the Dignity Battalions were being aligned to support specific PDF units. Rumors of PDF plans to use DIGBAT teams to take American hostages were widely circulated and raised concern. Two PDF plans nicknamed *Genesis* and *Exodus* called for the kidnapping of Americans and moving of them to the interior of the country in the event of an invasion. A companion PDF plan called Operation *Montana* directed elements of the PDF to take to the mountains and conduct guerrilla warfare. The American command was concerned that if the PDF implemented *Montana*, the DIGBATS would be well positioned to implement *Genesis* and *Exodus* and provide an intra-city information network as well as a recruitment and support base for PDF guerrilla forces. However, the initial focus of American military operations had to be the neutralization of the combat power of the PDF.

The American appreciation of the Panamanian military force structure was reflected in General Thurman's (and the XVIII Abn Corps) assessment of the PDF. General Thurman expected particular resistance from the following units dictating that they had to be high on the strike priorities.

- Battalion 2000, about 550 troops located at Fort Cimarron, 15 miles east of Panama City
- 2nd Infantry Company, with a troop strength of 200 located at Tocumen Airport
- 1st Heavy Weapons Company, some 200 troops with 122 mm long range mortars at the Tinajitas hilltop garrison (San Miguelito Barracks) midway between the airport and central Panama City
- 12th Cavalry Squadron some 150 solders split between Fort Cimarron and Garrison Panama Viejo
- Elements of the 6th, 7th and 8th Companies based at the PDF Headquarters - the Comandancia
- 5th Rifle Company, upwards of 300 troops at Fort Amador near the Bridge of Americas
- 6th and 7th Rifle Companies with a combined strength of some 400 troops at Base Rio Hato approximately 75 miles west of Panama City
- 8th Rifle Company with a strength of approximately 175 at Fort Espinar adjacent to Colon City

THE FINAL PLAN

The *Blue Spoon* Operations order, as revised in October, called for an expanded commitment of forces conducting a wider range of simultaneous actions. The Joint Special Operations Task Force (JSOTF) would operate under the tactical command of Major General Luck, the JSOC Commander.

The SOF operations would be part of the overall JTF assault plan. It included the use of the pre-positioned armored and infantry elements, and a series of separate, but coordinated raiding and seizure actions, followed by the introduction of additional conventional forces in two waves to guarantee success.

The missions of the original JSOTF had been modified over time. The Rangers were now targeted for the Torrijos and Rio Hato airfield seizures instead of an assault on the Comandancia. When the UESAT (antiterrorist unit) was relocated to Panama Viejo, the planned SEAL assault on Flamenco Island was canceled. Other special operations forces teams were targeted for the Muse prison rescue and the search for General Noriega. The Comandancia would now be the object of an armored task force. Other in-country forces would move to neutralize PDF forces that were garrisoned in close proximity to American housing areas or critical facilities while the PDF garrisons at Panama Viejo, Tinajitas and Fort Cimarron would be the initial combat focus of the 82nd Airborne Division.

The initial hours of the plan called for multiple objectives to be achieved. These included the capture of Noriega, the neutralization of the Comandancia, and the seizure of the Torrijos/Tocumen airport and the Rio Hato complex. Also on the timetable were the release of prisoners from two PDF prisons (Carcel Modelo and Renacer) and the neutralization of several PDF police facilities in Colon and Panama City, plus the blocking of several Noriega escape options. A total of 27 targets were scheduled for initial attention.

Simultaneously, defensive operations and measures were to be conducted to ensure the protection of U.S. facilities and citizens. Early in the planning process H-Hour had been selected as 1:00 AM. The selection was based on several factors including the limited nature of vehicle and pedestrian traffic in the city at that time and the normal lull in scheduled civilian airliner activity at Torrijos. This would also allow the American aircraft flying from the United States to accomplish the flight entirely under cover of darkness.

The concept called for a battalion-sized Army-Marine mechanized infantry Task Force (TF Gator) to isolate the Comandancia, and, with the help of Army and Air Force airborne gunships, to neutralize it as a PDF command and control point and rallying point. Although the Comandancia was located only 500 meters from the bottom of Ancon Hill, the bulk of the American force had to approach from the more distant Fort Clayton and Albrook areas, some four miles away. The final quarter mile of the approach was complicated by the Comandancia's location amidst the narrow streets of one of the poorest and most densely populated neighborhoods in the city, Barrio Chorrillo.

Meanwhile, other elements of the 193rd Infantry Brigade (Task Force Bayonet) were to secure the Curundu, Ancon Hill, and Balboa areas, and conduct a helicopter assault on Fort Amador, to isolate and neutralize the

PDF garrison located there. The Amador force was nicknamed as Task Force Red Devil after the 193rd unit which would comprise the main assault element.

Separately, Marine forces designated Task Force Semper Fi, reinforced with elements of an Army engineer battalion, would move to block the western approaches into the city by seizing several PDF police stations and securing the Bridge of the Americas.

Twelve miles away, at the far eastern edge of Panama City, an Army-Air Force strike force consisting of Army rangers and helicopter gunships, supported by USAF AC-130 *Spectre* gunships, would neutralize the PDF infantry and air force personnel stationed at Tocumen Airbase and seize the adjacent Torrijos International Airport. The ground combat force, a reinforced Ranger battalion, augmented by the USAF special tactics teams and Army PSYOP teams, would conduct a parachute assault onto the Tocumen and Torrijos runways. They would then move to neutralize the PDF forces and seize control of both the military and civilian portions of the airport complex. This task force was known as Task Force Red.

Simultaneously, a second Ranger force of slightly less than two battalions in strength, also augmented by USAF Special Tactics and Army PSYOP teams, supported by USAF *Spectre* gunships plus Army and USAF helicopters, were to conduct a parachute assault onto Rio Hato airfield. The mission was to seize the field and neutralize the PDF 6th and 7th Infantry Companies garrisoned there and secure the area for follow-on operations.

Farther west, on the other side of the isthmus, Task Force Atlantic, drawn largely from elements of the 7th Infantry Division from Fort Ord, had a series of separate missions. These were to isolate Colon, neutralize the PDF Naval Infantry Company at Coco Solo and the 8th Infantry company at Fort Espinar, and seize and protect Madden Dam (which was a source of water for Canal operations). Other TF Atlantic objectives included securing the PDF logistic depot at Cerro Tigre, clearing the town of Gamboa, and seizing nearby Renacer Prison where some of the participants in previous coup attempts were being held.

While these larger unit operations were underway, a range of smaller, pinpoint operations were to be conducted by various special operations units and teams under the control of the Joint Special Operations Task Force. These actions were to include disabling PDF naval patrol craft in Balboa Harbor, making a TV tower at Cerro Azul inoperative, and conducting a rescue assault on the Modelo Prison across the street from the Comandancia. Other SOF actions included denying the use of Paitilla airfield to the PDF and mounting quick reaction operations to capture General Noriega or rescue American hostages, as required.

Follow-on operations were to begin 45 minutes after the Ranger assault on Torrijos/Tocumen with the airdrop of a brigade–size task force from the 82nd Airborne Division on the secured airport. The troopers of the 82nd were then to pair up with Army helicopters of Task Force Hawk and conduct air assault operations against several PDF garrisons. First was the Panama Viejo barracks, which had become the new home of the PDF Special Forces unit (relocated from Flamenco Island after the Giroldi coup), second was the Tinajitas hilltop compound of the PDF 1st Heavy Weapons Infantry Company (and mortar school), which was close enough to rocket the Torrijos/Tocumen airhead, and third was Fort Cimarron to neutralize PDF Battalion 2000 and prevent any reinforcing action.

Third phase operations envisioned clearing and patrolling in Panama City and Colon to restore law and order, followed by operations in the interior provinces and cities to neutralize the PDF garrisons located there.

The original 1988 plan had not specifically addressed the capture of General Noriega but only the neutralization of the PDF as an institution. However, during the summer of 1989, changes in the strategic dimensions of the plan were made which included provisions for capturing the PDF Commander. The planners felt strongly that Noriega could be captured at the outset of operations if sufficient lead-time were available to adequately track his movements, establish a pattern, and set up a surveillance and tracking structure. Although there was no assumption that his capture could be guaranteed, the confidence factor was high. A special tracking and strike force package was created from selected elements of the Joint Special Operations Command (JSOC) and the 470th Military Intelligence Group, the principal intelligence element of U.S. Army South.

The simultaneous nature of execution meant that thorough planning and rehearsal of the various force elements was absolutely essential. This translated into a major joint planning effort not seen in more than five years. The effort involved a series of joint ground and air planning meetings, which over a period of time involved a complex, but straightforward, highly executable game plan. The initial round of meetings had begun in March 1988 and continued throughout the following 20 months. They increased in frequency and scope as the situation in Panama heated up, and the size and composition of the American forces evolved and increased.

During the last 70 days preceding the operation, the Plans section of the USARSO Deputy Chief of Staff Operations (DCSOPS) office hosted three major OPLAN 90-2 Planning Conferences. These occurred between October 11, 1989 and December 17, 1989. The conferences brought together all of the component service commanders and major subordinate commanders. They were chaired by either General Maxwell Thurman, CINC USSOUTHCOM, or Lieutenant General Carl Stiner, Commander, XVIII Airborne Corps. Beginning with the first of this series on October 11, 1989, the XVIII Airborne Corps maintained a five-man team of liaison officers (LNOs) on temporary duty (TDY) in Panama on a 30-day rotation.

Air support was to be provided by both USAF and Army in-country forces and units stationed in the United States. USAF units included the Panama-based 24th Composite Wing and 830th Air Division of the Tactical Air Command (TAC) and special operations aircraft from the MAC 23rd Air

Force 1st Special Operations Wing. The USAF helicopter forces were part of a larger helicopter fleet which included Army helicopter units from the 193rd Infantry Brigade in Panama, the 160th Special Operations Aviation Regiment (SOAR) from Fort Campbell, helicopters from the XVIII Airborne Corps, and the already deployed TF Hawk. A tremendous amount of airlift and refueling support from CONUS-based MAC transport units and SAC refueling units was also required. Air surveillance, electronic warfare, air defense cover, and selected bombing support were to be provided by aircraft from TAC.

More than 300 Air Force and 60 Army aircraft were to be employed on D-Day. Almost the entire spectrum of Air Force and Army aircraft, except the strategic bomber force, was to be involved. Fighter aircraft, AWACS control platforms, strategic and tactical tankers, as well as both strategic and tactical airlift transports were involved, along with rescue, airlift, attack, and gunship helicopters, plus electronic warfare platforms, and a range of rotary and fixed wing Special Operations aircraft.

The generation and integration of this multi-functional force required the active contribution and involvement of mission planners from four different Air Force commands and two Army aviation organizations. Eventually aircraft and crews from 20 different airbases and three Army posts across the length and breadth of the continental United States (CONUS) were involved. The aviation planners were charged to ensure that the right air asset was available at the right time to do the right job in direct concert with the ground plan. This philosophy was the guiding light to the host of air planners, operators and support personnel.

The D-Day operation required 250 USAF aircraft to depart the CONUS from 17 separate bases during a tightly controlled six-hour time window. The various types of aircraft (more than a dozen) would operate at different altitudes and air speeds. All had different operational characteristics and capabilities. It was a monumental planning effort to develop the flow schedule. It required extensive coordination and liaison with the Federal Aviation Administration (FAA) to allow the aircraft to enter and exit the U.S. air traffic control system without attracting attention and get them flowing south on schedule.

Mission planners had to contend not only with a time, distance, and time zones equation, but also the constraints of the physical, political, and surveillance environment between the United States and Panama.

There are only a few viable air routes between the southeastern United States and Panama that could provide some aspect of unobtrusive movement for a military force the size of *Just Cause*. An added factor was the need to conduct the movement without violating the sovereignty of other nations or risking detection by their air tracking and intelligence systems.

Although commercial airliners routinely overflew central Cuba enroute to and from the United States and Latin America, a military movement of this size was out of the question. Likewise, an unauthorized overflight of

Mexico or any of the Central American countries would be a political blunder. With Cuba and its radar surveillance and lethal air defense network on one side, and Mexico on the other, the options were limited. The planners were also concerned about what action Cuba might take, aside from possibly notifying General Noriega, if they did detect the air flow. Consideration was also given to the potential for detection by any Nicaraguan surveillance radars that might be operational.

The combination of these factors forced the air planners to develop a unique flight profile, eventually called a "gap profile." It was so named because it was designed to allow the aircraft to "shoot" the Cuba/Yucatan channel without being detected. The normal flight profiles were adjusted to have the aircraft begin descending from their cruise altitude well before they entered Cuba and Mexican radar coverage, remain low until they were past the point of detection and then gradually return to their normal flight altitude. It was believed that the use of this tactic, along with the imposition of radio silence, and the shutting down of key electronic emitters on board the American aircraft would allow the H-Hour elements of the force to approach Panamanian airspace with minimum chance of detection.

Although confidence was high among the planners that these tactics would work, provisions were made to have an AWACS aircraft airborne over the Gulf of Mexico and in a position to detect the launch of any Cuban fighters if the American transport flow were detected. The AWACS would be teamed with several flights of USAF F-15 fighters, from Eglin Air Force Base in the Florida panhandle, who would be flying a Combat Air Patrol (CAP) within radar coverage of the AWACS, but outside of Cuban coverage. Command responsibility for this protection shield rested with another U.S. Joint Command, U.S. Atlantic Command, referred to as LANTCOM, which also was prepared to provide maritime support if required.

The enroute planning was made more complicated by the fact that a significant number of the tactical and transport aircraft would require air refueling enroute while others would need to be topped off after they had delivered their cargo (troops, equipment, bullets and batteries) before returning to the States. Three airborne refueling tracks were planned and positioned in the northern part of the Gulf of Mexico, to support the aircraft requiring a top-off before proceeding south. Another 11 tracks were planned just north of Panama to support the aircraft that needed a top-off after completing their mission, before starting the long return flight to the United States.

A large amount of planning went into ensuring several of the other special support assets, in addition to the refuelers, were properly integrated into the H-Hour time schedule and the follow-on operations. Two orbits for Electronic Warfare (EW) aircraft were created off Panama, one off Panama City and another off Rio Hato. These C-130 aircraft, known by the nickname of *Compass Call*, were used as electronic jammers and were targeted against selected Panamanian command and control networks and specific frequencies within the overall PDF structure. In addition to the *Compass Call* EW aircraft, orbits were planned for two radio and TV broadcast C-130 aircraft, nicknamed *Volent Solo*. One orbit was placed over Panama City itself and the other southward off the Panamanian coast.

Another set of support capabilities involved planning for an additional electronic jamming orbit for two EF-111s (*Ravens*), the EW version of the swing-wing fighter-bomber aircraft flown by both TAC and SAC. The target for the *Ravens* was the cellular car phone network used by the PDF. Many of the senior PDF officers had grown accustomed to employing this new technology as a matter of convenience. In addition, the EFs were programmed to jam the Air Traffic Control (ATC) radar that was used by the PDF and the air controller at Torrijos Airport to track and monitor the approach and let-down into the airport complex. The radar was located on Perico Island, a small dot off the Amador causeway at the entrance to the Canal.

Besides these cells of specialty aircraft, two AWACS surveillance aircraft were incorporated into the air control plan. One AWACS orbit was positioned north of Panama to manage the inbound and outbound flow and coordinate the flow of aircraft to the orbiting tankers. The second AWACS was positioned in a high orbit over Panama City to coordinate the movement, flow, and routing of the hundreds of flights, both fixed wing and helicopter, that would take place during the initial hours of the operation.

As the revised and expanded air-ground plan was completed, it was reviewed by General Stiner and key staff officers of JTF SOUTH (XVIII ABC), the JSOTF, and JTF Panama. General Thurman approved the revised plan (OPORD 90-2) on Monday, October 30. It was then submitted to the JCS for national level approval. On Wednesday November 1, the plan was briefed to General Powell by Lt. General Kelley, the JCS J-3, Director of Operations. Within 72 hours, General Thurman, assisted by General Stiner and the JSOTF Commander, Major General Luck, briefed the plan to the JCS in Washington. The service chiefs approved the plan on November 3rd, less than 30 days after the attempted coup and General Thurman's call for a revised plan.

The following week it was presented to the Secretary of Defense who also approved it with the exception of one air target, which was deleted. The senior approval cleared the way for an accelerated and expanded cycle of training exercises and rehearsals and the forward deployment of additional quick reaction forces.

Following the formal approval, General Stiner recommended that a tactical force package with substantial firepower be added to the pre-positioned in-country force structure. General Thurman concurred and requested JCS and SECDEF approval. The deployment order was approved by the SECDEF on November 7, and this additional air and ground firepower package began movement south.

Up until this point, the heaviest mobile weapon system was the Marine Light Assault Vehicle (LAV) with its 25 mm Bushmaster chain gun. Something heavier was needed to augment the Army's deployed light infantry forces. The *Sheridan*, a Vietnam era tracked armored reconnaissance vehicle, which looked and sounded like a tank and sported a smooth bore 152mm gun, was the only feasible candidate. The only *Sheridans* still in the U.S. inventory were part of the 82nd Airborne Division and could be airlifted or airdropped by C-130 if need be. The decision was made to unobtrusively pre-position four of these vehicles in Panama early.

Within a few days the force package of four M-551 *Sheridans*, six AH-64 *Apache* attack helicopters armed with long range *Hellfire* missiles, and three OH-58 *Kiowa* scout helicopters were being prepared for air shipment to Howard. The delivery flights were purposefully spread out over several days, in single ship missions, to minimize the chance of detection.

In the latter half of November 1989, the four M551 *Sheridan* light armored reconnaissance vehicles from the 3rd Battalion of the 73rd Armored Regiment of the XVIII Airborne Corps were flown into Howard. Arriving at night and with their identities masked under tarpaulins, the *Sheridans* were moved to the Empire Range where the vehicles spent the next few weeks concealed under General Purpose Medium tents as part of a larger tent city complex.

Meanwhile, the *Sheridan* crews established a rigorous training and maintenance program and became familiar with several candidate routes from the range to the various U.S. installations. The *Sheridan* crews drove the routes both during the day and at night using high mobility multi-purpose wheeled vehicles (HMMWV) as surrogates for their *Sheridans*. The M551 crews confirmed each firing position, verified data and landmarks, and exercised the movements so frequently that the Panamanians came to accept the activities as routine.

As the increased firepower was arriving, American military dependents were being flown back to the United States, many on the same planes. The dependent exodus began on November 16. The dependent draw down had a goal of reducing the number of American military families remaining in Panama to approximately five hundred. A few days before Thanksgiving, General Stiner flew to Panama to get a first hand report on the details of the tactical planning. While he was in Panama, SOUTHCOM received information that narco-trafficantes were about to initiate a car bomb campaign in Panama against Americans. This prompted General Thurman to activate JTF-SOUTH and provide General Stiner the authority to act if force were necessary.

After some brief discussion, General Powell and the SECDEF approved General Thurman's emergency decision. Technically, Thurman could only activate JTF Panama, his own forces, not JTF-SOUTH. General Stiner and the XVIII ABC were not assigned to SOUTHCOM, but were under the command of the Army Forces Command (FORSCOM) which commanded the majority of CONUS based Army forces. General Powell was keenly aware of the protocols of such a situation, having only recently left the post of FORSCOM commander; however, he supported the SECDEF's after-the-fact concurrence of Thurman's action.

Tension between Panama and the United States increased on November 22nd when the U.S. declined to accept the Panamanian nominee for the position of Panama Canal Commission (PCC) Administrator. The position was to be turned over to a Panamanian on the first of January 1990. SOUTHCOM anticipated the American rejection might result in anti-U.S. demonstrations and riots, possible disruption of Canal shipping, or threats to the Canal's key facilities and American personnel. As a result, JTF-SOUTH OPORD 90-3 (*Vocal Cordon*) and JTF-Panama OPLAN 90-4 (*Acting Jack*) were prepared and published. *Vocal Cordon* called for U.S. military forces to protect the PCC Administration Building, key PCC facilities, PCC housing areas, and selected PCC personnel. While *Acting Jack* provided for the personal security of Mr. Fernando Manfredo, the PCC's Deputy Administrator, a Panamanian, who the American government would accept as the new Administrator. However, the situation did not go beyond an exchange of rhetoric, and neither of the plans had to be executed.

By the end of November, and with no evidence of a car bomb campaign or other hostile actions materializing, JTF-South was deactivated and reverted to a planning and training posture. General Stiner and the XVIII Airborne Corps members of his deployed battle staff returned to Fort Bragg. However, plans and schedules had been laid out to conduct a series of joint readiness exercises (JRXs) to further fine tune the *Blue Spoon* forces and their command and control structure.

On 29 November, the 82nd Airborne Division conducted a major field rehearsal under the guise of a routine emergency deployment readiness exercise (EDRE). The Division was placed on alert, marshaled the division ready brigade (DRB), rigged the brigade equipment for an airdrop, and proceeded to conduct a live airdrop involving fourteen MAC C-141 *Starlifters* at Sicily Drop Zone at Fort Bragg. Most of the personnel involved thought the exercise was just another of the many EDREs conducted each year; however, key JTF SOUTH leaders and planners used the exercise to validate the revised and expanded plan which had been developed during the preceding two months.

The Drop Zone had been configured to replicate the ground layout of the Panamanian air complex to include its key features. The personnel drop involved twenty C-141s, while the heavy equipment drop was only representative as the full complement of drop aircraft were not available. The balance of heavy equipment drop was pre-positioned on the ground in relative distance and direction to the intended troop DZ. Additionally, troop assembly areas and the helicopter link up points were marked where the three battalions were to meet the lift forces that would take them to the three 82nd Assault objectives - Panama Viejo, Tinajitas and Fort Cimarron.

During command and control discussions between the XVIII Corps and the JSOC, the idea of providing the Corps/JTF an Airborne Command, Control and Communications (ABCCC) configured C-130 and developing a fully integrated "execution checklist" were surfaced. Both ideas were readily accepted and integrated into the accelerating planning effort.

The 82nd Airborne Division's ready brigade conducted a full-scale rehearsal of its portion of the revised OPORDER on December 6th. During the rehearsal an Air Force and SOF augmented XVIII Airborne Corp Headquarters staff served as the JTF headquarters with General Stiner as the JTF Commander. The JTF executed its mission through three principle operational components: 12th Air Force, 82nd Airborne Division and the Joint Special Operations Command (JSOC) which served as the Joint Special Operations Task Force (JSOTF).

Meanwhile, U.S. Marine and Army elements in Panama on both sides of the isthmus were also conducting "rehearsals." A battalion of the 82nd Airborne already in–country conducted its training rehearsals on the nights of the 12th and 13th. Back in the states, the special operations forces rehearsed their major portions beginning on the 14th and concluding on the 15th. The timing of the special operations rehearsal could not have been better planned. The rehearsal provided two key SOF commanders (Major General Downing and the Ranger Regimental Commander Colonel Kernan), both new to their respective positions, an opportunity to become fully knowledgeable of the mission sequence. By mid-December, exercises (rehearsals) involving all the earmarked forces had been conducted. Collectively, they were considered a successful test of the concept, the tactical timing, and the current readiness of the forces should *Blue Spoon* have to be executed in the near future.

The new revised version of *Blue Spoon* as published at the end of October made it imperative that *Blind Logic,* the plan to reconstitute the Panamanian government and restore normal services, also be revised. SOUTHCOM J5 civil military planners perceived that the changes required were relatively minor except that civil military operations should be under JTF-SOUTH rather than remain under SOUTHCOM directly. The most logical candidate to assume this responsibility was U.S. Army South. One problem with this proposal was the fact that the USARSO staff would be almost entirely absorbed by JTF-SOUTH and *Blue Spoon* once it was activated.

In November, preliminary discussions on transferring *Blind Logic* were held between USARSO planners and SCJ5. While these preliminary discussions were taking place, Brigadier General Gann presented the proposal to General Thurman. Gann recommended that Major General Marc Cisneros, as commander of USARSO, be given the mission. General Thurman gave his consent. Following the CINC's approval additional discussions were held which resulted in a staff review of *Blind Logic* by USARSO. On December 12, a meeting was held to formally hand off responsibility for *Blind Logic*. The USARSO representative expressed the opinion USARSO could not execute *Blind Logic* as it stood, and stated that a USARSO plan would have to be developed which would involve coordination with the Embassy and other U.S. Government agencies. Although this caused some consternation in SCJ5, it was agreed in principle that the plan would be transferred to USARSO. Ninety-six hours later, on December 16th, the transfer of *Blind Logic* responsibility and future planning was overtaken by the death of Lt. Paz and the PDF assault on the Navy couple who witnessed the incident.

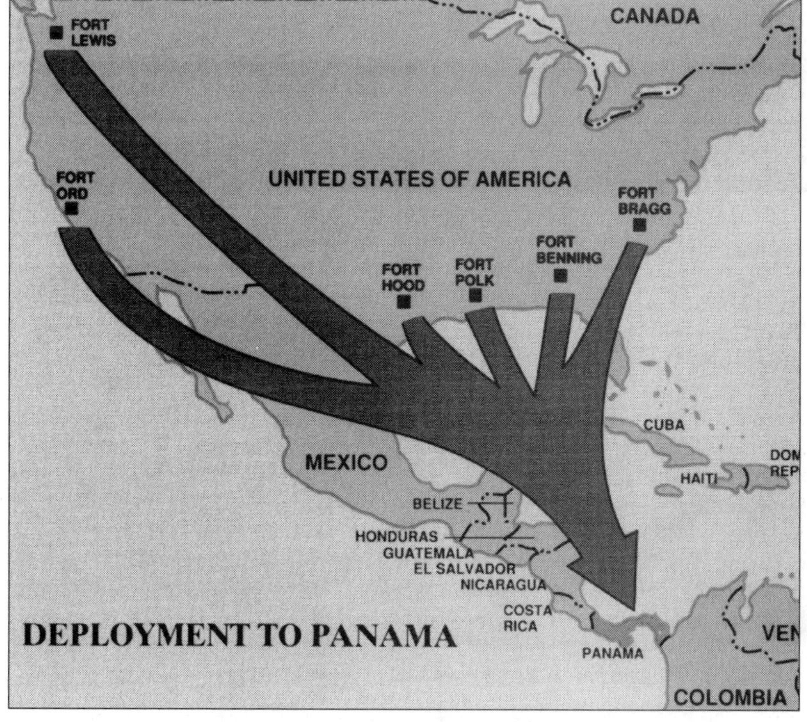

Deployment to Panama. Map courtesy U.S. Army Center for Military History.

View of Fort Amador main access road looking outward toward the vehicle checkpoint located approximately at position of car. Photo courtesy of the author.

Four of the PDF barracks at Fort Amador taken from location of American 105mm gun position adjacent to American family housing. Photo courtesy of the author.

CHAPTER EIGHT
CONFRONTATION IMMINENT

The loyalty to Noriega and rapid response of PDF units in countering the attempted Giroldi coup in October and the change in command personalities at SOUTHCOM had created a new framework of reference for a possible confrontation. The stepped-up tempo of American military movements and training in Panama characterized by some Americans as an aggressive assertion of our treaty rights, and by some members of the PDF as provocative, added a sober potential for confrontation. In the aggregate, however, none of these constituted the spark required to light the fuse of conflict. Even the death of Lt. Paz and the wounding of other officer occupants of the ill-fated car were by themselves insufficient cause to execute the *Blue Spoon Operations Order*. The death of the lieutenant, although tragic and regrettable, could be understood in some circles as the risk of running an armed roadblock. The deliberate and prolonged detention of the U.S. Navy couple, and particularly the unprovoked abuse of the wife, however, was too much for American sensitivities. From this point on, a military confrontation, although avoided previously, was now inevitable.

Prior to the death of Lt. Paz and the harassment of the Navy couple on December 16th, preparations for the Christmas holidays were at the forefront of most of the remaining American and Panamanian family activities – baking, decorating, wrapping gifts. The spirit of the season allowed many to ignore the political situation and concentrate on more pleasant thoughts.

Numerous Christmas parties were scheduled or already being held in both private homes with friends or in the various clubs. However, virtually all of the official functions were cancelled as a result of the incident.

The next day, the 17th, American armored personnel carriers were positioned at key points in the various American housing areas. Their presence became a topic of conversation at the small house parties and private get-togethers.

On Monday, the 18th, the American school children began their holiday vacation with the APCs strategically positionedand a visibly increased MP presence.

Tuesday, the 19th, was a busy day for most families with a lot of last minute shopping and running around. It was to be the last "normal" day for two weeks or more.

THE FINAL HOURS

After the events of the previous 48 hours, General Powell's telephone call to General Thurman on Sunday evening, December 17th, did not come as a surprise to the SOUTHCOM commander. Nor was it a surprise to most of his operations, communications and intelligence staff, who began going over the integrated execution checklist for the umpteenth time, looking for oversights or incompatibilities.

The checklist had been evolving in tandem with the changes in the various planning evolutions. It was going to be the script from which all monitoring and reporting would flow from the forces to the airborne command post to SOUTHCOM at Quarry Heights and then to the JCS and the National Command Authorities (NCA). General Powell's advance notification also started a series of quiet deployments and final preparations although the formal execute order for Operation *Just Cause* would not be issued until the next day, Monday the 18th.

Because of their early commitment some of the first movements and preparations involved the special operation forces. The USAF airlift and air support elements also had to be pre-positioned and postured to move the various ground forces. Typical of this sequence was the alerting of the HC-130 Mission Commander who had to provide the enroute refueling to the self deploying Army and Air Force SOF helicopters. Upon initial notification on the 17th, the Commander alerted the aircrews and maintenance personnel. Two of the HC-130 SOF tankers were prepped and launched, landing in Panama on the 18th. Meanwhile, other tanker aircraft crews were planning the final details of the sixteen blackout aerial refuelings they would provide to the deploying SOF helicopters, which were to launch southward on the night of the 18th.

Also typical of these early actions was the movement from California to Panama of the 7th ID's Aviation Brigade Tactical Command Post (TACP) which had to be on the ground on the 18th. Once on the ground it assumed command and control of Task Force Hawk, which was the initial aviation element organized in May to support the earlier *Nimrod Dancer* deployments. As more Army aviation assets flowed in, which included aircraft and support elements from virtually every Army aviation unit in the CONUS, Task Force Hawk gave way to Task Force Aviation. TF Aviation was then restructured into operational groupings in concert with the mission forces they would be supporting. These composite helicopter forces were designated TF 1-228 (82nd Abn Div), TF Hawk, and Team Wolf.

At the same time that the tankers and the TACP were being alerted (the evening of the 17th) the 55th Special Operations Squadron at Eglin AFB, Florida was directed to prepare four MH-60 *Pave Hawk* Special Operations Rescue helicopters for immediate deployment to Panama. Crews were alerted. Mobility personnel began preparing weapons, chemical defense gear, and aircrew support equipment. Maintenance personnel began to disassemble the aircraft for movement by a C-5A *Galaxy* transport. While the aircraft were enroute via the C-5A, the aircrews were pre-positioned via a SOFC-130. The last of the helicopter rescue force arrived at Howard in the early morning hours of the 19th. The four MH-60s were reassembled in two hours, test hopped and ready with crews in the cockpit prepared to provide medical evacuation coverage several hours before H-Hour.

During the midnight to 1:00 AM on the 18th (Monday), the JSOC elements and a mix of operational forces (a total of some 450 personnel and equipment) departed the Norfolk and Fayetteville areas, arriving in Panama about six hours later. The Command elements and planners immediately set up shop in a hangar at Howard, while the operational forces rechecked gear and attempted to get some rest. A few hours later, the advance coordination element of the JTF SOUTH (XVIII Airborne staff) departed Fort Bragg for Panama. General Stiner and the balance of his staff followed that afternoon.

General Stiner and his senior planning elements arrived on an Army C-20 executive turboprop on December 18th, a date picked earlier for a previously planned exercise coordination meeting which had been on the books for more than a month. Immediately after landing at Howard the small group met with General Thurman at his alternate Command Post, the Howard AFB Operations Center. This was essentially a pre-battle Council of the War that included the majority of the General Officers involved in the operation. The attendees included General Thurman, Lt. General Stiner, Lt. General Peter Kempf (the 12 AF Commander) and Major General Wayne Downing who had replaced Major General Gary Luck as the commander of the Joint Special Operations Command (JSOC) and as JSOTF only a few weeks earlier.

Also participating were Major General Cavezza, Commander of the 7th Infantry Division, Major General Marc Cisneros, Brigadier General Hartzog the SOUTHCOM Director of Operations, and Colonel Jorge Torres who was dual hatted as the SOUTHCOM Director of Communications and as the Commander of the Signal Brigade. Also in attendance were the Commander of SOUTHCOM's sub-unified Panama–based Special Operations Command (SOCSOUTH), Colonel Robert Jacobelly, and the Commander of the 7th Aviation Brigade who was in charge of virtually all Army helicopter forces and the Marine Forces Commander, Colonel Charles Richardson.

The purpose of the meeting was to review, once more, with all key parties in attendance, the mission purpose, the objectives, the priorities, the ROE and the Command and Reporting structure, and the timetable and force flow. Essentially it was the formal activation of JTF SOUTH with all operations matters now in the hands of Lt. General Carl Stiner as COMJTF. After the meeting, General Stiner and his party were flown from Howard to Fort Clayton where General Stiner entered Building 95 and proceeded to the USARSO Emergency Operations Center (EOC) which had been turned into the JTF SOUTH Operations Center.

The center had been used for previous planning sessions and had been evolving in both its capabilities and the mix of personnel working there during the past two months. It had changed from an exclusively USARSO manned Army Operations Center into a JTF advance coordination center with the addition of the XVIII Airborne Corps planning team in mid-September. On the 18th it became a full Joint Operations Center with the addition of liaison officers from the Air Force, the Navy, and the JTSOTF to name a few. Later in the evening, General Stiner, as COMJTF SOUTH, received the JCS Execution order which designated D-day/H-Hour as 20/0600z Dec 89 (1:00 AM Local, December 20, 1989).

The Operations Center was organized in accordance with XVIII Airborne Corps standards and procedures that had evolved (principally) during the previous three years. Map boards and event chronologies were displayed much the same way they had been during several of the large 82nd Airborne exercises conducted in the previous twelve months. Many of the same faces were witnesses and active participants in one or more of several large-scale exercises conducted during the previous year to include *Giant Step IV* which was conducted in the summer of 1989 and *Market Square* (Fort Bragg rehearsal) which was executed in the fall of 1989.

Collectively, these exercises and the detailed planning efforts of the October through mid-December time frame provided a tremendous degree of understanding and fostered an excellent working relationship among all the forces - the Marines, the Rangers, the 82nd, the 7th, the 193rd, the Special Operations Forces and the Air Force. This same degree of mutual support and understanding began, in the eyes of the XVIII CORPS Operations staff, with the superb relationship that existed between the SOUTHCOM Commander, General Thurman, and Lt. General Stiner in his role as the JTF Commander. They both had separate jobs to do and they both understood the role and responsibilities at the two levels - one highly strategic and political and the other highly complex and operational. General Stiner was particularly well equipped to accept his role and execute his responsibilities, having only recently completed a two year tour of duty as Commander of the Joint Special Operations Command and, in this role, had been a de facto JTF Commander on several real world contingency operations.

Physically, the JTF SOUTH/XVIII Airborne Corps TOC (Tactical Operations Center) was arrayed with maps, displays and various status boards across the front. Rows of action officer desks were echeloned by function (operations, intelligence, fire support, aviation, engineer and liaison) flowed away from the frontline "Information Central" displays. Because of space limitations, other staff elements (personnel, logistics and Military Police, etc.) were positioned outside of the main JOC/TOC.

Within the JOC/TOC the intelligence (enemy situation) map boards were on the left and the operations (friendly) map boards on the right. Various status boards to include the Execution Schedule, Significant Activities (SIGACTS) and on-going operations were strategically positioned to present a comprehensive picture in a highly coherent and quickly digestible manner. Operations were listed by Task Force, e.g. TF Atlantic (7th ID), TF Pacific (82nd), Semper Fi (Marines), Bayonet (193th) and the JSOTF.

The overall physical and information configuration was reflective of the layout used in Joint Operations Centers dating from the early days of US

STRIKECOM in the 1960s through the mid '70s and '80s life span of the U.S. Readiness Command. REDCOM as it was known was deactivated in 1987 to provide a home and billets for the then newly recreated US Special Operations Command. Both REDCOM and its predecessor STRIKECOM had been the focal point for much of the contingency planning and joint force training of those eras and regularly planned and conducted large scale JTF training exercises and participated in selected Ranger EDREs.

The Joint Operations Center was housed in Building 95, the USARSO headquarters, which had undergone a metamorphosis in the previous 24 hours from a staid eight to four five–day week, unguarded and essentially open-to-visitors building to a throbbing round-the-clock command, information, communications and logistics coordination center. A security perimeter was established and pushed out from the building and marked by triple rolls of razor sharp concertina wire with armed guards at all entry control points. Epitomizing the level that USARSO's "soldier" involvement extended was the fact that the guards manning the checkpoints and patrolling the perimeter and monitoring the surrounding area from observation points on the roof had, months before, put aside their normal occupational instruments and requalified on the M-16 rifle. The exterior guard force for Building 95 was the 79th U.S. Army Band, part of the 193rd Brigade. Initially, some members of the XVIII Corps staff were skeptical of their skills and commitment; however, after numerous checks the skepticism was replaced by recognition that the bandsmen were alert, meant business, were proud of what they were doing and were credited with doing a superb job. Very quickly, the XVIII Corps staff also recognized that an overriding factor in the smooth operation of the Operations Center was the teamwork approach exhibited by everyone from all branches of service and all ranks.

The XVIII Corps had run multiple target exercises previously, in November 1987 and again in March 1989. Procedures had been established which reflected a deployed XVIII Corps "Jump" Headquarters would run the overall operation as a JTF Headquarters while several highly competent subordinate headquarters/units functioned at the operational level. These units included the 82nd Airborne Division Headquarters, the Division's On-Call Ready Brigade, the Joint Special Operations Task Force (JSOTF), and its subordinate component elements, as well as 12th Air Force.

While preparations were being made to execute *Blue Spoon*, similar preparations were being made with respect to *Blind Logic,* the civil military affairs plan for reconstituting the Panamanian civil government. On the morning of December 17, the SOUTHCOM Director of Plans (the SCJ5) realized that SOUTHCOM might have to execute the CA plan, as the previously agreed hand-off to USARSO had not yet been accomplished.

On December 18 and 19, there was a crash effort to update and finalize *Blind Logic*, as well as to get an approved version back from JCS. By December 19, it was clear that, initially at least, SCJ5 would have to execute the CA plan. Numerous secure conversations were held with JCS as the SOUTHCOM planners sought to pre-coordinate the message which would constitute the OPORD for *Blind Logic*. The final version of the CA plan was sent to JCS for approval on December 20th. Among the changes included were the establishment of the long-term CMOTF under JTF-South and the renaming from *Blind Logic* to *Promote Liberty*.

Beginning in the late afternoon hours of the 19th and continuing well into the evening, the U.S. media, including a major television news network, began reporting an increase in air activity into Howard AFB, commenting that it was unusual and had been ongoing for several hours. The media also reported that elements of the 82nd Airborne Division were on alert and intimated the two activities were linked and related to events in Panama. This information was picked up by various members of the PDF officer corps, and communicated with accompanying opinions to General Noriega who was in Colon at the time. Not knowing the full details of the American movements, some PDF staff believed it was another flexing of the muscles or a major exercise or preparation for a major counter-narcotics operation. None took these early reports to reflect a direct threat to Panama or the PDF.

Both media stories had elements of the truth in them. The 82nd had been alerted the previous day at 9:00 AM under the guise of an EDRE. And in fact, 2,000 soldiers, mostly from the 1st Brigade, were being marshaled and moved to the Personnel Holding Area (PHA) near the adjacent Pope AFB where they would be isolated prior to being briefed on the actual mission.

During the 28 hours preceding H-Hour, no less than 30 transport aircraft arrived at Howard and delivered more than 430 aircrew and maintenance personnel, as well as the MH-60s mentioned earlier, and advance command and control teams from the follow-on stateside combat forces. Included in this flow was a 13-man advance command and control headquarters team from the 82nd led by the Assistant Division Commander.

At 6:30 PM, the aircraft designated to serve as the JTF SOUTH (XVIII CORPS) Airborne Command Post took off from Pope AFB. It was carrying Major General William Roosma (Deputy Commander XVIII CORPS) serving as Deputy COMJTF and a hand picked Army and Air Force battle staff. The early departure was required in order for the battle staff to be in position off Panama to monitor events from 90 minutes prior to H-Hour throughout the initial critical seven hours of the operation. Upon reaching Panama, the aircraft orbited approximately 35 miles off shore at an altitude above 15,000 feet. From this position, communications were excellent and contact was readily maintained with the aircraft carrying the deploying 82nd Airborne Division and all the other American forces and headquarters already in Panama. This included SOUTHCOM at Quarry Heights, the JTF SOUTH Operations Center at Fort Clayton and the Joint Special Operations Task Force at Howard.

The command post aircraft was one of a small, but highly reliable, fleet of EC-130's, based at Keesler AFB, Mississippi. The aircraft were configured to serve as Airborne Command, Control and Communication platforms and were usually referred to by the nickname AB triple C (ABCCC). The ABCCC was designed and engineered to accept a giant prefabricated room, the size of a 28-foot mobile home that, theoretically, could be slid in and out of most C-130's. However, the practicality of maintaining sophisticated communications and hundreds of electrical connections did not make the slide in/slide out operation a daily occurrence.

The flying command post would act more as communications monitor and network traffic cop as long as the mission sequence was proceeding according to plan. The aircraft was equipped to monitor virtually all the command and control networks. The duty position of each member of the small battle staff had been configured to allow that individual to monitor the two or three communication channels he needed to track the on-going activity he was responsible for. Each of the positions was wired to an internal network, which allowed the various battle staff members to communicate with each other. The same configuration included a "drop" to the communications controller, who could reconfigure any of the internal aircraft communications by pushing some buttons on his control panel.

Thirty minutes later, at 7:00 PM on the 19th, in the midst of the cold rain that had been pounding the Bragg/Pope area periodically since mid-morning, the 1st Brigade of the 82nd Airborne Division began boarding the twenty C-141s scheduled to deliver the brigade to Panama. This would be the Division's first night combat parachute assault since World War II.

At about the same time, and under the cover of darkness, the four *Sheridans* that had been airlifted to Panama in mid-November were moved into position on Quarry Heights, and began overwatch of the Comandancia. The *Sheridans*, with their 152mm gun, were to be a part of the direct fire capability that was to be brought to bear on the Comandancia.

Fifteen minutes before 9:00 PM on the 19th an American intelligence detachment began receiving indications that PDF forces at the Comandancia were increasing their alert status and reinforcing their security posture with rocket propelled grenade (RPG) teams and armored vehicles (Cadillac Gauge V150/V300). This was just one of the earliest reports of increased PDF uneasiness and defensive preparations. It was quickly relayed to the four key commanders: Thurman, Stiner, Cisneros, and Downing.

The two airborne Ranger strike forces and the dozens of other airborne elements were tied together via a secure communications network. All of the strike force aircraft were equipped with tactical satellite (TACSAT) communications and specially designed hatch-mounted antennas. The entire force could be contacted within minutes from the ABCCC. The airborne communication capability extended to the C-141 fleet carrying the first elements of the 1st Brigade of the 82nd during its six-hour flight from Fort Bragg to Panama. The hatch mounted antennas, and the associated TACSAT radios on the 82nd Aircraft, had been installed and were operated by personnel from the Joint Communications Support Element (JSCE). JSCE was a specially equipped and trained joint service communications unit designed and fielded in the early 1960's to support contingency deployments anywhere in the world. Elements of this one-of-a-kind unit had participated in virtually every major contingency that U.S. forces have been involved in dating back to the Congo in 1964.

The deploying forces were tied together by a series of distinct but interlinked communications networks. The link between the two Ranger strike packages and the 82nd brigade included a special operations liaison officer (LNO) onboard the 82nd Airborne Division command aircraft. The SOF LNO had monitoring access to a SOF intelligence network through which he could provide critical information to the deploying 82nd Commander. Complementing this SOF input, the 82nd Commander operated on a JTF joint command network coordinating with, and receiving directions from, the JTF Commander in Panama, and the Corps Headquarters at Bragg that was coordinating the follow-on phases of the 82nd launch. In addition, the 82nd Commander used a 82nd Signal Battalion UHF line of sight (LOS) communication system to pass critical information to the brigade commander and the three battalion commanders on the other command aircraft in the airflow. The UHF system was operated by signal soldiers from the 82nd and was small, occupying two jump seats.

At the Pentagon, the JCS was monitoring developments through its operations center in the National Military Command Center (NMCC) and the adjacent DIA run National Military Intelligence Center (NMIC). The DIA had earlier deployed an information exchange and liaison team called the National Military Intelligence Support Team (N-MIST) to support JTF SOUTH. The National Security Agency (NSA) likewise had deployed its counterpart signals intelligence support team to provide direct connectivity between the NSA Operations Center at Fort Meade and the JTF Commander.

In Panama, three command posts were monitoring the operation with their respective execution check list and accomplishing their verifications and reporting actions. The Special Operations Task Force operations center was located in a hangar at Howard and monitored all special operations actions, reporting accomplishments and mission, results to the JTF SOUTH Command Post located at Fort Clayton. JTF SOUTH monitored all non-special operations missions principally the actions of Task Force Bayonet and Task Force Atlantic. Both General Stiner, COMJTF SOUTH, and General Downing, the Special Operations Commander had direct secure communications with General Thurman at Quarry Heights; however, the normal information flow went from the JSOTF to JTF SOUTH and then to the SOUTHCOM Operations Center. From here the SOUTHCOM Operations Staff advised the NMCC duty team and General Thurman periodically communicated directly with General Powell.

General Thurman spent most of his time during the first several days of Operation *Just Cause*, at Quarry Heights communicating with Washington and coordinating with General Stiner. He made extensive use of the Quarry

Heights CAT during this period. The SOUTHCOM CAT was a very crucial command node that "sucked up" many of the essential support, administrative, and oversight functions required of an operation of this size and complexity, freeing JTF SOUTH (18th Airborne Corps) and the operational components to fight the war.

The senior American Commanders, General Maxwell Thurman (CINCSOUTH), Lt. General Carl Stiner, the overall tactical commander, (COMJTF SOUTH), and Major General Wayne Downing, the Joint Special Operations Task Force Commander, had all been receiving indications that the PDF alert posture (at least among some PDF units), was changing. As the quarter hours crept by, the three commanders began to look for ways to advance the American H-Hour.

By 10:00 PM additional indicators began to be received that at least a portion of the planned operation was compromised. In addition, the JTF SOUTH staff operating out of Building 95 at Fort Clayton received a request from one unit to execute early, followed shortly thereafter by another request - this to go somewhat later than H-Hour. A discussion ensued with a range of factors considered. These included the fact that the Operations Schedule (OPSKED) and the Execution (and reporting) Checklist were geared to the meticulously developed minute-by-minute timetable of actions and the movement plan that was well understood by all participants. Any significant change would involve more than 100 different ground, naval and air elements and a host of intermediate headquarters and lateral supporting elements. Changes, even if communicated to all parties, could beget confusion.

By eleven o'clock, General Thurman had seen and heard enough PDF activity and received enough intelligence data to confirm to his satisfaction; strategic surprise had been lost and the potential for tactical surprise was rapidly diminishing. However, for a wide variety of independent and valid reasons, concerns including three civilian cargo ships in the Miraflores Locks transit, and the relatively lengthy travel distances of various U.S. forces to reach their objectives, any H-hour adjustment would be minimal. The final decision was to "go-with-the-plan" with one fifteen-minute adjustment applied, and this only applied to those in-country forces that were in position to accommodate the H-Hour advancement. It was too late for the units coming from the United States to make up the time. H-Hour for them would remain 1:00 AM. The time change affected the SOF in-country forces the most, and in some cases severely reduced their ability to close with their objectives and accomplish their mission preparations prior to the new H-hour.

About the same time, a little less than two hours before H-Hour, President Elect Guillermo Endara and his Vice Presidents Ricardo Arias Calderon and Guillermo Ford were sworn into office at the Howard Air Force Base Officers Club by the President of the Panamanian Human Rights Committee. The men had been "invited" to dinner earlier that evening by the

American Chargé dé Affairs to discuss the impact of recent events. Following the brief ceremony and a toast, the three men were flown by helicopter to Fort Clayton where they remained under the protective shield of the American military in Quarters 72 for the first 24 hours of the operation.

At 11:00 PM on December 19, the 1st platoon, 534th Military Police Company departed Fort Clayton in groups of three vehicles with a five minute separation between groups. The platoon leader's vehicle led the first group out. The platoon was instructed to drive to the Cocoli housing area on the opposite, i.e. westbank, of the Panama Canal via the Swing Bridge across the nearby Miraflores Locks. Upon approaching the bridge, the MP's discovered it had not been swung into position and several ships were still being processed through the locks. The platoon immediately took the only alternate and much longer route, which was down Gaillard Avenue, to Calle Diablo, to Avenida Amador, then across the Bridge of Americas and back up the opposite side of the Canal to Cocoli. Along the way the American platoon noticed several PDF Police vehicles parked alongside the Pan American Highway, but the occupants did not move to interfere, and the platoon reached Cocoli just before midnight.

A few minutes after 11:00 PM, Major General Marc A. Cisneros moved from Fort Clayton to Fort Amador because of his concern for the safety of American dependents and civilians at this, the most vulnerable American housing complex.

Shortly before midnight, the change in H-Hour to 12:45 AM was disseminated and started to ripple throughout the forces. The notification reached the two airborne ranger strike groups headed for Torrijos/Tocumen and Rio Hato about forty minutes before H-Hour.

At 12:30 AM, General Cisneros ordered the Amador front gate reinforced and closed, along with the simultaneous detention of the PDF gate guards.

Coincidentally, as an American MP platoon was moving into a road block position near Balboa Harbor, it was fired upon by PDF guards at Pier 18. This precipitated a brief, but erratic exchange of fire, with the MP's winning out within 10 minutes.

Meanwhile, three minutes later at 12:33 AM, a PDF bus tried to crash its way out the gate at Fort Amador and was engaged by the American security force. Less than four minutes later, a PDF sedan also tried to flee Amador through the gate and was also engaged.

By 12:40 AM there was no question that some elements of the PDF, at least those at Amador and Balboa, were now aware that the U.S. had moved from its normal defensive and reactive posture to an offensive status and was using "real" bullets.

Earlier in the evening of the 19th, the Fort Clayton Prisoner Detention Commander received the order to cease normal operations and begin converting the facility into a Maximum Security Enemy Prisoner of War

(EPW) detention center. It was to be used as holding area for the top ranking and the most wanted officials of the Noriega regime.

At the time the order was received, the facility had a population of approximately ten U.S. military prisoners. The first step in the transformation was to relocate all U.S. military prisoners to a separate isolated cellblock. This was accomplished prior to midnight and the facility reconfigured to handle the Panamanian detainees.

Shortly before 1:00 AM, the first Panamanian EPWs were received. Two of the MPs on duty spoke Spanish and were instrumental in handling the initial interrogation and processing of PDF prisoners.

The facility was designed and equipped to hold 76 prisoners. Conditions became crowded when the inmate population reached 106 prisoners (96 PDF/10 U.S.). During the course of the operation, a total of 142 PDF personnel were processed through the facility. The last PDF prisoner was released on February 9, 1990.

Aerial view of the POW camp set up by Americans on the Empire Range training area to hold PDF personnel. Photo courtesy of the author.

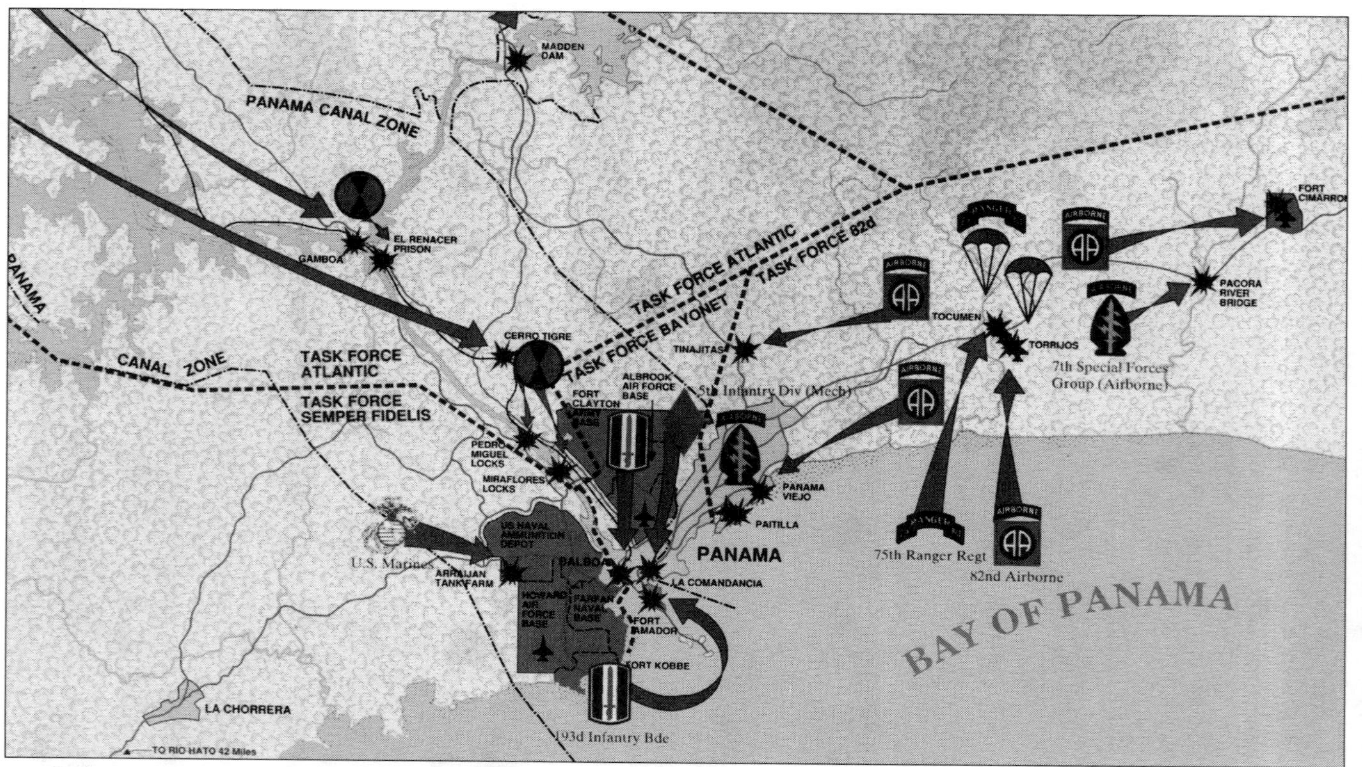

Operations in and around Panama City (Pacific). Map courtesy U.S. Army Institute of Military History.

PART THREE: COMBAT OPERATIONS

Each of the following four chapters deal with a major combat aspect of the first phase of the operation. Each tells a story on its own. Together, they reflect the fact that the operation called *Just Cause* had multiple facets which began with a series of pre-H-Hour small scale special operations, moved to simultaneous major ground force actions, and included a tremendous demonstration of aviation support throughout. The wide array of 2nd and 3rd phase follow-on security actions and essential support actions that were conducted are presented in Part Four.

A diverse range of combat and combat support and combat service units from virtually all the American military services were involved in the operation. *Just Cause* was to be the largest and most comprehensive single combat commitment of U.S. Forces since the early fifties and the Korean War. The collective American force that was coming together would eventually total 27,041 soldiers, sailors, airmen and marines. This number was to be exceeded a year later in *Desert Storm,* but only after a significant in-country build up lasting five months.

Just Cause was overshadowed in many ways by *Desert Shield/Desert Storm*. This was prompted by the proximity of time and eventually the scope of the 100 day air campaign and the sweeping success of the 100 hours of offensive ground operations, both of which were well conducted, heralded in the media and honored by the nation in a series of parades and ceremonies. None of this recognition accrued to the participants of *Just Cause* although many of the successes of *Desert Shield/Desert Storm* were first tested in *Just Cause*. Nevertheless, Operation *Just Cause* was real to its participants as typified by the following comment:

> "Nothing probably makes me angrier than to hear people say that *Just Cause* was not a real war or they had seen more combat than anyone from (in) Panama. These statements show the ignorance of the people making them and negate the performance of the soldiers who were here. *Just Cause* was not a game.
> All a person has to do is see the damage, feel the fear, inhale the smell of death, see what a 5.56mm round can do to a body, find parts of a body on a road or in a building, or know positively that someone out there is trying to kill you, to realize it was not a game. Additionally, nothing in the peacetime army accurately simulates war."

First Lieutenant Ken Miller, 5th Battalion, 87th Infantry.

Aerial view of Paitilla Airfield with East-West panoramic of the central segment of Panama City in background. SEAL engagement occurred near far end of airfield. Photo courtesy of the author.

CHAPTER NINE
INITIAL SOF OPERATIONS

Shortly after midnight on December 20th, a newscaster for the Southern Command TV and Radio Network (SCN) announced in a calm voice: "This is a SOUTHCOM special announcement. Once again. This is a SOUTHCOM special announcement. The command is currently at PML 'ECHO' (No unauthorized movement). The President of the United States has ordered military action against the Panama Defense Forces. There is fighting throughout Panama and all personnel should remain at home. Remain in place… all movement except by U.S. military forces is prohibited. Stay away from doors and windows. The operations are not directed against the people of Panama but rather Noriega and Panamanian Defense Forces. There is a threat to the lives of U.S. personnel. This has been a SOUTHCOM special announcement. Stay tuned to SCN radio and television, for further advisories."

Most people had turned in for the night and missed the initial SCN announcement. Many though, were wakened by the sound of low flying helicopters, or rounds being fired from AC-130 and helicopter gunships, and some by the crackle of small arms fire.

The American action groups were known as task forces and each had a unique name. The conventional task force (TF) designators were related to the heritage-origin of the dominant force: TF Semper Fi - Marines, TF Bayonet – taken from the shoulder patch of the 193rd Infantry Brigade, TF Gator-taken the home state of the 5th ID, Ft. Polk, Louisiana. Two of the larger and more organizational diverse Task Forces took their names from their geographic mission areas, TF Atlantic—7th ID, and TF Pacific—82nd Airborne Division. The individual special operations task forces (TF) were identified by a color code: TF White, Blue, Black, Red, Green, etc.

One of the early actions was the infiltration of a four-man team of USAF Special Tactics Combat Controllers into the inner confines of the Torrijos/Tocumen runway complex. Once inserted, their mission was to set up beacon equipment and a radio network to support the impending airdrop of Task Force Red, a Ranger strike force.

Another of the pre-H-Hour Special Operations quiet actions involved a team of Army Special Forces soldiers and two U.S. civilian antenna technicians from Task Force Black. The team fast-roped into the Cerro Azul TV-2 tower site from a blacked out helicopter and removed a critical module from the transmission facility, disabling the site and removing its signal from the airwaves.

A few minutes later, shortly after H-Hour, and using the same frequency as the disabled Panamanian station, the U.S. began the first of its information and psychological operations. The American signal was broadcast from an USAF EC-130, nicknamed *Volant Solo* (a special operations element from the Pennsylvania Air National Guard), which was orbiting the city. The American broadcast, rendered in Spanish, mirrored the SCN English language announcement and directed the Panamanian people to remain in their homes and not to resist the U.S. forces.

STAND AT THE PACORA

Meanwhile, another element of Task Force Black, which was responsible for surveilling the Pacora River Bridge east of the city and stopping any PDF forces attempting to across it, quickly realized that they had their hands full. The bridge is part of the road link between Fort Cimarron, the home of Battalion 2000 and the Torrijos/Tocumen airport complex. The team assigned this mission consisted of 22 SF troopers and a two man USAF Special Tactics Team. Airborne fire support was to be provided by an on-call AC-130.

On Monday, the 18th, the SF mission commander had received his mission directive to conduct final planning to seize the Pacora River Bridge at 1:00 AM December 20th, and hold it until relieved.

Task Force Red, a reinforced battalion of Army Rangers, was scheduled to parachute directly on to the Torrijos/Tocumen airfield complex and seize and secure it for the follow-on arrival of the 82nd Airborne's Division Ready Brigade (DRB).

The Rangers were skilled in seizing airfield objectives, but would have their hands full if a strong Panamanian force counter-attacked quickly.

The Pacora Bridge was the best interdiction point between Fort Cimarron and the Ranger airhead. The bridge was the confluence of two major highways, National Route One and the Pan American Highway. The two roads merged at the bridge and became one for less than a half mile. The western (Fort Cimarron) approach had a slight downhill grade before leveling off to cross the 400-foot bridge. The bridge approaches had steep side slopes, and in the middle, the bridge deck spanned the Rio Pacora at a height of 40 feet.

The original mission called for a 16-man Army/Air Force Special Operations element to be inserted near the bridge by MH-60 Black Hawk special operations helicopters just before H-Hour. The team began detailed planning based on the availability of only two helicopters. Rehearsals began immediately after receiving the mission order and continued almost non-stop into the evening of the 19th. The team conducted its last mission backbrief at 8:00 PM, that evening. As the force was conducting its final equipment inspections, the mission commander was notified that a third UH-60 helicopter was available to support the mission.

He made adjustments to the plan quickly, adding six men to the force and revising the load plans. As the team was moving to board the three helicopters at Albrook, their launch point, they began receiving small arms fire. The fire was coming from the PDF area across the divided tarmac of the Albrook runway/taxiway complex and from the perimeter fence line along Gaillard Highway.

At the same time, he was told that H-Hour had been moved up 15 minutes. This required an immediate take-off. Fortunately, the helicopters had their engines running. The force commander quickly moved to each helicopter and, through the noise of the spinning turbines, briefed the pilots on the time change while his men completed loading.

The erratic ground fire continued, but all the helicopters lifted off safely and none of the occupants were hit.

To make up for the 15-minute change, the pilots modified the flight route while airborne – a dangerous task because of the density of other American air traffic in the local area heading for other targets. However, the three choppers cleared the congested downtown airspace without incident and made the run to the bridge in record time, touching down precisely at 12:45 AM.

As the helicopters were making their final approach to the landing zone, a convoy of Panamanian military trucks was sighted less than a mile away, and closing fast from the direction of Fort Cimarron. The Americans quickly deployed and established three security elements and a blocking force positioned on both sides of the road.

As the PDF convoy approached to within 100 yards of the bridge, the SF mission commander directed a controlled firing sequence. The terrain around the bridge necessitated the Special Forces troopers move from their protected positions and stand in the middle of the road to get accurate hits on the approaching convoy. As other members of the force prepared to provide covering fire, three troopers each armed with a lightweight anti-tank (LAW) rocket, moved to the center of the road at five-second intervals and fired. All three of the LAWs were on the mark. The convoy stopped immediately with the lead vehicle consumed in flames.

Simultaneously, the Air Force Special Tactics Combat Controller established radio communications with the orbiting AC-130 gunship and prepared to bring a fire mission on the convoy. After receiving clearance from the Special Forces commander to fire, the AC-130 gunship began to engage the remaining vehicles in the convoy. The gunship fire was extremely effective. All the vehicles suffered direct hits in rapid succession. The occupants of the trucks did not wait around. As the AC-130 began firing down the convoy line, the PDF soldiers quickly scrambled out of the trucks and took cover along the roadside, some firing and moving toward the American positions.

The Special Forces troopers engaged the maneuvering PDF infantrymen while the AC-130 monitored the PDF movements and made surveillance reports. The AC also used its infrared search light to provide infrared illumination enhancing the utility of the Special Forces' own night vision equipment. Several elements of PDF soldiers attempted to cross the bridge, but were detected and engaged.

One PDF trooper was killed outright in the initial exchange and the remaining soldiers in his squad, although injured, elected to jump over the side of the bridge, tumbling down the steep slopes.

Firing continued sporadically, until one of the Special Forces soldiers threw several grenades under the bridge and the sounds of PDF foot movement stopped.

Events began to stabilize at 1:30 AM (forty-five minutes after initial contact) and the American troopers made security probes to confirm that no PDF troopers had succeeded in crossing the river to the American side. None had.

At first light, the Americans made a sweep of the area and disarmed the PDF wounded and treated their injuries. Several of the PDF wounded were found hiding in nearby civilian houses. Weapons and munitions were collected and prepared for movement out of the area. Security around the bridge was broadened and checkpoints were set up to inspect transiting vehicles for PDF personnel and weapons.

The PDF prisoners were processed and an initial interrogation conducted while their evacuation was coordinated. The special operations force was relieved by elements of the 82nd Airborne Division at 2:30 PM, 13 hours after the team had landed at the bridge site. At 5:30 PM, they and their PDF prisoners were airlifted back to Albrook where the prisoners were turned over to the MP detachment, and the team went into a mission debriefing.

TASK FORCE WHITE
NAVY SPECIAL WARFARE OPERATIONS

While the Special Forces/Special Tactics team of Task Force Black was busy at the Pacora River Bridge, Task Force White, consisting of Navy Special Warfare (NSW) elements, operating under the JSOTF, conducted two H-Hour maritime oriented missions. One was the securing of the Pacific side of the Panama Canal. The second was the neutralization of a PDF Navy boat used by General Noriega that could provide him with a seagoing means of escape. The boat was moored in Balboa Harbor across the Canal from Rodman Naval Station. The third was the interdiction of a Noriega air escape option. The PDF general maintained a Lear jet at the Paitilla Airport in downtown Panama City, less than a 10-minute drive from the Comandancia.

The NSW elements tasked to accomplish these missions departed Rodman well before midnight to get in position to execute them on the timetable of the original H-Hour (1:00 AM) The Paitilla force left their staging area, a small pier and beach on the backside of Fort Kobbe, shortly after ten o'clock. The Balboa element left their launch site last. The Panama Canal security element succeeded in their mission without encountering any significant problems or engaging the PDF.

BALBOA HARBOR OPERATION

An hour before midnight on December 19th, the task unit charged with the Balboa operation departed the west bank of the Panama Canal to conduct combat operations against the PDF patrol boat, *President Porras*. The vessel was considered by the American command authorities in Panama to be a potential escape platform for General Noriega and other senior PDF officers. The object of the mission was to destroy the boat and eliminate it as an escape platform. The *Porras* was moored to a floating dock adjacent to a PDF pier on the east side of the Canal in the northern portion of Balboa Harbor. The disabling action was planned to be conducted by two SEAL teams and to occur precisely at H-Hour, 1:00 AM, December 20, 1989.

Just before the force was to launch from Rodman, the task unit commander was informed that H-Hour had been advanced by 15 minutes, to 12:45 AM. The time change dictated a shift from the original swimmer insertion point to a point closer to the target vessel. The shorter distance was required to allow the swimmers to reach the *Porras*, plant their charges, and exit the immediate area before the chaos of the new H-Hour erupted.

The men departed Rodman in two Combat Rubber Raiding Craft (CRRC) powered by muffled outboard motors at 11:00 PM. Each CRRC carried five Americans, two of whom were the combat swimmers who would make the final approach to the PDF boat and plant the explosive charges. Each of the swim teams was equipped with a MK 138 Mod 1 demolition haversack, a preset MCS-1 timing clock, and a MK 39 Safety and Arming Device with a MK 96 detonator. When assembled, these components constituted the mission weapon.

Shore based fire support would be provided by a four man team of Navy Special Warfare personnel positioned near the Rodman launch site. Their weapons suite included a .50 caliber machine gun, a MK-19 40mm MG, and a 60mm mortar. Seven other heavily armed Navy Special Warfare personnel boarded a blacked out American patrol boat and slowly moved the craft to a position near mid-channel and held there. This element would serve as a contingency reaction force in the event the CRRCs or the swimmers were engaged by PDF forces.

Due to heavy boat traffic in the harbor and the Canal channel, the CRRCs had to take a circuitous route to the swimmer insertion point north of where the target vessel was moored. They moved at extremely low speeds to avoid creating a wake and to reduce the chances of visual, audio, and radar detection. Upon reaching the objective area, the CRRCs concealed themselves in the mangrove tree line north of the pier where the *Porras* was moored.

Just before the CRRCs were to move to the insertion-dive point, CRRC Two experienced motor problems and went dead in the water. The officer in command made the decision to insert dive pair #1 using CRRC One, and then return to tow CRRC Two to the insertion point. Shortly before 11:30 PM, CRRC One maneuvered to within 150 meters of the pier and inserted the first SEAL dive pair at 11:30. CRRC One then returned to the staging point and towed the disabled CRRC to the insertion point. Dive pair Two was inserted at 11:35.

The swimmers dived on a compass bearing to bring them to the target pier. They surfaced underneath the pier 20 minutes later. Both sets of swimmers moved under the pier, utilizing the cover provided by the supports and pilings. The swimmers navigated the length of the pier, alternating between surface and subsurface movement to conserve oxygen. Upon reaching the shore end of the pier and the floating dock to which the target vessel was moored, the SEALs began their final approach totally underwater.

Swim pair Two was the first to arrive, reaching the stern of the target vessel, at 12:11 AM. After positively identifying the vessel as the *Porras*, they attached the 20-pound demolition haversack to the port propeller shaft and armed the system.

Swim pair One arrived three minutes later and attached their demolition charge to the starboard shaft. After they armed the second system, the SEALS then tied detonation cord leads between the charges to insure dual priming. Just as the SEALs finished the arming sequence at 12:45, the engines of the *Porras* were started, but fortunately the propellers were not engaged. The SEALs quickly moved away from the vessel and sought temporary concealment at an adjacent pier.

As the swimmer teams began their egress from the immediate area, they were hit by pressure from nearby explosions. The divers sought cover behind pier pilings to minimize the shock effect. As the divers resumed their movement, they were subjected to the impact of four additional explosions in nearby waters. Since the explosions were not near them, the swimmers speculated the detonations were caused by PDF personnel throwing grenades into the water as a deterrent to any would-be underwater attackers.

The swimmers operated in separate pairs, alternating between surface and subsurface movement, moving beneath the adjacent pier towards the designated extraction point. Both of the teams were still under the adjacent pier when the mission charges detonated in accordance with the pre-set time at 1:00 AM.

Immediately following the detonation, many of the ships in the harbor started their engines and began turning their propellers as an anti-swimmer measure.

Shortly after the charges exploded, the divers departed the pier on an underwater course that brought them close to the main Canal channel. They heard a large, deep draft vessel approaching. This was probably the *SS Chaiten*, a Liberian registered refrigerator ship, one of two ships which cleared the Miraflores locks at 1:12 AM. The swimmers made an emergency descent to a depth of 45 feet. After waiting 10 minutes, the SEALs returned to their shallower swimming depth and continued their underwater movement.

The captain of the *SS Chaiten* dropped anchor in the Balboa Basin, five nautical miles from open sea. However, the second ship a smaller Chinese fishing vessel, the SS Chung Yong No.8, continued out to sea, sailing under the Bridge of the Americas, and past Fort Amador as the battle for that facility raged. Meanwhile, the two swimmer teams reached the security of the rendezvous pier, and then proceeded to the extraction site at the end of the pier.

Fifteen minutes before the charges exploded, the two CRRCs assigned to recover the swimmers departed for the rendezvous point. They arrived at the designated spot at 1:00 AM just as the *Porras* charges exploded. They took cover under the pier. While waiting for the swim teams, the CRRC crews heard small arms firing in the immediate vicinity, none of which was directed at them. They remained concealed at the designated extraction site while tracer rounds passed overhead. Operation *Just Cause* had been underway for fifteen minutes, and small arms and tracer fire could be seen and heard in many directions.

When it became apparent that the swim teams were late, the officer-in-charge sent one of the CRRCs to the adjacent pier to see if the divers had mistakenly gone to that location. The CRRC returned without sighting the divers.

Although both swim teams were equipped with short-range waterproof radios, they had been unable to communicate due to the extreme interference caused by the many obstructions and extensive boat traffic in the area. The first pair of swimmers arrived safely at the extraction point at 2:00 AM, more than fifteen minutes later than expected. The second team followed five minutes later, at 2:05.

After recovering both of the swimmer teams, the two CRRCs got underway and made radio contact with the task unit command element at Rodman informing them of mission accomplishment and that the CRRCs were returning to base with the swimmers.

The CRRCs arrived at Rodman at 2:20 AM, three hours and 20 minutes after departing from their starting point. The mission was a success and complete, except for the debriefing.

PAITILLA AIRFIELD OPERATION

Just as the Balboa swimmers heard the explosion of their demolition charges, the other element of the NSW force was racing to close with its mission objective, the northern hangar complex on Paitilla airfield. Situated adjacent to the affluent downtown highrise area, the airfield was water accessible by an approach from the broad expanse of Panama Bay. The 5,000-foot runway ran perpendicular to the coastline on a north-south axis.

The southern end of the runway stopped less than 50 yards from the coastline. The southern coastline was rocky with no discernable beach. The eastern coastline consisted of a shallow beach that was the normal resting place for a handful of beached fishing skiffs.

Most aircraft approaches were made over the water rather than over the landward side, which was populated by middle class private homes. On the west side, the airfield was overlooked by the last cluster of the downtown high-rise apartments, while on the north and east sides a major city road ran parallel to its perimeter fence. Midway along the eastern perimeter, the road turned east toward the Marriott hotel, the National Convention Hall, and Panama Viejo.

The small airport passenger terminal and business and customs offices were clustered at the north end on the west/downtown side within the airfield fence line. An aircraft parking area and three medium-sized hangars stretched southward from this northern cluster to a point just short of the mid-section of the runway. The relatively squat control tower was located on the opposite (east) side of the field, along with a string of small hangar sheds which were set back from the runway, and ran down the east side, ending just short of the runway midline.

At approximately 10:00 PM on December 19, three hours before the original H-Hour, a USN patrol boat from Special Boat Unit (SBU) 26, based at Rodman Naval Station, began the slow journey to Paitilla. SBU 26 had been created in early 1988 during the initial stages of the *Blue Spoon* contingency planning. The existing Panama based SEAL detachment had also been increased. This was due to SOUTHCOM's concern for potential terrorist activity against the Canal, as well as part of the DOD counter-narcotics effort in the area. However, the Panama-based SEALs and other elements of the SBU were busy preparing for a series of maritime interdiction missions at the Colon end of the Canal. The NSW force that was underway that night had arrived from the United States less than 72 hours earlier, and less than a week after they had rehearsed the mission scenario in Florida.

The Paitilla mission force, designated Task Unit Papa, included a 62 man landing force from Little Creek Amphibious Base near Norfolk, Virginia. The landing force consisted of three, 16 man SEAL platoons and a small Command and Control (C2) element from SEAL Team Four. The C2 element included the task unit commander, his radioman, two SEAL corpsmen, and a two man Air Force Special Tactics Combat Control element.

The darkened patrol boat moved quietly from its launch point on the backside (waterside) of the Kobbe/Howard complex. It was followed by more than a dozen CRRCs. Once clear of the shoreline, the small flotilla moved out into the open water of the Pacific, skirting the channel approach to the Canal. About 20 minutes out, they turned east and continued to steadily move eastward under blacked out conditions until they reached a point about a mile off Paitilla.

The CRRCs then left the patrol boat, and moved toward the shore, holding off shore about 300 yards. This kept the fragile flotilla outside the glow of the ambient lights from the city and beyond the surf line. At this point, a pair of SEALs slipped into the water and swam to shore, landing near the south end of the Paitilla runway. The swimmers were to conduct a reconnaissance of the landing area and scout out the ground situation at the northern half of the airfield.

Although the basic intent of the mission had not changed from that which was originally planned in the spring of 1988, the situation in Panama and the potential for PDF resistance had changed considerably. One of the earlier options was to put the runway and the aircraft parking area under surveillance from an offset location and interdict any aircraft that attempted to take off with standoff weapons. As the PDF potential for doing the unexpected increased, as witnessed by their unpredicted airlifting of forces from Rio Hato in response to the October coup, the complexion of the Paitilla mission changed. It became prudent to incorporate a capability to block the runway at several points and increase the size of the mission force. A key element of the mission was to insure that General Noriega could not use Paitilla as an emergency exit and flee the country. It was known that his Lear jet, an aircraft with sufficient range for such a purpose, was parked in the middle hangar at the north end of the field.

The tactical intent was to slip onto the airfield and move close enough to observe, and set up blocking positions around the northern hangar area without being detected. To do this meant landing at the southern end, and then moving almost a mile over open ground virtually devoid of any concealment. The first third of the distance was the easiest. Although open and flat, that area had no buildings or lights. The second third, although dark, had a half dozen small hangars and maintenance sheds along the left (west) side of the runway. A middle class housing area backed up to this section of the airfield and the potential for human detection was higher. Roughly parallel and opposite to this first string of structures sat another set of hangars, the control tower, and a row of sheds. This latter area held a greater chance for detection as it joined a cluster of buildings and sheds that supported a mix of airfield workers and private fishermen, some of whom could be expected to be up and about, even at this hour of the night. The potential for an alarm being sounded was much higher here. The corridor approach that allowed the best chance of passing between these two built-up areas undetected was up the runway and its adjacent grassy area.

Shortly after midnight, the landing force learned from the patrol boat (which was holding a half-mile offshore) that H-Hour had been advanced 15 minutes. This put the landing force commander and the three SEAL platoons who were waiting in the CRRCs (a few hundred yards offshore) in a catch up mode. Without waiting for the reconnaissance party to return, the Landing Force commander ordered the flotilla of rubber boats toward the beach.

The CRRCs reached the beach at 12:45 AM, and met the reconnaissance party who confirmed there were no guards or patrols on the southern third of the airfield, but reported they had not had time to scout the upper reaches of the airfield. In accordance with the plan they had rehearsed in Florida, they began moving inland. The landing force commander directed Bravo and Golf platoons to move briskly up the runway and close on their northern objectives while the C2 element and Delta platoon moved up the western side of the airfield. The C2 remained at the southern end of the runway setting up a mortar position and the tactical command post. In the meantime, the Air Force ST/CCT element charged with coordinating with the "on-call" AC-130 was finding it impossible to contact the aircraft on the assigned frequency.

The last minute adjustment in H-Hour, coupled with radio reports of the impending arrival of a PDF plane reported to be carrying Noriega, and the possibility of the imminent arrival of PDF armored vehicles, forced an acceleration in the plan. The radio reports forced the on-scene SEAL force commander to direct Golf and Bravo platoons to move up the runway at a faster than normal tactical closure speed. The third platoon (Delta) was directed to set a position from which it could ambush the "inbound" plane. Golf and Bravo platoons were task organized into four eight-man squads and were moving essentially in trail. The lead squad was to establish a security and blocking position north of the Noriega hangar. The second and third squads were to set up similar blocking positions in front of the hangar, where they would be in a position to block the runway with aircraft from the nearby hangars. The fourth eight-man squad was to take up a blocking position south of the hangars.

As the platoons came abreast of the string of sheds and hangars on the east side of the field, several Panamanian civilians called out verbally challenging the SEAL presence, telling the shadowy American figures to leave. The SEALs responded in Spanish telling the Panamanians not to get involved and stay out of the way. While the two platoons were maneuvering northward toward their objective, the landing force commander maintained radio contact with the task unit commander onboard the offshore patrol boat (who in turn was in contact with the Navy command element at Rodman). The lead Air Force combat controller was still trying unsuccessfully to establish radio contact with the airborne AC-130. Procedures and frequencies had been worked out and employed days before, during the joint rehearsal back in the United States, but unknown to the combat controllers, technical problems had been plaguing the AC-130 since its takeoff six hours earlier. However, the controller's teammate, another USAF CCT was in contact with the SOUTHCOM Joint Operations Center and had been passing mission reports as directed by the SEAL tactical commander.

The noisy verbal exchange between the SEALs and the Panamanian civilians and the explosions and noise from the ensuing battle at the Comandancia undoubtedly was heard by some of the PDF personnel who were on duty at the main west side hangar located a few hundred yards farther north. This gave the PDF a few minutes warning – time enough to prepare for the advancing Americans. The tarmac in front of the northern string of hangars was illuminated by overhead lights. Just as the lead SEAL squad was crossing in front of the first hangar, on the last leg of their land transit, the Golf platoon leader heard a Spanish voice from within the darkened space of the hangar give a preparatory fire order. Just as the American lieutenant began to yell a warning to his men, the relative quiet of the airfield was ripped by the sound of PDF small arms fire. Seven of the eight men in the lead squad were hit immediately, collapsing on the open ground, one an immediate fatality. The PDF gunners, firing from behind oil drums, had fired most of the rounds in their multi-round magazines in the initial burst of fire. Many of the rounds impacted low and short, adding shards of concrete to the spray of direct and ricocheting bullets.

The second SEAL squad immediately opened fire on the darkened interior of the hangar and continued moving forward, while calling for the second platoon (Bravo) to come to their aid. As the second squad closed with their wounded comrades, PDF soldiers inside the hangar again swept the tarmac with small arms fire hitting some of the earlier American wounded again. This second round of fire increased the fatalities in the first squad and injured some members of the second squad, including the assistant platoon leader, LTJG Conners, who died within minutes from wounds to his lower body cutting his femoral artery, raising the number of SEAL KIAs to three and WIAs to nine.

As Bravo platoon was closing with the remnant of Golf platoon and, engaging the PDF in the hangar area with a hail of intense fire, the landing force commander directed Delta platoon to reinforce Golf platoon. At the same time the SEAL force commander moved rapidly up the runway with the second corpsman and three other shooters from the C2 element, leaving the mortar element and the CCT to cover the southern end of the airfield. The sensor operators on board the orbiting AC-130 had been watching the two SEAL platoons during their ground movement, and saw the lead squad suffer the devastating effect of the first PDF barrage. Unfortunately, the AC-130 could not blindly commit its firepower to the ground situation without posing substantial risk to the SEALS.

However, the possibility of the arrival of Noriega's aircraft or of several PDF Cadillac Gage V-300 armored vehicles with their 90mm gun, prompted the SEAL ground force commander to reposition the wounded and dead. He chose the center of the grassy area between the bullet-torn tarmac and the runway and set up a three-point defensive perimeter while calling for immediate medical evacuation of the injured and continued support.

Shortly after the initial rounds of the deadly firefight, a SEAL had put a large hole in the forward section of the "Noriega" Lear jet with an AT-4 anti-tank rocket. As stillness settled on the airfield, the SEALs rolled several light aircraft onto the runway, then disabled them, making the runway unusable per the original SEAL mission order.

The AC-130 remained on station but communications were not established until some time later. Neither the phantom plane nor the wayward PDF armored personnel carriers showed up, and the PDF guard force withdrew from the scene with their own KIA and WIA (later confirmed to be three KIAs and eight WIAs).

The most pressing SEAL need was to evacuate the surviving wounded. All of the injured SEALS needed immediate medical assistance beyond what their corpsman could provide. The CCT element continued to contact the Joint Operation Center via SATCOM and the patrol boat offshore and again requested immediate MEDEVAC support. However, no helicopter extraction capability was immediately available as virtually all of the helicopter fleet (both the Army and Air Force) were already on mission assignments at this the original H-Hour, 1:00 AM. By this time, combat operations were in full swing throughout the country, particularly in the Panama City area.

Once the initial few minutes of rapid fire conflict, and the immediate emotion of the loss of lives had subsided, and after the wounded had been moved to the center of the SEAL defensive screen, a tense calmness and impatience came over the isolated force. The SEAL commander took a moment to speculate on the amount of conflict, violence, and destruction that was occurring at the Comandancia less than two miles away. Fires were raging, smoke was rolling, and the sound of almost continuous small arms and machine gun fire was punctuating the balmy winter night. Although the tremendous sounds and impacts of the initial American crescendo of 105mm and 40mm guns, mini-guns, and rocket fire laid on by the pair of Air Force *Spectre* gunships and the Army helicopter gunships had died away, the results of their work was still very much in evidence.

The nine miles between Paitilla and Torrijos airports diffused the sounds of conflict at the Ranger airhead, but the flames from the burning barracks and sounds of the invisible transport aircraft droning over the contested airhead was evident. Although scattered small arms fire continued near Paitilla, the SEALs were not attacked, though they were well prepared to make it a costly effort for the PDF if an assault were attempted. As time passed, the SEAL commander became more confident that the remaining force of 40-plus men, backed up by the AC-130, could hold the field and insure it was not used as an escape window for Noriega or anyone else. Reinforcements were desirable, but not immediately essential.

An Army helicopter was tasked with the SEAL medical extraction mission at 1:15 AM, but upon reaching Paitilla, it waved itself off because of small arms fire. It returned to its staging point and advised the JSOTF of its aborted attempt. Action was initiated to launch another aircraft. After some scrambling, the mission was given to an USAF Special Operations

MH-60 *Pave Hawk* rescue crew from the 55th Special Operations Squadron (55th SOS). It was approaching an hour after the Army "bird" aborted when the Air Force MH-60 *Pave Hawk* landed at Paitilla and evacuated the Navy wounded. Regrettably, one of the wounded SEALS later succumbed to his wounds on board an Air Force MEDEVAC C-141 while enroute to a military trauma center in the United States. Within a few hours, other USAF MH-60s from the 55th SOS brought in additional SEAL elements to reinforce the initial platoons. A replacement AC-130 arrived on station at 3:20 AM and with it good direct communications were established between the SEAL/CCT force and the orbiting gunship.

The SEALs remained at Paitilla until relieved by elements of a Ranger company (A/1-75) the next day (D+1), the 21st at 2:00 PM. The Rangers were airlifted into the airfield perimeter by two Army CH-47 heavy-lift helicopters. The Rangers remained at Paitilla until they were relieved late on D+2, December 22nd, by A Company 3/505th of the 82nd Airborne. That evening an 82nd trooper was killed by sniper fire as his squad began their first patrol outside of the airfield. This fatality raised the total number of Americans killed at Paitilla to five with eight others wounded.

While these actions had been going on, other small American elements were monitoring key PDF installations that were further down the American timetable. These included Fort Cimarron, home of Battalion 2000, which was monitored by a special forces team with backup by an AH-64 *Apache* helicopter operating in a standoff surveillance mode at a distance of 3-5 kilometers. This placed the helicopter outside of PDF visual detection and small arms range, but within the surveillance capability of its own night vision equipment and the engagement range of its *Hellfire* attack missiles. Variations of this tactic were also used to monitor the PDF garrison at Tinajitas which was in a position to mortar the Torrijos/Tocumen airhead with its 120mm mortars. The surveillance team detected no significant activity at Tinajitas during their night watch and did not have to engage the garrison.

A portion of the hilltop PDF Tinajitas barracks with Barrio San Miguelito in background. Photo courtesy of the author.

Frontal view of Balboa High School. Site of Initial Refugee Camp. Photo courtesy of the author.

Rear view of high rise in working class barrio of Panama City. Photo courtesy of the author.

CHAPTER TEN
MARINE FORCE OPERATIONS

The Marine story began long before December 1989 and must be put in perspective by the events that preceded the execution of *Just Cause*.

A permanent Marine barracks was established in Panama in 1923 at the U.S. Naval Submarine Base, Coco Solo. Over the following decades, Marine forces in Panama went through periods of expansion and contraction, reaching a peak of 36 officers, three warrant officers, and 1,571 enlisted men in February 1945. They also went through a number of redesignations and relocations. In August 1987, the official title was changed to Marine Corps Security Force Company, Panama with a complement of approximately five officers and 125 Marines garrisoned at Rodman Naval Station located on the west bank of the Canal near the Pacific Ocean terminus. This USMC garrison was reinforced in March 1988.

The initial Marine augmentation force was a Fleet Anti-terrorist Security Team (FAST) from the Fleet Marine Force Atlantic, Security Force Battalion based at Norfolk, Virginia. The FAST unit was a platoon-sized element of Marine infantrymen, specially trained in building and room clearing operations. The FAST platoon arrived in Panama on March 14, 1988. FAST personnel were trained in security and close-quarter battle techniques. The plan called for a FAST platoon to be rotated through Panama every 60-90 days.

After an orientation period, the platoon was given the mission of patrolling the Arraijan Tank Farm (ATF). The "farm" included 37 underground fuel tanks and was the source of much of the fuel used by American forces in Panama. The tank farm covered approximately two square kilometers of rolling grassland, surrounding by dense jungle that provided excellent concealment during any approach. Once in the surrounding jungle, visibility was often limited to ten feet during the day and half that at night without the assistance of some type of night vision augmentation. Under all circumstances, movement was slow and could be exhausting. The rule of thumb was that a squad could effectively patrol no more than 500 meters in one hour.

The Naval Ammunition Depot bounded the ATF on the north. Also referred to as the Ammunition Supply Point (ASP), the munitions depot was fenced. However, the majority of the Tank Farm perimeter was not and bordered the Pan-American Highway a well traveled public road at almost any time of the day or night. Under the circumstances, it was nearly impossible for Marine forces to totally secure both the tank farm and the adjacent ammunition storage area.

On April 1st, the Department of Defense formally announced that 1,300 additional U.S. troops would be sent to Panama. Marine reinforcements, a company drawn from the 2nd Marine Division augmented by a Service

Support Group of 40 Marines, began flowing into Panama on April 6th. Before deploying, the company was reinforced by an 81mm mortar section of two mortars, a Surveillance and Target Acquisition (STA) platoon, a counter-intelligence team, and a squad of engineers.

On April 7th the unit was given the mission of insuring the integrity of the tank farm, as well as other nearby installations. The young commander, a Captain, in analyzing the tactical situation and considering the terrain and the ease of nighttime closure by intruders, realized the mission responsibilities were somewhat ambitious given the highway, the jungle, and the threat. He decided to patrol, as opposed to manning fixed positions. He assessed that rather than waste time and effort periodically moving command post and communications equipment, it would be more efficient to find and improve one set of good positions. Accordingly, he divided the tank farm into two zones and assigned each platoon a zone of responsibility.

Two days later, on the 9th operational control of Marine Forces Panama passed from US Naval Forces South (NAVSO) to the newly activated SOUTHCOM Joint Task Force Panama.

Shortly after the two infantry platoons relieved the FAST platoon unknown intruders began to probe the Marine positions. On the night of April 11, a Marine squad-sized patrol operating in the northeast sector of the tank farm made contact with an unidentified group of intruders. The patrol split into two elements in an attempt to trap the intruders. When a flare misfired, igniting with a "pop" like a gunshot, one Marine element opened fire mistaking the ignition of the flare for an "intruder" action. Unfortunately, the hail of American bullets hit a Marine in the other element seriously wounding him. The injured Marine was evacuated to Gorgas Hospital and died the next day.

At dusk on the 12th, U.S. Army remote battlefield sensors on loan to the Marines detected approximately 40 persons approaching the tank farm from the direction of the Pan-American Highway. The sensor activation was confirmed by the detachment of Surveillance and Target Acquisition (STA), Marines from 3d Battalion, 4th Marines. The detachment, located some 700 meters from the company command post, reported by radio that they had seen and heard intruders. A specially equipped Air Force AC-130 Specter orbiting the area also confirmed the sightings. Shortly thereafter, approximately 12 intruders were spotted between the highway and the tank farm. Soon , the Marines received and returned fire, aiming back along the line of tracers that came at them. Separately, the 13-man surveillance detachment reported some of the intruders were probing their positions, and requested illumination fire. An 81mm mortar team responded with illumination rounds. Putting the illumination rounds to good use, the STA NCO reported that he could see the intruders were armed and moving like professional soldiers. When the intruders continued to advance he called for the mortars to drop high-explosive rounds on pre-plotted targets forward of the Marine positions. The company commander authorized the fire missions, and the STA squad to return fire. The mortars fired 16 high-explosive rounds. A few minutes later, the company headquarters position received fire from a ravine to its front. The commander directed the First Sergeant to return fire with a Mark 19 chain gun, subsequently firing a total of 222 40mm rounds. The Mark 19 barrages, along with the fire from the 81mm mortars, concluded the exchange.

At dawn, teams of Marines swept the area looking for evidence to confirm the presence of the intruders. There were signs that bodies had been dragged through the area, and there was debris such as fresh, foreign–made battle dressings, scraps of camouflage uniforms, and chemical light sticks, but there were neither bodies nor spent ammunition shells. The Marines later learned that many of the automatic weapons carried by Panamanian soldiers were equipped with brass-catchers. Following the incidents of the 11/12th, the Marines stood down for a few days of on-post rest and recreation at Rodman. Meanwhile a reinforced Army battalion took their place.

On the 14th, Army sentries guarding the Ammunitions Supply Point (ASP) verbally challenged a small group of intruders who responded with gunfire. Separately, an Army Special Forces patrol from the 3rd Battalion, 7th SF Group, operating west of Howard Air Force Base engaged another group of well-disciplined intruders. The month that followed was a period of relative calm. In addition to routine patrolling, day and night, the company improved and hardened six observation and listening posts in both the tank farm and ammunition supply point. Although the ASP remained a Marine responsibility, Army units frequently patrolled the area. In the months that followed, there were occasional incidents, but nothing on the scale of the April 12th firefight.

According to information obtained from Panamanian Officers following *Just Cause*, the intruders were identified as being members the 7th Rifle Company, known as the "Macho de Monte," together with members of the Special Anti-terrorist Security Unit (UESAT) and possibly one or more Cuban military advisors. Considering the timing of the attack, a few days after the arrival of Marine reinforcements and supported by documents seized in December 1989, the object of the "intrusions" was to embarrass and harass the Marines while testing the versatility and competence of the Panamanian military elite.

The period of relative calm came to an end around 1900 on July 19th, when sensor activations alerted the Marines of Company L, 3rd Battalion, 4th Marines, which had relieved Company I in June, to the approach of approximately 20 intruders. Marines and Army forces moved to insert blocking forces in an attempt to capture the intruders. However, the ground movement was a tortuously slow proposition at night and no Panamanians were captured, apparently melting away before daylight. The pattern of intrusions in August and September was similar, but less dramatic, with only a limited number of sporadic sightings and brief firefights in the tank farm and near the ASP.

Air Force and Navy dog teams regularly joined the Marines on patrol. Army specialists helped the Marines set up a speaker system which, when triggered, informed intruders in Spanish that they were on U.S. government property and that it was in their best interest to immediately return to where they had come. At night, the Air Force continued to fly AC-130 Specter surveillance and security missions in support of the Marines, using Low Level Light TV and Infrared Systems to search for and track intruders.

On October 31st there was another major firefight, much like that of April 12th. Over a period of roughly two and one-half hours, there were seven separate incidents throughout the Arraijan Tank Farm. In five of the incidents, the intruders fired first, but did not hit any Americans. In the other two engagements, Marines from Company M, 3d Battalion, 8th Marines, which had replaced Company L, fired first with unknown results.

The repercussions of the October firefights were predictable. The Panamanians exploited the Halloween theme, showing cartoons of Marines shooting at witches flying through the palm trees. For its part, Southern Command directed the Joint Task Force to place limits on nighttime patrolling and the deployment of observation and listening post in the jungle. Limits also were placed on the number of Marines permitted in the tank farm at any one time. This meant that there was a reinforced platoon in The Arraijan Tank- Farm, one platoon patrolling the ammunition depot and one in reserve giving the Marines an opportunity to rest and train.

In December, Operation *Rabbit Hunt* was launched in the ammunition reservation. It was essentially a large scale joint cordon and search operation conducted by Marine Forces Panama and an entire Army airborne infantry battalion, the lst Battalion, 508th Infantry. The two forces swept through the ASP during the early morning hours of December 19th while Army military police and engineers patrolled the perimeter. Although no intruders were captured, the sweep apparently had a deterrent effect.

THE NEW YEAR – 1989

Although there were incidents in January 1989, especially in the ASP, the New Year brought a period of relative calm and a virtual end to confrontation at both facilities. The situation was so quiet that a rumor that the Marines were going home in February made the rounds. However, the execute order never came.

The May 10th attack on Vice President-elect Guillermo Ford was immortalized by a sequence of photographs of Dignity Battalion personnel attacking the defenseless politician with sticks and clubs, leaving him injured and bleeding profusely.

Within days of the event, as part of the Presidentially directed 1,900-man "beef-up" of U.S. security, additional Army and Marine reinforcements were on their way to Panama. Since freedom of movement was now one of the central treaty issues, General Woerner wanted mobile forces that suited the terrain and the situation. The Marine Light Assault Vehicle (LAV) was faster and more maneuverable than most of the alternatives. It was also formidable looking, standing high on an eight-wheeled chassis topped with a cupola housing, a 25mm Bushmaster chain gun and 7.62mm machine gun. Depending upon their configuration, most LAVs could also carry eight infantrymen.

The Marine reinforcements were drawn from Company A, 2d Light Amphibious Infantry (LAI) Battalion, 2nd Marine Division based at Camp Lejeune, N.C. which was equipped with light assault vehicles (LAVs). Accompanied by a battalion command group the 17 LAVs, "Tanquitos" - little tanks, as the Panamanians soon labeled them, were airlifted into Howard by six Air Force C-141s and three C-5 transports arriving on the 12th of May.

The companies were normally rotated every 90 days. Alpha company which had deployed in the May was replaced in mid-summer and then again in late October 1989. It was K (Kilo) Company, 3rd Bn, 6th Marine Regiment and D (Delta) Company, 2nd LAI Bn that were in Panama when *Just Cause* was executed.

The LAV force included 14 LAV-25s assault variants, two logistics variants (LAV-L), and one command and control (C2) variant, as well as 10 four-man scout teams. Within days of their arrival, the LAVs were very active, overtly signifying their presence and mobility. This was an intentional tactic designed to keep the Panamanian Defense Forces off balance. Their effect on the PDF was clear in incidents like that of May 23rd when Panamanian military police stopped a column of LAVs returning to Rodman from a routine patrol, claiming that the LAVs were machines of war and therefore required an escort. The LAI platoon commander replied that, by stopping his vehicles, the Panamanians had violated his right to freedom of movement. He gave the policemen a card written in Spanish that spelled out American treaty rights and instructed them they had two minutes to consult with their superiors before he would "carry out his mission." After attempting to call a superior, the Panamanian soldiers waved the column through.

A few days later, the LAVs swam the Canal in an exercise named Operation Big Show designed to test and demonstrate the American ability to reinforce and/or secure Fort Amador without using the Bridge of the Americas. The tactic caught the Panamanians off guard, and was repeated successfully on June 20th, 23rd, and 26th. One month later, on July 22nd, the LAV company executed Operation *Hippocrates*, designed to create a diversion and place a blocking force on the Panama City side of the canal.

Over time, LAV operations became more ambitious and ranged farther afield, as in the case of Operation *Lola*. The operation was a 300 kilometer motorized reconnaissance that began on September 23rd, a little more than a month after Company B replaced Company A. The operation took the company west through jungle and rolling terrain.

Throughout the period, the Marine forces conducted training exercises. At first, these were in-house exercises involving the deployment of mobile reaction forces to trouble spots. The reaction forces included HMMWVs carrying heavy machine guns and TOW missiles. Then, there were a series of exercises with other American forces. These were nicknamed *Purple Storm* for offensive evolutions and *Purple Blitz* for defensive evolutions and casualty evacuation drills.

MISSION PREPARATION

Following the initial deployment in May, the Marine commander, just as the other force commanders had done, had directed the development of tactical plans for several contingency options to meet the missions contained in the *Blue Spoon* Operation Orders. Detailed training plans were developed almost simultaneously. The internal Marine preparation plan was nicknamed *Spartan Gap*. All of this effort was designed to prepare the Marine forces to execute their assigned missions from a no-notice, standing start posture.

Mission requirements directly drove the training initiatives. Shortly after the ill-fated Giroldi coup attempt of October 5, the LAV company commander created three specially–configured scout-assault squads, and began intensive building assault and weapons training under a wide range of field conditions.

During the latter part of October (24-26), Delta Company and the first FAST platoon relieved their predecessors in Panama and began a seven day workweek of non-stop training. The program included urban warfare training and conducting freedom of movement exercises in concert with the SouthCom goal of conditioning the PDF to American military movements. The Marines also established a program of "sand table" discussions within their leadership cadre. At these discussions, each force or unit commander would lay out his scheme of maneuver and the sequence of the anticipated tactical operation. The follow-on questions and dialogue reduced the potential for confusion during the initial operations, and in several cases aided in positive refinements to the tactical and support arrangements. Part of the overall program included the activation and use of fire support and aviation coordination communication networks. These included practicing air support request procedures for USAF combat support from the Howard based A-7 fighters, the OA-37 air control/observation aircraft, and the deployed special operations AC-130 gunships.

In late November, Delta Company was called upon to conduct three counter-roadblock and breaching drills at three separate PDF roadblocks in one day. The company had established contingency procedures for virtually all possible PDF actions by creating breaching and riot control teams within the newly created scout-assault platoon. Upon reaching a PDF manned roadblock, the LAVs would take up interlocking fire positions, and the American force commander would demand the removal of the roadblock obstacles. If a positive response were not forthcoming, the riot control teams would dismount the LAVs, and, on order, move forward to provide a defensive screen in front of the LAVs and the follow-on breaching teams. The breaching teams would then dismount the LAVs, move to the blocking obstacle(s) (usually vehicles), hook cables to them, and pull them out of the way using a retriever variant of the LAV. In all three of the November 22 instances, the PDF blockades were quickly cleared without any shooting or bloodletting.

Less than two weeks later, Delta Company was given an immediate action mission to capture and secure PDF Traffic Station #2 of the Department of Transportation (DNTT) which sat astride the Pan-American Highway, slightly more than two miles west of Rodman. The mission was directed for both punitive and deterrent purposes. It was believed PDF personnel from the station had fired on a passing U.S. van. Operational planning was initiated, options analyzed, and tactical planning coordinated down to the fire team level. Shortly before execution, the mission was called off when it was learned the firing had not originated from the station, but from some unidentified transient personnel. Nevertheless, the incident spurred further MOUT (Military Operations in Urban Terrain) training within Delta Company.

The Marine segment of the *Blue Spoon* Operations Order was known as "Ghostbuster," and called for Marine forces to accomplish several diverse and critical missions during the first hour of *Just Cause* and then revert to a strategic security force prepared to conduct follow-on missions. The initial Marine missions included gaining total control of the Bridge of the Americas, neutralizing PDF Traffic Station #2, and the PDF police station at Arraijan, as well as providing a section of four LAVs to assist in the combined arms assault on the Comandancia.

These combat missions were in addition to the normal, but expanded, Marine security mission. The standing missions included providing a guard force at the U.S. Embassy in Panama City and security reaction units and patrols at Rodman Naval Station. Other tasks included providing security at the Arraijan Petroleum Storage (tank farm) area and the Naval Ammunition Depot as well as a rotating guard force of 40 Marines at the Naval security site at Galeta Island on the Atlantic coast. All of these locations, with the exception of the Embassy, were critical to the U.S. combat effort.

THE OCTOBER COUP AND ITS AFTERMATH

The day immediately before the actual coup attempt, the Marine Force was placed on standby alert with orders to prepare to block the approaches to Panama City from the west, preventing possible ground movement by the 6th and 7th PDF Companies from their Rio Hato base. The order to execute came around 11:00 AM on the 3rd. While other Marine units moved to staging areas, 33 FAST Marines moved out along with a detachment of

Army engineers and a reaction force of LAI Marines in light armored vehicles. FAST Marines established a roadblock approximately two kilometers west of the tank farm, where the Pan-American Highway intersected a north-south highway. The engineers placed obstacles, while the LAI Marines waited in reserve nearby. Air support was on station. Artillery targets were pre-plotted. No PDF forces attempted to use the road, unknowingly bypassing the American roadblocks through their use of airlift to move from their base into Panama City. The American force was withdrawn in two hours.

On October 31st, Company B encountered a roadblock at La Chorerra, several kilometers west of the Canal Zone along the Pan-American Highway, during an exercise movement. The Marines were disappointed when JTF Panama ordered them to turn around rather than accept the risk of collateral damage to surrounding civilian property which any attempts to breach the roadblock would have entailed.

On November 22nd, the situation was different for the next company of LAI Marines to serve in Panama, Company D, 2nd LAI Battalion. A movement exercise dubbed Operation *Rough Rider* was intended to familiarize the fresh company with the towns of Nuevo Emperador, Nuevo Guarare, Vista Alegre and Arraijan. The operation called for the deployment of 12 LAV's and three HMMWVs, supported by an Army Psychological Operations detachment and two USARSO Treaty Affairs officers, as well as an OH-58 helicopter serving as an airborne scout. On the outskirts of Vista Alegre, the American force stopped 75 meters short of an impromptu Panamanian roadblock. After a dialogue between the American Treaty Affairs officers and the Panamanians manning the roadblock produced nothing except a shouting match, the Marine Commander through the Army PSYOP Team warned the personnel at the roadblock to clear a passage as the American unit was coming through. The Marine force contracted into a column and slowly advanced through the obstacles to the cheers and applause of a friendly crowd of townspeople. Within minutes the column encountered two more roadblock attempts. These were also cleared without injuries to either side and without an exchange of fire.

Panamanian block and Marine counterblock tactics continued to evolve. The Panamanians often placed junkyard vehicles at key locations to create roadblocks, and stacked old tires in front of them, ready to set them on fire. The Marines countered by acquiring grappling hooks and fire extinguishers.

Other LAI Marines worked with the Army's Task Force Gator, charged with the mission of neutralizing the Comandancia if OPORD 90-1 had to be executed. After witnessing the accuracy of LAV gunnery, and conducting extensive tests, including firing into windows at ranges up to 2,000 meters, Army planners concluded that the LAV was a valuable adjunct to the Comandancia mission force. It was deemed a particularly effective weapon for engaging targets inside the PDF headquarters complex. The result was that one LAI platoon was permanently attached to Task Force Gator, the Comandancia takedown force.

By December 1989, the total Marine force in Panama numbered approximately 700 personnel. This included the small Embassy guard force, which reported to the Ambassador, the security forces company, the Fleet FAST team, a rifle company (K CO-3rd Bn, 6th Regt), and the light armored infantry company (D Co-2nd LAI Bn), which were responsive to the Marine task force commander.

MISSION ORDER

The Marine Force Commander, Colonel Richardson, was briefed on the Presidential decision on December 18th and logistical and maintenance preparations were initiated extending through the day of the 19th.

Company D, 2d LAI Battalion was to attack and seize PDF/DNTT Traffic Station 2 and the PDF station in Arraijan, and screen west of Arraijan. Company D's 2d Platoon was to support Task Force Gator. Company I, 3d Battalion, was to establish a roadblock south of Howard AFB and seize the PDF station in Vera Cruz, while maintaining the security of the tank farm. When relieved it was to occupy the high ground west of Howard and screen the approaches to the airfield. The reinforced detachment from Brigade Service Support Group 6 (BSSG-6) was to form a provisional rifle platoon, seize and hold the Bridge of the Americas. The Marine Security Force Company was to relieve Company I in the tank farm, follow in trace of Company D and establish a roadblock west of the fuel storage facility on the Pan American Highway and maintain security at other U.S. Navy installations. The FAST Platoon, in addition to serving as the command's reserve, would be prepared to reinforce the Marine Detachment at the U.S. Embassy and provide a close-quarter battle element for Company D in its seizure and clearing operations.

Beginning at 6:00 PM the Marine Commander, Colonel Richardson began briefing the officers on the impending operation. This included the command personnel of the attached 534th Army Military Police Company and the 536th Army Engineer Battalion. The tactical commanders began briefing their enlisted personnel at 8:00 PM.

At 9:00 PM the Delta Company commander briefed the company on the impending operation. Each of the specially trained and created scout-assault squads was attached to a specific LAV platoon. The three LAV platoons each had a distinct mission. The first platoon was to capture the Arraijan PDF station, some seven miles west. The second platoon was to marry up with the Army assault units aimed at the Comandancia in downtown Panama City. The third platoon was targeted against DNTT Traffic Station 2, a little more than two miles west of Rodman.

The assault plan called for three LAVs to crash through the gate of the DNTT station, with their M-60 machine guns suppressing any reaction from the PDF bunker located in front of the station building. It was hoped the PDF would surrender at this point. However, if resistance were encountered, the assault squad would dismount the LAVs with the squad machine gunner taking a covering position at the right corner of the station to cover that side and the access road. The remaining squad members would then forcibly enter the station and clear it within 10 minutes leaving a small security element, and then move on to link up with the first platoon at Arraijan.

The two platoons targeted against DNTT #2 and Arraijan departed Rodman Naval Station at the same time. The 3rd platoon, targeted for the DNTT station, was in the lead with the Arraijan-bound 1st platoon in trail. The 2nd platoon, targeted for the Comandancia, had departed earlier, and was headed for the swing bridge at Miraflores Locks to join with the Army components of the Comandancia-bound Task Force. The Marine platoon (four Marine LAVs) linked up with Task Force Bayonet forces at Fort Clayton.

H-HOUR ACTIONS

It was shortly after midnight when the Marine elements comprising Task Force Semper Fi, the designation given Marine Forces Panama and its attached units under 90-2, moved out of their staging area with several sub-elements proceeding directly to their individual objectives. The primary mission for Task Force Semper Fi was multi-fold. It included responsibility: to gain control of the western approaches to Panama City, including the Bridge of the Americas, protect U.S. facilities at Rodman/Fort Kobbe, seize the port of Vaca Monte, and neutralize all PDF threats in its AO including police stations in the towns of Arraijan and Vera Cruz.

One of the key targets was the Bridge of the Americas, the only public land route to Panama City from the west. Thirty minutes before H-Hour, a combined service task force of Army MPs, combat engineers and Marines seized the east end of the Bridge of the Americas. The terrain was exposed high ground with no fortifications or protective cover. The force was split into three teams. The largest element of about 40 soldiers was sent to block both ends of the bridge, while another team was sent to block the nearby road junction to Vera Cruz. The roadblocks were emplaced and defensive positions established on the approaches. These were augmented by Claymore mines placed on the most likely PDF approach routes. Automatic weapons teams were deployed under the bridge to ensure the bridge supports were not damaged or destroyed by PDF or DIGBAT demolition teams. An outer checkpoint was established on the west end to stop any civilians from trying to use the bridge. Although the Marines had planned to do the same on the Panama City approach, they found the PDF had already blocked the lower end of the approach and were diverting all traffic. The Marines held fast on the high ground of the bridge roadway.

Approximately, five minutes prior to the advanced H-Hour, the Marines received a report that Panamanian V-300 APCs were on the move in the vicinity of Rodman. Within ten minutes, thirteen (13) of Company D LAVs moved out, loaded with the scout platoon, and a Detachment of FAST Marines. As the LAN's approached DNTT Traffic Station 2, the PDF opened fire with small arms from nearby bunkers. While 1st Platoon proceeded towards its objective at Arraijan despite the fire, 3d platoon turned its attention on the station. With rounds pinging off their armor, three of its LAVs burst into the station compound, firing their M-60 coaxial machine guns; they did not fire their main guns, the 25mm Bushmasters, in order to limit collateral damage. Two of the vehicles stopped about 20 meters from the station and continued to fire while a squad of scouts dismounted and closed with the building. The front door was opened with buckshot rounds from Marine M-203 grenade launchers.

During a brief lull in the firing, a Marine corporal kicked the door open and firing his weapon, started into the room. He was hit by PDF fire while still in the doorway, and fell back to the ground. In the next instant, one of the other Marines fired buckshot into the room, and, seconds later, yet another Marine sprayed the room. Then the Marines threw a grenade into the room temporarily neutralizing any further resistance. The squad carried the injured corporal outside and left him in the care of the corpsman on the logistics LAV. They then continued on to Arraijan in accordance with their orders to spend no more than ten minutes at their first assignment. A few minutes later, another team of Marines from Company D swept through the station. In the room where Marine corporal had been hit, they found a severely wounded PDF soldier, who reached for his weapon when he saw the Marines. He was killed before he succeeded.

While moving west on the Pan-American Highway, 1st Platoon encountered a roadblock outside Arraijan at approximately 1:20 AM. The roadblock was built around two gasoline tank trucks. The American LAVs stopped about 1,500 meters from the roadblock in order to guard against a possible rocket-propelled grenade attack. The scouts then deployed, conducted a brief reconnaissance and reported 20 to 30 armed personnel were with the two tankers. In the meantime, 3d Platoon arrived and established an overwatch position, while the FAST Marines provided forward, rear, and flank security. The assault leader was reluctant to engage the tankers due to the risk of a major explosion; however, after some minutes, and no signs of the opposition pulling out, he requested permission to do so. Marine Force headquarters gave him permission. Fortunately the tankers turned out to be non-volatile and the Marine fire dispersed the opposition without further incident.

Within minutes, 1st Platoon arrived at its next target, the PDF substation in Arraijan. Fifteen scouts dismounted and took cover against the wall surrounding the small two-story building. Finding both the wall and the building impervious to small arms fire, they pulled back, and permitted the vehicles' main guns to create openings for them. The scouts ran through the openings and, learning from the injured corporal's experience, used fragmentation grenades to secure the building, which ultimately burst into flames. Within the hour, it was little more than a smoking ruin.

Meanwhile, Marines of 3d Platoon proceeded to the other target in Arraijan, the local headquarters of Noriega's political party. They, too, found it difficult to force an entry. All the doors and windows were protected by grillwork that was locked into place. The situation called for a different method of operations. The FAST Marines, who had been following in trail and were specialists in forcible entry techniques, were called forward. They now advanced on the building. While the LAI Marines and the LAVs provided perimeter security, the FAST Marines used shotguns to break the locks. They then warned the occupants of the building in Spanish and then threw a stun grenade into the building. A single unarmed Panamanian, visibly shaken by the effects of the grenade but otherwise uninjured, staggered out into the night air and was taken into custody. The FAST Marines proceeded to secure the building without any casualties.

At H-Hour (20/01:00 AM), Marine elements had, with the assistance of a team of Army engineers, set up a roadblock between the tank farm and the village of Arraijan. Another element of Marines had established a security roadblock, on their side of Miraflores Locks and the swing bridge.

As the Marine task force elements were moving, PDF mortar rounds began landing on the American side of the Canal, between Rodman and the Cocoli housing area. The first rounds hit at 12:45 AM, the new H-Hour.

The 3rd platoon's lead LAV, christened "Highway" by its enlisted commander, began receiving small arms fire at 12:55 AM, as it approached DNTT Station 2. The PDF bullets produced an erratic rain dance on the hull of the vehicle. All three of the LAVs returned the PDF fire with their own M-60 7.62mm machine guns, and proceeded to crash through the gate. They came to a stop about 60 feet from the station building. The scout-assault squad quickly dismounted, took up a skirmish line, and began to put additional suppressive fire on the building. The senior NCO gave the order to cease-fire; then he and the squad leader led the charge on the building, bypassing the empty bunker. The glass door was too heavy to kick in, so it was shot out with two loads of heavy gauge buckshot from the M590 militarized shotguns they carried. The squad leader then kicked out the remaining glass and entered the station while spraying the room with automatic fire.

Once inside the dimly lit building, the squad began to receive fire from a darkened hallway on the right. The NCO who was closest to the firing emptied a magazine down the hall, and directed a two-man element to start room-clearing operations. As the team dashed down the hall to the first room, more shots erupted from the far end of the hallway with rounds appearing to impact everywhere except on the quick–moving Marines. As the men leapfrogged from one room to another, clearing rooms as they went, the firing continued intermittently. As they approached the end of the hall, a figure dashed through an end door and closed it. The firing stopped with the closing of the door. The squad leader stood to one side of the door and kicked it open. He began firing as he entered the room, but was hit by PDF return fire and knocked backwards, falling just outside of the room. The Marine standing on the other side of the door was directed by the NCO to throw a grenade into the room.

As soon as the grenade was detonated, the injured Marine was moved outside of the building to the fourth LAV, "Blackjack," and treated by the platoon corpsman. The assault element then remounted their LAVs and, leaving their wounded comrade in the care of the corpsman and the empty station in the hands of the security element, proceeded at top speed to Arraijan to join the 1st platoon at Arraijan. The scout-assault elements had neutralized the PDF station within 10 minutes and turned it over to the security team as planned.

Within a few minutes, the security team swept the station. On entering the last room, they found a severely wounded PDF trooper hiding behind a desk. The soldier reached for his rifle, but before he could use it, he was dead from Marine bullets. The rest of the building was cleared without incident.

Meanwhile, the assault on the PDF station at Arraijan began with a roadblock clearing. The LAV column found a fuel tanker blocking the main intersection to the town. The American commander had the attached PSYOP team make an announcement in Spanish warning the PDF to remove the vehicle immediately or the Marines would open fire. The time limit quickly expired without any PDF movement, and the commander of the lead LAV, aptly named "Predator," was given the order to fire a three-round burst of high explosive 25mm fire into the PDF headquarters building that lay behind the tanker.

The two-story building had been built in a fortress style with iron bars on the windows and doors, and its walls were impenetrable to small arms fire, but not the shells from the Bushmaster. Reports of fleeing PDF troopers were relayed from one Marine to another as the Marines approached the station which sat at the intersection of a highways, and General Torrijos Boulevard on the edge of the town. The fifteen-man scout-assault element dismounted the LAVs and proceeded to enter the building through the entrances made by the Bushmaster.

The combination of the sound and fury from the 25mm Bushmaster, exploding fragmentation grenades, the sharp snap of M-16 rifles, M-60 rounds, and the flat sound of AK-47 fire split the normally quiet humidity of the night with a mixture of sounds and darts of red and yellow flame.

As the main building was being subdued by the scouts, the close-quarter battle team from the FAST element seized and cleared the nearby PRD political headquarters. Once the sun was up, the LAI's, rifle squads, and the FAST team began to comb the town searching for arms caches and pockets of resistance, and clearing the homes of known Noriega loyalists. Once the clearing operations had been completed, security of the town was assumed, as planned, by a composite force consisting of a reinforced rifle platoon, a LAV platoon and a platoon of MPs.

While Delta Company, the FAST team and the Embassy detachment were occupied with events around Panama City, the other Marine infantry company, Company K, had moved to the coastal fishing village of Vera Cruz, located behind Howard AFB, and successfully occupied the town. At approximately 1:40, the 2d Platoon approached the village of Vera Cruz. The night seemed so unnaturally quiet to the platoon leader who wondered if he was leading his Marines into an ambush. When they arrived at their first objective, the Panamanian Defense Force station in Vera Cruz, there was no one to be found. The station was strewn with clothing, equipment, and documents of all kinds, including passports, shot records, school certificates, and checkbooks. There was even a half-eaten meal, further proof that the occupants had left in a hurry. After securing the station, the platoon withdrew from the town and set up a blocking position from which they could patrol the area. Beginning at 6:00 PM on December 22nd, combined U.S. and Panamanian Security patrols were operating in Vera Cruz, enforcing the curfew and initiating a return to civil order.

By 4:30 AM, Task Force Semper Fi had neutralized its three major targets, and was in complete control of the main highway on the west side of the Canal and both approaches to the Bridge of the Americas and all the PDF installations within 10 miles.

HARASSMENT AT THE U.S. EMBASSY COMPOUND

The presence and significance of the American Embassy compound had become more symbolic and less substantive after the departure of Ambassador Davis and the downsizing of the staff to skeleton force in May and June. There was no decrease or increase in either the security posture, or the size of the Marine guard force, or a change in the mission scope. The Marine responsibility was still to protect American lives and property.

During the first six hours of *Just Cause*, the U.S. Embassy compound in downtown Panama City was the target of several rocket attacks, while its skeleton staff and the small Marine guard detachment were the target of a parallel psychological warfare effort by unidentified PDF/DIGBAT elements. At 1:22 AM, a salvo of rocket-propelled grenades (RPGs), were fired from a position across the broad boulevard in front of the embassy. None of the eight-man Marine guard force was hit and the PDF did not follow-up with a ground attack or sniper fire. However, the rocket assault was followed within minutes by a telephone call advising the defenders that elements of Battalion 2000 were enroute and were only five miles away. An hour later, at 2:25 AM, a second rocket attack impacted the compound this time launched from a building across the street in the rear of the compound. The attack set a car on fire, but inflicted no other damage. Twenty minutes after the second attack, the telephone caller announced that

Battalion 2000 was now two miles away. At 3:00 AM another salvo of rockets were fired at the compound, again with no significant effect. Fifteen minutes later, the telephone caller stated members of Battalion 2000 were now within four blocks of the compound.

The Embassy communicated their situation to the SOUTHCOM Command Post at 3:20 AM. The Embassy was told assistance would be there soon. Less than ten minutes later, the mysterious caller advised that members of Battalion 2000 had arrived and were taking up positions around the Embassy. Just as the defenders' tension level reached new heights, they heard a loud explosion outside the compound and the sounds of American helicopters, followed by an American voice booming out of a loudspeaker calling on them to stay put. Assistance had arrived. This initial air assistance was followed up by the arrival of a LAV/M-113 armored team that had been detached from the Comandancia assault force.

The two and a half-mile ground movement of the reinforcing element took more than two hours to complete. During the tedious movement through the narrow streets, the column was provided extended eyes and an airborne escort by an AC-130 gunship. The *Spectre* monitored the movement route and the adjacent cross streets and was prepared to counter any ambush attempts by PDF or DIGBAT elements. The Embassy was formally declared secured at 4:45 AM.

LA CHORRERA – THE FIRST TIME

Early on the morning of D-Day December 20th, the Marine Forces headquarters received a verbal order from JTF SOUTH to secure the headquarters of the PDF 10th Military Zone (MZ) headquarters in La Chorrera, Panama's third largest city with a population of 80,000. It was an unexpected mission that would take Marine units west of their originally assigned area of operations. Colonel Richardson assigned the mission to Company D and its FAST detachment.

At 3:30 PM, the company began moving west on the Pan-American Highway. Ten minutes later a Marine pilot was airborne in an Army OH-58 *Kiowa* helicopter serving as an aerial observer, scout and fire control coordinator for the advancing Marine column. At 3:47 PM, the company encountered a roadblock built around a number of buses. The LAV's began to take small arms fire from the roadblock and an adjoining hill. As the tempo of the fire increased, the column commander decided to take the initiative and ordered an assault. Led by two LAVs, advancing side by side at a steady but brisk speed and firing their main guns, the assault was over almost as soon as it began as the bus drivers quickly started their vehicles and drove away, clearing the road.

As the roadblock evaporated, the OH-58 moved on and the Marine observer focused on the MZ Headquarters and the immediate surroundings. The MZ headquarters was a block-long compound containing four large buildings surrounded by a six-foot concrete wall that was studded with firing ports. The approach of the helicopter drew tracer–laden small arms fire from the compound. Impressed by the volume of the PDF fire and concerned that the small Marine task force might be outnumbered and possibly outgunned, the airborne Marine requested close air support. The Marine forces headquarters concurred and forwarded the request to JTF SOUTH for final approval. After some discussion, and evaluating the risk of collateral damage to be low, COMJTF General Stiner approved the request.

Within the hour, three USAF aircraft were on station. One was an OA-37 Dragonfly to mark the target and two Virginia National Guard A-7 Corsairs to attack it. The airborne Marine pilot acted as Forward Air Controller and from his standoff position, in the Army OH-58, coordinated and controlled the USAF firing runs. The OA-37 went in first, marking the main building with a white phosphorous rocket. After confirming a "good" mark, the Marine pilot then cleared the two A-7's in "hot." The Corsairs pilots stitched the compound with 20mm cannon fire without damaging any buildings outside its wall. Seconds after the last cannon round struck the compound, the Marine pilot cleared the LAV company commander to commence the ground assault.

The LAV force had been poised to make the closure movement some 2,000 meters from the objective outside the village proper. The LAVs closed with the objective before the smoke from the airstrikes had cleared, and entered the compound gate firing their 25mm Bushmaster main guns. The remnants of the PDF garrison, reported to have been 265 strong on December 10th, fled in disarray. The only opposition came from a few snipers who continued to fire while FAST Marines and LAI scouts cleared the buildings. Within 10 minutes, resistance had ended and the compound was secure. The Marines seized a large quantity of weapons and documents, and then returned to Arraijan since the force was not strong enough to immediately maintain a presence in La Chorrera and support the other pending security missions

ARRAIJAN

Early in the evening of D-day, the Marine command had learned that a crowd of 200 to 300 Panamanians was looting and burning buildings in Arraijan. Because of the need to quell this action, the primary mission for the next day was to stabilize Arraijan, capture any PDF and Dignity Battalion personnel who were still at large, and extend the American sphere of control to the nearby towns of Nuevo Arraijan and Vista Allegre.

Late in the morning on the 21st, the Marines received an unexpected windfall that helped to accomplish its new missions. A Panamanian lieutenant surrendered to Marines at the western roadblock near Arraijan, and said that his men were ready to surrender if promised good treatment. After receiving that assurance, the lieutenant kept his word, and, over the next two days, helped to arrange the surrender of more than 400 Panamanian soldiers.

Once the initial series of targets were secured, the Marine task force turned its attention farther west and began clearing operations in other nearby coastal villages in conjunction with Navy SEAL and special boat units.

One of the first search and secure operations was conducted on December 21 and 22nd. It involved elements of Delta Company and the FAST platoon in the take-down and clearing of a ranch complex owned by a known drug smuggler, which was also reported to be a staging base for DIGBAT personnel. The complex was seized, searched and secured without any resistance as the occupants had apparently fled hours earlier.

On the 22nd, Company K Marines returned to the center of Vera Cruz to deter snipers and looters, and quickly was offered the surrender of 53 PDF soldiers. The Marines decided to capitalize on the opportunity and use a number of the former soldiers to guide security patrols. The company commander also enlisted the services of a Panamanian woman who had been elected mayor of Vera Cruz, but was denied office by the Noriega regime. The new mayor helped the Marines with the restoration of city services including the distribution of food and water that had been cut off since the 20th. Beginning at 6:00 PM on the 22nd, combined U.S. and Panamanian security patrols were operating in the Vera Cruz, enforcing the curfew and initiating a return to civil order.

Also on the 22nd, an ad hoc platoon sized Security Task Force, commanded by a Marine Corps military police officer, was created. It was composed of a group of some 70 Marines and Soldiers and was created as a contingency measure. The unit arrived in Arraijan on December 22th to help fill the law and order vacuum. Its initial focus was helping to manage the Arraijan area POW/EPW/detainee collection point. When the flood of detainees ebbed, the task force focused on preventing crime and restoring order with the welcome assistance of a detachment of civil affairs specialists from the Army's 96th Civil Affairs Battalion. There was food to distribute, a clinic to reopen, and a police force to organize. The task force installed the rightfully elected major who, as other Panamanian politicians, had been elected in May 1989 but denied office, and, alongside him a police chief chosen by the townspeople. They helped him to recruit a police force, which ran joint patrols with the Marines.

At first, the population was somewhat standoffish, hesitant to work with the Marines. However, after Noriega surrendered on January 3rd, there was a turning point in Arraijan, as in other towns. The PDF having been defeated, it was now safe for Panamanians to help the Americans, and many did so willingly. They offered information on arms caches, pointed out former PDF and Dignity Battalion members for arrest and in general helped to restore order. The EPW/Detainee process began with the capturing unit forwarding the individual to a designated collection point, such as the one in Arraijan.

Hundreds of detainees poured into that site, which after December 22nd was under the control of the U.S. Army's 534th Military Police company, 16th Military Police Brigade. Working with the Marines at Arraijan, the military police assisted in the searching, tagging, and processing the detainees before evacuating them to the Marine holding facility at Rodman. The holding facility was a former softball field converted to a POW compound by the presence of military tents and portable toilets surrounded by barbed wire and guard towers.

At the height of *Just Cause*, ten 140 man Military Police Companies were operating throughout Panama, many in conjunction with infantry units. Often operating in four-man teams with a M-60 machine gun mounted on their HMMWV they provide tremendous mobility, flexible presence and added firepower if needed, particularly in the urban environment of the larger cities.

Between December 20th and January 5th more than 2,000 Panamanians passed through the facility, and were checked against the data bases that had been put together in the months before the operation. Senior PDF prisoners helped to maintain order while armed sailors with dogs manned the perimeter. There were no recorded instances of attempts to escape, either from Rodman or from Arraijan. Within days, the Navy and Marine Corps detainees were transferred to the JTF camp at Empire Range near the Canal for further disposition.

LA CHORRERA – REVISITED

After receiving reports of a rally by 500 Dignity Battalion members in La Chorrera on the morning of December 22nd, and being directed by JTF SOUTH to maintain a presence in the city, the Marine Force Commander made preparations to again deploy a force into the city. Before drafting the mission order for the impending operation, the Marine Force Commander and Marine Force Operations Officer conducted a helicopter reconnaissance of the town (which had been the site of the 10th Military Zone Headquarters destroyed two days earlier) that afternoon, scattering "Surrender" leaflets in the process.

This second mission force would include LAI Company K, its attached elements and a newly arrived Army reinforcing unit. The unit was the 2d Battalion, 27th Regiment, 7th Infantry Division (Light). In addition, the Army engineers that had been attached to Bridge of Americas Marine Task Force were withdrawn from the Bridge on the 22nd and executed a mobile link-up with the Marine force the next day (the 23rd) at La Chorrera.

Company K, with their LAVs, was given the mission order at midday on December 22 and quickly set out to cover the distance while the Army battalion prepared for an air assault insertion. Upon reaching the eastern approaches to the town, the LAI and FAST Marines backed up by the LAVs, established blocking and screening positions and waited for the next phase of the operation to begin - the Army helicopter insertion. However, even before the Army battalion appeared 75 PDF soldiers surrendered as a consequence of the earlier leaflet drop.

The next to final event of the operation was the insertion of the first wave of the Army battalion by helicopter on the other side of town. The battalion immediately swept through the city from southwest to northeast, driving a number of Panamanian soldiers toward the LAI and FAST Marines position to the east. The balance of the Army battalion was airlifted into the town the next morning and conducted another sweep picking up some more detainees. Overall the operation yielded approximately 200 PDF soldiers and hostile civilians.

VACA MONTE

One of the larger search operations took place the same day, December 23rd. The operation involved another team effort with Marine, Army, and Navy elements working together to apprehend Dignity Battalion and PDF personnel. More than 250 Marines, sailors, and soldiers were involved. The town Vaca Monte was of particular concern because it was the hub of a large Cuban fishing fleet operation and was suspected of being involved in drug trafficking.

Field reporting indicated Noriega's 100-strong antiterrorist unit maintained a small operating/staging base in the town. Task Force Bulldog, composed of Company B, 2d Battalion, 27th Infantry, the LAI company, still reinforced with a detachment of FAST Marines and a detachment of Security Force Marines, was created and given the mission. The mission was to presume the reports were true, secure the facility and detain any members of the PDF. The Marine units began a motor march to the west, while a supporting Army company started from La Chorrera, moving east to meet the Marines at the intersection of the Pan-American Highway and the road to Vaca Monte. The American forces rendezvoused at 3:30 PM on the 23rd.

With the Marine observer once again reconnoitering from the air, the units coordinated their plans while on the move. The airborne coordination served its purpose, preventing the task force from inadvertently firing on U.S. Navy SEALs who were heading north in high speed boats towards the same objective to block the seaward flank. While the Navy units screened that flank, the task force entered the port and encountered a crowd of looters, many of whom were trying to drive away with trucks heavily laden with stolen goods. The Marines stopped and boarded the lead trucks, depositing the contraband on the ground. As word of the Americans' arrival spread, other civilians (including looters, foreign nationals and former members of the PDF) began to stream toward the only remaining exit point, in an attempt to escape. However, that portal was also under American control. The task force detained some 400 people for counterintelligence teams to process. The detainees included Cuban, German, Peruvian, and Nicaraguan seamen, all from ships docked at Vaca Monte. By midnight, all of the foreigners had been released, and the number of detainees had fallen to 100 Panamanians, including 13 regular Panamanian soldiers assigned to Vaca Monte. None of the reported PDF anti-terrorist force was encountered or captured; however, the search did yield more than 240 pounds of TNT.

MARINE CORPS CHRISTMAS EVE

The operation against Vaca Monte was the last action that carried with it the threat of hostilities on a large scale. By Christmas Eve, the Marine commanders realized that the fight was all but over, especially after Noriega sought refuge in the Papal Nunciatura. When the news spread, crowds of Panamanians celebrated in the streets. In Vera Cruz, they produced a large portrait of the legitimately elected president, Guillermo Endara, and hung it at the local PDF station. The hanging of the portrait of Endara marked the end of hostilities in Vera Cruz and the surrounding area.

CHRISTMAS DAY AND AFTER

During the days that followed, the Marines slipped into a routine of search and seizure operations, and conventional patrolling. The searches were mainly focused on finding PDF cadre or weapons and fell into either roadblocks, screening, or building, i.e, property searches. The roadblocks and the associated screening were conducted by line infantry while the property searches were largely conducted by FAST Marines supported by LAI Marines. Typically, the LAIs Marines secured the perimeter while FAST cleared the objective. All told, they cleared approximately 40 multistory, multiroom buildings. The targets included a radio station and possible tunnel complex in the town of Nuevo Emperador. During these operations, LAI and FAST Marines captured a number of Noriega's affiliates without causing any civilian casualties. The most important capture happened almost by chance. It was during a vehicle recovery operation on Christmas Day that a detachment of support group Marines captured local strongman Rigoberto Paredes, the owner of the drug ranch that had been raided earlier while passing through Nuevo Arraijan. Paredes, who was high on JTF SOUTH's wanted list, had eluded U.S. forces for several days. When the Marine detachment appeared in the village to recover the vehicle, they found local citizens chasing Paredes down the street. After the American force had taken Paredes into custody, several local Panamanians pleaded with the American detachment commander to kill him. Their request was denied.

Three days later, on the 28th, the original Marine area of responsibility, some 200 square miles, was expanded to cover more than 600 square miles. At the same time, the original Marine contingent was reinforced by an additional rifle company (I Co 3rd Bn/6th Regt), which was augmented with an engineer element, TOW teams, heavy machine gun sections, and 81mm mortar squads, plus a transportation element.

During operations in the expanded area, the Marines were augmented by Army military police teams with gun jeeps, and infantry squads from the 7th Infantry Division which had been airlifted into Panama immediately after the initiation of operations to help in the country-wide follow-on clearing and security operations. Throughout these operations, emphasis was placed on a deliberate and measured use of force necessary to accomplish the mission. Special care was taken in all built-up areas to avoid inflicting any unnecessary damage to civilian property or personnel.

By the time *Just Cause* officially ended a few days later, the Marine command, which numbered about four percent of the American forces, had captured some 1,320 PDF and Dignity Battalion personnel, about 25 percent of the total number detained by the collective American joint task forces.

Total Marine casualties were: one killed in action, three wounded in action, two non-battle injuries, and Lieutenant Robert Paz whose death, on December 15th, was one of the trip wires that had changed the *Blue Spoon* contingency planning effort into the execution of Operation *Just Cause*.

OPERATION PROMOTE LIBERTY

After the initial fighting, Operation *Just Cause* was replaced by Operation *Promote Liberty*. Its purpose was "to promote democracy, promote Panamanian confidence in its democratically elected government, and support the nation-building process."

Accordingly, the Marine presence in each town was reduced to a few men, occasionally augmented by small detachments to help patrol or provide replacements for observation and listening posts. Marine Reservists from the 4th Civil Affairs Group on two-week tours of active duty were among the augmentees. They coordinated relief efforts, screened candidates for government positions, documented claims against the U.S. government, and conducted liaison with local officials.

In early February, the LAI company deployed to the towns of Santiago and Sona, and, in late February, an infantry task force deployed to the Azuero Peninsula. During March, a completely motorized and mechanized task force launched Operation *Texas Rangers*, a reconnaissance force and around the towns of David, Volcan, and Rio Sereno in Chiriqui province. Built around Company C, 2d LAI Battalion, the task force covered 1,500 kilometers. During the operation, the Marines enjoyed the support of courageous Panamanians like the Mayor of Rio Sereno, who rode along with the LAV's, pointing out potential cache sites and approving search warrants. In the process, the task force uncovered a cache of falsified passports and large amounts of American currency. In addition to search and seizure operations, the Marines conducted civil affairs work to include setting up field expedient roadside medical clinics and providing care to the local citizenry wherever feasible.

In late March, Marines replaced Army troops at the former Panamanian Defense Force base at Rio Hato, located some 80 kilometers west of the Canal. The mission was to maintain a presence and a forward refueling site.

The Marine command used Rio Hato to support its LAI task force operations further west. The task force comprised of 80 Marines and Sailors and was built around a rifle platoon and a LAI platoon. The task force operated for the next 51 days.

The Marines and Sailors worked hard to establish rapport with their neighbors in the provincial towns. Over time, the Americans won the support of the local citizenry. The Marines quickly discovered they could use their "Tanquitos" to accomplish their peacetime mission. The oversized lumbering armored vehicle was a people-magnet. They quickly attracted throngs of the curious simply by appearing. The Marines would then distribute candy to the children, and take the opportunity to make contact with the local officials and the population of all ages. They built on this foundation by subsequently ferrying members of the new National Police around the countryside in the "Tanquitos" and then introducing them to people the Marines had met during earlier visits. After learning that a number of children had been wounded by unexploded ordnance, Marines conducted a series of classes in local schools, describing the dangers and telling the children what to do if they found ordnance. The program was a success and proved to be yet another way to get close to the Panamanian people and convince them of the true purpose of the intervention: to help them.

Security Patrol in one of the "Tanquitos," Marine LAV (Light Assault Vehicle)
Photo courtesy US Southern Command Public Information Office.

CHAPTER ELEVEN
ASSAULT ON THE COMANDANCIA (TASK FORCE BAYONET)

The main missions of Task Force Bayonet (193rd Inf. Bde [L]) and its attached elements were to isolate and clear the Comandancia, seize and secure the PDF engineer battalion compound and the PDF portions of Ft. Amador, seize the Balboa and Ancon police stations, and protect U.S. housing areas and critical U.S. defense sites. The intent was to initially fix (isolate) the enemy forces in place and offer them the opportunity to surrender, then assault only if the surrender invitation were ignored.

Specific H-Hour assault objectives for Task Force Bayonet included:

- PDF Headquarters (the Comandancia), Chorrillo
- Fifth Company Infantry facilities, Fort Amador
- Balboa Police & Investigation Station (DENI)
- Panama Traffic Bureau (DNTT), Ancon
- Ancon Investigation Station (DENI)
- PDF Engineer Compound, Curundu
- Balboa Harbor (Pier 18)
- PDF Dog Compound, Curundu
- The emplacement of 15 roadblocks to secure the line of march to the Comandancia

Task Force Bayonet had been conducting contingency planning for defensive and offensive operations for the previous 20 months, beginning shortly following the March 1988 coup attempt. Each battalion and company of the 193rd had produced a "Battle Book" detailing every aspect of its mission and plan. The result of this effort was a detailed game plan that was fully understood by the chain of command and which most of the troops had unwittingly rehearsed on several occasions as a *Sand Flea* or *Purple Storm* exercise.

Beginning in October 1989, the task force began an intensive live fire training program spanning from individual up through company exercises. The 193rd shifted its training focus from jungle warfare to urban warfare. Although training facilities for MOUT - Military Operations in Urban Training - (i.e. fighting in cities) did not exist in Panama, innovative steps were taken at the company level to construct jury-rigged MOUT props as live fire objectives in a simulated urban setting at Fort Sherman. An essential element of these exercises was the inclusion of simulated non-combatants and surrounding enemy targets, as the troop leaders knew target identification would be critical in MOUT fighting if they were to operate within the intent of the established rules of engagement (ROE).

For purposes of training and OPORD execution, Task Force Bayonet was broken down into several separate combined arms task forces.

The largest of these was nicknamed Task Force Gator. TF Gator had the H-Hour mission to conduct offensive operations to isolate, place a close cordon around the Comandancia complex and the nearby Carcel Modelo prison, and, on order, seize and secure the Comandancia complex. Task Force Gator consisted of a mixture of Army and Marine infantry and attached MP and specialty units. This task force was equipped with Army M-113 Armored Personnel Carriers (APCs) and Marine Light Armored Amphibious Vehicles (LAAVs).

The second group, Task Force Wildcat, was composed of three infantry companies of the 5th Bn, 87th Infantry Regiment, 193rd Infantry Brigade based in Panama, and a mechanized infantry company of the 4th Bn, 6th Infantry, 5th Division from Fort Polk, Louisiana. Its H-Hour objectives were the neutralization of the PDF elements at the PDF engineer compound, and the nearby DNTT complex, as well as the DENI Stations at Ancon and Balboa.

The third mission group, designated Task Force Black Devil, was composed of two companies of the 1st Battalion (Airborne), 508th Infantry (1/508), from Fort Kobbe and one mechanized company from the 4-6th Infantry (Mechanized)/5th ID. The 1/508th Airborne was known locally as the "Red Devils," but, since the 82nd Airborne Division, included a unit with the identical nickname, the 1/508th was renamed Task Force Black Devil (for the operation) to avoid confusion. The H-Hour mission of Task Force Black Devil was the neutralization of PDF forces at Fort Amador and the protection of U.S. personnel quartered there.

Task Force Bayonet also included the 519th Military Police Battalion, which controlled five military police companies. Several military police platoons were directly attached to the three operational task forces.

The 59th Engineer Company provided direct support by attaching a platoon of combat engineers to both Task Force Wildcat and Task Force Red Devil. The 193rd Brigade maintained one mechanized company, minus a platoon, as a ready reserve.

The execution of H-Hour assaults entailed a complex movement of 14 separate companies over two separate routes, and a two-phased battalion air assault, all to be completed within a 30-minute window.

Task Force Gator, the Comandancia assault force, which was built around the 4th Battalion, of the 6th Infantry (Mechanized), of the 5th Infantry Division (5th ID) from Fort Polk had the toughest job. Although not designed, or normally used, in urban environments, the M-113 armored personnel carriers (APCs) of the 5th ID were selected for their mobility, shock action, and ability to provide an added degree of protection to the infantry assault troops. The assault force included two companies (B and D) with a strength of nine platoons of mechanized infantry mounted in M-113s, an engineer platoon and airborne infantry company from the 508th-193rd (based at Fort Kobbe), four M-551 *Sheridans* from the 82nd Airborne Division, four U.S. Marine Corps LAAVs, and two military police platoons in HMMWVs equipped with 50 caliber machine guns.

It was not until the evening of December 19 that the task force soldiers were briefed on the full details of their part in the impending operation. At 6:00 PM, the soldiers of B and D Companies, 4th Battalion, 6th Infantry, 5th ID were briefed on the details of the plan to secure the Comandancia. H-Hour was scheduled to be 1:00 AM the next morning, December 20, less than seven hours away. Heavy resistance was expected.

After the initial briefing, the team leaders took over and final preparations and double checks of weapons, ammunition, radios, personnel gear, and the M-113s began in deadly earnest. One of these measures was covering the top of the M-113s with three layers of sandbags. This provided an extra degree of protection to the troops who would be riding in the cargo compartments.

The timetable and sequence of the assault had been worked out in detail during the course of the past nine months and further refined in the last three with key segments rehearsed several times. The execution of Task Force Bayonet's H-Hour assaults involved the movement of most of the forces more than four miles from their assembly points to their objectives.

Combat deployment began with two MP companies crossing the Miraflores Swing Bridge to the east bank, securing the bridge as they went, while another MP unit secured the lock and control buildings. Other HMMWV-mounted MP patrols moved out to establish roadblocks along the two main axes of advance and neutralize selected PDF positions, as needed.

Several of the MP units, which were moving into position along Gaillard Highway connecting Fort Clayton to downtown Panama City, were the target of some of the first shots of the operation. At one of the American roadblocks, an MP who was manning an M-60 machine gun mounted on a HMMWV, was hit by rifle fire from a PDF sniper. The round struck the MP's helmet, knocking him out of the gunner cupola onto the hood of the vehicle. His patrol–mates returned the fire and silenced the PDF position. The injured MP suffered a concussion from the impact of the shell hitting his helmet, but the kevlar material stopped the bullet. The same type of shot would have penetrated the old steel helmet used in World War II, Korea, and Vietnam.

Major ground movement for the assault began twenty minutes after midnight, when the two 6th Infantry mechanized infantry companies departed their assembly points and moved along their separate routes to the assault jump off points closer to the Comandancia. At the same time, the attached Military Police units employing HMMWV (with machine guns mounted) moved to establish roadblocks at key intersections along the route of advance.

At 12:21 AM, Bravo Company of the 4th Bn, 6th Regiment (Mechanized) led off from its staging site at Corozal, while Delta company rumbled out of the SCN (North) gate of Fort Clayton on its road march. The 193rd Airborne company and the engineers followed the M-113s of Delta company. The engineers were to breach the Comandancia compound wall once closure was attained, and then set up a holding area for PDF prisoners of war (POW) to be manned by the MPs. The airborne company was to be held in readiness as a clearing force.

Two hundred yards short of the designated line of departure (Avenue de Fourth of July), the lead units of the Task Force Gator began to receive fire from a PDF roadblock. The fire was returned and the roadblock was crashed. Three PDF soldiers were killed in this fast-moving action.

At 12:45 AM, the lead elements of the two American columns crossed the line of departure, from their jump off points on either side of Ancon Hill. Both elements received PDF fire within twenty seconds.

As the Bravo Company column closed with the congested tangle of narrow-city streets surrounding the Comandancia, they were confronted by PDF roadblocks and heavy small arms fire. The PDF had positioned dump trucks to block the key approach intersection. The lead American APC platoon swung up onto the sidewalk, rolled over a fire hydrant, and continued its forward movement under heavy fire. At another PDF roadblock, one M-113 had to ram the first PDF roadblock, which was made up of several vehicles, four times before creating a bypass corridor. As another APC moved forward, it was hit by a rocket propelled grenade (RPG) and small arms fire. Its young commander was killed.

Meanwhile, a pair of AC-130 *Spectre* gunships were entering their firing orbit overhead. The AC-130s were to provide direct preplanned fire on the Comandancia, while Army helicopter gunships attacked PDF fighting positions in the adjacent high-rise building. The advancing American ground forces coordinated with the airborne gunships through a team of U.S. Air Force combat controllers located in the command APC. Less than one minute after H-Hour, PDF sniper, automatic weapons, heavy machine gun and RPG fire was crisscrossing the air a few feet above the advancing APCs.

As the four APCs platoons approached the Comandancia they were faced with additional roadblocks and barricades, sandbagged gun positions, and PDF troopers firing from street level, from balconies, building roofs, and apartment windows. The amount of small arms and machine gun fire from the PDF was intense during the initial phases of the American advance.

The streets surrounding the Comandancia were barely wide enough for the M-113s. This made the vehicles moving shields for the American engineers and infantrymen, but it did not provide any room for the vehicle commanders to maneuver their massive machines. In one of the lead platoons, 26 of the 29 troopers were wounded. Most of the wounds were on arms and legs as all the infantrymen were wearing body armor vest that, although hot and heavy, did provide better protection than the older, more cumbersome and rarely worn flak jackets of the Vietnam era.

With the objective in sight, the tank commanders pressed on through the erratic but heavy fire, responding with their own .50 caliber machine guns. It was apparent to the advancing Americans that they had been expected and the PDF was prepared to put up a stiff fight.

When the follow-on infantry elements, Charlie Company, 1st Battalion,

508th Infantry Regiment, crested the rise near the base of Ancon Hill a few minutes after 1:00 AM, they caught their first look at the objective and its surroundings. Many of the young soldiers were not totally prepared for the sights and sounds of destruction that assailed their senses and awaited them less than 150 yards away.

Flames from the Comandancia were shooting into the air, casting a reddish-orange glow and dancing shadows. The picture also included streams of tracers and the crackle of .50 caliber ammunition being expended by the M-113 tracks firing at the PDF roadblocks and enemy sniper positions in the surrounding buildings, the most prominent was named "24 December". Charlie Company quickly dismounted its trucks and moved across the line of departure (4th of July Avenue), and down to the grassy area on the other side of the highway, and into the first alleyway in Chorrillo. The unit worked its way through the alleys, with fire teams providing covering fire at the end of each alley, while the rest of the platoon was sandwiched in between, until they cleared the first several streets. At this point they started receiving heavy sniper fire from the dominant high rise.

Once the American infantrymen started working their way through the streets, every movement was very time consuming. Progress was measured building by building. The Americans were fighting determined pockets of Panamanian resistance indistinguishable between Dignity Battalion and PDF, as both were wearing civilian clothes. In addition to the street level barricades and firing from within the Comandancia, the PDF had established machine gun positions and sniper teams in the sixteen story, high-rise apartment building adjacent to the Comandancia. The Panamanian positions were peppering the approaching U.S. ground forces. The four LAVs attached to Task Force Gator were providing covering fire for the Army assault on the Comandancia. They fired more than one hundred 25mm rounds through specific windows in the PDF headquarters building.

The Panamanians were contesting the American advance at every building and street intersection. As soon as the Americans would clear one building, the DIGBAT/PDF fighters would run out the back door, then relocate to the next building, reload and reinitiate the duel of bullets.

The resulting smoke and flames severely reduced the utility of the four *Sheridans* that had occupied their two firing positions (Bull 1 and 2), on the Quarry Heights "backgate" road at 12:47 AM. Although the positions overlooked the Comandancia and the Carcel Modelo, the smoke largely obscured the Comandancia, making visual gunnery a risky proposition. The *Sheridan* crews did not have any personal night-vision equipment, nor was the *Sheridan* equipped with a sensor-equipped target acquisition capability.

Although the smoke obscured the sights of the overwatching *Sheridans*, the attacking ground element and the attached engineers breached the wall surrounding the Comandancia at approximately 2:00 AM. However, the American forces were told to hold their positions and not enter the burning compound.

CONFRONTATION ZONE

Fifteen minutes earlier, with closure on the Comandancia assured, a mixed armor force consisting of M-113 APCs, Marine Light Armored Vehicles (LAVs) were detached from the main force and ordered to proceed to the U.S. Embassy compound to reinforce its small Marine guard force. The nearly two mile, 27 block movement took approximately two hours. The Embassy was officially reported secure at 4:45 AM, after the armored force had established an interlocking protective overwatch screen on the possible PDF/DIGBAT avenues of approach.

In the meantime, the Comandancia continued to burn out of control. The men and vehicles of Task Force Gator kept vigil from their blocking positions, periodically returning fire, as PDF snipers ventured sporadic shots.

By dawn, only two of the original four M-551s remained on Ancon Hill, the other two having been attached to maneuver forces to support clearing and security action on the city streets. The *Sheridans* attached to the maneuver elements were employed in one breaching and two suppression engagements, as well as presenting an intimidating force at blocking positions and roadblocks. The breaching mission required only two rounds, the first suppression mission involved five rounds and the second six rounds. Another fire mission occurred at 8:18 AM when the American cordon received a fierce burst of heavy machine gun fire from the second floor of the Comandancia. The PDF position was silenced by direct fire from a *Sheridan*. All the *Sheridan* fire missions were direct fire upon well defined, hostile targets, i.e., barricaded heavy weapons positions.

Hellfire missiles from *Apache* helicopters fire were also used selectively to neutralize particularly lethal PDF points of heavy weapons and antiaircraft fire that were inaccessible to the ground forces. One of these was a PDF heavy machine gun anti-aircraft position located on the roof of a majestic masonry building at the point of the French Quarter promenade overlooking Panama Bay. This PDF vantage point had an unobstructed view across the shallow inlet to the American housing area at Fort Amador, and commanded a potentially lethal field of fire on the Fort Amador H-Hour helicopter landing zone and its flight approach. The gun position was obliterated by a Hellfire missile launched from an *Apache* several kilometers distant.

COMBINED AIR SUPPORT

As the American APCs crossed the line of departure to begin their approach to the Comandancia, a brace of Army MH-6 helicopter gunships and a pair of USAF AC-130 *Spectre* gunships began to lay in a pattern of direct fire on pre-selected PDF targets in and near the Comandancia.

Intense PDF ground-to-air fire erupted just prior to the helicopters reaching their firing point. Despite the heavy fire, the chopper crews began suppressing PDF sniper and weapons positions on the sixteen-story high-rise apartment building, which sat adjacent to the Comandancia overlooking it like a giant father protector. The view from the roof and the upper stories provided a clear panorama of the entire downtown skyline and unobstructed views of the Bridge of the Americas, Fort Amador, and Albrook Air Station, and the road approaches from Quarry Heights and Fort Clayton.

The PDF had taken advantage of its strategic and tactical value by pre-positioning observers and gun positions at key locations and heights, including some on the lower floors. From here, a direct view of several of the key approach streets could be had. However, all these PDF military precautions were taken without evacuating the occupants or changing the basic character and day-to-day residential function of the building.

The American helicopter crews were keenly aware, as were all American forces, of the ROE dictating the application of the minimum force needed to meet the mission objective. Based on this philosophy, the helicopter crew used only its 7.62mm mini-guns to engage the PDF positions, refraining from employing its less precise, but more destructive, rocket capability.

After sweeping the apartment rooftops, the helicopter crew turned their aircraft to direct its fire at the Comandancia itself. As the crew began its gun run, the helicopter was hit by ground fire and the flight controls no longer responded correctly. The copilot noticed the pilot was having difficulty pulling the aircraft out of its gun run, so he grabbed the controls to assist.

The aircraft failed to respond to their combined efforts and continued its descent towards the urban clutter below. With no response from one of the helicopter controls and limited response from another, the crew attempted to aim the aircraft toward an open spot that they observed on the ground. They managed to barely level the aircraft before it slammed into the ground, slid sixty feet across a courtyard, and hit a concrete pillar. Almost immediately after impact, it caught fire. The pilot quickly exited the crippled machine. However, the copilot's door was blocked by a stone wall and debris. Some of the debris pulled at his vest and flight suit, temporarily trapping him in the burning machine. He struggled and tore free, scrambling over the pilot's empty seat and out the other side of the aircraft. He then joined the pilot in front of the fire.

The pair made a hasty assessment of the situation, although unsure of their exact location, they stayed in the shadows and moved away from the glow of the fire and the sound of the small arms fire they could hear close by. With the help of their knee-board schematics of the Comandancia and the surrounding landmarks, they confirmed they had crashed inside the Comandancia complex, although in one of the less critical sub-areas. Both crew members unsuccessfully attempted to contact friendly forces with their PRC-90 rescue radios and had to change locations several times to avoid contact with the PDF defenders.

The aircrew's immediate fear was being trapped inside the compound in close proximity to some of the critical targets when the *Spectres* began their firing runs. The first impacts from the AC-130s started quite a distance from the helicopter crew, but both men realized that they had to clear the compound. PDF small arms fire from several locations forced the aviators to abandon their initial attempt to move to a nearby corner of the compound and scale the wall.

The combination of fire from the orbiting AC-130s and the PDF frustrated several attempts to exit the compound. There was a lull in the firing at about 2:15 AM, so the aircrew decided to make another attempt to reach the outer wall. The two men moved slowly between the jumble of buildings and sheds, staying in the shadows wherever possible until they finally reached an exterior wall topped by a single strand of concertina wire.

Concerned about being shot by friendlies, the aviators decided that one of them should go over the wall and approach the suspected U.S. locations yelling "BULLDOG," the password. Just then they heard the sound of movement coming from some nearby bushes and brought their pistols to bear on the noise. Although prepared to shoot, they held their fire. A PDF soldier with his hands raised in the air hesitantly emerged from the bushes stating he wanted to surrender. He claimed that all of the 200 plus PDF garrison, who had not been killed or seriously injured, had abandoned the fight and left the compound.

The pilot, who still had one tube of his night vision goggles, threw his flak jacket over the concertina wire and slid over the wall to maintain a low profile. Quietly lowering himself to the ground, he surveyed the dark street with the NVG tube and cautiously moved toward an American position. He quietly called to the American troopers. After a few tense minutes, with the helicopter pilot speaking English and the American infantrymen speaking Spanish, the troopers recognized the pilot as an American and allowed him to return for the copilot and the Panamanian soldier.

Just as the copilot was assisting the PDF trooper over the wall, an AC-130 opened fire. The copilot vaulted over the startled PDF soldier to the relative safety of the outside of the compound. When the gunship ceased firing, the two aviators pulled the petrified PDF soldier from his location on top of the wall, and quickly moved to the American ground force position.

The three men passed the next several hours in the belly of the command M-113 of Delta Company, 4th Bn, 6th Infantry, listening to the slowly diminishing sounds of the battle. After the fighting subsided, the American infantrymen evacuated the trio to Balboa High School where the battalion support elements had set up a medical aid station, a civilian refugee camp, and a POW detention center. The aviators turned their prisoner over to an Army intelligence detachment for debriefing and contacted their unit for a pick-up.

AC-130 FIRE SUPPORT

The original H-Hour (1:00 AM) was only five minutes away as the American ground assault units were moving to isolate the Comandancia. Two AC-130 *Spectre* gunships (of the USAF 1st Special Operations Wing from Hurlburt Field, Florida) arrived overhead and began systematically laying 105mm artillery and 40mm cannon fire onto pre-selected targets within the compound.

Prior to departing the United States, the two aircrews were briefed that the Comandancia was the most heavily defended of the various PDF strongholds and fierce resistance was expected. The lead aircraft was tasked to destroy nine specific targets within the complex. These included the barracks and arms rooms, and several antiaircraft artillery positions, which were also capable of bringing fire on the advancing U.S. ground forces.

The two aircrews had developed special tactics during numerous rehearsals on the firing range and training sites in CONUS. The tactic called for firing within fifty feet of the other gunship while both ships were in a controlled very tight turn. The intent was to maintain total sensor surveillance on the compound, and be able to bring all six weapons systems to bear on any location in the compound and the immediate surrounding area.

As the aircraft rolled into their firing orbit, the night sky lit up with machine gun and antiaircraft artillery fire. The lead aircraft was the upper aircraft in the two-ship formation. The aircrew of the lead/upper ship reduced each of their nine assigned targets to smoldering rubble within the first two minutes of their five-minute firing window. The aircrew scored 14 direct hits with their 105mm gun in those two minutes. Their first round set off a huge secondary explosion that lit up the compound briefly and then flooded the area with a mixture of rolling smoke interspersed with climbing flames.

Two minutes into the preplanned attack, the aircrew received an unexpected radio call from the U.S. ground force requesting them to suppress enemy fire coming from the Comandancia headquarters building. The aircrew elected to employ the 40mm Bofors system to satisfy this request because of its faster fire rate and a slight edge in accuracy over the heavier 105mm. The first target was a PDF gun position firing RPGs at the advancing U.S. ground forces. The position was knocked out with the first few rounds. The aircrew then proceeded to systematically lay down a near continuous barrage of accurate fire on other PDF firing positions for the next three to four minutes.

This barrage of suppressive fire was critical to a separate U.S. assault on the nearby Carcel Modelo Prison, and also allowed the advancing ground forces to gain access to the main street in front of the Comandancia.

While this sequence of events was unfolding, the second *Spectre* delivered 35 rounds of 105mm fire on its three targets in less than four minutes. Shortly before the U.S. ground forces closed with the compound, the advancing Americans again started receiving hostile fire from the upper levels of the headquarters building. The ground forces asked the AC crew to put additional 105mm rounds on the building even though the American forces were within the normal danger zone from such fire. Carefully selecting its aiming points and monitoring exactly where the U.S. forces were, the aircrew began the requested bombardment with deadly accuracy, bringing the impacts within 50 feet of the U.S. forces. Within two minutes, the targeted section of the building had been reduced to a smoking shell and the ground forces resumed their advance.

Once this task was accomplished, the aircrew began searching the complex and surrounding area for any potential threats to the U.S. ground forces. In the closing minute of their firing window, the aircrew found and destroyed four .50-caliber heavy machine gun positions and one mortar position which were engaging U.S. forces.

After the initial aerial onslaught on the Comandancia, one of the *Spectres* was released and ordered to provide airborne surveillance and protective fire support to the Marine detachment holding the U.S. Embassy two miles away. The aircrew was also given the task of providing airborne surveillance and fire protection for the 27-block movement of the Marine LAVs, and Army mechanized infantry platoon that were being detached from Task Force Gator to reinforce the embassy detachment. The *Spectre* crew used its surveillance capability to scout for and guide the relief column through the rabbit warren of streets that separated them from the embassy compound. During the course of this transit, the AC engaged a PDF armored vehicle that was trying to ambush the American column.

Despite the determined PDF resistance, the Comandancia was isolated and neutralized as a command and control entity by 3:30 AM, two and half-hours after H-Hour. However, scattered small arms fire persisted for several more hours.

The men of Task Force Gator kept vigil from their blocking positions throughout the day. In mid-afternoon the final ground assault occurred. It was preceded at 3:45 PM by a suppressive Hellfire missile strike from an AH-64 *Apache* standing off the coast. The target was a heavy weapons machine gun position. A Ranger company had been added to the ground strength, and the Rangers joined the paratroopers of Charlie Company, lst Battalion, 508th Infantry Regiment and began clearing the Comandancia complex, building by building, room by room.

The Rangers cleared building one, the multi-storied headquarters building, while Charlie Company cleared the other smaller buildings in the complex. Task Force Bayonet reported the La Comandancia secure at 6:00 PM. In terms of casualties, the battle for the Comandancia was the bloodiest of the entire operation. Although the intensive fighting lasted less than three hours, the PDF resistance was fierce. The Task Force Bayonet cost was five soldiers killed and 56 wounded.

MODELO RESCUE OPERATION

While the lead elements of Task Force Gator had been moving into the maelstrom surrounding the Comandancia, a specially trained Army Special Forces Unit (1st SFOD-D), with air support from Army Special Operations helicopters of the 160th Aviation Group, assaulted the nearby national prison known as Carcel Modelo. Their mission was to free the American civilian Frederick Muse, who had been arrested by the PDF in April and had been imprisoned on the allegation that he was involved in operating a clandestine radio broadcast station for the opposition movement.

The American Embassy had been trying unsuccessfully to obtain his release in the intervening months; however, no progress had been made. There was concern that he would be an immediate PDF target of revenge should the U.S. undertake military actions. This concern was reinforced by Muse, who told his periodic visitors of screams coming from the basement of the three-story prison, confirming that physical torture was employed by the PDF police as a means of gaining information.

The rescue plan had been developed separately from other aspects of the special operations and the general contingency options so it could be implemented as a stand-alone gambit if the situation dictated. However, as tensions between the two nations increased, the rescue option was folded into the timetable of the overall military plan. The rescue sequence had been rehearsed many times, as had most other aspects of *Just Cause*. The insertion of the force, the neutralization of the prison guards, and the safe extraction of the prisoner and the rescue force were extremely time sensitive. This was compounded by the potential for guards in other parts of the prison to respond to the noise of the rescue and the prison's proximity to the Comandancia.

The force planners decided a vertical insertion directly onto the prison roof, followed by an explosive forced entry into the American's cellblock, and by a vertical extraction was the best tactic to increase the probability of mission success. A militarized version of the Hughes' 500 helicopter known as an MH-6 was selected as the insertion platform. Its small size, high lift capacity, and excellent maneuverability were all essential to operating in the high-density urban environment of Panama City. The SOF MH-6 was a derivative of the Vietnam war vintage OH-6 that was recovered from the Army National Guard in 1980 during preparations for a second Iranian rescue attempt. The small but powerful helicopters quickly came to be referred to as "*Little Birds*."

Shortly before H-Hour, an Army special operations MH-6 *Little Bird,* carrying the small but well-armed rescue team, swooped down onto the prison roof and disgorged its human cargo of black-clad troopers.

Within seconds the rescuers had set a demolition charge and blasted an entryway through the rooftop and into the corridor leading to the American's cell. The team quickly descended to the corridor floor, engaging and neutralizing several guards before they could react.

A portion of the team raced down the hallway to the designated cell, confirmed Muse was in the room, and instructed him to move away from the metal door. Once he signaled he was clear, the team blew the lock mechanism and entered the room. They then put a bullet-proof vest and protective headgear on the anxious prisoner and hustled him back down the corridor and up onto the roof. Muse was quickly and unceremoniously shoved into the belly of the waiting chopper. The rescue team then quickly strapped themselves onto special benches mounted on the helicopter's exposed landing skids.

As soon as the rescue team and the "precious cargo" were onboard, the MH-6 pilot pulled pitch, and the flying bubble lifted off and started on the planned escape route. Almost instantly, the aircraft was hit by ground fire and the controls became sluggish. The pilot was able to maintain directional control but could not gain any altitude. Within seconds it was apparent a crash landing was imminent. The aircraft began losing altitude and taking additional hits from PDF gunners including one round that hit a member of the rescue team. The pilot struggled with the crippled machine and managed to guide it to a hard but upright skid type landing similar to that of his Comandancia counterpart minutes earlier. The aircraft came to a halt in a side street less than a block from the Comandancia.

Several members of the ground rescue team were injured during the landing but they, the pilot and the former prisoner, moved away from the disabled and potentially explosive helicopter. Using a parked vehicle as a partial shield, they set up a defensive perimeter and called for assistance.

The call was reacted to quickly and within two minutes, three American M-113s rumbled down the street, pulling abreast and slightly forward of the American position, forming a protective cordon around the small band of Americans. Within 90 seconds all of the rescue force, including the pilot and the former prisoner, were inside the APCs and moving toward the American area of control.

While the rescue team had been focused on the airborne assault and safe release of the American prisoner, another American force consisting of three mechanized infantry platoons had initiated a ground assault to isolate the prison complex and provide a contingency reaction force if needed. The armored ground movement succeeded in focusing PDF attention on itself, to the benefit of the air assault team. It was from this force that the three M-113s were detached to aid the SOF rescue party.

Subsequent to the SOF rescue, the armored spearhead succeeded in breaching the prison compound and freeing a number of other prisoners on the lower floors, including a Costa Rican government pilot shot down and imprisoned two weeks earlier, and several PDF officers involved in the earlier coup attempts.

Once clear of the immediate combat zone, the rescuers, the pilot, and Kurt Muse were taken directly to the American medical station that had been set up at Balboa High School. The injured troopers were treated immediately and the critically wounded, as well as the former prisoner, were promptly air evacuated to the joint field surgical hospital at Howard.

Shortly after the conclusion of the release of Muse and the clearing of the Carcel Modelo, General Downing, the overall special operations force commander (COMJSOTF), formed a highly mobile armored quick reaction sub-task force under his direct control. At the time, Downing was in operational control of all U.S. forces involved in the initial phases of the assault on the Comandancia. This command arrangement was essential due to the high degree of precision and coordination required in the employment of SOF air assets (Army and USAF) in support of the Comandancia ground assault, and the separate but simultaneous assault on the nearby national prison (Carcel Modelo). The armored group, informally referred to as the Panzer Gruppe, included a detachment of Army special mission unit (SMU) close-quarter-combat specialists, four Army M113s, four USMC LAV's, two *Sheridans* and a former PDF 2 1/2-ton truck and a school bus. Its initial mission was to move to the American Embassy and provide a security cordon. The Gruppe was often augmented by aerial surveillance and standby firepower from special operations helicopters. This composite strike force was used extensively during the first four days of the operation. It was able to move with impunity throughout Panama City. It would cordon off a city block, a compound or a specific building and, acting on captured PDF documents, intercepted telephone calls, prisoner debriefings and informant leads was able to "roll up" a significant number of infrastructure captures. These were key members of the PDF and PRD that had supported the Noriega regime.

TASK FORCE WILDCAT – SECURING BALBOA

Less than three-quarters of a mile away from the prison, on the other side of Ancon Hill, but within hearing range of the noise of the Comandancia struggle and the glow from the burning tinder boxes of Barrio Chorrillo, Task Force Wildcat was moving to secure several PDF facilities within the old Canal Zone that could pose a threat to U.S. lives.

Task Force Wildcat consisted of the 5th Bn, 87th Infantry and the attached Co. A, 4th Bn., 6th Infantry (Mech.) from Ft. Polk, La. Neutralizing six PDF objectives, securing two American housing areas, and emplacing a series of roadblocks around the Comandancia was its part in the American scheme of maneuver.

At H-Hour, Task Force Wildcat launched out the back gate of Fort Clayton, splitting into its sub-elements as it moved. TF Wildcat quickly secured the U.S. housing areas at Curundu and Curundu Heights. Some PDF resistance was encountered during this move at the nearby PDF dog kennels. The PDF troopers lost out to the soldiers of a U.S. military police platoon that seized the facility.

The balance of the task force moved across the Albrook Airfield to their objectives. These included the headquarters compound of the PDF Traffic Police at the base of Ancon Hill, the site of the PDF-US standoff over the detention of nine American school buses. The compound was taken without any serious physical damage to the buildings and later became a training site for the new Panamanian police force.

Meanwhile, other task force elements closed with the sprawling 11-building PDF engineering compound while still other elements moved to seize the Balboa and Ancon DENI buildings. During the building-by-building clearing of the rambling engineer compound, the American forces captured 19 PDF, including a lieutenant. The captured soldiers reported 20-25 well-armed Macho de Monte troopers plus 70 PDF combat engineers were hiding in the remaining buildings; however, none of these forces were located during the sweeps which continued until noon on D-Day.

The American force targeted against the Ancon DENI complex located on the city side of Ancon Hill (less than an eighth of a mile from Gorgas American Military Hospital) broke away from the main force and proceeded a few short blocks up the slight incline to their target. The station was taken with relative ease and no significant battle action occurred.

However, this was not to be the case at the Balboa station located on the other side of Ancon Hill, in the heart of the former American Canal Zone capital. The station had, at one time, been the Canal Zone Police station. It was situated in the midst of the Balboa residential area at the intersection of a "Y" in the road; a YMCA complex was on one side and a Catholic church overlooked the intersection from the other.

The station was located less than 100 yards from an unfenced, unguarded American military family housing area, and only 150 yards from a set of steep steps leading to a pedestrian back gate of the U.S. SOUTHCOM headquarters in the Quarry Heights compound.

The attack on the Balboa Police and DENI station complex was conducted by the 2nd Platoon, Company B, 5th Battalion, 87th Infantry. It consisted of a four-prong approach with three squads establishing blocking positions and the fourth squad establishing an overwatch position on nearby high ground. One infantry squad took up a position to the left (at the YMCA), the second established its position to the rear (at the Marco Polo restaurant), and the third in the front (at the *Christian Science Monitor* building across the street). The fourth squad was positioned to the right on the high ground of Saint Mary's Church that overlooked the entire area.

PDF resistance was immediately evident to the Americans as they rolled into the area and took up their positions. The American call to surrender was answered with a barrage of fire. The American ground forces returned the fire and again called on the PDF defenders to surrender.

The PDF response was more weapons fire. Due to the need to minimize any damage to the surrounding area and civilian personnel, the American ground commander called for air support and received fire support from an AC-130 gunship. The DENI headquarters building was destroyed quickly and surgically, leaving only the exterior walls standing, while a nearby PDF police sedan and Christmas nativity scene were unscratched.

Following the successful completion of its D-Day missions, various elements of Task Force Wildcat performed security missions at the Papal Nunciatura, Quarry Heights, Balboa Heights, Diablo Heights, and Fort Amador. These operations continued until January 22, when the task force was relieved by the 3rd Bn., 6th Infantry (Mech.), 7th Infantry Division.

ASSAULT AT AMADOR

Simultaneously with the assault on the Comandancia, the 1st Battalion, 508th Airborne Infantry Regiment, (Task Force Black Devil) in conjunction with the helicopters and crews of the Aviation Task Force, conducted an airmobile assault into Fort Amador to neutralize the PDF forces garrisoned there.

Amador was home to the PDF 5th Company plus a PDF MP honor guard unit and navy guard detachment. The PDF units were housed in a series of two-story cement barracks lined up along the Canal side of the post facing the parade ground and the back of the American housing units located some 100 yards distant.

The assault LZ was a low-lying segment of the golf course located behind the exposed American housing units. A few minutes before the assault troops landed, the American families that lived in the endangered housing units were removed quietly and quickly to safer locations.

The 1st Battalion, 508th had been kept close to their billets on Fort Kobbe all day December 19th. Some of the young squad leaders speculated they were about to be deployed on another field training exercise. Everyone was told to stay in the immediate area. At 9:00 PM the battalion and company leaders were called together to receive the operations order and the assault timetable. Troop briefings followed immediately. Final tactical preparations were begun in earnest at 10:00 PM.

The PDF complex formed an inverted "L." The row of troop barracks constituted the long southern waterside leg, backing up to the Pacific approach to the Canal. The fenced Combined Headquarters building and the adjacent gymnasium comprised the short northern land leg.

The barracks were numbered one through six with the support building, the gymnasium and the combined headquarters building numbered seven, eight and nine.

In order to surprise and isolate the PDF units, the American battalion planned to air assault onto the golf course behind the American housing, then quickly move forward and establish defensive positions between the American housing area and the phalanx of opposing PDF buildings. The plan called for Alpha company to assault the north end of the PDF complex, beginning with building 1. Meanwhile, B Company would simultaneously initiate its assault on the opposite end of the PDF complex. The headquarters company would provide support with special teams of snipers, assault scouts, anti-tank crew-served weapons. Heavier fire support included an attached 105mm howitzer with its gun crew under the supervision of the Battalion Fire Support officer.

The troop leaders conducted the final back brief an hour before the scheduled loadout.

Due to an apparent increase in PDF alertness, and as part of the American Command's decision to advance H-Hour, the unit was ordered (shortly after midnight) to immediately seal off Fort Amador. Two reserve platoons from Fort Kobbe were dispatched by truck over the Bridge of the Americas to secure the Amador main gate. Shortly after the Americans reached the gate and had begun to establish a roadblock, two PDF vehicles loaded with troops attempted to shoot their way out of the complex. The first, a bus, was destroyed on the spot, but the other succeeded in running the incomplete American roadblock and disappeared into the night. The roadblock was completed within the next few minutes and Amador was sealed off.

Meanwhile, the air-assault force lifted off from Fort Kobbe five minutes before H-Hour. Once clear of the U.S. buildings, the pilots turned the dozen helicopters toward the ocean. Almost as soon as the aircraft cleared Fort Kobbe, their occupants (14 troops each) could see the beginning of the Comandancia firefight. As the helicopters turned inbound over Panama Bay toward For. Amador and the landing zone (LZ), they became aware that several of the aircraft had been hit.

Everyone grew intent as the tracers flew by. Some of the troops mentally ran down the list of tasks to be accomplished once they hit the LZ; others reviewed ditching procedures. The pilots concentrated on the LZ and flareout. The helicopters touched down safely and were empty in record time. The squad leaders quickly set up local security. Then the company moved off the LZ and up the surrounding embankment and began to set up screening positions between the American housing units facing the PDF barracks.

Three hours earlier, the battalion commander and executive officer had pre-positioned themselves at Fort Amador and set up their command post for the impending action in the basement of Quarters 20 near the zone of confrontation. Half a mile away, the parking lot at the Fort Amador Officer's Club was programmed to be converted to an EPW/POW holding compound shortly after H-Hour.

The air assault began with Bravo Company arriving first. Its mission was to move from the LZ and establish overwatch and staging positions to counter the PDF 5th Infantry Company.

Alpha Company came in next and moved north. Its mission was to secure the adjacent U.S. naval housing area, evacuate friendlies in that area, and then assist in protecting the northern area of the post which included a critical communications center and the U.S. Navy headquarters building.

Simultaneous with the heliborne insertion, the scout platoon and anti-tank platoon (which had been prepositioned piecemeal throughout the day in composite squads and fire teams) moved to clear and secure three other PDF buildings located on the causeway connecting Amador and the PDF-controlled Flamenco Island.

A second mixed scout/anti-tank fire team reinforced the roadblock team at the main gate and engaged another PDF bus loaded with armed troopers that tried to crash the gate to reinforce the 5th Company. The American teams quickly stopped the bus, causing the PDF inside to withdraw in haste. Most went out the rear emergency door, leaving weapons, military equipment, and even some uniforms behind.

Meanwhile, part of Alpha Company moved laterally to secure the U.S. Naval Headquarters and the adjacent U.S. communications center which were even closer to the PDF area. Shortly thereafter, elements of Alpha Company moved into positions supporting the front gate. A platoon sergeant was dispatched with radio and night vision equipment to establish an observation post and coordinate U.S. control of the open area between the Naval Headquarters building and the "A" Company positions at the front gate.

By 1:30 AM, the American forces had isolated the PDF barracks, and the attached PSYOP team began broadcasting surrender terms, however, the Panamanian garrison refused to comply. The PSYOP teams broadcast the surrender demands in-between U.S. firepower demonstrations, which continued periodically until just after 5:00 AM. The concept was initially to place selective fire on unoccupied buildings (such as the PDF mess hall) as a demonstration of the power available to the U.S. forces, and then press for a peaceful surrender. Following each unsuccessful surrender call, the destructive level of the firepower was gradually increased.

One of the most potent capabilities available to the battalion resided in the attached 105mm howitzer section from D-Battery, 320th Field Artillery. The section had been flown in from Kobbe on the second helo-lift, suspended in slings. The two guns were positioned to provide direct fire on each PDF barracks in turn.

At 5:45 AM the howitzer section chief was directed to place one round each into support buildings 7, 8 and 9. The effect was dramatic. As Bravo Company moved into its assault jump-off positions, several dozen PDF soldiers were sighted exiting the rear of the barracks. The PDF troopers threw their weapons down the rock embankment along the water and made a dash for the safety of the Canal waters less than 150 feet behind the buildings.

At 6:30 AM the platoon sergeant was recalled from his mid-field observation post (OP), and assumed command of a platoon ordered to clear the PDF housing units located just outside the front gate. The new mission order specifically included the residence of the Commander of the PDF 5th Infantry Company. The sweep was made and the PDF Commander's house seized and searched. The search revealed not only military weapons, as might be expected, but, in addition, a large amount of explosives and the components to create a car bomb. The platoon quickly cleared the balance of the homes, and then returned to the company staging area and took up positions from which they would initiate the ground assault on the PDF barracks.

Clearing operations began shortly before 10:00 AM. The movement was to be as simultaneous and methodical as had been the show of force. As Bravo Company began clearing buildings 8 and 9 at the north end of the PDF complex, Alpha Company began receiving fire from buildings 2 and 3 at the south end. Despite the PDF fire, the lead platoon from Alpha company moved into their final jump-off position and at 10:00 began to systematically clear the southernmost structure, building one. The clearing was done without the usual employment of fragmentation grenades, a normal precursor to an assault entry. This option was not used in order to reduce needless PDF casualties.

Tension ran high throughout the clearing operation, but as one squad leader put it, "Everyone was really professional. They (the individual troops) understood we didn't want to just shoot and destroy everything in sight and (they) worked hard at using only what (force) was necessary."

The day began to get warm and the tension was taking its toll, but the men of A and B Companies continued the tedious mission of clearing each building, floor by floor, room by room. The loudspeaker teams preceded each assault, and gradually only a small contingent of diehard PDF troopers were left holding out.

PDF resistance at Amador ended in the gymnasium located at the elbow of the "L" (the last building to be cleared). Twelve PDF soldiers refused to surrender and were firing on the advancing American paratroopers from the gymnasium. The American battalion commander called forward two M-113 Armored Personnel Carriers which had been attached to the battalion from the 5th Mechanized Division.

Following several bursts of concentrated fire from the .50 caliber heavy machine guns of the M-113s, the guns of the diehards went silent and the PSYOP Teams, speaking in Spanish, coaxed the PDF troopers out of the building and guided them to the surrender point.

Meanwhile, the clearing teams of A and B Companies had linked up with the Delta Company teams at building three, completing the initial sweep of the buildings. A follow-on detailed search of each building was already underway by other battalion elements and local security was in place. The American families that had been evacuated from their homes near the battle scene the night before were told they could return to their homes.

The following day, 35 PDF soldiers were found hiding in and under the nearby Balboa Yacht Club, where they had taken refuge after fleeing the barracks during the American fire power demonstrations of D-Day.

Throughout the remainder of the operation, TF Red Devil conducted a variety of security and civil military operations. Together with the 5th Bn., 87th Infantry, the troops of TF Red Devil swept the San Felipe, Santa Ana, El Maranon, and Chorrillo districts of the city on D+2.

Partial interior view of Comandancia Compound with PDF Monument statue on left . Photo courtesy U.S. Army Center for Military History.

View of the Comandancia taken the day after the initiation of Operation. *Just Cause*. Photo courtesy U.S. Southern Command Public Information Office.

Torrijos Airfield approach, with civilian terminal complex (white buildings) and older military runway behind terminal in background. Photo courtesy of U.S. Army Center for Military History.

CHAPTER TWELVE
PARACHUTE OPERATIONS – AIRHEAD SEIZURES

THE SEIZURE OF TORRIJOS/TOCUMEN

At the opposite end of the city, precisely at 1:00 AM, a *Spectre* gunship opened fire on the PDF 2nd Rifle Company Barracks at Tocumen Airfield. Simultaneously, Army helicopter gunships attacked other pre-selected targets within the complex. Three minutes after the gunships completed their combined fire missions, three companies of Rangers from the 1st Bn., 75 Ranger Regiment, from Fort Stewart, Georgia, augmented by Charlie Company of the 3rd Bn., 75th Ranger Regiment, out of Fort Benning, Georgia, and PSYOP teams from Fort Bragg and USAF Special Tactics Personnel parachuted onto the tarmac at Tocumen.

The Ranger forces had been designated Task Force Red and was one of several special operations task forces operating under the control of the Joint Special Operations Task Force (JSOTF). The Ranger regiment had been involved in the Panamanian contingency planning since early in the spring of 1988, when General Woerner had requested and obtained the cooperation of General Jim Lindsay, the Commander of the U.S. Special Operations Command to form the initial JSOTF. The Ranger regimental staff had seen the options evolve during the intervening twenty months and had completed a week of rehearsals less than 36 hours earlier.

The task force had four priority objectives: the barracks of the PDF 2nd Rifle Company (Pumas de Tocumen), the barracks of the Panamanian Air Force (FAP), the Tocumen military terminal, and the International Civil Air Terminal at Torrijos. The objectives lay on a line almost a mile and half long, diagonally bisecting the two offset runways. The three military targets were in close proximity to each other at the northern end of Tocumen, while the giant civil air terminal was more than a mile south, adjacent to the newer Torrijos runway. The selection of the objectives was based upon an assessment of the anticipated Panamanian resistance, as well as American requirements to use the airhead to land follow-on forces.

The three companies of the 1st Battalion drew the three northern objectives, which had the potential to provide the greatest resistance. The PDF 2nd Rifle Company barracks was estimated to house 200 soldiers and the FAP barracks 150 airmen. The civilian terminal, although larger, had a smaller guard force estimated to be less than 50 personnel. This objective was assigned to Charlie Company of the 3rd Battalion. This assignment of missions by company permitted the force elements to train and repeatedly rehearse their actions, while at their home post, maintaining a low operations security (OPSEC) profile.

The Regiment Commander received notice of the impending deployment on the evening of December 17, 1989. Charlie Company, 3rd

Battalion was one of the first alerted. The company left Fort Benning in the early morning hours of December 18, and deployed to Hunter Army Airfield, a former SAC bomber base near Savannah, Georgia where it joined the 1st Ranger Battalion.

Charlie Company's movement and the face-to-face link-up with the 1st Battalion staff at Sabre Hall, the old SAC alert facility, went smoothly. The OPORD review and coordination meeting took place about 11:00 AM on December 18. Charlie Company was given responsibility for seizing key points within the Torrijos complex and clearing the main civilian terminal.

Specifically, the company mission was to conduct an airborne assault on Torrijos runway at 1:00 AM, then quickly move to isolate and secure the multi-level rambling main terminal (designated Objective Bear), eliminate any enemy resistance, and prevent PDF forces from interfering with follow-on battle plans.

Early in the planning cycle, intelligence had indicated that there were normally very few people in the main terminal at 1:00 AM, the planned H-Hour. However, as is normal with commercial air flights in Latin America, and the Third World in general, adherence to flight schedules is rare. This was the case at Torrijos. Shortly after midnight, two unscheduled international charter flights landed at the airport. The terminal was still fully operational. In fact the passengers from a Brazilian airliner, which landed only minutes before the American paradrop, witnessed the descent of the Rangers and the harassment fire from the PDF forces on the ground. Later, the Rangers found out there were a total of 398 civilians of various nationalities in the terminal as the Rangers exited the darkened C-130s. (Author's note: The American execution timetable could not have been changed significantly even if the American authorities had learned of the chartered flights earlier.)

Troop leading procedures and a review of sub-unit tasks took place on the morning of December 19. The Rangers and their attached CCT and PSYOP elements were marshaled into 16 jump elements referred to as chalks 1 through 16. Within the overall drop plan, chalks 13-16 were composed of Company C personnel. The force took off that night a few hours after dark.

Because of U.S. media broadcast about the alert of the 82nd, the reported influx of transports into Howard earlier in the day, the initiation of combat at Fort Amador, and the advance on the Comandancia, the PDF troopers at Torrijos/Tocumen PDF were alert and manning anti-aircraft (AA) gun positions. However, the preparatory fire delivered by the Army helicopters and a USAF AC-130 gunship neutralized the most lethal, but not all, of the PDF defenses before the Rangers exited the jump aircraft.

The AC-130 destroyed three .50 caliber machine gun positions and one Soviet made four-barrel ZPU-4 AA gun position during its pre-assault missions, as well as collapsing the horseshoe-shaped 2nd Rifle Company barracks. The AH-6 helicopters took out the PDF guard tower and three-machine gun positions. About 30 PDF and FAP soldiers tried unsuccessfully to shoot down the AH-6s as the two helicopters were making their attack runs on the FAP communications and arms building. The helicopters reported mission complete.

The flight track of the Ranger drop transports came in from the east over the bay and made a 90 degree turn, then a second turn, and then drove straight down a line between the two offset runways. Four C-130's made the initial pass dropping four reinforced platoons of Rangers, plus the attached Special Tactics and PSYOP loudspeaker teams. The lead formation was followed shortly thereafter by another 12 C-130s coming in over the drop zone from the other direction. The two drops were considered near perfect, with most of the Rangers landing within a few meters of where they had planned.

The jump was executed from an altitude of 500 feet. The jumpers were all heavily laden with rucksacks that bulged with enough ammunition, batteries, radios, water, and rations to last three days. Given the low jump altitude and the heavy loads, the value of reserve chutes was questionable. A minimum of 250-300 feet is normally required to fully deploy a parachute. If an individual's main chute did not deploy properly, there would have been little time or altitude left to manually throw out the reserve; however, the Ranger commander did not preclude the possibility, and contrary to media hearsay, the Rangers did jump with their emergency reserve parachutes. Happily, and with great credit to the parachute riggers, all the main chutes worked, and there were no jump fatalities.

The low jump altitude combined with the heavy loads and impacting on the unyielding concrete and tarmac of the airfield, however, did inflict more than a score of injuries. Fifteen (2 percent) of the seven hundred and fifty jumpers suffered some degree of minor injury. Most injuries were sprained ankles, a few torn ligaments, and some bruised ribs, etc. Some of the injuries were caused by younger troopers not releasing their rucksacks on the drop lines. The rucksacks were intended to be released and hang below the parachutist on a suspension line. This separation of the pack and trooper during landing would decrease the soldier's impact weight and allow him to execute a proper parachute landing fall (PLF).

The Ranger assault timetable was tight. The exact status of PDF Battalion 2000 was unknown, but the potential for a counterattack was recognized. In addition, the transports carrying the first heavy equipment drop of the follow-on unit, a brigade from the 82nd Airborne Division was due overhead in 45 minutes. Within 15 minutes of exiting the C-130 aircraft, the lead Ranger elements were fully assembled and enroute to their assault objectives. While most of the Rangers were moving to their objectives, the USAF Special Tactics personnel rushed to clear and prepare the airhead for the second wave, while the Spanish speaking PSYOP teams mated with designated Ranger elements.

During the initial minutes of the assault, as the Rangers were descending on the north (military) end of the Tocumen runway, several cars and light trucks escaped to the north. The vehicles lost themselves in the village of Tocumen; however, not before the PDF soldiers in the departing vehicles emptied their pistols and rifles at the American parachutists. Not all the PDF fled the battle area. Approximately one dozen PDF stood their ground and attempted to defend the multi-storied old Tocumen terminal, placing accurate rifle fire on the 1st Bn., 75th Ranger Regiment as they were getting out of their parachute harnesses on the landing zone. PDF soldiers also stood their ground at the military fire station and emptied their rifles at the approaching Rangers. The Rangers also encountered rifle and light machine gun fire from maneuvering squad sized units in the FAP (Panamanian Air Force) area. In addition, one truckload of armed PDF chose to drive south along the Tocumen taxiway and ran into the bulk of a Ranger company. During the ensuing firefight, which the PDF lost, one Ranger was killed, the only American fatality at Tocumen.

A little after 2:00 AM, just as two Ranger companies were about to conduct the final clearing assaults on the PDF and FAP barracks areas, the first personnel drop of the 82nd Airborne brigade occurred. Some of the 82nd personnel landed near the two PDF barracks areas targeted by the Rangers. The Ranger companies immediately stopped their forward movement and held their fire. Using the loudspeakers of attached PSYOP teams, the Rangers directed the 82nd troopers safely out of the engagement areas. Due to the darkness, enemy fire, and the 82nd troops' lack of familiarity with the complex, the extraction and passage of the 82nd through the Rangers took nearly 90 minutes.

Shortly thereafter, about 3:30 AM, the Rangers resumed their forward movement and began conducting an extensive building and room clearing of the entire PDF/FAP complex. During the sweep, four armed PDF troopers were found and taken prisoner in the military terminal without any additional bloodshed. The Tocumen complex was declared clear shortly after first light. In total, four PDF/FAP personnel were confirmed killed in the northern assault and 34 captured. In addition, four operational machine gun positions were found abandoned with full ammunition belts already fed into the guns. Although sporadic, PDF rifle fire continued from the northwest perimeter until sunrise. It was inaccurate and did not cause any additional Ranger casualties.

At the south (Torrijos-Civil) end of the complex, the platoons of Charlie Company of the 3rd Ranger Battalion had been faced with a different situation. The 1st Platoon's initial mission was to secure a restaurant building next to the southern section of the terminal. The second was to control the main road entrance to the airport complex and establish a blocking position, and the third, to establish a second blocking position to isolate the terminal from any westward approach.

Upon reaching the restaurant building, the platoon found it was operational. A number of civilian airport employees were inside eating and talking, apparently oblivious to events outside the cafe. The 1st squad was assigned the mission of clearing the building and, after scaling a chain link fence, they used their Spanish speaker to tell the workers to open the doors and surrender and they would not be hurt. The 18 workers immediately complied and became the first civilian detainees. They were handcuffed with plastic bands called flexcuffs, and moved to the designated detainee assembly area. The building was cleared systematically and no casualties were suffered.

When the 2nd squad reached the PDF guard shack at the entrance to the airfield complex, they found the shack leveled and the PDF sentries dead as a result of the earlier helicopter attack. They marked the shack as under U.S. control and established their blocking position without any opposition. At 1:25 AM, an AC-130 was called in to destroy a PDF vehicle harassing the Ranger position. The AC provided the requested support, destroying the vehicle.

Meanwhile, the 3rd squad had moved to the west side of the civilian terminal and set up an observation post to overwatch the front of the terminal and the broad expanses of the huge parking lot. The 3rd squad maintained security around the building while the 2nd squad cut through two chain link fences to move outward to battle position two, the main entrance to Omar Torrijos Airport. An additional Ranger element arrived about the same time with a gun jeep (extracted from the heavy equipment drop) to reinforce the position.

The 2nd platoon had also assembled on the move and raced to its initial assault objective, the Eastern Air Lines (EAL) support building, and a nearby pre-determined link-up point (LP-92) which then isolated the terminal from the south. The platoon encountered ten Panamanian civilians all identified as EAL employees at the support building. The EAL employees were classified as detainees, flexcuffed, and put under protective custody.

The 3rd platoon had the mission of clearing the Airport Fire Station and establishing LP- 91 and isolating the terminal from any PDF movement from the north. The platoon captured 15 PDF fire personnel during the seizure of the fire station and held them as Enemy Prisoners of War (EPW).

The Ranger heavy weapons platoon, equipped with mortars and heavy machine guns, assembled on the grassy area 100 meters infield of the runway east of LP-92. Once the LP was declared clear by the 2nd platoon, the weapons platoon moved to and assumed security responsibility for the LP. The location had been designated as the linkup point for the lead elements of the 82nd Airborne Division Jump Command Post that was expected within 90 minutes.

Almost immediately, the Rangers came under fire from a pair of PDF soldiers firing from an upper level of the passenger terminal. The platoon quickly moved into the terminal, and a squad isolated the PDF personnel in a men's bathroom. As two of the Rangers entered the room, one of the PDF soldiers, concealed in a stall, fired three rounds, hitting the lead Ranger with all three, knocking him to the ground inside the room. The American's teammate attempted to return fire, but his weapon malfunctioned, and he was forced to withdraw from the doorway. He quickly briefed the three-man backup team of the situation, and they immediately entered the latrine.

Two of the Rangers pulled their wounded comrade out of the entranceway, while the third Ranger provided security overwatch. The wounded Ranger was lucid and gave the Rangers a "SALUTE" report as he was being administered first aid. After throwing a grenade into the room, two of the Rangers reentered, with the third assuming security overwatch outside. Although the grenade provided some distraction and shock, it was tactically ineffective as the PDF soldiers were protected by the stall partitions. The lead Ranger was carrying a squad automatic weapon (SAW) that malfunctioned as he attempted to charge it. He quickly discarded the SAW and retrieved the M-16 weapon dropped earlier by his wounded comrade.

As the two Rangers quietly crouched against the interior wall, one to the right and the other to the left, assessing the situation for sounds or movement, there were no indications of a willingness to surrender by the PDF personnel. Within seconds, a PDF soldier with his weapon at the ready, peered around a corner of a stall. He was shot by the lead Ranger. Simultaneously, the other PDF soldier jumped out and attempted to grab the second Ranger's weapon. He was shot by the first Ranger and died instantly.

Simultaneously, a third enemy soldier charged down the hallway attempting to unholster his pistol. The Ranger that was on security overwatch stopped him with a kick that sent the PDF soldier staggering backwards through a glass wall and out onto the tarmac, where he again attempted to draw his pistol. A nearby Ranger witnessed the latter phases of this action and shot the determined PDF trooper, killing him instantly.

At the same time that the 3rd platoon had received its initial barrage of PDF small arms fire from the terminal, the 2nd platoon was entering the terminal from the south with one squad assigned to clear each of the three floors. Upon entering the third floor, the 1st squad came under PDF fire. The culprits were engaged and withdrew into the Airport Security Office with the Ranger squad in hot pursuit. Once in the office, the PDF personnel started a fire with the stacks of paper scattered throughout the office. The purpose was unclear to the Rangers, but again there was no indication of any intent to surrender, so the Rangers threw a single grenade into the room as a surrender stimuli and waited for the occupants to surrender.

There was no response from the PDF. The American squad cautiously entered the room, quickly learning that the former occupants had departed. The Rangers attempted to beat the fire out, but failing in their initial efforts, they activated the built-in overhead sprinkler system which suppressed the fire. They cleared the remainder of the third floor without any further encounters.

Meanwhile, on the second floor, a Ranger squad made brief contact with an undetermined number of PDF. While pursuing the contact, the Rangers found a large group of Panamanian civilians clustered in one room. Not knowing who among the group might be PDF personnel (wearing civilian clothes), the entire group was flexcuffed and searched, then escorted to the EPW collection point for screening.

Meanwhile, the squad responsible for clearing the first floor encountered and cornered a group of PDF trying to flee the building using American civilians as hostage-shields. The hostages included women and at least one infant. The Ranger platoon leader and company commander were immediately notified of the situation. The company commander directed the platoon leader to seal off the entire area using the reserve (4th) squad and elements of the other squads.

The platoon leader was the first American officer to reach the scene. He immediately made contact with the airport security manager, a Panamanian civilian, who was willing to help negotiate a solution. The Americans used the manager as a go-between, with two Spanish-speaking Rangers ensuring the accuracy of the dialogue and the integrity of his actions. After two hours of negotiations, the PDF soldiers freed the hostages and surrendered. The PDF troopers were added to the more than 100 EPW already collected by the Rangers.

The 1st platoon established an EPW collection point outside on the second floor three-lane wide vehicle unloading area. Meanwhile the 1st squad collected the original 18 detainees and 30 more from the Avis car rental facility and moved them to the civilian detainee point. The 2nd and 3rd squads swept the building again, finding another 40 civilians along the way.

At the conclusion of the follow-on sweeps (once the terminal was considered clear of combatants), the nature of the American activity turned from close order combat and room clearing to managing the hundreds of civilian detainees (and the dozens of sullen PDF prisoners).

The Panamanian detainees and PDF EPWs were separated from the civilian population and each other. The first two groups were flexcuffed and closely guarded while confirmed civilians were asked to sit down and remain calm. The final number for the terminal totaled 398 civilian detainees and 21 PDF EPWs. The tactical aspects of the operation resulted in three PDF KIA and one Ranger WIA.

After two to three hours had elapsed, approximately 10 children, aged 6 months to 10 years, became hungry and were fed through an arrangement with the restaurant manager, the U.S. forces assuming responsibility for the cost. One civilian woman, who suffered from smoke inhalation, was treated by a Ranger medic and recovered quickly.

Shortly after 7:00 AM, military police elements of the 82nd Airborne Division linked-up with the Rangers. The PDF EPWs, the Panamanian civil detainees (mostly Panamanian government workers), and the confiscated documents and weapons were turned over to the 82nd MP company commander. The Ranger company, relieved of its human charges, reverted to a reserve force status. It had completed its first mission in *Just Cause*. The mission began with combat, but ended with police and humanitarian assistance. Meanwhile, other Ranger elements were still hard at work.

At the same time, a Ranger scout element began moving overland towards Fort Cimarron, where they were to reconnoiter the post. The element passed through the Special Forces control point at the Pacora River Bridge about 8:00 AM, reaching the Cimarron area about midday, where they linked up with an SF team which had the earlier phase of the surveillance mission. Both teams assumed a coordinated overwatch and began waiting for the 82nd to be helo-lifted in for the seize and secure segments of the mission.

At 7:45 AM the JSOTF commander, General Downing at the request of COMJTF General Stiner, ordered a company of Rangers be detached from Task Force Red and attached to Task Force Gator to assist in clearing La Comandancia. The Ranger Regiment designated Charlie Company of the 3rd of the 75th (Fort Benning), which had just cleared the air terminal to conduct the mission.

At 9:00 AM the Ranger liaison officer assigned to the 82nd linked up with the Rangers at Torrijos. By 10:30 AM lead elements of the 82nd begin to relieve the Rangers at Torrijos/Tocumen, while other 82nd units began to assemble for the follow-on heliborne assaults into Tinajitas and Cimarron.

The Military Airlift Command (MAC) began landing C-141s and C-5s at noon on the now American-controlled dual runways. The aircraft brought in the last wave of the 82nd Airborne combat troops and the first follow-on elements of the 7th Infantry Division from Fort Ord, California.

At 12:30 PM Charlie Company, 3rd Bn., 75th Ranger Regiment, the company designated for Comandancia clearing operations, was helo-lifted to Fort Amador by two Army CH-47's and a USAF MH-53. From Amador, the company was transported across the Bridge of the Americas by truck to the staging site where they married up with Task Force Gator and the 508th Paratroopers.

The parachute assault on the Torrijos/Tocumen complex was a success and, unbeknownst to the Rangers, they nearly accomplished an unassigned but vital mission: the capture of Manuel Noriega. The PDF commander had been visiting Colon on the other side of the isthmus the previous afternoon, and had been driven to Tocumen to spend the night at the PDF Air Force Recreation Center at Ceremi, a former motel complex adjacent to the main gate of Tocumen.

Upon hearing the devastation being visited on the nearby military facilities by the AC-130s and the helicopter gunships, General Noriega, his officer aide and bodyguard team fled the recreation center in several vehicles. Initially, the small convoy turned toward Tocumen and the presumed safety of the PDF Barracks. A Ranger squad, seeing the approaching vehicles, took them under fire. There was a brief but brisk exchange of fire. The PDF drivers, trained in evasion and anti-terrorist tactics, spun the cars around and took off in the other direction, disappearing into the darkness of the night.

RANGERS AT RIO HATO

Meanwhile, the other half of Task Force Red was engaged in its own major action halfway across the isthmus at Rio Hato. During the initial U.S. contingency planning in the spring of 1988, Rio Hato had not figured prominently in the concept, although it was decidedly a candidate that was examined and monitored. Initially its importance was keyed to the fact that General Noriega maintained a seaside villa overlooking the beach near the coastal end of the garrison's 4,380 ft. runway. However, the quick response of the Rio Hato-based 6th and 7th Companies and their rapid airlift to Panama City in October had changed the significance of the installation and the threat posed by the two PDF companies. The 6th was a mechanized infantry company equipped with machine gun armored cars while the 7th, Maches de Monte, was an elite light infantry jungle warfare force.

The subsequent upgrading of the Comandancia defenses and the increase in the PDF reaction capability in October had prompted the U.S. planners to change the composition of the Comandancia assault force. The original spring of 1988 force, a heliborne Ranger quick strike element was changed to a mechanized infantry task force and a Ranger force was reinforced against Rio Hato.

In October, the Ranger regiment was given the mission to seize and secure both the Torrijos/Tocumen complex and Rio Hato airfield and neutralize all PDF forces at both sites. The Regimental commander decided to dedicate five Ranger companies to the Rio Hato task. The forces included the 2nd Ranger Battalion from Fort Lewis, Washington and two companies from the 3rd Battalion in Fort Benning, Georgia.

During the initial stages of Rio Hato planning, the proximity of the PDF barracks to the intended Ranger drop zone (less than 200 yards) dictated some manner of fire support or diversionary tactic to delay the PDF forces from effectively reacting before the Rangers hit the ground. Staying within one of the long standing planning ROE, minimum loss of Panamanian life, a diversionary strike was selected as the preferred tactic rather than a direct air attack on the barracks. The weapons system chosen needed to close with the target and deposit its ordnance with precision without compromising its presence until the munitions went off.

Although the AC-130 had the accuracy, the lumbering transport was not fast or quiet enough to do the job, nor were there any to spare. The newest addition to the USAF tactical fighter fleet, the radar elusive F-117 *Nighthawk,* was chosen. The mission called for two F-117's to each drop a 2,000 pound bomb in the open field in front of the barracks, discouraging the

PDF soldiers from advancing on the Ranger landing zone—the runway area. The planners anticipated that the noise, concussion and shock of the bomb explosions would create confusion within the PDF forces and provide the necessary delay.

The F-117s, which had departed their home base in Nevada several hours and multi-midair refuelings earlier, entered Panamanian airspace over the north coast (Caribbean) 22 minutes before H-Hour and crossed the isthmus undetected, exiting over the Pacific. The two aircraft then reversed their track, turned back toward land, and assumed an inbound flight path heading for their drop point.

The low altitude atmospherics along the coastline were not the best that night. Visibility was limited. This type of localized effect was normal for the area and that time of year, but unpredictable in any precise sense. The speed of the aircraft, combined with the low altitude and poor visibility, severely limited the amount of time the lead pilot had to check for identification features and pinpoint the selected impact point, in this case, a set of coordinates without any physically distinctive features. The lead pilot had less than 60 seconds to visually identify a recognition feature, position his crosshair on this point, fix the locational data, feed it to the onboard computer, move his crosshair to the desired impact point, and then allow the computer to solve the release solution.

General Thurman's earlier direction to advance H-Hour by fifteen minutes reached the two airborne Ranger strike groups about 30 minutes before H-Hour. On at least one plane, bound for Rio Hato, the news that the element of surprise had been lost, and that the PDF guns would be manned and operational caused an audible cry of "O-Shit" from the jumpers.

The PDF threat at Rio Hato was estimated at 470 personnel, approximately 200 in each of the infantry companies, plus an engineer platoon. There was also the potential for up to 250 recruits and a training cadre at the nearby Herrera-Ruiz Infantry Training School. The range of weapons available to the two infantry companies included 40 machine guns, 24 mortars and 200 rocket propelled grenade (RPG) launchers, plus rifles, pistols and grenades. The PDF also had ground mobility in the form of 19 armored cars and 15 motorcycles. Air defense weapons included at least three Soviet/Chinese made ZPU AA heavy machine-guns. The priority of attack for the Rangers was the two infantry barracks and the motor pool where the armored vehicles and motorcycles were stored, followed by the communication center, then the training school and, lastly, the engineer barracks.

The Ranger commander had organized his forces into three major components. A headquarters and fire support element and two assault forces. The headquarters element, identified as Team Black, included the attached Army Special Operations Aviation element, the USAF Special Tactics team (Combat Controllers, and Pararescue medics), and the supporting USAF aircraft. The two assault forces were cored around the two battalion cadres and their companies, plus a PSYOP team, a Special Tactics element and a civil affairs element.

Exactly at 1:00 AM, the two fighter aircraft dropped their 2,000 pound bombs in the open field about 50 meters in front of the barracks housing the PDF 7th Infantry Company. Within 30 seconds following the F-117 strike, additional pre-assault fire was delivered by a combination of USAF special operations MH-53/MH-60, and Army attack helicopters AH-6 and AH-64. Three minutes after the F-117 bomb drop, and one minute after the gunship fire missions on the known and detected AA and heavy machine gun positions, 15 C-130s carrying the Rangers flew low over the drop zone.

In spite of the F-117 strike and the other American air suppression measures, the troop transports were met with a hail of small arms and anti-aircraft heavy machine gun fire from the ground shortly before they reached the drop zone, confirming the U.S. SOUTHCOM warning. All the pilots held their aircraft steady, despite the stream of tracers reaching up to meet them. Eleven of the thirteen C-130s involved in the Rio Hato air operation received battle damage from AA and small arms fire. One Ranger was wounded before he could exit his plane; however, he was pulled out of the way and treated for his wound while his fellow troopers continued the jump.

At 1:03 AM, the Rangers, accompanied by a PSYOP team, a Special Tactics team and a refueling team from the 160th Aviation Battalion, began exiting their C-130s. The drop aircraft were lined up 100 yards to the right (upwind) of the runway, so the eastward wind would make the Rangers land on or close to the runway, which was obstructed with several vehicles placed by the PDF defenders to impede an airlanding option.

Once on the ground, the Rangers quickly moved to their assembly points and then to their immediate objectives. Company tasks included attacking each of the PDF barracks simultaneously.

The 2nd Battalion assaulted and seized the two infantry company barracks and the training school. The 3rd Battalion seized the post headquarters, the communications center, the engineer barracks and the motor pool, and established roadblocks on the Pan-American Highway, which bisected the post and the runway. The Rangers were hampered in their initial movement toward their objectives by random charges from small groups of PDF in armored vehicles with guns blazing racing up and down the roads that ran through the complex.

Other PDF soldiers initially offered resistance from the protection of the barracks, then quickly withdrew out the rear of the building as the Rangers closed with the targeted buildings. Some of the retreating PDF hastily took up ambush positions in the treeline behind the barracks and engaged the Rangers as they exited the rear of the buildings. The PDF then faded into the surrounding forest, where some of them continued to offer sporadic resistance in the form of sniper and machine gun fire and occasional mortar attacks until several hours past daylight.

While the assault forces were engaged clearing the primary combat objectives, the Special Tactics teams, assisted by Rangers, were busy clearing the runway of PDF, blocking material including several vehicles and the hundreds of American parachutes shucked by the assault forces. The Special Tactics teams established control points, and set up beacons for the following airlanding operation. Meanwhile, the 160th aviation troopers set about establishing the first of two forward area refueling (and rearming) points (FARP) for the follow-on helicopter support. Within 45 minutes, the combat initiative lay with the Rangers, and they had sufficient control of the airhead to call in the follow-on air landing force. One hour and fifty-three minutes after the combined air and parachute assault had begun, the first of the follow-on contingent landed.

This air–land group consisted of five C-130s (three MC-130s and two C-130 SOF low-level equipped troop transports). The aircraft made blackout landings using a combination of night vision devices and landing beacons implanted by the Special Tactics Teams (STTs). The aircraft carried gun jeeps and other tactical vehicles to allow the Rangers and the SSTs to expand their perimeter and control runways and the surrounding area. Other equipment that was delivered included portable gasoline storage tanks and pumps needed to turn the captured airhead into a full-fledged refueling and rearming point. One of the MC-130s that had been configured with extra internal fuel tanks remained on the ground for three hours, serving as a refueling station for the Army and USAF helicopter gunships which were supporting the Rangers.

Seven minutes after the air–land phase began, the Rangers were ordered to execute an on-order mission: seize, search, and secure the Farallon-Noriega beach house complex. The hacienda was quickly seized without any combat action, nor any sign of General Noriega.

The PDF equipment captured at Rio Hato largely mirrored the threat estimate with the noticeable exception of an increase in anti-aircraft guns. Eleven Soviet-made 23mm, 4 barrel, ZPU-4s were captured; fortunately, most had not been deployed or manned.

Four Rangers were killed and eighteen wounded in the ground action. Ranger jump injuries at Rio Hato totaled 36. Most were not totally debilitating, and many of the injured jumpers continued with the initial phases of their mission. Most of the Ranger combat casualties were suffered during the clearing of the two PDF infantry barracks. Thirty-four PDF soldiers died in the fighting and 362 were captured.

Unit crest for the PDF *El Macho De Monte* (Men of the Mountain) company located in front of their barracks at Rio Hato with unit slogan proclaiming in bold letters *Vive La Guerra* (Long Live War). Photo courtesy U.S. Southern Command Public Information Office.

CHAPTER THIRTEEN
THE AIR SUPPORT EQUATION

During the first 15 minutes of Operation *Just Cause* (12:45-1:00 AM) all of the major H-Hour objectives had been attacked. The Panama-based U.S. forces had moved by foot, flippers, truck, bus, HMMWV, APC, landing craft, amphibious vehicles, boats and helicopters from their in-country jump-off points, while the lead elements of the CONUS-based forces had moved by strategic and tactical airlift directly to their objectives, descending via parachute. In the final analysis, the prodigious efforts of the airlift planners, the dedication of the aviation ground crews and the competence of the Army and Air Force flight crews counted as much toward the ultimate victory as the valor of the forces engaged on the ground.

Although advancing technology often gets the credit, the key to success is not technology, but the human beings who must blend together into the aircrews that function as smoothly as the complicated machines they fly. In *Just Cause*, it was the Army and Air Force helicopter crews and USAF transport, command and control, tanker crews, the "old and new" of the Tactical Air Command and the AC-130s of the Air Force Special Operations Command, that provided some of the most lethal support.

The air support story of *Just Cause* is not one of sustained heroic airlift such as the Berlin Airlift of 1948. Nor is it one of the 100 days of deep strikes that ate away at the combat power and infrastructure of Iraq in 1991, and undoubtedly saved the lives of thousands of American, allied and Iraqi ground forces. The air support story of *Just Cause* was more an orchestration of 1,000 small actions in the air and on the ground, compressed essentially into a 72-hour window, that had one unifying purpose – support the ground forces where and when they needed it.

ARMY AVIATION

Company A of the 1st Battalion, 22nd Aviation Brigade (the Talons), a Panama-based unit stationed at Fort Kobbe, was typical of the Army aviation elements. Other Army aviation units included the 160th Special Operations Aviation Regiment from Fort Campbell, Kentucky, elements of the 7th Aviation Brigade of the Seventh Infantry Division, and the 82nd Airborne Division's AH-64 *Apache* helicopters.

The *Apache*, equipped with the Hellfire missile, saw its first combat in *Just Cause* although only seven of the highly accurate and destructive Hellfires were launched because of the tight safety concerns and Rules of Engagement. All seven were direct hits against active PDF gun positions that, if left unattended, could have played havoc with several aspects of the air operation.

Overall, 172 helicopters were employed in the operation. Sixty (60) Army and Air Force special operations helicopters supported the operation.

An additional 112 Army helicopters were involved including 11 *Apache* (AH-64), 11 *Cobra* (AH-1), 64 *Blackhawks* (UH-60), 17 *Kiowa* (OH-58), and nine *Chinook* (CH-47).

During the first 24 hours of Operation *Just Cause*, Company A, 1/22nd Aviation Bn (193rd Infantry Brigade), along with its sister unit Company A, 3/123rd Aviation Bn (7th ID), flew their MH-60 *Blackhawks* on four successive combat air assaults. For both the aircrews and the aircraft, December 20, 1989 marked an introduction to the realities of war. Fortunately, the company commander had been preparing them for the transformation. His story is a reflection of all the unit commanders of all the services who strove to insure that the personnel of their unit were prepared for the mission challenges they would face.

Alpha Company (1/22/193rd) had changed commanders seven months earlier (June 1989) just as the political situation in Panama entered a new phase of tensions. In addition to coping with the already taxing demands of maintaining the helicopters in the tropical climate, and guiding the soldiers through the turbulence caused by the phased withdrawal of many of their families, the commander began working to increase the readiness and reliability of the men and machines. Training schedules were reworked to increase the unit's ability to fly at night. The unit conducted numerous air assault operations in conjunction with Company A of the 3rd Bn of the 123rd Aviation, and the paratroopers of the 1st Bn of the 508th Infantry Regiment stationed at Kobbe.

By the time of the Giroldi coup attempt on October 3, the personnel of the two aviation companies and the 508th Paratroopers had come together as a team. The aircrews and maintenance personnel had achieved a high-level of confidence in their comrades and themselves. The key challenge was sustaining those qualities over an indefinite period while conducting the detailed planning and training necessary to conduct the four successive air assaults called for in the plan.

Late in the afternoon of December 19, the word came down that Operation *Just Cause* would begin that night. During the pre-mission flight meeting, eight hours before the designated H-Hour, the young commander gave the aircrews one last minute "pep talk," stressing the need to adhere to the routines that they had practiced so often and to approach each situation in a methodical manner.

Shortly before H-Hour, the helicopters lifted off from a darkened corner of the Howard tarmac with the 508th paratroopers packed inside. The objective was the PDF portion of Fort Amador. The flight route carried them out into the darkness over the Pacific Ocean well outside the range of small arms or rocket fire from Flamenco Island, which was suspected to possibly house a residual element of the PDF Special Operations Force.

During the approach to the Fort Amador landing zone, all of the personnel onboard the helicopters observed the tracers, explosions, and fires engulfing La Comandancia less than a mile away. The aircrews put the *Blackhawks* down exactly on target. The 508th Infantrymen unloaded in a matter of seconds. As the last man exited, each chopper lifted off and took up a flight path to a FARP (refueling location) at Empire Range. There they awaited word of the arrival of the 82nd Airborne Division at Torrijos, which would signal the beginning of their second air assault mission.

THE AIR FORCE MIX

Most of the USAF CONUS-based forces had been alerted on December 17th and began their deployment preparations and, in some cases, actual deployment immediately. USAF special operations elements were among the earliest to move. This included the air coordination elements, combat control specialists, and selected aircraft. Two gunships, five MH-53J *Pave Low* long-range penetration helicopters, and seven HC-130 *Combat Shadow* tankers self-deployed the 1,500 miles to Panama on December 18th, refueling enroute.

Two SOF HC-130 tankers from Eglin AFB, Florida supported Army MH-47s and other Air Force MH-53 helicopters with 16 mid-air refuelings during their flight south. These SOF aircraft joined two Air Force Reserve "A" model C-130 gunships that were already in Panama on a rotational training deployment. Also on December 18th, four MH-60G *Pave Hawk*, medium-range penetrator helicopters were flown into Howard in the belly of a C-5 transport, as were the *Apache*s of the 82nd Airborne. During the evening of the 19th, five additional AC-130 gunships flew south as part of the H-Hour commitment.

Other units that were involved included A-7 fixed wing fighters and Forward Air Controller OA-37 aircraft from the National Guard and Tactical Air Command that were in Panama on rotational tours. TAC also contributed the F-117 strike package that was part of the pre-assault suppression effort at Rio Hato, as well as the JTF's flying command post (ABCCC) and the Electronic Warfare EF-111s. A total of 392 close air support (CAS) and fire suppression sorties were flown by TAC aircrews.

The Military Airlift Command (MAC) played the largest Air Force role, with aircraft drawn from all three of its Numbered Air Forces (21st, 22nd and 23rd). This involved 24 active duty units, as well as nine Air National Guard and nine Air Force Reserve units. The initial employment phase of the operation included 84-airdrop sorties and 27-combat air-land missions. These missions involved 22 C-130, 77 C-141, and 12 C-5 aircraft. Forty C-141s and thirteen C-5s provided airlift to the follow-on force build-up and sustainment phase. Overall, MAC flew 784 airlift sorties, almost evenly split between intra-theater and long haul CONUS-to-Panama missions. The majority of the CONUS-Panama missions could not have been accomplished without the active support of the Strategic

Air Command's "flying gas stations," KC-135 and KC-10 tankers which flew almost 200 refueling sorties.

INITIAL LAUNCH PHASE

The December 19th launch phase was complicated by unexpected, unseasonable, and persistently poor weather at several of the East Coast departure airfields. Weather is the one factor that is totally uncontrollable, often the most unpredictable, and can have a very dramatic effect on the success or failure of a military operation.

In the case of Operation *Just Cause*, weather had a disruptive effect on the launch of the second echelon parachute force (the 82nd Airborne Division), but was pretty good during the execution phase, with only a minor degradation in one action. The weather problems were most severe in North Carolina, at Fort Bragg and neighboring Pope Air Force Base, from which the Division Ready Brigade of the 82nd Airborne Division was to launch, although some California (7th ID) launch sites had their own weather problems.

The 20 C-141 drop aircraft (that were scheduled to carry the brigade) plus several ground spares, were de–iced during the late morning and early afternoon. The weather forecasters had correctly predicted the arrival of the ice storms that had come through that morning, but they had also expected the storms to move out of the region, in time for the launch to be conducted on time that night. However, about an hour prior to takeoff, the ice storms reversed course. They doubled back and recoated the mission aircraft with a thick layer of ice. This changed the aircraft takeoff weight and impeded proper performance of control surfaces such as the flaps, ailerons, and rudder.

The ground crews, working in bitter cold and windy conditions, immediately began the de-icing process again, but only seven aircraft were airworthy at the planned takeoff time. These seven jets launched on time, to be followed within 10 minutes by another three. All ten of these transports made their original drop times at Torrijos; however, it took another three hours to de–ice, refuel, and launch the second half of the 82nd airdrop fleet. Fortunately, the aircraft projected to accomplish the 82nd's heavy equipment drop had been loaded the day before and had been repositioned to Charleston Air Force Base in South Carolina and thus were not hit by the ice storm.

The ice storm also had a negative effect on tanker operations at Seymour-Johnson AFB, Goldsboro, NC. Johnson was a Strategic Air Command (SAC) base and home to a wing of long-range tankers, some of which were scheduled to refuel the drop-transports and other *Just Cause* aircraft. A winter ice storm is rare, but not unknown at Fort Bragg; however, they are rarer at Johnson and, consequently, the base had a limited ability to de-ice its mission aircraft. Reacting quickly, SAC with its nation-wide basing structure replaced the icebound Seymour-Johnson tankers with KC-135 and KC-10 aircraft from Barksdale AFB, Louisiana and MacDill AFB, Florida. This in itself presented another last minute challenge to the air planners and mission flow coordinators. Quiet but urgent detailed coordination with Federal Aviation Administration (FAA) liaison personnel in Washington, Florida, and Louisiana was required to ensure the substitution did not compromise the mission security or the transport flow.

PARADROP OPERATIONS

Within 12 minutes of the first Rangers starting their parachute descent over Tocumen and Rio Hato, 31 C-130 *Hercules* transports had delivered more than 1,000 U.S. paratroopers into the two active battle zones, on time and on target. This exceeded the combined Ranger and 82nd Airborne Divisions paradrops conducted in Grenada in 1983.

During the initial strike operations, AC-130s were in orbit over seven different ground objectives providing fire and surveillance support to a range of ground forces engaging the PDF. The *Spectre*s were overhead at Rio Hato, Tocumen, the Comandancia, Paitilla, the Pacora River Bridge, Tinajitas, and Colon. During the first hours of the operation, more than 200 American military aircraft were operating in the skies over Panama under total blackout conditions.

At 1:45 AM, the first elements of the 82nd Airborne Division were delivered into the battle zone by MAC transports. The 82nd airflow was originally designed to be an air bridge composed of 51 C-141s; however, due to the icing problems at Fort Bragg, only 41 aircraft participated in the initial two phases of the air drop.

The first 28 C-141s were the heavy equipment drop. These aircraft had been the first to load out at Fort Bragg and had been flown to Charleston Air Force Base where they were staged awaiting execution launch. The aircraft were loaded with armored personnel carriers, HMMWV and other support-type equipment. The 28-ship heavy equipment drop was followed by a cell of three C-141s. These unloaded strings of containerized delivery system (CDS) units contained munitions, food and other sustainment items. These two logistic drops were then followed at 2:00 AM by an eight ship formation delivering the first wave of 82nd paratroopers. The remainder of the brigade arrived about three hours later via another 12 C-141s in several small groups. These were the aircraft that had suffered the ice storm delay. Altogether, the 82nd delivery included 2,176 soldiers and more than one million pounds of equipment.

82ND DROPS ON TORRIJOS

Major General James Johnson, the commander of the 82nd Airborne Division, was the first 82nd jumper to "hit the silk." It was a few minutes after 2:00 AM as he stood in the door on the left side of the aircraft waiting for the green jump light. A cloud obscured the moon, reducing his ability to clearly see the drop zone and the wing of the C-141 blocked his forward view. However, there was enough illumination for him to recognize he was farther up the drop track than he wanted to be and off to the right of the runway, but inside the perimeter fence as desired. Upon exiting the aircraft he could see the civilian air terminal off to his left, a firefight to the north – the military end of the field and the dark blobs of the earlier heavy equipment drop off to right. He got the impression that many of loads had landed outside the perimeter fence in the adjacent jungle grass and marsh area.

During the numerous planning meetings and discussions with the MAC airdrop planners, many considerations were tabled by the Army planners, some driven home repeatedly. These included no heavy equipment on the runway, minimum personnel chutes on the runway, favor the right of the runway, the band of clear grassy area between the right edge of the runway and the perimeter fence. Heavy equipment on the runway would increase damage to both the runway, which was vital to the follow-on airland operations, and to the equipment. Several hundred personnel parachutes and associated gear shucked by the 82nd jumpers once they hit the ground would substantially complicate the runway clearing operations and create a tremendous potential for a mishap with the mass of helicopters that would descend on the airhead in the next few hours.

According to the 1:12,500 scale topographic chart of the area, the designed drop zone was in excess of 6,000 feet long, but barely 900 feet wide. The combat DZ was substantially smaller than overall Sicily (rehearsal) DZ back at Bragg. Based on an aircraft speed of 130 knots, the drop window for any given aircraft was less than 50 seconds. Given the darkness and the probability for even a slight 1-3 knot cross wind, the potential was high for some of the exiting paratroopers to land off the DZ, i.e. outside the perimeter fence. It would have been a tight squeeze under ideal conditions. General Johnson was part of the 50-60 percent that landed inside the fence line.

Approximately three minutes later, the paratroopers of Chalk Three, the third aircraft in the drop stream, exited their aluminum taxicab. The moon was no longer obscured and the lead jumper surveyed the area as he descended from the drop altitude of 500 feet. He made three twists on his way down and could see a building burning to the north. He presumed it was the PDF 2nd Infantry Company barracks that had been hit by AC-130. The civilian passenger terminal was lit and he remembers thinking, "Boy, it looks just like the photos." His view was helped by a clear night with at least thirty to forty percent moon illumination and the light from tracers, some looked red, others white and green. He drifted right, propelled by a slight crosswind, and landed in the elephant grass outside the fence.

Most of the personnel from Chalk Three and Four also landed outside the fence. In the final analysis approximately half the jumpers landed outside the DZ, with some of the troopers coming down in elephant grass that stood fifteen to twenty feet in height. The time taken to get to the fence ranged from 20-30 minutes to an hour depending on the distance involved and the mixture of elephant grass and swamp that had be navigated. Once at the fence, orientation became easy and many troopers, typically now in small groups, cut through the fence with their M-9 bayonets. Once through the fence, maneuvering became easier, but scattered firefights were still occurring and care had to exercised. It took the better part of the next two hours for many of the troopers to reach their designated rendezvous points. By 5:00 AM, a greater semblance of order was evident.

Twelve hours after the Rangers first parachuted into the night skies of Panama, a third massive airlift flow descended on Panamanian soil. This time, 31 heavy transports, 21 C-141s and 10 giant C-5s began landing operations at Tocumen. The delivery of the third major wave of U.S. forces, the 2nd Brigade of the 7th Infantry Division from Fort Ord, California, had begun.

REFUELING A KEY TO FLEXIBILITY

Airborne refueling operations were an essential underpinning of virtually all other air operations. Refueling support included both strategic tankers (KC-135s and KC-10s) from 15 Strategic Air Command units and tactical (HC-130) tankers from the Air Force Special Operations Command. The volume of fuel transferred ranged into the millions of pounds and several hundred airborne transfers. The small HC fleet itself conducted 65 successful low-level tactical air refuelings, most to helicopters. A high percentage of these operations were conducted at night and under blackout night vision goggles (NVG) conditions. Nearly 500,000 pounds of fuel were transferred in these tactical operations.

The strategic tankers more than tripled these figures, flying 170 missions and transferring one and a half million pounds of fuel in 270 mid-air linkups. Most of the combined total of 335 transfers and two million pounds of fuel was accomplished in the first 36 hours of the operation. In addition to the air refueling conducted by the SAC tankers and the SOF HC-130s, other aircraft, including Army CH-47 *Chinooks* helicopters, were used as refueling vehicles. One tactic involved a CH-47 refueling from an airborne HC-130, then landing at a tactical FARP and transferring fuel to smaller tactical helicopters on the ground. Several SOF C-130s also refueled in mid-air then landed at forward FARPs and transferred fuel in the ground mode to helicopters, often two at a time.

One minute after H-Hour, the F-117s that had struck Rio Hato turned north and flew out of Panama airspace. They rendezvoused with a KC-135 and refueled, then flew nonstop back to the United States. The transports that dropped the Rangers also took up a northerly heading and rendezvoused with the SAC tankers on the northbound refueling track. However, the two airborne SAC KC-135 refueling orbits did not have enough capacity to refuel all elements of the assault fleet. This shortfall was recognized early in the planning cycle, and the air planners had developed a four legged flight track, called a "Timing pattern," which allowed sufficient spacing between aircraft to permit safe blackout landings, refuelings, and takeoffs on Howard's single runway. Twenty-four of the shorter ranged C-130s used this procedure to land at Howard for refueling before returning to the United States.

AIRBORNE COMMAND & CONTROL COMMUNICATIONS

The TAC EC-130 Airborne Command, Control and Communications (ABCCC) aircraft from Keesler AFB were an integral portion of the initial six to eight hours of the air operation. An ABCCC carrying a JTF SOUTH coordination element maintained communications with the assault forces while they were enroute, passing intelligence data and operational modifications such as adjustments to "no fire zones" and link-up operations. In addition, the ABCCC coordinated refueling missions for that portion of the enroute force that was late due to the weather delay.

AIRBORNE FORWARD AIR CONTROLLERS

The OA-37s of the 24th Tactical Air Support Squadron based at Howard provided a weapon system that had both psychological and firepower attributes and contributed to saving both American and Panamanian lives on more than a half-dozen occasions. Not only did they provide airborne eyes and extend the vision and situation awareness of the ground forces, but they proved to be a flexible weapon system that could switch from reconnaissance to close air support-strike or a PSYOP role with ease. Operating within the constraints of the mission ROE that strictly controlled firing in populated areas, the pilots on numerous occasions resorted to making dry-gun "buzzing" passes on enemy positions in spite of enemy ground fire. On at least one occasion, the combination of airborne day-night reconnaissance and "dry-fire" strafing runs broke up a PDF/DIGBAT ambush of an American truck convoy.

HOWARD/KOBBE AIRDROME AIR OPERATIONS

No discussion of Operation *Just Cause* would be complete without covering the crucial role performed by the men and women that made the Howard-Kobbe complex the successful nerve center it was. The parking ramp at Howard itself was, in spots, literally sinking from the sustained weight of the aircraft it was supporting during the initial 72 hours.

At any given time, there were 30 or more C-130 transports being serviced, several different fighter aircraft, and an assortment of 160 helicopters, plus 10 heavy-lift transports (a mix of C-141s and C-5s). In addition to the dramatic explosion in the number of aircraft, the base population almost quadrupled in the span of 1-2 days. The normal (assigned) strength of 2,500 quickly grew to close to 10,000.

The permanent personnel were phenomenal in their ability to absorb the increase, and feed and bed down the rapid influx of personnel that rolled into the theater. The accommodations varied from opening up recently emptied family housing units to small groups of five personnel to one organization that chose to squeeze 42 people into one house to preserve unit integrity and responsiveness.

The success of the ground servicing operations was unprecedented. Despite working in a very congested environment, largely under blackout conditions, landing, downloading, maintenance, repair, refueling, rearming, and marshalling was accomplished without any significant problems. The sleepy training complex was transformed into a beehive of operational, logistic, and medical activity, in addition to a high tempo of fixed and rotary wing launch and recovery operations.

The compact airdrome was also the epicenter for a wide range of multi-unit, multi-command, and multi-service operations involving all Air Force combat commands, the full range of Army and Air Force Special Operations Forces, and a varied spectrum of the conventional forces from the active and reserve components of both services. Throughout all of this there was not a single accident. All in all, it was an incredible record: aircraft suffering bullet holes were patched on the tarmac in the dark, refueling was conducted with engines running, ordnance uploaded and a steady stream of severely injured personnel delivered, treated, and air evacuated back to the United States. The fuels handling personnel pumped more than a half million gallons of gasoline in the first 24 hours.

Typical of the many support personnel of the services were two young communications technicians. The airmen were the first American support personnel to arrive at Torrijos/Tocumen Airport. They arrived in the first aircraft to land, rather than parachute its cargo into the airhead. This small team was responsible for setting up a field repair and issue point for communication equipment to support the combat control operations throughout the country. The team ensured the communication vehicles and power generation equipment was available and operational to support the wide ranging follow-on combat and combat support operations. Throughout the entire operation, the two technicians consolidated their knowledge of the systems being utilized, adapted to all situations, and responded to a shifting set of priorities and challenges. In addition to maintaining, repairing, and reissuing critical equipment, they organized and conducted in-the-field hands-on training sessions for non-communications personnel who were being issued the equipment for the first time. Their efforts were mirrored by other small teams of enlisted specialists in all services throughout the entire operation.

ENLISTED TACTICAL AIR CONTROLLERS

The demarcation line on Albrook between the USAF-controlled real estate and Panamanian-controlled acreage was an eight-foot high chain link fence. It separated the broad expanse of open tarmac in front of the two sets of 1950's vintage hangars on the U.S. side and the deteriorating PDF-controlled runway and a grouping of larger hangars used by the PDF Police and the Panamanian Air Force to support their helicopter flight detachment. The distance from the PDF hangars to the American hangars at the north end, which were serving as furniture storage warehouses, was less than 500 yards. The distance to the functional American hangars at the south end, which until only months earlier had served as the hands-on training facilities for the Inter-American Air Force Academy, was less than a mile. Both sets of American hangars as well as a major segment of the densely populated family housing areas at Albrook and nearby Curundu were within easy range of PDF mortars.

Three 2-man teams of Enlisted Tactical Air Controllers (ETAC) from the 24th Tactical Air Support Squadron at Howard had been assigned to Albrook to coordinate air operations when it was decided to use the inactive hangars as a Special Operations helicopter staging/launch base. Twenty minutes before the in-country H-Hour of 12:45 AM, the PDF began firing at the southern hangar area where several Army *Blackhawk* helicopters were loading the Special Forces Pacora River Bridge interdiction team. Within two minutes, the three ETAC teams working together triangulated the source of the PDF rifle and mortar fire and vectored an airborne AC-130 *Spectre* gunship onto the target which was one of the PDF hangars. The impact of the AC-130's firepower stopped the PDF fire and collapsed a major portion of the hangar.

Other ETAC teams were attached to and operated with Army units at Fort Amador during that clearing operation, and with the Army elements that seized and secured the PDF logistics complex at Cerro Tigre. Located mid-way across the isthmus, Cerro Tigre yielded a cache of 2,000 weapons composed of new AK-47 assault rifles and .50 caliber machine guns – more than enough to equip three 600-man infantry battalions.

SPECIAL TACTICS TEAMS

After being alerted on December 17th, six Special Tactics personnel from the Air Force Special Operations Command (AFSOC) were among the first CONUS-based personnel to arrive in Panama following receipt of the alert order. Upon arrival at Howard, they reported to the Joint Special Operations Task Force (JSOTF) headquarters that had been established in a Howard hangar. Three of these combat air traffic control qualified specialists immediately went into session with air planners from both the U.S.

Southern Command and the JSOTF. The other three NCOs began a detailed survey of the Howard tarmac area designated to be the SOF aircraft maintenance, refueling, arming, and loading area. They were instrumental in converting the Howard tarmac into an operating base from which practically all SOF combat missions would launch. This team also aided in integrating the flow of the inbound special operations fleet into the already saturated airdrome. During the early morning hours of December 18th, they developed a comprehensive airfield marshaling and support plan, which included traffic patterns, parking plans, helicopter refueling and rearming areas, and finalized the siting of the Joint Army/Air Force emergency field hospital.

The USAF Special Tactics force was created in the reconstructive aftermath of the aborted Iranian Rescue by merging the skills and training of two highly professional combat support specialties - Combat Controllers and Pararescue personnel. Every trainee undergoes the same combat skills indoctrination, combat diver, parachutist, freefall parachutist, and aircrew survival training. Those designated for combat controller duty attend Air Traffic Control and communications training, while those selected for the Pararescue specialty undergo extensive medical training. All special tactics personnel are trained in DZ/LZ and extraction zone marking. Functions such as surveys, planning and control of the assault zone requires more expertise and is normally the domain the CCT qualified team member, while rescue, recovery and medical care are the domain of the PJ. In addition, all special tactics personnel have extensive small arms, radio communication and land navigation skills with many attending the Army Ranger training program.

On December 20th, during the initial hours of the operation, two of the original special tactics combat controllers augmented the Howard "peacetime" air traffic controllers and provided blackout landing expertise and tactical communication links between mission aircraft and the joint operations center. The other four personnel managed the ground movement of blacked out special operations aircraft. Utilizing night vision goggles, they marshaled and parked aircraft, provided follow-me services using motorcycles, and assisted field hospital personnel with the unloading of wounded soldiers from medical evacuation helicopters. Using their inter-team radios, they maintained contact with the Howard tower, and advised their counterparts in the tower of the ground movement situation. They established a procedure whereby they gave the trauma teams at the field hospital advance warning as to the type of injuries and treatment that would be required for the incoming wounded. The six men provided these critical services continuously during the first 72 hours without rest.

SUPPORT TO TASK FORCE BLUE

Two other members of the original Special Tactics Squadron were detached to support Task Force (TF) Blue, one of the Naval Special Warfare

Task Forces. This team participated in two-ship assaults with Navy SEAL personnel. These operations resulted in the capture of two Panamanian boats in the Canal, which were believed to be carrying PDF teams who were eavesdropping on sensitive U. S. radio transmissions. The Special Tactics Team (STT) provided airborne fire support coordination with supporting helicopters and gunships. The communication link was essential to the success of these missions.

SUPPORT TO RANGER OPERATIONS

A separate 27-man contingent from the USAF Special Operations Command's 1724th Special Tactics Squadron at Pope AFB, North Carolina was assigned to support Ranger operations at Torrijos/Tocumen. The Special Tactics (ST) contingent was alerted on December 17th and, within three hours, had deployed. Four ST NCOs flew to Panama to prepare for a covert pre-H-Hour mission, which involved the infiltration of the Torrijos/Tocumen drop zone. Upon reaching Howard, the team immediately went into execution planning with the JSOTF staff. The four-man special tactics team was tasked to prepare the Torrijos drop zone for the American parachute assault. The infiltration aspects of the mission were particularly risky due to the active presence of the Panamanian Air Force, and a company of PDF infantry, plus roving PDF Police elements.

The balance of the ST personnel, 14 USAF Special Tactics Combat Controllers and nine Combat Medical Specialists (PJs), deployed from Bragg to Fort Benning, Georgia. There they linked-up and participated in final planning with the 3rd Bn/75th Rangers and the USAF special operations aircrews that would provide the airdrop, surveillance and fire support for the Torrijos assault.

Final planning, coordination, and equipment checks consumed the majority of December 18th, continuing well into the morning of the l9th. The Fort Benning contingent, now integrated with the paratroopers of the 3/75, boarded the C-130s and C-141s early on the evening of December 19th for the long flight to Panama.

Five hours later, as the Ranger aircraft were passing Nicaragua, the four Combat Controllers who were already in Panama infiltrated the Torrijos/Tocumen runway complex.

During the 25 minutes prior to the airdrop, the advance team positioned navigational beacons at pre-designated locations, took wind and weather observations, and relayed this data, as well as on-site intelligence on the PDF posture and guard post, to the command elements of the inbound assault force.

The advance team also established an air traffic control and fire direction net with the tactical fire support aircraft (USAF AC-130s and Army gunship helicopters). They also established a secure communications link with the ABCCC which was carrying a JTF cadre and a joint special operations coordination element.

Twenty minutes before jump time, the inbound Ranger assault force received word from SOUTHCOM that the PDF had increased their alert status, and the upcoming drop would be into a hot landing zone. The 16-ship assault formation began receiving substantial ground fire from PDF gunners as the aircraft began the final leg of the jump pass. The ST personnel had been cross-loaded with the Rangers, in accordance with normal procedures, and made the drop without incurring any injuries.

Once the team leader had insured that all ST personnel were accounted for and had established a communications link with the Ranger Tactical Operations Center (TOC), he initiated the ground tactical plan. Under sporadic, but largely ineffective, fire from several PDF positions, the team moved across a thousand yards of essentially open terrain, reaching the preselected point on schedule and without any personnel losses.

After the first 16 aircraft dropped the Ranger assault force, the ground infiltrated advance team repositioned the navigational beacons adjacent to a taxiway on the south end of Torrijos/Tocumen runway in preparation for the 82nd Airborne Division heavy drop. In the process, the team captured a Panamanian soldier and interrogated him in Spanish and passed on additional intelligence on PDF ground positions to the Ranger's TOC. The team also treated several American troopers injured in the paradrop and two civilian casualties, one of whom would have died if he had not been treated immediately.

Although the target area had been prepped by AC-130 gunfire prior to the airdrop, the defending PDF troopers were well-placed to contest control of the area. Immediately after reaching the rendezvous point, the main ST element began taking direct PDF fire. A STS NCO had been attached to the Ranger TOC to coordinate requests for close air fire support and medical evacuation of the wounded. A request for fire support was issued and responded to within minutes, and the individual ST sub-teams began their separate missions.

The original plan of action began to require adjustments as numerous fire-fights broke out between the PDF and the maneuvering Rangers. The overall scheme was further complicated 30 minutes later by the dispersed nature of the 82nd Division's heavy equipment drop. Many of the ST's All Terrain Vehicles (ATVs) had been part of the drop, and were inaccessible due to landing in the marshy area adjacent to the drop zone.

NORTHERN AREA SUPPORT

During the early stages of mission planning, six members of the 27 man STS contingent were directly attached to maneuver elements of the 1st Battalion, 75th Ranger Regiment which had the mission to subdue and neutralize the PDF forces at the northern Tocumen complex. After the paradrop, a junior ST NCO linked up with the Ranger company TOC in accordance with the plan, and became an integral part of their fire control support in the northern area. While engaged in a fire-fight for control of the old military terminal, he coordinated and directed several helicopter close air support missions to neutralize PDF strongholds. Once the Ranger company began its advance, it quickly secured the terminal and set up defensive positions. The ST NCO then moved out alone to survey the northern end of the runway for follow-on landing operations. He assessed the condition of the ramp and movement area, and passed this information to the clearing team leader. Taking sporadic sniper fire from the unsecured secondary objective, the Panamanian Air Force (FAP) barracks, he remained in his forward position and reported intelligence observations to the Ranger TOC and was responsible for identifying a concealed PDF machine gun position. Once located, the position was quickly destroyed by coordinated Ranger fire.

Another ST NCO linked up with the Ranger company responsible for the primary military stronghold at the airfield (the PDF Infantry Barracks). The ST trooper maneuvered with the Rangers and engaged the target. While coordinating for helicopter gunships to support the Rangers, he also moved into a forward observation point. He identified the source of the PDF opposition, and relayed this information to the Ranger fire support element that directed mortar fire on the target. After passing vital location adjustments to the Ranger TOC, and monitoring the successful mortar mission, he then led a four-man Ranger team in clearing parachutes, miscellaneous debris and unexploded ordnance from the runway and primary movement areas. The joint team continued clearing until the runway was ready to receive the impending operation.

Due to the dynamics of the ongoing ground situation and, in some cases, prolonged engagements, the ST team leader had to revise the aircraft ground movement and parking plan. The plan had been designed weeks earlier during one of the numerous planning meetings using reconnaissance photography. While attempting to assess and measure the parking ramp and taxiways for operational usability, he became engaged in several firefights, but eventually succeeded in devising an alternate parking and taxi scheme.

After ensuring the runway was clear, and coordinating the U.S. defensive security posture and force disposition with the Rangers, the ST team leader reported the north Tocumen runway was ready to receive the third wave of the force.

SOUTHERN AREA SUPPORT

Meanwhile, at the southern (Torrijos) Tactical Control Point (TCP), the ST NCO was the primary coordinator between the JTF-South ABCCC which was carrying the Deputy Commander of the XVIII Corps, who was in contact with the follow-on 82nd personnel airdrop formation. Plagued with weather delays in the CONUS, the C-141 aircraft arrived in intermittent waves, requiring intensive coordination on the already saturated radio nets.

The battle for the airfield complex was still going on, and fire-fights were occurring near the southern TCP as they had at the northern (Tocumen) TCP.

As the 82nd Division aircraft approached the still "hot" Drop Zone (DZ), the southern TCP team monitored the status of the electronic navigational aids (Navaids) and provided visual alignment information to the incoming air formation. Although the ST position came under fire several times, the team held in place and continued to pass vital control information to the lead aircraft, and assess where the different force loads were landing. On several occasions, recently landed jumpers from the 82nd Airborne Division came upon the team and were provided ground guide services to insure they went to the proper assembly location for their helicopter transload.

Meanwhile, another young ST NCO had doggedly fought with the marshy terrain where the vehicles had landed, finally managing to retrieve an ATR motorcycle. He then proceeded to deliver essential equipment to the north runway by repeatedly maneuvering through two separate fire-fights. He made a run, positioned the equipment and returned to the drop zone for another load – again, to negotiate the danger area and come under enemy fire. Once this was accomplished, he assisted with the recovery of other essential vehicles and the establishment of a helicopter rearm and refueling point, and provided terminal flight guidance and security for the Forward Arming and Refueling Points (FARP) site during the next 12 hours.

Two other members of the team coordinated a search and recovery operation for the remainder of the ST vehicles, derigging numerous vehicles, and directing their movement to the proper unit. Throughout the night and well into the next day, the STS troopers were involved in the movement of essential equipment to the northern runway for trans-loading. In one instance, after engaging in a firefight near the runway, they commandeered a jeep and transported recently wounded Army personnel to the Casualty Collection Point (CCP) for medical evacuation directly to the Joint Casualty Collection Point (JCCP) at Howard for treatment.

At the same time, two other junior ST NCOs were attempting to gain entrance to the Torrijos civil air traffic control tower. Integrated with a Ranger fire maneuver team, they advanced slowly due to the unexpected PDF resistance encountered within the main (i.e., civilian) terminal. After three hours of fighting alongside the Rangers, as they cleared the multi-level terminal, the two airmen finally gained ground floor entrance to the five-story control tower. With the arrival of the airlanding force imminent, the two-man Air Force element climbed the stairwell, cleared each floor, and entered the tower cab without incident.

After establishing secure command and control communications with the American Air Control Network, they activated the civil air traffic control communications and began to transmit a warning to all civilian aircraft to remain clear of the airport. They located the regular Panamanian air traffic controllers and, with their cooperation, established an Air Traffic Control zone and coordination procedures to safely conduct landing operations for the impending wave of logistics operations. Next, they began the coordination process of directing the arriving 82nd Airborne Division troops to where they were to link-up with the helicopters of the Army Aviation Task Force for the air assault operations at Panama Viejo, Tinajitas, and Fort Cimarron. The STS forces were augmented and, eventually, relieved by an 18 man conventional USAF combat control team from the 1721st CCS, that parachuted in with the 82nd and teamed up with the SOF STS personnel.

The STS team was relieved by the 1721st personnel eight hours after the SOF STS team had parachuted on the Torrijos/Tocumen tarmac. The handoff went smoothly. The turn-over and transition of air traffic control functions from the SOF STT to the 82nd CCT enabled the U.S. forces to continue the high tempo of strategic air-land operations on the dual runways as well as support helicopter flight operations on the recently established refuel and rearm points.

Within a few hours, the C-141 and C-5 transports carrying the 7th Infantry Division began to arrive on time and in accordance with the original flow plan.

COMBAT MEDICS AT TORRIJOS

Meanwhile the nine USAF special tactics Pararescuemen (PJ) that were attached to the 1st Battalion, 75th Ranger Regiment at Torrijos/Tocumen International Airport on December 20th had been busy with their own mission responsibilities. One of these responsibilities was to set up the Joint Casualty Collection Point (JCCP) and provide a command and control network for all medical services to be performed on the airhead. This responsibility included coordinating search and recovery operations and prioritizing the air evacuation of the wounded.

Three of the special tactics PJs had been tasked to participate in the runway clearing operations. This critical task was complicated by the initial loss of several of the team's specially-built Rescue All Terrain Vehicles (RATVs) to the neighboring marsh. The loss severely reduced the PJ's mobility. However, the three air medics began clearing the 8,000-foot runway on foot and in spite of small arms fire from PDF elements, also emplaced the infrared runway lights for the impending landing operations. Two other PJs emplaced navigational aids for the follow-on airdrop and then assisted in the runway clearing effort.

Immediately after the airdrop, several of the PJs wrestled with the marsh that had mired their airdropped RATVs, managing to recover some of the unique vehicles. The PJ/RATV element was immediately called upon to respond to several urgent requests for medical assistance from the Rangers. The RATV teams maneuvered the ungainly looking vehicles over rough terrain and through intermittent zones of hostile fire to reach the injured. The teams successfully reached all locations and administered life-saving emergency medical treatment. The PJs then moved the injured to the Joint Casualty Collection Point (JCCP) for evacuation by helicopter to the Howard JCCP, where they were treated and stabilized for air evacuation to the United States.

Once the runway was cleared and secured, five of the PJs were dispatched to separate locations on the airfield to establish aid stations and administer emergency medical treatment to both military and civilian casualties and coordinate their evacuation. Once these immediate tasks had been accomplished, the PJs not involved in medical emergencies aided in locating and derigging the essential support equipment.

RIO HATO CCT FOLLOW-ON OPS

Seven other Special Tactics Combat Controllers, upon airlanding at Rio Hato Airfield, assumed landing zone control duties from the initial ST team that had parachuted in with the Ranger force. Immediately upon landing, the follow-on element unloaded their tactical vehicle and one member of the team proceeded to a Ranger squad's position to evacuate a gravely wounded Ranger who was under direct sniper fire. The airman tasked with this mission recovered the wounded soldier and rushed him to the Casualty Collection Point. Meanwhile, other members of the team positioned and activated their vehicular mounted ground radio communications and assumed radio operator duties from the initial assault force. This element also established a communications link to the main Air Traffic Control (ATC) Center at Howard and assumed the ATC responsibilities for the Rio Hato airhead.

Working in blackout conditions and exposed to enemy small arms fire and random mortar rounds, the STS team broke down to working elements. Collectively, the team established helicopter landing zones, marshaled fixed and rotary wing aircraft into refueling points, implanted and serviced infrared runway and taxi lights, and made runway surface checks between the surges of air operations to insure unimpeded landings and takeoffs could be made.

While checking the runway and taxiway shoulders to remove parachute canopies and other debris from within the safety zone, the STS troopers found and disposed of a range of unexploded ordnance including a damaged LAW rocket, two live hand grenades and a dud 40 mm round.

Although PDF mortars periodically landed within 35 meters of their control point, the small team continued to operate the airfield without delays. They also performed the duties of an Airlift Control Element (ALCE), which entailed parking aircraft, directing combat unloading, manifesting personnel and equipment, and relaying flight-following information to the Airlift Control Center (ACC) at Howard. They also coordinated the expeditious movement of battlefield casualties from the

CCP to the awaiting aircraft. Throughout the invasion night and the following day they transmitted vital intelligence, air movement and weather information through the command and control communications net to the Special Operations Joint Operations Center at Howard.

During the first 24 hours the STS team safely controlled the air movement of more than 300 aircraft in and out of Rio Hato airfield and coordinated the marshaling and transfer of more than 350 PDF prisoners of war and more than two dozen Ranger injured.

NORIEGA PURSUIT OPERATIONS

Shortly before the initial H-Hour assault operations began, two of the original Howard ST advance element deployed to Nuevo Guararre Airport located in a back country area midway between Colon and Panama City to support Task Force Green. TF Green was one of the sub-elements of the Joint Special Operations Task Force (JSOTF) charged with Noriega search operations.

The small remote airstrip was sufficient to support parking, servicing, refueling, and transloading operations safely and was designated to be a focal point for search and reaction teams in pursuit of General Noriega.

The initial task was to confirm an earlier assessment as to the ability of the airstrip to support military air operations. The survey reaffirmed the previous assessment, and the team proceeded to activate Air Traffic Control (ATC) services and establish command and control communications from the remote airstrip back to the JSOTF headquarters via a satellite communications link.

Once the basic services were established the team provided air and ground coordination to the Army and USAF aircraft staging out of the airhead. The aircraft in turn provided airlift and fire support to the specially trained ground search forces.

The number of chase operations increased from the initial half-dozen planned. The primary airlift for the reactions teams were Air Force MH-53s and MH-60s. During the subsequent ten days, SF and SEAL elements of the JSOTF raided many of General Noriega's former haunts and numerous locations where he was reported to be hiding. The chase teams narrowly missed him several times. More than twenty such missions were conducted.

CHRISTMAS AIR OPERATIONS

On Christmas Eve at Hurlburt AFB, a special operations C-130 aircrew was alerted for an immediate deployment mission to Panama. The crew launched within hours of the alert, arriving in Panama that evening, and immediately put into crew rest without any mission orders. Early the next morning, Christmas Day, the crew was alerted for an immediate out and back mission to Enrique Malek Airfield near David in the western province of Chiriqui.

Earlier that morning, three of the original special operations combat controllers assigned to Howard during the initial days of the operation had deployed to the David Airfield with elements of the 1st Bn/75th Ranger Regiment. The force was to be part of the U.S. campaign to neutralize the PDF in the outlying reaches of the country.

The initial mission was to assess the usability of the airhead to support sustained operations of heavy lift fixed-wing aircraft. The three-man team accomplished the airfield survey within 90 minutes, then assisted with runway repairs, provided air traffic control (ATC) services, and established command and control communications back to the rear echelon headquarters. The team was tasked to orchestrate the smooth flow of the follow-on air assets and coordinate the evacuation of the local PDF commander, Colonel Del Cid.

Del Cid was one of the two other PDF officers named in the Florida Grand Jury drug indictments of February 1988 along with Manuel Noriega. Del Cid had surrendered himself and his garrison to the American Special Forces and their accompanying AC-130 reaction force. The Hurlburt Field C-130 was to pick up Del Cid and deliver him to Howard where the formal process of his extradition would begin. At Howard he was to be transferred from U.S. military control to a Federal Marshal and a Drug Enforcement Administration (DEA) escort for his follow-on flight to the United States.

The SOF aircrew had the C-130 engines running, and were ready for takeoff from Howard in less than 30 minutes after receiving the mission order. They flew a low-level route, avoiding areas of suspected PDF activity. As they prepared to set up their final approach, they were advised that the runway had suffered significant damage through deterioration, and only the first 3,000 feet was useable. The crew put the aircraft down within the allotted distance, then maneuvered around numerous potholes during roll out.

The PDF prisoner, along with an American security force, was loaded on with the engines running and the aircraft was airborne again within three minutes of its touch down time. Once on the ground at Howard, the crew maneuvered the aircraft close to another SOF C-130 that was waiting with its engines running for the next leg of the journey to Florida. As soon as the legal transfer from the military security team to the civil law enforcement agents had been accomplished, the second C-130 taxied out and began its delivery mission.

The original aircrew was then tasked with a series of immediate follow-on missions. The first, an afternoon mission, took them from Howard to Torrijos Airport to drop off hot Christmas dinners. The follow-on night flight took them back to David to deliver a team of U.S. Army engineers to assess the runway repair requirements. The night landing was made with the assistance of runway markers implanted earlier by the ST team. This stop also was a quick turn around. The David cargo this time was a planeload of flexcuffed PDF prisoners captured during the previous

72 hours. The last and fifth flight took the crew and the aircraft back to Howard where the POWs were transferred to military police custody, and the aircraft to the custody of the crew chief. Then the crew headed for the maintenance, operations, and intelligence debriefing points.

The Headquarters of the Department of National Investigations (DENI), the Panamanian equivalent of the FBI located in Balboa City shown after AC-130 air strike in support of Task Force Bayonet. Note PDF sandbaged fighting position in forground. Courtesy U.S. Army Center for Military History.

Comandancia under attack. Photo courtesy U.S. Army Center for Military History.

Closeup of one PDF barracks at Fort Amador showing the results of the American assault. Photo courtesy U.S. Southern Command Public Information Office.

Aerial view of the Renacer Prison Compound. Photo courtesy of the author.

PART FOUR: THE OTHER HALF OF COMBAT OPERATIONS

The success of the initial series of major actions would have been for naught, if the dozens of smaller actions and follow-on missions had not been completed successfully. The next three chapters provide a detailed look at the other, less visible half of the combat equation. This includes operations in the Colon, i.e., on the Atlantic side of the Isthmus, the air assault operations of phase two, and a host of widespread follow-on actions which continued through early January.

CHAPTER FOURTEEN ATLANTIC COAST OPERATIONS

During the three hours preceding H-Hour, U.S. forces on the Atlantic side of the isthmus had also been moving into position to execute their portion of *Just Cause*. A brigade task force built around the 3rd Brigade of the 7th Infantry Division from Fort Ord, California was charged with coordinating operations in the Atlantic provinces.

Task Force Atlantic, as it was called, was responsible for the simultaneous execution of a range of diverse missions including securing of the vital Gatun Locks and the Madden Dam as well as securing the U.S. installations in its area of operations. The task force also had to isolate and neutralize the PDF forces in the Colon City area. This included the 100-man PDF Naval Infantry unit at Coco Solo on the outskirts of Colon City. Coco Solo was a joint U.S.-Panamanian installation similar to Fort Amador where only a few hundred feet separated American dependents from the PDF "Marine" barracks.

RENACER PRISON

Task Force Atlantic also had the mission of rescuing the prisoners being held in the PDF Renacer Prison near Gamboa, midway between Colon and Panama City. Many of the prisoners were former PDF who had taken part in the March 1988 coup while others had participated in the October 1989 attempt. U.S. planners hoped that by rescuing these men, some could be persuaded to help the new government.

Charlie Company 3rd Bn, 504th Infantry drew this mission and expected PDF resistance and a firefight. This estimate was reinforced a few days before mission execution during the execution of a CRE near the prison. The American assault commander and the PDF site commander had a highly vocal toe-to-toe debate about the rights of American forces to conduct combat maneuvers in close proximity to sovereign PDF installations. Although the PDF officer held firm in his position that such exercises were provocative, dangerous and could lead to loss of life, the confrontation did not proceed beyond the exchange of verbal missives.

The CRE was one of two conducted the same night. The other CRE was conducted against Madden Dam. The CREs gave the personnel of the two units an excellent opportunity to survey their respective objective and its approaches. The CREs were very much a duplication of the mission, short of execution. The CREs stopped at the fence line of the objectives although they were executed with weapons loaded should the PDF react with hostility.

The tight little prison complex sat on the bank of the Panama Canal in an isolated jungle area near the confluence of the Chagres River. The prison was bounded on two sides by water and on the third side by a heavily vegetated jungle ridge. It consisted of a collection of 20 or so cinderblock and wooden buildings with tin roofs. The fenced-in area included the prison barracks, a recreation shed, and the exercise yard that measured no more than 40 by 70 meters.

The guard force consisted of 20-25 PDF soldiers. Duty at the isolated compound was not considered a good assignment or career enhancing. Part of the guard force included members of Battalion 2000 who, because of various discipline infractions, were serving punishment tours as guards.

Their weapons consisted of a variety of automatic rifles – mostly communist AK-47s and a Chinese manufactured version of the U.S. M-16, the T65. It was estimated that a number of machine guns were mounted in the tin roofed guard towers.

The seizure of Renacer Prison and securing the release of the prisoners had become one of the key missions for Task Force Atlantic in late October. Execution of this lifesaving mission was expected to be extremely difficult due to the close proximity of the prisoners and guards, and the danger of American fire hitting the prisoners.

If U.S. forces did not gain control of the compound quickly, the rescue attempt could easily turn into a hostage situation with the guards holding up to 64 hostages. The mission had to be executed quickly and precisely, with maximum surprise, and using a measured but overwhelming application of force.

The mission fell to a battalion of the 82nd Airborne Division from Fort Bragg that was in Panama undergoing field training as part of the Jungle Operations Training Program. Shortly after the Battalion's initial inbrief and processing at Fort Sherman, the site of the Jungle Warfare School, the senior battalion staff was briefed on *Blue Spoon*, and the battalion was integrated into the SOUTHCOM joint planning and training program as part of Task Force Atlantic.

The rescue mission evolved into another example of the blending of diverse capabilities into an integrated combined arms team. The core element of the team was C Company, 3rd Battalion, 504th Parachute Infantry Regiment (3-504th PIR), 82nd Airborne Division. The unit was ideally suited by previous training and current location for the operation. Three of the company's rifle platoons were directly committed to the rescue mission.

Three UH-1, *Huey* helicopters, from the 1st Battalion, 228th Aviation Regiment, stationed in Panama, were to provide airlift and combat assault, while *Cobra* attack helicopters from the 7th Infantry Division would provide aerial firepower. In addition, an engineer team from the 82nd Airborne Division's 307th Engineer Battalion was attached to provide demolition support to break through doors and walls. A Landing Craft Medium (LCM) from the Panama-based Army 1097th Transportation Company (Medium Boat) was to provide an amphibious assault and delivery capability. A team of three military policemen rounded out the mission task force.

The plan involved a simultaneous air and amphibious assault at H-Hour. The door gunners on the assault helicopters would engage specific pre-planned targets, while a *Cobra* attack helicopter would take the guard barracks under fire. The two assault *Hueys*, each carrying eleven paratroopers and flown by pilots using night vision goggles, would land the *Hueys* inside the cramped prison yard. The troops would rapidly disembark and immediately search and secure the two major buildings within the fenced area – the recreation building and the prisoners' barracks.

The heliborne rescue-assault element consisted of two squads from the 2nd Platoon. The remainder of the 2nd Platoon would assault from the LCM as it landed on a nearby Canal bank. The LCM force would provide fire support and security for the rescue force. The LCM squads would carry five M60 machine guns and AT-4 anti-tank weapons. The latter was to be available for use against buildings to create entry holes or against armored vehicles should the PDF choose to reinforce or counterattack.

The 3rd Platoon was also sandwiched on board the LCM. Its mission was to clear and secure the 18 exterior buildings outside the prison fence. In addition, an OH-58 scout helicopter carrying a sniper team would be orbiting nearby with a full overview of the compound. Meanwhile, a third *Huey* would land outside the prison with 10-infantry scouts who would set up blocking positions to stop any PDF reinforcements from entering the fray.

During November and December, the various teams rehearsed repeatedly, both separately and collectively, honing their skills in building clearing, fire control, and exiting the helicopters and the LCM. The prison layout was marked out with cloth tape using an empty American barracks as the cornerstone of the compound's profile. Numerous nighttime drills were conducted.

In addition, the force conducted field training and exercises around the prison. These "freedom of movement" exercises were part of the "*Sand Flea*" series that were conducted by American forces throughout Panama. Some of the Renacer associated exercises involved team elements conducting amphibious landings near the prison, and then maneuvering through the area in a tactical manner.

These "drills" were considered absolutely invaluable for several reasons. First, they lulled the PDF into a certain degree of complacency.

Second, the American force elements became familiar with their individual roles and missions. Third, the American soldiers were able to "eyeball" their future target and gain a situational awareness not normally available. Specific knowledge gained included target configuration, construction, type and size of fences, and details concerning the guard force such as size, armament, level of alertness, and state of training.

The rescue force received the mission order late in the evening of December 19th. The weather was poor for night flying, with the cloud base at about 500 feet and very little ambient light for NVG flight operations.

Shortly before H-Hour, the two OH-58 observation helicopters flew down the Canal as programmed and as they had done numerous other times. However, this time when they were abreast of the prison on their return pass, they opened fire on the two principal guard positions. While the OH-58s were exchanging fire with the PDF positions, the two *Hueys* carrying the initial assault forces began their descent into the prison yard. They were met with a hail of PDF ground fire.

As the pilots fought to maneuver their descending machines precisely to the preplanned landing locations, only the gunners on the right side of the aircraft were allowed to return the PDF fire. The gunners on the left side of the aircraft had to hold their fire to prevent hitting the prisoners' barracks. The barrage from the two right side door gunners was magnified by fire from three members of the 11-man assault teams that were positioned in the open door. Automatic weapons and grenade launchers were added to the firepower of the door gunner's machine gun.

Although the prison guards responded, and tracers were passing all around the two *Hueys*, neither of the aircraft nor their occupants was hit. Within seconds the two choppers touched down inside the compound while the third *Huey* with the heavily armed scout squad landed at the blocking position. Within fifteen seconds, the LCM's ramp came crashing down on the shore at its designated spot, discharging the support element of 2nd Platoon with their phalanx of five machine guns. Overhead, the *Cobra* gunship let loose with its 20mm Gatling gun on the guard barracks.

The floodlights in the yard went out seconds later, probably due to a severed power line. Once on the ground, the 1st Squad, 2nd Platoon moved quickly to the main prisoner barracks and blew open the metal door. One of the American troopers was hit in the arm and went down, but the rest of the squad continued to press forward. Once the door was clear, the 3rd Squad quickly moved inside, taking up covering positions and assessing the situation. Americans found the prisoners unharmed, laying on the floor covering themselves with their mattresses. The 2nd Squad simultaneously secured the recreation building without any confrontation or injuries.

The five covering machine guns from the LCM were in position within 40 seconds of leaving the LCM. As the machine gunners settled in, the 3rd Platoon, which had followed them off the LCM, moved through the machine gun positions and began to clear the remainder of the buildings. Seeing two PDF soldiers running between the buildings, one of the LCM troops notified the machine gun squad. An American M-60 gunner, whose responsibility it was for that zone, spotted the two PDF troopers and opened fire, killing both.

However, not everything went strictly according to plan. A 10-foot high fence, positioned under the overhang of the office and PDF headquarters building, was a surprise. It had not been visible in the aerial photos the unit had used to plan the assault. The troopers found that neither grenades nor claymore mines were effective in opening a passage in the heavy gauge metal. Frustrated by the ineffectiveness of the munitions, two paratroopers crawled forward and cut a hole in the barrier with their M-9 bayonets.

Meanwhile, an American fire team moved into the darkened headquarters building and were met with a cloud of tear gas. Unfazed, they withdrew, donned their protective masks, and reentered the building. As the team moved through the building, they spotted a trail of blood and followed it outside. Once outside the building, the American team spotted the source. Hunched down beside the building, and within 10 feet of other unsuspecting American paratroopers, were two PDF troopers. The PDF soldiers sensed the additional American presence behind them and began to swing their weapons towards the team. The American leader saw the movement and fired first, killing both of them.

While the events at the prison headquarters had been unfolding, the 1st squad had moved up the jungle ridge to clear a couple of the out buildings, one was a duplex-style family residence. One apartment was cleared without incident. Then the Americans heard a woman crying, "Don't shoot!" The squad held its fire and discovered a PDF lieutenant, his wife, and child in the second apartment. None were injured. The lieutenant was taken prisoner, and the woman and child put into detainee status.

By daylight, the prison and all its occupants and facilities were in American hands with all the prisoners accounted for and unharmed. Five PDF guards were killed and 22 captured (six of these were wounded). Four U.S. soldiers were also wounded in the operation, but none fatally.

GAMBOA VILLAGE AND BRIDGE

Alpha Company had drawn a two-fold mission: clear the village of any PDF forces and secure the nearby road bridge that spanned the Chagres river. The bridge was crucial to the uninterrupted flow of road traffic from the Atlantic to Pacific and linked Gamboa with the nearby Renacer Prison. Steady and careful restraint was required in sweeping the village due to the intermix of American and Panamanian residents, most of whom were employees of the Panama Canal Commission (PCC). This operation was also a combined arms air mobile and amphibious landing (LCM) operation. The original plan called for an air assault into two LZs outside of town, then move in on the ground. Based upon the presumption that the PDF forces in the town may have gone to a increased alert posture, the LZ location was changed. The new LZ area was a soccer field (McGrath Field) in the center of the town. The first helicopter in was a UH-1 carried eleven fully-equipped soldiers with a high ratio of automatic weapons. Their responsibility was to secure the LZ and return any fire that was directed at the LZ or the follow-on helicopters.

The two CH-47s that followed each carried a max load of fifty troopers, almost equivalent to three platoons, each targeted at a different objective. One platoon was targeted at the PDF female training school (Escuela de Formacion Femenina 'Rufina Alfaro'). It was unknown if the cadre would resist, but it was known that they had access to weapons and were well trained. However, the Americans did not encounter any organized resistance at the school. Another platoon quickly took down the police station and then moved to secure the bridge over the Chagres. The third platoon was assigned to seize, clear and secure the Forest Police Barracks and Headquarters. This building was critical because of its proximity to surrounding American residences. An element of the Forest Police resisted. The building clearing turned into a major operation during which the platoon suffered two wounded, however, they succeeded in clearing and securing the objective without any damage to the surrounding American quarters.

MADDEN DAM

Just as the Renacer Mission Task Force had planned, practiced, and rehearsed their mission, so had a sister company from the 504th PIR worked with a different set of constraints and assets to prepare for their critical mission. Madden Dam is the key to capturing the tropical rains of Panama, and storing the water which is then used to replenish the millions of gallons of water expended into the sea every time a ship exits the Canal. If the dam were to be severely damaged, tremendous flood damage would occur across the length of the entire Canal. If its controls were damaged, the smooth operation of the Canal would be severely interrupted until repairs could be made. The continued safety and operation of the dam was essential from multiple perspectives, including humanitarian, ecological, and economical.

The mission of seizing and protecting the Madden Dam and its crucial water flow Control Center was one of several assigned to the 3rd Bn, 504th Infantry of the 82nd Airborne Division. The battalion commander assigned the dam seizure mission to two platoons from Delta Company because the mission best fit the training and capabilities of the company. Delta Company was a relatively new addition to the Battalion capabilities and was trained as a mechanized cavalry element with an additional mission of dismounted reconnaissance and patrolling. The movement to and closure with the dam was to be by vehicle road march. The movement from Fort Sherman to Fort Davis to the Dam required an hour and a half drive. Because of the distance and travel time required the Delta Company convoy began its movement long before H-Hour. The small convoy departed Sherman at 10:00 PM in order to allow ample time to clear the Gatun Locks and be positioned to leave its jump off point (Fort Davis) at 11:30. The assault convoy was similar in composition to the configuration used only a few nights before in a SOUTHCOM Contingency Reaction Exercise (CRE).

The mission convoy included a command and control HMMWV, four other HMMWVs sporting 50 caliber machine guns and three "Deuce & Half" (2 1/2 ton) trucks. An extra challenge was the requirement to clear through three PDF checkpoints enroute without raising an alarm or causing an incident. The convoy commander, the CO of Delta Company, had orders to bluff his way through the checkpoints and not engage in a firefight unless the PDF initiated the exchange.

The battalion commander's level of concern was particularly high because of a PDF broadcast at 11:00 PM. The broadcast indicated the PDF had advance warning of the U.S. H-Hour announcing 1:00 as being "the time for the party to occur." The broadcast included orders (authorization) that any American intervening with any PDF operations could be shot.

The battalion CO was relieved as he learned the convoy was clearing each of the checkpoints on time and without encountering any trouble. The American force came within striking range of the Dam fifteen minutes prior to H-Hour. The company commander pulled the convoy off the road and out of earshot of the dam and waited for H-hour. The final closure was quick and followed the same general approach scenario that was exercised in the CRE. Although some small arms fire was encountered, there was no significant PDF resistance. The American commander, mindful of the ROE and the seeking to avoid the needless loss of lives or destruction to the Dam's control mechanisms, openly approached the Panamanian custodian of the dam's control center. The captain had made a point to engage the same man in brief, but congenial conversations during earlier survey visits. This foresight paid off and the Panamanian unlocked the gate and surrendered the control facility to the care of the Americans. Contrary to some earlier speculation, no hidden explosive chambers or demolition charges were found on the dam or in the control center. An American guard force remained at the Dam for more than two weeks.

During this period, the battalion commander periodically made visits to the isolated guard force as he did to the other scattered battalion locations. During one of these visits he and his command helicopter were nearly the cause (and caught in the middle) of a potentially disastrous case of misidentification and friendly fire fratricide. As the CO's helicopter was departing after one of these visits, he noticed an AC-130 circling the area and four Army Special Operations helicopters. After some close maneuvers by the SPECOP helos, he ordered his pilot to return to the dam and land. The pilot dutifully complied. Once on the ground, the pilot and the battalion commander watched three of the SPECOP Helos and wondered where number four was. Suddenly, it dropped out of sky near them, depositing a cluster of black-clad, heavily armed special operations assault forces who circled the helicopter weapons at the ready. The special operation force, one of those charged with capturing General Noriega and acting on information from Panamanians in the nearby village, had been dispatched to the area. The battalion commander's helicopter had attracted attention as a possible Noriega escape platform and prompted the actions of the men on helo number four.

However, given the distance separating the Delta Company guard force located on the dam from the helicopter landing site, all that the Delta personnel could discern was that their battalion CO was being held at gun point by an unknown force of men in black Ninja-style clothing. Not being aware of the American special operations force, or its mission, the guard force assumed the black-clad men were members of the Panamanian special operations force on which they had been briefed and began to fire on the American force.

The battalion CO quickly detached himself from the cluster of men near the helicopters and, running toward the dam, shouted to his troopers to cease fire. Fortunately, none of those initial rounds found a human mark although they left several holes in the commander's helicopter.

COCO SOLO AND THE PDF 1ST NAVAL INFANTRY COMPANY

The mission order given to the 4th Battalion, 17th Infantry Regiment, 7th Division, United States Army read as follows:

> "Commencing at 0100, 20 December 1989, the 4-17 Infantry will (take action to): protect the lives of U.S. citizens in zone, neutralize the PDF naval infantry company at Coco Solo, capture the PDF boats at the Coco Solo dock, establish a roadblock at the neck of the Colon Peninsula, establish a roadblock on the Boyd-Roosevelt Highway, protect the Galeta Island Facility, disable all multi-engine aircraft on France Airfield, and on-order conduct follow-on operations to neutralize the PDF at Military Zone headquarters, in Colon City, and secure key Canal facilities."

Colon is the major Panamanian port on the Atlantic side and the eastern terminus of the Canal. It boasts a population of approximately 60,000 and a massive "international free trade zone," the profits from which are an important part of the Panamanian national economy. The city lies at the northern tip of a half-mile long peninsula commonly referred to as the Colon Bottleneck.

One half mile to the east across a small water inlet is the village of Coco

Solo. Adjacent to the village was a joint American-Panamanian military garrison by the same name. A pair of large identical buildings sit parallel to each other and dominate the landscape. The northern building housed the Cristobal Junior/Senior High School, a U.S. facility, and the barracks used by one of the U.S. infantry companies on rotation from the States.

The southern building served several purposes, including being the barracks for the PDF 1st Naval Infantry Company, a garment factory, and a Chinese restaurant known as the "noodle shop." Fifty yards to the east across a stretch of green grass was a small U.S. family housing area consisting of two dozen houses. Many of the units were unoccupied on the night of December 19, 1989, the occupants having returned to the United States months earlier. The PDF boat docks were located 200 yards behind the southern-most PDF building, and several armed patrol boats were nestled next to the docks.

The U.S. battalion commander's intent was to quickly neutralize the PDF units in Coco Solo before they could harm the nearby American dependents, sealing off the city of Colon (by controlling the causeway). He would then posture his force for an attack into Colon to neutralize any PDF that chose to resist. The PDF Military Zone headquarters that was located in the city would be among the first targets in the move on the city.

Although the mission statement was lengthy, each objective was assigned to an individual maneuver element within the battalion down to the platoon and squad level. Each of the unit leaders developed a tactical plan and training schedule designed to achieve mission success. Once approved by the company commanders and the battalion commander, training began on a unit-by-unit basis. Most of the actions were rehearsed as part of the overall SOUTHCOM training and conditioning program.

Charlie Company (4Bn/17Inf/7ID) drew the mission of neutralizing the PDF Naval Infantry Company. The American company had been billeted in an unused wing of the high school building since its arrival in mid-November, 33 days earlier. During normal patrolling and security operations, the Americans often came in contact or close proximity to the PDF infantry and often had to restrain themselves from reacting to insulting gestures from the PDF soldiers.

The total force available to the company commander included his three organic rifle platoons, a rifle platoon from 3-504th Infantry (of the 82nd Abn Division), two Vulcan rapid fire Gatling guns from the 2-62 Air Defense Artillery (ADA) Battalion. In addition, the force included a communications detachment from the 127th Signal Battalion, a platoon of military police from the 549th MP Company, and a medical team from the battalion support platoon. The total troop strength approximated 200 soldiers. The 2nd platoon was charged with clearing the PDF barracks.

Late in the afternoon and continuing into the evening of December 19th, some of the company troopers began to sense that the tranquility of the past month, was about to change. One of the indicators came home to a squad leader when his platoon leader called him to the U.S. guard post opposite the PDF Naval Infantry barracks and together they conducted a casual reconnaissance of the area. After the survey was completed, the platoon leader told the squad leader to retire to the American barracks and draft the tactical operations plan for his squad. This same procedure was followed for each of the squad leaders. Rumors began to circulate about two hours later that the president had given the directive to execute the takedown of the PDF.

Beginning about 8:00 PM, the company commander quietly began to assemble his forces in small unit groups and issue ammunition in combat loads. New radio call signs were assigned and a schedule of unit operations briefings was set up. During the unit briefings, H-Hour was announced as 1:00 the next morning.

Mission anticipation rose steadily during the next several hours. The main focus of the tactical leaders, after reviewing the mission sequence to ensure nothing had been left to chance, was the mental and physical condition of their troops and gear.

The Charlie Company plan was simple: seal-off the area using one rifle platoon and a military police element, then prepare to conduct an assault on the PDF section of the southern building, using a second platoon supported by 20mm fire provided by the Vulcan cannon from the air defense unit. The infantry platoon would also be equipped with machine guns and shoulder-fired anti-tank rockets in addition to its M-16s.

A third platoon would be positioned at the rear of the high school to cover the back door of the PDF barracks and the dock area. From this location, the platoon would be able to assault the dock and capture the patrol boats before they could be put in action. A fourth platoon would be poised to seize the high school gym, located between the PDF barracks and the American high school and, from there, clear the PDF barracks after it had been brought under fire by the Vulcans.

The company commander planned to initiate the attack precisely at H-Hour with two minutes of carefully directed Vulcan and anti-tank weapon fire. This would be followed by a call over the bullhorn, in Spanish, for a full and immediate PDF surrender.

Shortly after midnight, the eight American families living in the first row of buildings in the American housing area, which were in the direct line of fire from the PDF barracks, were quietly evacuated to neighbors' quarters one row of buildings away.

At about the same time, the two Vulcan systems were wheeled into position, just as they had been every night for the past several months. The troopers were again becoming adjusted to the feel of their kevlar body armor vest, and now the additional weight of a full combat-load of ammunition. The tactical leaders reviewed the sequence of actions with their squads for the last time. Then the battalion commander quietly spoke to the men, reminding them they had the training, the weapons, the leadership, and the individual discipline to make the plan succeed. The commander was followed by the Chaplain, who said a prayer and blessed the assembled men. In the background, a tape of Hank Williams singing "A Country Boy Can Survive" could be heard in the stillness of the night.

About ten minutes before H-hour, two platoons from Delta Company, equipped with M-2 (.50 caliber) machine guns mounted on HMMWVs, established a roadblock near Cristobal High School and the PDF Naval Infantry barracks complex, isolating the area. The mission to establish and hold a blocking position at Fuerte Espinar, the key land approach to Colon, was assigned to a composite platoon size force composed of headquarters staff and garrison support troops including parachute riggers and cooks as well as administrative, supply and air defense personnel commanded by the Headquarters Company commander. Although originally conceived as a static security mission, it evolved to have a very active component when the composite platoon became involved in the clearing of the nearby the former U.S. Army School of Americas building.

Charlie company had been in its jump-off positions for five minutes and the individual soldiers had started to settle in with their own thoughts for a nervous 15 minutes when three shots were heard coming from the vicinity of the main gate to the village of Coco Solo. The shots were answered immediately by a burst of fire from a M-60 machine gun from the American platoon enroute towards the dock area. The company commander promptly gave the signal for the brace of Vulcans to begin the preplanned two-minute barrage of fire. The gunners followed the plan, alternating the guns, and firing in 10 round burst at pre-selected targets.

When the thunder of the Vulcans shattered the remnants of the quiet night, the American troopers began to move. The company commander had positioned a sergeant, a seasoned squad leader with Ranger training, on the second floor of the American-controlled building where he could watch over the movement of the first squad and provide covering fire.

As the squad began to move, the sergeant rapidly fired several rounds from his grenade launcher into the courtyard of the PDF facility. By the time the squad was half way across the gap, rifle and machine gun fire could be heard and seen coming from all around the PDF barracks. The light from the various tracer rounds being used by the two forces turned the black night into brilliant eerie flashes of color. The covering barrage of grenades suppressed local PDF action long enough for the lead squad to cross the exposed space and enter the target building unscathed.

Just as the squad reached the building, the Vulcans completed their two-minute burst and other sounds became audible as the deep growl of the guns faded away and the ground vibrations stopped. The quasi-silence was immediately punctured with the American loudspeakers, calling in Spanish on the PDF troopers to surrender. Instead of a surrender response, the American call was answered by renewed fire from the PDF barracks.

By this time, all four squads of the 2nd Platoon were in the building and clearing operations were initiated.

The first obstacle encountered was the 17-member Chinese family who operated the "Noodle Factory" restaurant and lived in an adjacent cluster of rooms. Although confusion and fear had seized the terrified family, the American soldiers held their fire and managed to gain control of the human turmoil of crying children and screaming women, and get the entire family out of the building and into safe hands without any injuries.

The Americans then blew down the door separating the restaurant/factory area from the PDF-controlled area using a well-placed C-4 explosive charge. Before the smoke had cleared, the squad had moved through the fiery door frame and into the darkened gymnasium, which occupied the ground floor. Still in the dark, the lead squad crossed the open floor and took up clearing positions on the stairs leading to the second floor barracks area.

As the American squad prepared to move up the stairs, the Vulcans concluded their second volley, which was immediately followed by a declaration of surrender from some PDF troopers. The American squad leader disarmed the 11 PDF troopers and held them under close guard until he was assured that the remainder of the building had been thoroughly cleared. When the Americans were sure that there were no further pockets of resistance, a Spanish-speaking American private formally accepted the surrender of the senior PDF prisoner, a captain who had assumed command of the PDF unit only 10 hours before.

During the four hours of the operation, Charlie Company captured 27 PDF troopers at a cost of no U.S. casualties.

CERRO TIGRE – LOGISTICS DEPOT

The logistics depot complex was the largest target assigned to the 3 Bn/504th Infantry. It had more buildings than of any of the other 3/504th targets and given its nature was the key ingredient in any large scale PDF resistance. Bravo Company, 3rd Battalion/504th was assigned this mission. The depot guard force was estimated to be a company-sized force with a strength of 160-200, plus an unknown number of instructors and possibly students at the collocated Explosive Ordnance School (Escuela de Explosivs, Demolicion Y Sabotaje). The complex sat in a partial bowl with higher ground covered with deep jungle foliage on three sides. Internally, it was sub-divided into several functional areas, warehouses, barracks, headquarters and the Explosive Ordnance School.

The initial American attack plan called for two UH-1 helicopters, each carrying a squad to land and secure two landing zones (LZs) in the center of the compound directly opposite the guard force billets. The *Hueys* were to be followed by Chinook H-47 heavy lift troop carriers delivering the balance of the assault forces that were targeted against the three primary functional areas. However, after learning that some elements of the PDF were alert to the impending American actions and presuming the guard force at the depot could be one of those, the choice of LZs was shifted to an area outside the complex. The alternative sites were located on the nearby golf course just south of the fenced complex. The golf course LZ's had been used in a recent CRE (Contingency Reaction Exercises) and the helo pilots were familiar with them. This factor reduced the problems normally associated with the last minute change of a LZ particularly in a night operation such as this.

When the two *Hueys* began their approach they received fire from positions north of the golf course, which had been established by the PDF in reaction to an earlier CRE. However a rocket run by the accompanying AH-1G *Cobra* gunship, who was on station waiting for such a PDF reaction, quickly silenced the PDF gunners and the two *Huey's* deposited their squads on target without any losses. Within 30 seconds of the *Huey's* liftoff, the first CH-47 Chinook delivered its platoon of American reinforcements. A second CH-47 deposited the remainder of the force within a few minutes.

The original assault plan called for a forceful breech of the perimeter chain link fence with the platoons then fanning out to secure their individual objectives. However, once on the ground the lead American elements found an open gate, set up a protective overwatch position inside the gate and in rapid succession all three elements were inside the complex and moving away from each other and toward their assigned targets. One unit swung northwest to the warehouse and mess hall area, a second headed for the troop barracks and the third made a beeline for the headquarters complex. The American forces were the target of scattered small arms fire but no sustained PDF resistance was encountered, although there were several brief engagements during the clearing of the warehouses and the barracks. The potentially most lethal threat to the advancing Americans was a series of booby traps discovered in the final approach to the PDF Explosive Ordnance School.

The school was located at the north end of the depot in the vicinity of the initial small arms fire. The American force cordoned off the school area until dawn and then the area was gingerly swept for PDF troopers. None were found. The Delta company infantryman did not attempt to disarm any of the booby traps. This work was left to U.S. EOD teams that were called in to sweep the area.

By dawn, all of the Atlantic area H-Hour targets had been successfully secured and Colon City isolated.

Unidentified U.S. Infantry troopers loading onto *Blackhawks* (UH-60). Photo courtesy U.S. Army Center for Military History.

Aerial view of Panama Viejo Complex with PDF barrack on left, old ruins in center and horse stables on right. Courtesy of US Army Center for Military History.

CHAPTER FIFTEEN
PHASE TWO: AIR ASSAULT OPERATIONS

Operational timing was a critical factor during the execution of phase one (H-Hour) operations and was affected by scattered patches of PDF anticipation, nervousness, and readiness. Timing was no less critical during the deployment and execution of phase two operations. The timing and surprise of the planned follow-on air assault operations were also severely affected by weather delays in the strategic deployment, and the slow assembly at Torrijos of the units of 82nd Airborne Division.

The brigade airdrop had been scheduled in two increments. A 28-ship heavy equipment drop was to be followed by the personnel drop. The heavy drop included eight *Sheridans*, four 105mm howitzers, and 72 HMMWVs plus an assortment of STS motorcycles and PJ all-terrain vehicles (ATVs). Some of the HMMWVs were specially configured as air-droppable Assault Command Post Vehicles (ACPV) and were equipped with a mixture of communication capabilities. The typical ACPV included three TACSAT radios, four FM radios, plus teletype and facsimile terminals. Other heavy equipment included vehicles carrying power generators. The heavy equipment drop occurred on time, 45 minutes after H-Hour, with the 28 C-141s disgorging hundreds of tons of equipment. Some landed to the right of the LZ in the adjacent marshy swamp which severely complicated recovery and immediate use.

However, the icing problem at Pope AFB caused a greater challenge. The weather delay split the follow-on personnel drop into several elements. The first group of eight aircraft arrived over Torrijos shortly after 2:00 AM, approximately 30 minutes behind schedule. It was another 90 minutes before the next two aircraft arrived. Two more arrived at 3:50 AM, three more at 4:00, another pair at 4:55, and the last five at 5:15 AM.

The initial eight aircraft approached the small, i.e., narrow, drop zone (400 meters versus the preferred 800 meters) in a trailing, echeloned to-the-right pattern. The combination of the narrower drop zone, the prevailing winds and the echelon pattern put several loads of paratroopers landing far to the right of the drop zone and into a mixture of marsh and tall Kuna (elephant) grass. It took the troopers that landed some distance off the DZ (in some cases as much as 800 meters), and outside the airfield's chainlink fence, more than an hour to slog their way to firm ground near the runways. Typically, they linked up in small groups and, using their bayonets (and in a few cases machetes), followed a compass heading toward the sounds of the fighting. One group stumbled on a heavy drop HMMWV, proceeded to strip the parachutes and drop lines from it, and drove it to the unit assembly area. Most of the troopers were not that lucky and had to plod their way out of thick vegetation.

CONFRONTATION ZONE

Once on firm recognizable ground, the paratroopers quickly moved to their assembly points and began the wait for the helicopters that would deliver them against the three second tier PDF garrisons that were their combat objectives.

At 5:00 AM, fifteen minutes before the arrival of the last two aircraft over the drop zone, the 82nd Airborne Division commander radioed General Stiner (COMJTF SOUTH) that the 82nd had officially linked up with the Ranger command element. At 6:00 the 82nd CG assumed operational control of the Rangers and, with the bulk of his force assembled, advised General Stiner he was prepared to execute the three air assault missions in the planned sequence: Panama Viejo, then Tinajitas (San Miguelito) and, last, Fort Cimarron.

The brigade commander planned to use the majority of a battalion on each of the objectives delivering the forces in nominal, company-sized increments. The three air assault operations marked the initiation of the second major phase of offensive operations.

PANAMA VIEJO

Panama Viejo (Old Panama), the original Spanish settlement, was established in the 1519, burned by pirates, and rebuilt of stone in the 1600's. Weather, neglect, and age had reduced the stone remnants to skeletons. The ruins of the church tower and surrounding shells of the old complex stand on a scenic point of land looking out across the Bay of Panama along the eastern shoreline of the city. Most days of the year it is a calm and peaceful place, with balmy breezes and tall palm trees – normally a very pleasant location.

Behind the ruins is a collection of horse stables and corrals. The nearby PDF barracks had a capacity of 250 soldiers. The barracks sat beside and to the front of the ruins, with its rear parallel to the shoreline and its front facing inland across a small cobblestone road that led to the ruins. According to the PDF Order of Battle, 180 of these troops were from the 1st Cavalry Squadron, a unit providing guards and ceremonial support to the Panamanian President. The squadron had 48 horses at the nearby stable. The remaining 70 soldiers were members of UESAT, the elite Panamanian anti-terrorist unit. These highly-trained soldiers had been stationed on Flamenco Island at the far end of Fort Amador, but after the October coup showed them to be too isolated, the unit was moved to Panama Viejo.

The UESAT troopers were armed and trained in a wide variety of weapons, including Uzi submachine guns with night sights, anti-tank rockets, sniper rifles, and grenade launchers. Additionally, they possessed state-of-the-art body armor and were skilled snipers. For added defense, a .50 caliber machine gun had been mounted on the roof of the two-story barracks, and a Soviet-bloc 4-barreled anti-aircraft gun (ZPU 23-4) was positioned on the shoreline. Both commanded an unobstructed view out over the bay. The combination of the two automatic weapons posed a limited but lethal threat.

The mission to seize and secure Panama Viejo was assigned to the 2nd Battalion of the 504th Parachute Infantry Regiment (2-504), of the 82nd Airborne Division.

The battalion had been scheduled to parachute into Torrijos two hours after the Rangers conducted the initial 1:00 AM combat assault. Following the airdrop, the battalion was to assemble near the Tocumen runway and wait for transloading to a fleet of UH-60 *Blackhawk* helicopters for a short 12 minute flight to two LZs bracketing the PDF barracks at Panama Viejo. Ground maneuver planning, to include selection of the proposed LZs, had been conducted by the battalion staff while at Fort Bragg and the air movement sequence prepared by Army aviation units in Panama.

The intent was to accomplish the mission through the measured application of overwhelming force, while avoiding the indiscriminate use of firepower. The area was to be cordoned off by the 2-504 rifle companies, and the PDF were to be told of the opportunity to surrender by the Psychological Operations team via loudspeaker.

Two landing zones had been selected for the near simultaneous troop insertion. They were LZ Bobcat, an overgrown soccer field located immediately north of the barracks that was covered in (a Panamanian version of) elephant grass and LZ Lion on the south side, along the exposed mud flats of the bay shoreline.

AH-1 *Cobra* gunship helicopters from the 7th Infantry Division would escort the troop delivery H-60 *Blackhawks*, which were from the 7th Infantry Division, and the 228th Aviation Regiment stationed at Fort Kobbe. This was the second combat lift of the operation for the helicopter crews. At H-Hour, they had delivered the paratroopers of the 508th into Ft. Amador.

The Panama Viejo plan also called for an anti-tank company, mounted in HMMWVs, sporting .50 caliber machine guns, and two *Sheridans* with their 152mm guns, to quickly transit the six miles between the Torrijos/Tocumen airhead and Panama Viejo, and reinforce the helicopter-inserted paratroopers.

Leaving Fort Bragg and the freezing rain behind shortly after midnight, the 504th paratroopers exited their MAC C-141 transports over the Torrijos complex three to four hours later. They jumped into a hot, humid Panamanian sky punctuated with small arms and tracer fire. The fires at the Comandancia could still be seen in the distance, and a sporadic spray of tracers laced the horizon as the troopers exited the aircraft. Many of the jumpers landed in the tall grass, marsh, and trees that populated the area along the north side of the runway more than a hundred yards from their intended landing zone.

After suffering some initial disorientation, the 82nd soldiers shucked their parachute harnesses and attempted to reach their designated assembly areas. Although the assembly went slower than planned, most of the troopers reached their assembly areas within 40 minutes and began to form into their assault groups.

Meanwhile, during the predawn hours, the aircrews of the helicopter task force had tried to get some rest after delivering the 508th to Amador. They lay on the ground near their refueled aircraft and took some quiet pride in the fact they had accomplished their initial mission without any casualties to either personnel or machines.

Their thoughts and rest were interrupted shortly after daylight when word was received that the 82nd Airborne was on the ground at Torrijos and ready to conduct the assault missions. Within minutes, the two-company aviation task force lifted off from its Empire Range nest and headed for the pickup location at Torrijos some 30 minutes away.

The two-aviation company commanders anticipated a far greater threat from enemy fire at Panama Viejo than they had encountered at Ft. Amador earlier and had prepared their aircrews for this possibility. The air assault against the PDF complex at Panama Viejo began shortly before 7:00 AM, later than planned, due to the delayed and staggered arrival of the 82nd. The first wave of helicopters went into LZ Lion, the landing zone along the beach. The second wave inserted its troopers in LZ Bobcat on the land-side of the PDF cuartel (barracks).

The approach of first lift and its subsequent touch down sparked intense automatic and small arms fire from the barracks and the surrounding area. Despite the firing, the *Blackhawks* held a steady formation, preserving the unit integrity of the assault forces. The *Cobra* gunships withheld their fire, not wanting to fire unless a very clear target was presented. The ZPU 23-4 sitting on the beach presented such a target. The PDF troopers manning the anti-aircraft gun fled without firing a shot as a *Cobra* gunship rolled in and took aim on their exposed position.

Although both insertions were made without casualties to the aircrews, some of the infantrymen inserted "along the beach" had a few terrifying moments. The troops who disembarked close to the shoreline had no problem. But the last of the follow-on aircraft discharged their passengers farther out, over the deceptively firm-looking mud flats. Dropping a few feet from the helicopters, many of the heavily loaded troopers quickly sank into the soft muck up to their armpits. The door gunners were the first to witness the predicament of the mired paratroopers. They immediately alerted their pilots who maneuvered the helicopters back over the struggling troops and, despite persistent PDF fire, went into a hover and slowly descended until the stranded soldiers could grab the landing gear and be pulled free. Some Panamanian civilians witnessing the scene quickly set up a human chain running from shore to the American soldiers, helping them attain the safety of solid land.

Meanwhile, things were hot on LZ Bobcat. Automatic fire from (communist-built) AK-47 assault rifles and pistols sprayed the area. The LZ was covered with tall grass, which protected the American troopers from

PDF fire, but at the same time, made it extremely difficult for the Americans to orient themselves, or find each other, or the sources of the PDF fire. A sergeant from C Company located one of the PDF weapon positions, and called for a grenade launcher. After firing several rounds and exposing himself to a return hail of PDF gunfire, he took careful aim and launched several grenade rounds at the position. He then directed the fire of a U.S. machine gun team and neutralized the PDF position, allowing the American troopers to move off the LZ.

Once assembled, the American squads moved to seal off the immediate area and seize the barracks. After a short fire-fight with some defenders, the Americans entered the barracks and began to sweep the internal areas. Quickly searching the barracks, the paratroopers found an eating area with half-eaten breakfast and the weapons room in great disarray. Shortly after the American unit had established control of the complex, they captured several unarmed PDF members who, unaware of the events of the preceding seven hours, blissfully drove up to the cuartel in their cars ready to put in another routine workday. It was discovered later that many of the hard core PDF, including most of the UESAT soldiers, had left the barracks during the night and had taken up positions in nearby civilian buildings.

Shortly after 9:00 AM, a convoy of seven vehicles, including two *Sheridans,* began to move out of the airport complex to reinforce the paratroopers at Panama Viejo. Their path was blocked at a small bridge just outside of the airport by two burned-out vehicles and a PDF element with automatic weapons. A brief but intense firefight followed as the Americans cleared and forced the blockade. While the American troopers were engaged in this effort, some of the PDF force retired and assumed positions in a building some 200 meters behind the bridge and began bringing machine gun fire on the advancing Americans. A combination of American rifle fire and an LAW rocket silenced the PDF weapons team. Eleven PDF died in the subsequent room clearing operation before the American convoy could resume its movement to Panama Viejo.

The contest for the picturesque site continued periodically throughout the day. A typical tactic involved a “civilian” car approaching an American position along the public road. As the vehicle closed with the position, heads, followed by guns would appear in the passenger seats and let loose with automatic weapons fire. Nearly a dozen cars full of armed PDF or Dignity Battalion members drove by the American guard positions. Nine vehicles were stopped or destroyed by fire from American grenades and machine gun fire. A PDF V-300 armored car, one of the nine, met its demise at the hands of an 82nd trooper wielding a shoulder-fired AT-4 anti-armor rocket similar to the weapons used by the SF team at the Pacora Bridge and the SEALs at Paitilla. A total of five additional V-300 vehicles were destroyed by AH-64 *Apache* attack helicopters (from the 82nd Airborne Division) during the securing of the Panama Viejo area. Intermittent sniper fire continued throughout the day and three PDF mortar rounds slammed into the area, but did not cause any American casualties.

Around 7:00 PM that evening, the 2nd Battalion of the 504th was ordered to send a company overland along the coast road toward Panama City to secure the Marriott Hotel from possible attacks by DIGBATs or PDF. After some quick planning, B Company with an engineer squad and the brigade surgeon attached, moved out on foot along the road leading to the hotel. The American force got no further than 150 meters before being ambushed by four PDF regulars. All four were killed without injury to the paratroopers, and the march continued.

Scarcely 300 meters past the ambush scene, a large truck suddenly careened onto the semi-dark street and its occupants began wildly spewing machine gun and AK-47 fire in the direction of the American column. The truck quickly closed with the slow-moving American troops, spraying the length of the column, wounding two of the marching troopers. The lead platoon returned fire almost to a man, raking the truck as it accelerated past the Americans. A person in the cab was firing a pistol and threw a grenade as the truck passed the American column. The grenade sailed harmlessly over the American troops and landed in the bay.

The 3rd Platoon, coming up the road behind the 1st platoon, heard the commotion and saw the oncoming truck, which by now was moving at about 35 mph. Stepping directly into the path of the truck, one of the troopers took aim with his M203 grenade launcher and let fly. The round detonated on the passenger side of the cab, blowing off the arm of the pistol-firer, but the truck kept coming. The trooper stood his ground, loaded a second grenade and fired again. This time the round exploded on the driver's windshield; the truck swerved and crashed into a nearby building. The result was five Panamanians killed and two wounded. The truck yielded three machine guns with hot barrels and three AK-47s with almost empty clips. The company quickly resumed its march in the growing darkness with a small sense of elation and greatly heightened alertness.

During all of this, one of the battalion medics and a radio operator had found a white civilian van and converted it into a combat ambulance. Following the advancing company, the pair began a series of round trips, delivering wounded to the 82nd's aid station which had been set up at Panama Viejo. During the third of these trips, the vehicle was ambushed. The windshield was blasted away and one member of the self-appointed, two-man ambulance service was wounded. The vehicle was still operative and the remaining soldier was preparing to resume his shuttle when the brigade commander stopped him because of the danger.

Meanwhile, the paratrooper column, reinforced with a *Sheridan* and a truck, and now advancing under the protective night eyes and firepower of an AC-130 (on a surveillance and fire support mission), resumed the march to the Marriott. Twice during the movement, the ACs night capabilities proved useful. In one case, an early observation allowed the ground force to bypass a PDF ambush and in another case the 40mm gun of the AC was called upon to eliminate an active PDF sniper position. The convoy reached the Marriott Hotel about 9:00 PM and began the tedious process of clearing the multistory, several hundred room building. Two and half hours later, the hotel was declared secured and 106 civilians, including 29 Americans, plus the hotel staff were safe. The next day the American civilians were driven to Panama Viejo in an armed convoy and from there were transported by helicopter to Howard for evacuation back to the United States.

TINAJITAS
SAN MIGUELITO BARRACKS

While the 504th was busy at Panama Viejo, the helicopters and aircrews of Task Force Talon conducted their third mission of the day. After dropping the 504th at Panama Viejo, the helicopters had returned to Torrijos to pick up another element of the 82nd. This force was to be delivered to a set of LZs near the PDF barracks at San Miguelito which sits on a hilltop called Tinajitas.

Surprise was no longer possible. Visibility from Cerro Tinajitas was essentially unobstructed. Located a mile and a half north of the main road to the airport on the tallest landmass in the area, the PDF could see the approaching choppers from virtually any direction. The approach path was dictated by the location of the LZs. The PDF had deployed fire teams on the surrounding hills, and they began firing and continued firing as the helicopters deposited the American infantrymen on the lower fully exposed LZs.

For these reasons, and the proximity of Panamanian civilian housing, the American paratroopers were inserted on an adjacent but lower hill more than 500 yards from, but within lethal small arms range of, the PDF positions.

The 82nd paratroopers were picked up by *Blackhawk* (UH-60) helicopters on the main runway. The boarding went quickly and the liftoff smoothly. Once airborne the choppers formed up and circled over the runway and took up heading for the LZ. The built-up, i.e. metropolitan, area of Panama City could be seen out the left side of the aircraft with the more rural areas to the right. The initial lift numbered eight troop carrying helicopters, down from the ten planned. Two of the aircraft had received extensive damage going into Panama Viejo earlier and had been declared temporarily unserviceable. Each of the *Blackhawks* carried in excess of twenty troopers. The troop lift was escorted by two *Apache* attack helicopters.

As the lead choppers approached the LZ, they came within small arms range and began being peppered about 300 meters short of the LZ. To some of the troopers, the small arms fire sounded like popcorn exploding accompanied by a tic-tic-tic as the shells hit the aluminum skin of the helicopter. The helicopter crew chiefs, doubling as door gunners on the run-in, returned the PDF fire with bursts from their swivel-mounted M-60 machine gun. As they identified targets, the *Apache*s turned loose with their weapons.

The initial lift touched down at 8:30 AM. Both of the lead helicopters received small arms fire during their approach and flare-out, but the *Blackhawks* delivered the 82nd troopers unscathed. The 82nd soldiers unloaded in 10 seconds and then set up a base of fire for the touchdown of the follow-on helicopters.

Because of the severity of the PDF fire, some of the helicopters did not land, and in those cases the troopers exited the aircraft by jumping/dropping 10-20-30 feet to the ground which in many areas was covered by stands of elephant grass. The LZ was a lower hill mass than the PDF garrison and had been picked, at least partially, because it was not in the line of fire from the PDF garrison. However, the PDF soldiers had taken up positions outside of the compound proper which gave them a clear field of fire on the helicopters and the LZ and part of the higher hill mass.

Again, the minimum loss of life ROE came into play. It was decided not to attack the PDF barracks with gunship fire or land the U.S. troopers directly inside the PDF compound. The former because of the predictable loss of Panamanian lives, and the latter because of the potential loss of American lives during the insertion which would have been made in broad daylight.

The Tinajitas air assault involved three separate lifts on two LZ, putting the helicopters and their aircrews into the maelstrom of PDF fire for the fifth or sixth time that morning. Every helicopter involved in the lift received extensive hits during the final run-ins, but no aircrews or American troopers were seriously injured.

The PDF ground fire complicated life somewhat for the aircrews, but more so for the assaulting infantrymen who had to contend with the PDF fire during the majority of their uphill climb. The original battalion plan called for one company to fix the front of the hill and the PDF defenders while the other two companies maneuvered around and up the flanks. However, circumstances on the ground, including the broader PDF disposition and the terrain, i.e. the steepness of the hill and density of the foliage, dictated otherwise. Alpha company was in the lead and received fire support from an AC-130 *Spectre* and two OA-37 *Dragonflys* that provided suppressive fire during the long slow climb. The OA-37s a small, agile, observation attack aircraft were armed with 14 high-explosive and 14 white phosphorous (Willy Pete) anti-armor rockets and a rapid-fire 7.62mm mini-gun.

Charlie and Bravo companies followed Alpha up the hill. All three companies basically went straight up, climbing and clawing their way toward the top. During the tortuous climb, the battalion fire support officer, in partnership with the unit USAF Air Liaison Officer who was controlling the airstrikes, could, using binoculars, see a PDF 120mm mortar crew firing the weapon. Due to the proximity of civilian on-lookers, some less than 100 meters from the mortar, the FSO chose not to engage the mortar crew with air strikes. However, the company's own 60mm mortars were used quite effectively during the hill climb.

It took the lead elements two hours under the hot sun to maneuver up the steep hillside to the highest point, which was offset from the plateau where the PDF complex was sited. After reaching the higher crest, the paratroopers then came down on the PDF garrison, encountering little resistance during this maneuver. Upon reaching the garrison, the Americans learned the PDF defenders had retired in good order, melting into the surrounding *barrios* and jungle. At 2:33 PM, after a thorough search, the American battalion commander declared the hilltop and the barracks secured. The cost was two American fatalities, one on the LZ and one during the climb.

PDF sniper fire and an occasional mortar round continued to visit the Americans paratroopers throughout the balance of the day and into the night. The next morning, the surrounding barrio became the focus of deliberate clearing operations by the American infantrymen, and the harassing fire almost ceased.

The Americans captured two French-made 120s long-range mortars when they took the barracks. A third was captured by a patrol initiated on the basis of information received from Panamanian civilians. The fourth tube in the battery was destroyed on D-Day plus One by a two ship A-37 airstrike called in after an American patrol had conducted a reconnaissance and pinpointed the mortar launch site. The site was a warehouse from which a PDF/Dignity Battalion team would run the mortar out, launch a few rounds and run it back inside. The warehouse was hit by two salvos of 2.75 inch HE rockets which tore through the outer walls causing a series of explosions. The American observers did not see anyone leave the demolished building nor were any more mortars rounds launched from the site.

On D+Two, the 82nd paratroopers began patrolling off the hill and into the congested civilian neighborhoods that stretched out around the base of the hill and along the highway that ran from the airport to Panama City. During the first few days, American convoys transiting the road from the airport would be ambushed by small arms fire and find burning vehicles blocking the roadway. The convoys, with *Sheridans* in the lead and air support overhead, would blast their way through the choke points and continue on their way to the Americans garrisoned at the former PDF hilltop compound.

FORT CIMARRON

The fourth airlift of the day for the two aviation companies involved another return to Torrijos to pick-up another load of paratroopers, and then a flight eastward past the Pacora Bridge to Fort Cimarron. The 4th Battalion, 325th Infantry Regiment was scheduled to make the final major air assault of the day into the sprawling ranch-like campus which was the home of PDF Battalion 2000. The PDF Battalion took its name from the purpose of its creation and its mission: assumption of security for the Canal on January 1, 2000. The PDF battalion was a hybrid-combined arms organization with an airborne company, an air assault company and an armored vehicle company plus a heavy weapons unit which included mobile rapid fire anti-aircraft guns. The armored company was equipped with a combination of V-150 and V-300 Cadillac-Gage Armored cars with some of the V-300 vehicles mounting 90mm guns. In the words of one 82nd Airborne artillery officer, “All in all a pretty high velocity ‘cop’ to go against,” in a reference to the PDF being largely a police force.

The American Battalion’s assault plan included using its Delta company’s platoons, with their .50 caliber equipped HMMWV, to establish blocking and support positions while the heli-lift would deliver the initial forces to be followed in close order by a ground convoy with additional forces.

The lead chopper touched down at 12:05 PM. During the course of the next hour, two companies of 82nd troopers were deposited on two LZs some distance removed from the garrison proper. This was accomplished without any PDF interference. The 82nd paratroopers were not the first Americans to visit Cimarron. A Special Forces team had maintained surveillance on the installation since H-Hour, and a small Ranger reconnaissance element had moved overland during the early daylight hours. The Rangers had linked up with the SF troopers and the combined element constituted a small blocking force. They were supported by an on-call airborne AC-130 *Spectre* gunship and an Army *Apache*.

Once the full heliborne force was on the ground, one company initiated patrols to the south and the west. The second company moved to the high ground and by late afternoon had assumed an overwatch position of the complex. The PDF detected this movement and fired on the maneuvering Americans. Following the prevailing ROE, the American commander had the attached PSYOP team broadcast a surrender call and a warning of air strikes if the PDF did not lay down its arms. The American surrender call and warning went unheeded. After an appropriate wait, the ground commander requested air assistance. A flight of two USAF OA-37 *Dragonfly* aircraft out of Howard provided the first assistance.

As one aircraft dropped illumination flares, the other fired high-explosive rockets into the garrison motor pool where the PDF had positioned three long-range 120mm mortars and a row of armored cars. The two aircraft continued to alternate roles until all the mortars and the armored vehicles were considered inoperable. In the meantime, heavy machine gun fire erupted from one of the PDF barracks, pinning down some of the 82nd troopers. One of OA-37s made repeated single-rocket attacks on the position, surgically silencing the PDF fire. Meanwhile, the other *Dragonfly*, now out of ordnance, was radioing coordinates to an AC-130 that was assuming a firing orbit as a prelude to bringing its guns to bear on the barracks from which the PDF fire originated. However, the FACs also called in a pair of A-7D strike fighters, which flew two strafing runs at PDF ground positions expending 1,000 rounds of 20mm ammunition during each pass.

The AC-130 was then cleared to engage the last active PDF position. The AC-130 conducted the fire mission as requested and suppressed the PDF fire. The barracks fell silent. The AC-130 remained on station above the 82nd for the next four hours (9:00 PM to 1:00 AM). Early the next morning, December 21st, the 82nd troopers conducted a sweep of the complex. At 7:30 AM, the American commander reported the complex secured. The bodies of 13 PDF soldiers were found in the sweep and 10 PDF combat vehicles were confirmed destroyed. No PDF injured or wounded were found and no PDF soldiers were captured or surrendered. They apparently took to the jungles during or after the air missions.

Initially, the lack of PDF troopers at the Battalion 2000 complex presented the American command with the troublesome question of where the battalion and its combat companies were. Had Operation *Montana* been initiated during the night of December 19th or had other PDF contingency plans been put into action? Had the battalion taken to the countryside or the city in small sniper/assault groups?

A segment of the sprawling Fort Cimarron complex located several miles west of the Torrijos/Tocumen airport. Photo courtesy of the author.

Unidentified 82nd Airborne Trooper. Photo courtesy U.S. Army Center for Military History.

CHAPTER SIXTEEN
THIRD PHASE OPERATIONS

The initial phases of *Blue Spoon* had, in spite of the bad weather and the resulting delay of the 82nd, been executed successfully. All the major U.S. objectives, except the capture of General Noriega, had been accomplished in the first 12 hours of the operation. Although many PDF units, elements, and individuals initially resisted, no major PDF units had conducted counterattacks against U.S. forces.

By dawn on D-day, the 193rd Brigade had effectively sealed off the western sections of Panama City within an arc that ran from the back of Fort Clayton all the way through Balboa to Fort Amador. By mid-day on D plus One, the eastern segment of the cordon was sealed off by elements of the 82nd and the Ranger battalions that had moved westward after securing Torrijos, Tinajitas and Panama Viejo.

As the Commanding General of the 82nd Airborne Division (Task Force Pacific) reviewed the situation on the evening of D-Day (December 20th), units of his Task Force occupied key positions from the eastern edge of Panama City to Fort Cimarron; however, both Panama City and Colon remained lethal environments.

COLON NEUTRALIZATION

Meanwhile, Task Force Atlantic, after completing its series of initial combat and security actions outside of Colon, closed off the city and waited. The city was sealed off on night one and after a full day of PSYOP broadcast and leaflet drops the American forces elected to move into the city on the second night. The PSYOP campaign had advised the population that the American objective was to clear the city and disarm any remaining PDF and Dignity Battalion forces and restore order and civilian rule as quickly as possible. The population was also advised for safety's sake to remain in their houses. There was no need to rush American troops into the highly congested rabbit warren that was peninsula Colon. The impact of the American cordon settled in on PDF soldiers trapped within the city and they began surrendering to the American element holding the only land exit. Nicknamed the Colon Bottleneck, this narrow stretch of land, a causeway, originally built in 1851by the Panama railroad, was the sight of such a continuing tempo of PDF surrenders that the American military entry into the city was intentionally postponed until D+3, December 22th.

On D+3, three American rifle companies, squeezed into an LCM of the 1097th Boat Transportation Company conducted the second Army amphibious assault of the operation. The LCM company delivered the force into the warehouse and shop district known as the "duty free zone." While the three companies moved off the LCMs into the eastern part of the city, two other American companies advanced overland into the city from the

Bottleneck. The advancing ground forces were met by sporadic sniper fire, but continued their movement to their key objectives: the PDF Military Zone (MZ) headquarters, the Department of Investigation (DENI) Station and the PDF naval facilities at Cristobal Pier. All three of the objectives were quickly seized and secured with minimum resistance.

Task Force Atlantic immediately began security patrols throughout the city with infantry squads and military police patrols. The next day, D+4, December 23rd, the task force switched modes and moved from combat and combat security operations to the maintenance of law and order, and the initiation of Civil Military Operations (CMO). CMO is reconstruction and humanitarian aid.

On Day Four, General Thurman switched his operating location, spending more time away from Quarry Heights and a growing amount of that time at Ft. Clayton where he was closer to General Stiner and the JTF SOUTH Tactical Operations Center (TOC).

PROMOTE LIBERTY

Although the dozen civilians, including one American who had been taken hostage by the PDF in the Marriott hotel bar 15 minutes before H-Hour, had been released unharmed after being detained for five hours, there was concern among senior officers that the potential for future hostage situations still existed. In addition, Operation *Montana* was still a possibility.

Beginning at noon on D-Day, the balance of the 7th Infantry Division, the 1st and 2nd Brigades, along with additional MP units, began landing at Torrijos which was now operating under U.S. military control. The American troop flow would continue for the next several days. It was now time to shift mind sets and begin follow-on clearing and stability operations as part of the third phase "pacification and rebuilding."

The 7th Infantry Division's (Task Force Atlantic) plan of action was developed at the brigade level as this was the force that was called upon in the original SOUTHCOM plan (OPORD 90-1) and the subsequent XVIII Corps Plan (OPORD 90-2). Colonel Dave Hale was the Commander of the lead 7th ID brigade (the 1st) to deploy to Panama and was the senior 7th ID officer on the ground during the earlier security reinforcement known as *Nimrod Dancer*. The SOUTHCOM and Army South Commanders at the time that Hale's 1st Brigade was deployed were General Woerner and Major General Loeffke. Hale's brigade set the pattern for the follow-on brigades. The 3rd Brigade rotated in next. Under the command of Colonel Keith Kellogg, the 3rd refined the plan and established the training parameters for his brigade and its rotation replacement the 2nd Brigade. It was the 2nd Brigade, under Colonel Linwood Burney, that was in Panama when the operation began.

The balance of the 7th Infantry Division at Fort Ord, California had received the alert order on the 18th and began its 18-hour "wheels-in-well" marshaling and mobilization sequence. In contrast to the proximity enjoyed by the XVIII Corps and the 82nd Airborne to the adjacent departure airfield, Pope Air Force Base, the 7th had to move its personnel 152 miles by road to its principal departure field, Travis Air Force Base. Because of the extended travel distance, the bulk of the Ready Brigade's equipment was pre-positioned at Travis and rotated as each of the brigades assumed the "alert status." The equipment was under the control and care of the Division's logistics support element, i.e. the Division's Departure Airfield Control Group (DACG) which was based at Travis and married to the Air Force's 62nd Airlift Wing. The 152 mile geographic separation required a very tight and well-rehearsed deployment system. The process was fully exercised on a monthly basis with at least a full battalion moving to the airhead each month and a full brigade quarterly.

The first *Just Cause* movement for the 7th ID began in the late afternoon of December 19th. The weather was bad and the Christmas shopping traffic added to the potential for road mishaps and travel time. The road trip typically took four hours, but, recognizing the potential for the unexpected delay and interruption, the Division advanced the "roll-out" convoy departure time by two hours. This was a fortunate decision as a heavy layer of fog began to blanket parts of the California coast. A major concentration occurred at Travis Air Force Base where, even with Air Force ground guides, it was difficult to see the gray-green Air Force C-141 and C-5 transports until within 30-40 feet and had to be much closer to read the subdued black tail numbers. In spite of the weather and the need to reconfigure some of the pre-grouped loads (because of the greater use of giant C-5s over the typically available C-141s), the lead aircraft departed Travis at 12:56 AM on the 20th. This was four minutes ahead of its scheduled 1:00 AM 18-hour wheels-up time. The balance of the flow went smoothly until the weather and airfield overload conditions forced the activation of another departure airfield.

The second field pressed into use was a civilian airfield at Monterey, CA on the 22nd. A splinter, i.e. second, DACG was created to handle the loadout at Monterey. Teamed with Air Force ground crews, refuelers, cargo handlers and loadmasters this operation was soon running smoothly.

As elements of the 7th ID arrived at Tocumen beginning on D-Day, the Division Commander, Major General Cavezza, was faced with a major logistic challenge. He had no way to move his troops to the back country. He asked the commander of a group of C-130 transports from the South Carolina National Guard (who were in between missions) to move his troops. The Guard commander responded positively and with the concurrence of the Air Force Commander, Lt. General Kempf, a shuttle operation was begun. The Guard aircraft moved the 7th ID Brigade across half the country from Tocumen to Malek airfield adjacent to the provincial capital of David near to the Costa Rican border. The operation was conducted without mishap.

Subsequent to the initial use of the Guard C-130s, the Division was forced to pump fuel directly from the C-130s wing-fuel tanks to support helicopter operations at David when it was learned that the Panamanian fuel stored at the airfield was contaminated and could not be used in the Division's helicopters. This direct "wet-wing" refueling expediency was quickly replaced with the excess C-130 fuel being transferred into fuel bladders from which the helicopter fleet drew its gas. Without this type of cross-service cooperation, the job of the 7th ID in expanding and controlling its very extensive area of operation, which extended to the Costa Rican border on the north and the Colombian border on the south, would have been far more difficult.

As the 7th ID flowed in, and the brigades and battalions were assigned to their individual and widely dispersed areas of operations, the Division decided to break down the Division's Medical battalion into direct support elements. Medical teams were attached directly to the brigades who integrated this crucial capability with the maneuver units. The decision proved to be highly effective, and the close attachment earned a number of these forward-deployed medics the Combat Medic Badge.

Later, as part of the transition from combat to security and nation building, the 7th Special Forces Group (SFG) brought in an additional battalion. The battalion picked up responsibility for the "outback" from the 7th ID which then withdrew and distributed selected elements of its brigades and battalions into the city, relieving the 82nd Airborne Division. However, the 7th ID still maintained a presence in the countryside by conducting mobile operations (in coordination with the 7th SFG teams) throughout the western provinces for the better part of a month.

One of the first of the many nation building efforts was given to Task Force Bayonet (the 193rd Infantry) during the early evening hours of D-day. The mission: make all arrangements, protocol, presentation, and security, for the inauguration of the new Panamanian government. The inauguration was to take place at the Legislative Palace in the middle of downtown Panama City at approximately 11:00 AM the next morning, D+One.

A company of APCs were dispatched at approximately 6:00 PM to initiate clearing and securing the palace. Beginning at 8:00 PM, a cross-section of support and security personnel assembled at Fort Clayton to conduct the planning and preparations for the ceremony and reception.

Four personnel from the protocol office were tasked with transforming the sterile auditorium into an appropriate diplomatic and ceremonial setting. The team included two American civilian women who were knowledgeable about the protocol and presentation requirements, and two soldiers to assist them in the physical arrangements. The convoy carrying the team arrived at the palace shortly before the building and the immediate surrounding area were declared secured by Task Force Bayonet infantry and MP units. Small arms fire could be heard in the vicinity, and it was impossible to know who was doing the shooting or who were the targets.

The protocol team entered the building quickly, using the bulk of the APCs to provide some cover from potential sniper fire. Once inside, the team made its way to the auditorium and surveyed the designated inauguration site. The site survey was concluded within an hour. A small HMMWV convoy returned to Fort Clayton to pick up the material deemed essential and appropriate to the decorum of the impending event.

The APCs remained at the site to insure security. The protocol team and full setup crew returned at approximately 4:00 AM. Setup activities began in earnest before dawn and were completed ahead of schedule, but not without some problems.

Approximately two hours before the scheduled swearing-in time, one of the security teams stopped a civilian car within two blocks of the palace at the outer edge of the American security cordon. The occupants, two men, were apprehended without incident, searched, and found to be carrying PDF identification cards. The car was searched and two loaded AK-47 assault rifles, three 9 mm pistols, and large amounts of ammunition for both types of weapons were found. The men were detained and preparations for the ceremony continued. Panamanian dignitaries began to arrive earlier than expected, complicating the final preparations and increasing security concerns.

President Elect Endara and Vice Presidents Calderon and Ford arrived at approximately 10:30 AM. The official ceremony was carried out as planned at 11:00 AM.

REFUGEE SUPPORT

Five and a half hours earlier, as dawn broke on D+1 (Thursday the 21st), the number of homeless refugees from "El Chorrillo," who had sought safety at the U.S. Balboa High School grounds and the nearby athletic stadium, was in the thousands and growing. The entire stadium was filled with squatters. Portions of the stadium were flooded from open showers and garbage was quickly accumulating everywhere.

By mid-morning U.S. Army civil affairs teams were on-site trying to organize the displaced families. Portions of the high school were converted into infirmaries. Access to the overloaded toilet facilities in the gymnasium and the Balboa stadium had to be controlled. U.S. Army civilian engineers, most of who were Panamanian civilians, were called in to help. They provided plumbing services including much needed additional toilet facilities, showers, garbage collection and disposal points, and clothes washing sinks. The engineers also improved the drainage of the stadium and adjacent areas. Within 13 hours, the chaos of the stadium was transformed into a safe, sanitary, and orderly refugee center.

Elsewhere, sniping and drive-by attacks on American positions similar to those that had occurred on D-Day at Panama Viejo were taking place throughout the inner city. Beginning in mid-morning, the extreme disadvantaged and criminal elements of the civilian population, including members of the Dignity Battalions, began looting the stores and businesses in the unpoliced central part of the city. Video footage of the wholesale looting became grist for the world media, although much of it was repetitious.

With the seating of the new President at noon, the Legislative Palace became another security requirement for Task Force Bayonet. Other unexpected security needs cropped up, such as requirements to protect a growing number of Embassies, and other key sites including Government Ministry buildings. Additional missions included requirements to secure and assist in food distribution. These essential humanitarian assistance missions diverted two maneuver companies from conducting security patrols in the areas where looting was ongoing.

On Friday D+2, a two-battalion (1,200 man) sweep was conducted of the Balboa area gradually extending the American zone of control outward from the Canal area. The objective was to clear the area of PDF and DIGBAT elements, bring the refugee situation under control and move the displaced civilians into the Balboa Camp. With the bulk of the Task Force Bayonet forces tied down protecting critical American and Panamanian facilities (many of them outside the American security cordon) the looting continued unabated.

D-Day + 2 was also the day of the highly publicized "Attack on Quarry Heights." Although the media reported the attack was aimed at the Southern Command's hilltop garrison, its actual target was a former PDF cantonment area near the foot of Ancon Hill.

The site, the old *Transito* (traffic) police compound, was more than a steep half a mile from the SOUTHCOM fence line. American MPs were using the site to screen former members of the PDF who were volunteering for the new police force. Suddenly, a mortar and small arms "attack" erupted which was short lived and highly inaccurate, both in weapons accuracy and media reporting. It caused only a brief interruption in the processing and no American or police lives were lost. However, it was costly in terms of property loss and civilian lives.

At approximately 11 AM, PDF/DIGBAT sniper and mortar fire aimed at the screening site began. It came from two directions, an adjacent warehouse area and the jungle line across the road at the base of Ancon Hill. Both the nearby Christian Servicemen's Center and an American household goods warehouse (located 100 yards beyond the site) suffered misplaced but direct mortar hits and caught fire.

About 20 minutes into the exchange of small arms fire, an American Army sergeant noticed two children and their mother standing by a nearby fence and yelled to another soldier to assist them. The second soldier could not see the children or their mother from his position and communicated this to the first soldier. The first soldier, a NCO, shucked off his load-bearing equipment and dropped his M-16 to the ground. He then raced 100 meters across the open parking lot under enemy gunfire and reached the petrified family. His actions saved the mother and two children; however, a third child and a man died in his arms. Both were shot by the attackers while the young American was attempting to move them to safety.

The next day, December 23rd, the 5th Battalion, 87th Infantry and 1st Battalion, 508th Infantry, both elements of Task Force Bayonet, conducted a sweep of the Chorrillo, San Felipe, and Santa Ana barrios (neighborhoods) of Panama City. By D+3, almost the entire 7th Division was incountry and deployed in a security role. The 7th ID was the single largest contributor of Army forces, almost 10,000 troops, squeezing out the U.S. Army South (USARSO) strength and more than doubling the size of the 82nd Airborne Division contribution (one brigade plus). The combined high density of American troops accelerated the restoration of civil order. Incidents of sniper-fire were defeated by well-trained counter-sniper teams. Combined American-Panamanian security-police patrols were initiated on December 24th.

Although the PDF had ceased to exist as an organized force by Christmas Eve, and the danger of a major counter effort by the PDF was declining rapidly, the Bush administration was anxious to speed the capture of General Noriega and close out possible PDF military operations. The Department of State announced that a one million-dollar reward was being offered for information leading to the apprehension of the former commander of the PDF. The announcement was publicized in the late morning, and the news quickly spread throughout the city. By early afternoon, a flood of speculative phone calls and reports began to pour into the American forces switchboards.

Later that afternoon, General Noriega contacted the Papal Nuncio (Vatican's Ambassador), Monsignor Sebastian Laboa, and requested asylum within the walls of the Holy See's Embassy.

The Monsignor contacted General Cisneros and informed him of the Noriega request and the intent of the Vatican to honor it just as it honored similar requests during previous years. Later that afternoon, Manuel Noriega rendezvoused with a car sent by the Monsignor in a parking lot in downtown Panama. He entered the sanctuary of the Vatican Embassy Compound, the Papal Nunciatura, within 30 minutes. It was late Christmas Eve afternoon, not quite 90 hours since H-Hour and his brief encounter with a squad of American Rangers near Tocumen Airport five evenings earlier.

Vatican authorities in Rome and in Panama were adamant about the sanctity of asylum. They were opposed to granting American forces permission to enter the compound and seize General Noriega or any of the other Panamanian officials sequestered within its walls. This position, although understood by American officials, was extremely frustrating and taxed their patience and diplomatic skills.

The next day, American forces cordoned off the Nicaraguan, Cuban, and Libyan embassies to preclude any additional asylum attempts while continuing to secure the American and British Embassies, the Legislative

Palace, and the Panamanian Ministries of the Treasury, Foreign Affairs, and Health.

General Noriega spent the next ten days partly cut off from the world, and semi-isolated in a small room in one wing of the Embassy. During much of this period, he and everyone else in the compound and surrounding area were bombarded by a variety of rock and roll music. The modern day version of the Chinese water torture blared from loud speaker units mounted on two American armored vehicles that were part of the cordon. The music was initially prompted by the media's use of high fidelity directional microphones to eavesdrop on discussions between General Thurman and General Cisneros regarding the situation inside the Nuncio. It was quickly seen by some as a delightful psychological warfare technique. However, the continuous loud booming of rock music and country and western songs just as quickly became annoying to a larger audience than General Noriega and the other dozen or so political refugees who had been granted asylum in the Nuncio.

WINNING THE WEST - OPERATION SURRENDER

Although the majority of the initial combat operations were conducted in proximity to Panama City, the former Canal Zone and Colon, several large PDF garrisons elsewhere in the country were also potential threats.

The American command felt it was critical that all available means be used to achieve a peaceful surrender. Being forced to fight for every cuartel would result in numerous casualties on both sides and have a bitter, long-term, negative effect.

The language capabilities and regional expertise of Special Forces, Civil Affairs (CA), and Psychological Operations (PSYOP) units were critical to the success of these follow-on "stability and security" operations. Most of the conventional units were short of Spanish speakers and had no one knowledgeable on the local customs and cultural nuances of Panama. SOF elements filled these voids and provided the specialty skills and interface with the local population, while conventional forces provided security and reaction forces.

On December 22, 1989, the commander of A Company, 3rd Battalion, 7th Special Forces Group (Airborne) received a Warning Order to prepare for operations to pacify the districts of Herrera, Cocle, Los Santos and Veraguas. The mission was to operate in conjunction with elements of the 2nd Brigade, 7th Division Infantry Division (L) and negotiate the surrender of the PDF cuartels throughout the western military districts. The intent was to gain the surrender through minimal force, limiting the number of both U.S. and Panamanian casualties. The Special Forces commander made initial coordination with the commander of the 2nd Brigade of the 7th ID at Albrook Air Station and then flew with his company to Rio Hato to begin detailed planning.

The ground-work for many of the follow-on bloodless surrenders had been laid by General Cisneros. During his initial how-goes-it survey visit to the Colon area on December 20th, General Cisneros met with a senior PDF prisoner, who professed no love for the Noriega regime, and offered his assistance to induce the outlying garrison commanders to surrender. The prisoner was released to the Cisneros's custody and accompanied the American general back to Fort Clayton. From here, the two officers initiated a combined telephone campaign to the far-flung garrisons, updating them about the events that had transpired, the uselessness of resistance and outlining a surrender procedure.

The Special Forces commander developed an operational concept (subset of the General Cisnernos'telephone technique) that came to be entitled the "Ma Bell Approach." The concept had two phases. The first phase was to insert a Special Forces element into the town to assess the situation. If no PDF efforts to resist an American move were noted, the plan was to present the PDF the terms under which they were to surrender. After the surrender was effected, the second phase was for the American elements to take PDF soldiers into custody and set up law and order in the town.

A part of phase one was "on call" back-up support provided by an AC-130 or several helicopter gunships, as well as an infantry company from 2nd Brigade 7th ID. The SF commander typically chose the airfield in each of the towns as the initial landing zone for his element. He intended to contact by phone the local PDF commander, who would be told the terms of surrender.

The terms were simple and clear: first, the surrender would be unconditional; second, all weapons would be placed in the arms room; and third, the entire garrison would assemble on the parade field in unit formation. The American commander would then fly over in a helicopter to insure the terms were being followed. If the cuartel resisted, the orbiting AC-130 would be ordered to fire on a pre-selected point in or near the cuartel to demonstrate that the Americans were prepared to use force if necessary.

The second phase of the process had the Special Forces elements search the compound and begin processing the unarmed Panamanian soldiers. Once the processing was completed, the infantry company from 7th ID would occupy the town and, in conjunction with an MP element, establish law and order in the community. Their mission was to prevent looting and forestall any reprisals the population might intend against the Panamanian soldiers or PDF police who had surrendered.

At 2:00 PM on December 23rd, D+3, the first mission was launched into the town of Santiago. Helicopters from Task Force Hawk of 7th ID and 617th Aviation moved the SF commander and the reaction force to Santiago. The lead SF team landed at the airport and quickly gained the surrender of three PDF personnel at the airfield. The American commander immediately attempted to contact the PDF commander, but was unsuccessful. He then decided to lead a small five-man SF team into the cuartel. As the American helicopter carrying the team approached the cuartel, the Americans found the majority of the weaponless Panamanian forces assembling on the open parade field, apparently preparing to surrender gracefully. However, as the Americans exited the chopper, one PDF trooper attempted to fire on the American party. The soldier was quickly subdued by other members of the PDF. There were no casualties.

The American commander then called the remainder of the SF company forward, and they searched and cleared the cuartel. The American captain commanding the infantry company was then placed in charge of the cuartel. A Special Forces detachment was left behind to provide a linguistic capability and assist the infantry commander in working with the local community.

The infantry company had four functions. First, to gather intelligence on the location of weapons caches and PDF and Dignity Battalion personnel who had not surrendered. Second, to assist the local officials in re-establishing the civilian infrastructure. Third, to conduct an assessment of the public utilities, medical facilities, and law and order capabilities and recommend priorities for follow-on civil/military operations. Fourth, to conduct joint U.S. and Panamanian patrols throughout the town to reestablish law and order in the community. All the functions were accomplished without any major incidents.

At 6:30 the next morning, on December 24th, the SF commander launched the second surrender mission into the town of Chitre. The pattern repeated itself with one PDF trooper captured at the airport without a fight, and then quick telephone contact with the commander of the cuartel who surrendered himself and his soldiers without resistance. Operations in the town followed those established in Santiago and all missions were accomplished without incident.

At 9:00 on Christmas morning, the Americans moved into town number three, Las Tablas. The American commander again employed a helicopter to carry him and the lead element. This time they landed in an open field on the edge of the town as there was no airfield. The SF Commander walked to a nearby housing area and contacted the cuartel commander by phone. The PDF commander surrendered and the American forces entered the cuartel. Shortly after securing the cuartel and the garrison, the American commander noticed that a large number of the local population had gathered outside the PDF compound. Not knowing precisely the mood of the crowd, he assembled all the U.S. and Panamanian forces on the parade field, called them to attention, gave them present arms and raised the Panamanian flag. This act of respect gained the cooperation of the population who willingly provided assistance and information to the American forces.

The same day, the PDF garrison at David was surrendered by its commander. David was the de facto capital and center of power in the interior provinces. The David Commander, Colonel Del Cid, had begun coordinating the surrender on Christmas Eve. Del Cid was not only a high ranking PDF officer, he was one of two PDF officers indicted with General Noriega in the Florida Grand Jury Narcotics indictments of the previous February.

A Special Forces team, supported by an orbiting AC-130 and a contingent of the 1st Bn/75th Rangers, accepted the PDF surrender. The three-man USAF special tactics team that accompanied the Rangers immediately conducted a survey to assess the capability of the decaying runway to support sustained heavy-lift fixed wing air operations. The survey was accomplished within 90 minutes with positive results. ATC and command and control communications were setup while runway repairs began. Shortly after the surrender, the former PDF colonel was flown to Howard aboard a SOF C-130 and immediately transferred to another C-130 for the flight to the United States to stand trial on narcotics charges.

The Special Forces "Ma Bell" technique resulted in the surrender of no less than six major PDF garrisons without bloodshed.

Following these initial operations, elements of the 2nd Brigade of 7th ID were deployed to Rio Hato to relieve the Rangers who had been there since D-Day. A lieutenant colonel from the 7th ID was made the U.S. area commander and was given a small force to secure the area. The SF major reverted to duty as adviser and interpreter for the new area commander. Together the two officers proceeded to visit all the cuartels and towns in the region. They established liaison with the newly appointed Panamanian garrison commanders, and the governors and mayors throughout the area. The first priority was to establish a working relationship between the former PDF personnel and the local government officials. This was not an easy task due to PDF police abuses in the past.

The two American officers, working as a team, were instrumental in convincing the governors to allow the new Panamanian security forces to carry side-arms and begin assuming the responsibility for civil law and order. The American cadre also established programs to train the Panamanian security forces to work with the local population as a protective police force and not a dominating Gestapo-like presence.

The Special Forces commander continued to receive numerous intelligence reports from the local population about arms caches and PDF holdouts. He felt they needed to react to this intelligence quickly or its value would fade. The two commanders reassessed the situation and felt that there were not enough U.S. forces deployed to properly pacify the region. Further, they saw a need to demonstrate to the local governors that U.S. forces would take measures to purge the area of any hostile forces that may be forming to threaten them.

The SF major, accompanied by his 7th ID counterpart, flew to David to discuss the issue with the 7th ID brigade commander. The two officers succeeded in convincing the 2nd Brigade commander to move a battalion to Rio Hato, and conduct airmobile reconnaissance operations throughout the region from that location. These operations resulted in the capture of several large weapons caches and additional PDF and Dignity Battalion personnel who had gone underground. In one instance, 180 members of the elite PDF 7th Infantry Company known as the "Macho De Montes" (Men of the Mountains), part of the Rio Hato force package, were tracked down and captured without a fight using the "carrot and stick" technique.

The 3rd Battalion/504th Infantry/82nd Airborne Division was involved in its own version of Ma Bell. Although the approach was different, it was just as effective. No less than three towns, Chilibre, Sabanitas and Buena Vista were cleared in the following fashion. The night before the main American force was set to move into the town the scout platoon was dropped off some distance outside of the town between one and two in the morning. From there, they moved to positions from which they observed the activities and tempo of life in the town for the next 24-30 hours. Before dawn on day two, at approximately 4:00 AM, a full company would quietly filter into town. When the people of the town awoke and ventured outside, the first thing they were likely to see was an alert, clean shaven, well armed, helmeted American paratrooper sans warpaint (camouflage makeup). The company would remain for 24 hours during which it would distribute food and set up a "cash for arms" turn-in point. In the case of Chilibre, Sabanitas and Buena Vista, the former PDF police stations became the operating base for a Joint Police Unit composed of American Military Police and the newly-created Panamanian Public Defense Force.

THE SURRENDER OF GENERAL NORIEGA

Late in the afternoon on January 3rd, General Manuel Antonio Noriega decided his active tenure as a Panamanian military leader and de facto Head of State was at an end. His surrender decision was communicated to the American commander, General Thurman, by the Papal Nuncio Monsignor Sebestian Laboa at 5:30 PM.

Several American agencies were involved in the physical and formal act which had to be conducted quietly, efficiently, and legally. It was determined that the best and safest way to extract Noriega from the downtown residential area was by helicopter. DEA agents and U.S. Marshals were alerted as well as a medical team and the site security commander. A SOF quick reaction force, part of the American security blanket around and above the Nunciatura, included two Special Tactics Combat Controllers, who were advised of the air extraction intent, quickly identified, surveyed, and marked a landing zone directly across the street from the Papal Nunciatura.

The landing space was tight, but after taking the measurements, they determined it was large enough to fit two *Blackhawk* helicopters if the landings and spotting were done precisely. In addition to spotting and emplacing the landing markers, the team selected and coordinated the exchange of the discrete radio frequencies that would be used for the ground to air terminal guidance between the helicopter pilots and themselves. They then stood by, waiting to activate the markers and talk the helicopter crews into the tight landing zone. The two choppers made precision landings as anticipated, and went into a waiting mode with their engines running.

A short time later, General Noriega, immaculately dressed in PDF uniform, walked out of the Nunciatura and surrendered to U.S. special operations forces, who immediately searched him and briskly walked him to the lead *Blackhawk*. Generals Thurman and Cisneros watched from a short distance away as the last major objective of *Just Cause* was achieved.

Once the passengers were on board, the helicopter lifted off and flew directly to Howard where it ground maneuvered to within a hundred feet of an MC-130 that was waiting to accomplish its part of this 1,000-mile relay.

The MC-130 aircrew was notified of the impending mission as Noriega departed the Nunciatura. The crew reacted with a special sense of urgency and cool professionalism. Notifying the flight engineer to initiate flight preparations via a handheld radio, the crew did a weather and flight clearance check at the Operations Center and reached the aircraft within six minutes of notification. In 12 minutes, the engines were running. While the navigators were confirming a flight route and obtaining the necessary clearances, the loadmasters worked out a transfer sequence which included the enplaning and deplaning of representatives from several different U.S. government agencies, as well as a medical team and photographers.

Immediately upon exiting the *Blackhawks*, the SOF escort team walked Noriega directly up the tail gate of the waiting MC-130 and turned Noriega over to two Drug Enforcement Agency (DEA) agents. The agents formally placed the former PDF commander under arrest on charges of drug trafficking and money laundering and read him his rights. Within minutes, Noriega was photographed, given a medical examination and had traded his trim PDF uniform for a lose fitting sage green American flight suit. He was handcuffed and took the seat designated for him between the two civil law enforcement agents who would accompany him on the flight to Florida.

Due to the expediency required as well as the safety of the prisoner, his escorts, and the aircraft, the aircrew elected to perform the takeoff and departure with minimum communication and reduced lighting. Once clear of the Howard control zone, the crew employed minimum communications and a varied altitude profile to further conceal their route of flight. Just short of the mid-mission point, the navigators detected three separate thunderstorm systems blocking their planned route. The navigators computed airborne weather avoidance vectors, and the pilots, using night vision goggles, visually confirmed and fine-tuned their flight maneuvers, picking their way through and around the thunderstorms for more than an hour. During the entire flight, the communications systems operator maintained a continuous, secure, low visibility radio link with Washington, periodically advising them of the flight status. In-flight secure communications via a satellite link was provided to the inbound Drug Enforcement Administration (DEA) agents, allowing them to coordinate and confirm the terminal arrival plan and transfer of the prisoner.

After a five hour and 14 minute flight, the MC-130 carrying General Noriega and his DEA escort landed at Homestead AFB, 25 miles south of Miami, at 2:45 AM January 4, 1990. Six minutes after touch down, Manuel Antonio Noriega was enroute to the Federal Courthouse in Miami where he was arraigned.

Footnote: In his book *America's Prisoner* (Random House-1997) co-authored with Peter Eisner from his prison cell in Florida, General Noriega lays out the political events that, from his perspective, led to the American intervention in 1989 and his subsequent trial, conviction and imprisonment. He lays the blame on political elements in Washington that were annoyed at his refusal to train CONTRAS on Panamanian territory, and use Panamanian forces to conduct raids into Nicaragua. He claims that these same elements encouraged and funded the Civilista movement and recruited Mr. Muse to set up a clandestine opposition radio. In the final analysis, General Noriega did not believe that America would take such overwhelming military action against Panama. He expected a more singular and pointed move to remove him after more than a year of cajoling and inferred bribes failed to gain his acquiescence or departure.

General Noriega transferred from Military Custody to DEA for flight back to United States. Photo courtesy U.S. Southern Command Public Information Office.

Block of burned out tenements of Barrio Chorrillo. Photo courtesy U.S. Southern Command Public Information Office.

Site of initial refugee camp set up on the grounds of Balboa High School. Photo courtesy U.S. Southern Command Public Information Office.

PART FIVE: THE SUPPORT EQUATION

The preceding chapters presented the story of many, but not all, of the combat actions that transpired during *Just Cause*. The next three chapters present the breadth of skills and commitment exhibited by the support forces.

It is impossible to present every facet of the support equation, just as it was impossible to capture every combat action. However, the efforts of medical, communications, logistic and civil affairs personnel are representative of the thousands of support personnel, civilian and military, active duty and reserve, that contributed to the success of the combat operations and the larger success of *Just Cause*.

CHAPTER SEVENTEEN MEDICAL HEROES AND ANGELS

This chapter presents a snapshot of the medical support provided to Americans (and Panamanians) during *Just Cause* from initial injury to (for Americans) full hospitalization in the United States.

Although there was determined resistance during the initial phases of the fighting and sporadic sniper attacks during the first few days, the U.S. casualty rate was comparatively light with less than one percent of the U.S. force sustaining injuries. The low rate was the result of a combination of factors: detailed planning and rehearsals, the widespread use of body armor, the non-use of heavy weapons by the PDF, and the immediate availability of medical aid. The medical system had been structured during the planning phases to provide for complete care from initial on-scene battlefield treatment to immediate trauma care in Panama, and air evacuation back to full service medical centers in the United States.

Early in the planning phase, medical planners from all the Services were involved in the development of a near-seamless joint treatment and evacuation system. It was decided to consolidate much of the crucial medical assets and collocate them at a single integrated Joint Casualty Collection Point (JCCP) at Howard, where trauma and surgical assistance could be provided in conjunction with immediate access to strategic medical evacuation aircraft and their medical aircrews.

Within two minutes of the first American parachutist exiting their aircraft, there were medical injuries. Within ten minutes most of the injured who wanted assistance (some soldiers ignored their injuries and proceeded with their initial missions) were receiving treatment at the hands of combat medics. Within two hours, most had been air evacuated from their injury site to the Joint Casualty Collection Point (JCCP) at Howard. After being treated and their basic signs stabilized, they were evacuated by air to Kelly AFB in

San Antonio, Texas. From Kelly, the injured were transferred directly to either the trauma unit at USAF Wilford Hall Medical Center on the south side or to Brooke Army Medical Center on the north side of San Antonio.

Due to its location, Gorgas Army Hospital, less than two hundred meters from the Ancon DENI building and four hundred from the built-up area surrounding the Comandancia, was not considered to be a viable focal point for medical support, at least during the initial 48 hours of operations. This security concern was compounded by the uncertain availability and reliability of its Panamanian staff which constituted 80 percent of the civilian work force at Gorgas. Although the Howard AFB and Fort Clayton clinics were in better security positions than Gorgas, neither of them had sufficient staff or space to handle a large and rapid flood of casualties, nor the immediate access to the evacuation airlift. Any critically injured would require the specialized services available at Wilford Hall and Brooke Medical Center in San Antonio.

For this reason, it was planned to establish a Joint Casualty Collection (and treatment) Point (JCCP) adjacent to the Howard runway to handle all the combat casualties, with aid stations and initial treatment medical teams attached to the major force elements. The creation of the Howard JCCP involved the mating of two deployable Army Forward Surgical Teams (FST) from the 44th Medical Brigade out of Fort Bragg with the Air Force 1st Aeromedical Evacuation Squadron based at Howard. The medical outpost presented an image reminiscent of a Korean War hospital tent complex, as portrayed in the long running TV show "MASH." During the final planning phases consideration had been given to deploying a full sized USAF surgical field hospital, but the expected brevity of the operation and the airlift cost (more than a half dozen sorties) negated the option.

Although a wide range of vehicles, including military ambulances and helicopters, were included in the medical planning and positioning, other vehicles were pressed into service. Helicopter support was provided by the Army's local 214th Medical Detachment flying UH-1s, and a USAF MH-60 helicopter element from the 55th Rescue Squadron out of Eglin Air Force Base, Florida, as well as a scattering of other non-medical/rescue helicopters, to be used as the tactical situation dictated.

In October and November 1989, the 142nd Medical Battalion, part of the in-country Army structure, developed, planned, and coordinated the essential in-country medical support required for Operation *Just Cause*. The battalion was given the mission to provide direct support to the 193rd Infantry Brigade plus a general support role for other units operating in the theater.

The 216th Medical Detachment (Veterinary Services) was assigned the mission of supporting all U.S. Army elements in the areas of inspecting food, controlling zoonotic diseases and providing care to military working dogs. The Field Medical Training Site (FMTS) was ordered to provide equipment and personnel to support deployed U.S. forces.

On December 19th, the day before D-Day, coordination was made with Gorgas Army Hospital for professional augmentees. Three military physicians were designated to join the 142nd Medical Battalion. That evening, all personnel were recalled and the battalion was attached to the 44th Medical Brigade. Vehicles were loaded and medical supplies inventoried. Radios were keyed and checked. Weapons, ammunition, flags, and glint tape were issued. A treatment team and two ambulances were deployed to the 5/87th Infantry Battalion (TF Wildcat, Objective PDF Engineer Compound). A second treatment team and an ambulance were deployed to the 1/508th Infantry Battalion (Airborne) (TF Black Devil, Objective Fort Amador). Two ambulances were also deployed to the 4/6 Infantry Battalion (Mechanized) (TF Gator, Objective La Comandancia). In addition, a treatment team and two ambulances were deployed to Building 519, the U.S. Army South Headquarters at Fort Clayton to provide an immediate treatment center and temporary patient holding facility. Similar arrangements were in place in the Colon area.

By 11:00 PM, all the tactical medical teams were ready to move to their assigned locations. Shortly after midnight, the last teams closed on their assigned sites. Patients began to arrive shortly after H-Hour. Most patients seen by the 142nd Medical Battalion on December 20, 1989 were Panamanian civilians, not U.S. military personnel. The injured were stabilized, treated and, later in the day, were transported to Gorgas Army Hospital as roads were opened and secured. Also, early on D-Day, a preventive medicine team was dispatched to conduct a site survey of the PDF/EPW (Enemy Prisoner of War) camp that had been established late in the afternoon the day before D-Day. Based upon this assessment, the battalion began providing on-site medical support to the EPW camp that evening (D-Day).

At the same time, as the two Ranger strike forces were exiting their planes, the duty officer at Wilford Hall Medical Center at Lackland AFB, Texas was alerted to the ongoing operation and the impending flow of wounded. The center's "Contingency Reaction" plan was immediately activated. The initial task was to assess the number and composition of the on-duty staff in relation to the potential trauma requirements of combat casualties. The normal night complement included two dozen doctors and nearly 100 nurses, plus a limited support staff. However, more than half of these numbers could not be shifted from the care of the more than 500 patients that were already in residence at the center.

A recall notice went out to one of the two quick reaction "mobility groups" that constituted the center's deployable capability. The group included 100 off-duty medical personnel (doctors, nurses, technicians, pharmacists, and administrators). The groups are already organized into teams by task, and prepared to deploy anywhere in the world and set up a field hospital. The initial mission brief for the majority of the alerted group began less than an hour after the center received its warning order. The exact number of casualties was unpredictable, so they planned for the worst.

Meanwhile, in Panama, at the north end of runway 36 at Howard AFB, the JCCP field hospital had been set up that afternoon to handle the wounded. Two USAF Special Operations MH-60 *Pave Hawk* rescue helicopters were on alert with crews in the cockpit at H-Hour. The two aircraft were part of a four-ship detachment that had been flown in earlier that day (D-1) in the belly of a C-5A transport. The other two rescue aircraft were airborne as part of a large nine helicopter special operations force enroute to Colon. The force was to conduct a raid on a known habitat of General Noriega. It was known that he often frequented this location when visiting the Colon area as he had done that afternoon.

Army personnel from the 44th Medical Brigade had deployed to Howard on the 19th and joined with the USAF trauma-trained personnel from the Howard AFB hospital to establish the JCCP. The field hospital was a collection of tents organized and positioned to provide medical sorting, i.e., triage area, a pre-operation area, a surgical operation area, and a post-operation/pre-flight evacuation area.

Immediately upon reaching the JCCP, the medical condition of each patient was evaluated and the patient assigned to one of four treatment categories. The least crucial category (Minimal Care Required) included patients who could walk and might not need surgery. The next group (Delayed Care) was composed of personnel who would need surgery, but did not need it immediately. The third group (Immediate Care Required), was composed of those patients suffering from a critical wound or combination of wounds that required immediate surgery (a life or death situation). Patients classified as "Immediate" were the highest priority and the first to receive treatment. The fourth, and last group, was labeled "Expectant." This category consisted of patients expected to die regardless of the extent of attention or treatment they received. Although they were the lowest priority for treatment they were not forgotten or abandoned.

During the early morning hours of D-Day, the medic attending the "Expectant" group noticed one of his most severely wounded charges who had been in a comatose state, when originally classified, showed signs of movement. The corpsmen promptly checked the soldier's vital signs, noticed an improvement over those recorded during the classification process, and immediately alerted the supervising doctor. The soldier was quickly moved to the treatment area, prepared for surgery and almost immediately put in the operating room. He survived the emergency operation, was stabilized, and flown to San Antonio for further treatment. He fully recovered.

The first CONUS-bound medical evacuation flight was a C-141 transport that had been reconfigured into a flying hospital at Howard after it delivered its inbound cargo. Most of the injured on this initial evacuation flight had high-velocity gunshot wounds, shell fragment (shrapnel type) wounds or both. The aircraft and its medical staff of a dozen departed Panama less than four hours after H-Hour with 43 patients. It arrived at

Kelly AFB about nine hours after H-Hour with 40 patients. Three soldiers died enroute.

Upon arrival at Wilford Hall, all 40 surviving patients were taken immediately to the first floor emergency treatment area. A triage assessment team of six doctors began the crucial resorting process.

Fifteen patients were identified as "Immediate" and one as "Expectant;" however, since the treatment capability of the trauma unit staff exceeded the fifteen "Immediates," the sole "Expectant" was treated as an "Immediate." Emergency surgery was performed. Regrettably, the triage assessment had been correct; neither the surgery nor the efforts of the operating team could save the life of the sole "expectant."

In the normal course of events, patients needing surgery normally trickle into a trauma center/emergency room at an irregular rate that often depends on the availability and capacity of the transportation being used. Based on this normal trickle-in principle, the number of pre-operation "prep" rooms are limited and designed to accommodate one patient at a time. In the case of *Just Cause* and the lead C-141 with its fifteen "Immediates," the limited number of "prep" rooms was immediately recognized as being insufficient. The solution was to reverse the normal flow. The large "open" bay area normally used as the post-operation recovery and patient-monitoring area was made the "mass" preparation area. From here the patients were funneled into one of the dozen operating rooms.

During the treatment of the first set of "Immediate" patients, a medical team that was about to begin work on a young soldier, learned they had an unexpected uphill battle on their hands. The soldier was suffering from multiple gunshot wounds, and in operating room jargon was "crashing" just as he was being placed on the operating table. The term is used to describe a patient whose vital signs suddenly drop, an indicator of impending failure of the full life support system.

In the case of older, less fit patients, the drop is more like a slow slide downhill and is easier to monitor and more time is available to react. Normally with younger and better fit patients, the body continues the fight up to a point of exhaustion and then the system starts to shut down very rapidly. There is usually very little time for the attending medical team to react and counter such a precipitous change.

In the case of the wounded soldier, he was bleeding to death, and if he had not been on the operating room table at the time, he probably would have died within two minutes. The attending team accomplished three medical procedures almost simultaneously. They inserted a breathing tube down his throat, opened his stomach cavity, and quickly put a clamp on the bleeding aorta, stopping the hemorrhaging before it was fatal. Other procedures then followed, and the patient slowly stabilized with near normal vital signs. The soldier subsequently recovered.

The different modes of transportation in a combat or emergency evacuation can create additional problems, depending on the nature and location of the wound. If the same "vital signs" incident had occurred during the C-141 flight, the probability of the airborne medical team having the success of the operating room team is low. In the case of a fast moving helicopter with only a paramedic on board, the odds are even slimmer, should the "plunge" occur. Either way, the transport gamble is always taken, particularly in a combat environment. The helicopter has saved many a soldier's life. However, its normal flight attitude for rapid forward flight is often nose down. This angle can exacerbate the condition of a soldier who has sustained a bleeding head wound if he is loaded aboard with his head toward the front of the aircraft. These considerations were paramount in the minds of the field medics and the stabilization teams as they prepared the patients for movement.

Beginning with the arrival of the second medical evacuation flight in San Antonio, which landed six and half hours after the first, an arrangement to divide the arriving patients between the two medical centers was implemented. This was done long before an overload point was reached at Wilford. The early splitting of the workload eliminated any potential for any inconsistency or drop in treatment quality which could have occurred if all the patients had been funneled through Wilford Hall until it reached capacity and its staff reached exhaustion. As it was, the military surgeons at both centers essentially worked non-stop for the first 48 hours.

Meanwhile, in Panama, the Howard JCCP composite medical teams worked straight through the first 36 hours before there was a break in the flow of injured. In spite of the dusty and humid tent environment, incessant noise and backwash of hundreds of helicopter and fixed wing sorties, and changing weather, which alternated from tropical heat and blowing dust to torrential rainstorms, the JCCP personnel treated more than 300 American and Panamanian injured. Three surgical teams performed more than 70 operations, with one team performing 27 of the procedures. Remarkably, none of the surgeries performed by this team required further surgical intervention upon reaching San Antonio.

The normal tension of the operating room was compounded by the urgency of the need for treatment and several unusual events. At one point, the JCCP operating area was crowded with three doctors and teams of five medical technicians feverishly working simultaneously to save the lives of nine casualties. One of the patients was a severely wounded Ranger, covered essentially from head to foot with large clumps of blood-soaked bandages and hastily applied field dressings. The collection masked the full extent of his injuries. One of the medical technicians and a doctor began to unwrap the dressings to gauge the extent of the multiple injuries. Traumatized with pain and fear, the young Ranger passed out in a state of shock.

As the doctor rolled him over onto his back to help his breathing and begin treatment, the Ranger awoke in a delirious rage, brandishing a cocked 9mm pistol directly in the face of the surprised surgeon. An assisting medical technician (MedTech) quickly placed himself between the doctor and the raging patient. As others in the area sought cover, the MedTech began to verbally soothe the Ranger. After a few seconds, he slowly reached over the barrel of the cocked weapon which was now aimed at him, and gently but firmly removed the pistol from the Ranger's grip. At this point the doctor determined the Ranger was drowning in his own blood and immediately began to put a tube down the soldier's throat to allow him to breath. The MedTech stopped the doctor in mid-movement. He had spotted four live hand grenades with the detonating handles secured only by rubber bands nestled in the Ranger's web gear. The technician gingerly removed the grenades and inserted makeshift safety pins. The doctor promptly resumed the process of inserting the breathing tube. The balance of the medical procedure was uneventful. The Ranger survived.

In another case, a physician was the object of a choke attack by a Panamanian prisoner as the doctor removed the prisoner's restraints preparatory to treating him for multiple injuries. Surprised, but undaunted by the attack, the doctor and two nearby medical technicians wrestled the soldier to the ground, spoke to him in Spanish, succeeded in calming him down, and then proceeded to treat and dress the bullet wounds in the prisoner's chest and legs.

Not all the drama occurred within the operating area. In another situation, a young medic was the only medical staff available at the moment when a young soldier, who had been shot in the face, near death and drowning in his own blood, was delivered to JCCP. Working alone, the MedTech quickly created an airway to enable the soldier to regain breathing. He then held the passageway open for an extended period until other medical personnel were available to insert intravenous lines and gingerly move the victim to the critical care area where he was operated on immediately and successfully.

Other incidents required medical skill, persistence, and patience. One soldier arrived at the triage point in deep shock due to severe blood loss that had allowed most of his veins to collapse. Despite several unsuccessful attempts by other MedTechs and Physicians' Assistants to insert an intravenous line, one young medic persisted and managed to skillfully insert two intravenous lines, allowing blood to "flow" into the arteries, literally saving the young soldier's life.

Some of the medical heroes were flying angels. Thirty minutes before H-Hour, two USAF MH-60G *Pave Hawk* special operations rescue helicopters took off from a SOF forward staging base as chalk 15 and 16 of a 16-ship joint special operations Army-Air Force assault force destined for Colon. The force mission was to conduct a vertical combat assault at 1:00 AM on a known Noriega hideaway. The mission of the two rescue crews was to provide overwater recovery and medical evacuation coverage during the raid mission. The assault went exactly as planned, with the American force encountering only light resistance from small arms ground fire. The American assault force suffered no casualties and after a thorough search of the target building, extraction of the assault elements began.

Following the departure of the main force, an Army observation helicopter that had been providing a stand-by gunfire interdiction capability, discovered that one of the U.S. seven-man blocking teams had not been extracted. The observation aircraft was too small to extract the team and all of the larger troop helicopters had departed the area. The mission fell to the two MH-60 *Pave Hawk* rescue crews. The flight lead coordinated the extraction procedure via secure radio with the ground force, and then made a NVG tactical approach into a vacant lot beside a four-story apartment building. The second *Pave Hawk* provided top cover flying gunship patterns. Although the lead crew did encounter some small arms fire during the pick-up and extraction, none of the blocking team or aircrew sustained wounds. All three helicopters landed safely at Howard 30 minutes later.

After dropping off the blocking force, the two *Pave Hawks* repositioned themselves to a helicopter FARP off the main runway and were rapidly refueled. Shortly after the refueling was completed, the flight was notified of an immediate request from the 82nd Airborne Division to evacuate a critically wounded 82nd trooper from the Torrijos/Tocumen airhead. The flight was conducted at a low-level and over the water to avoid any unsuppressed PDF anti-aircraft or small arms fire. When the two crews arrived at Torrijos, they found the airfield complex pockmarked by a series of firefights. They slowed their approach and moved at treetop level, maneuvering under the guidance of a ground ST/CCT to a hastily prepared recovery point. The PJ (combat medics) members of the helicopter crews departed the aircraft and immediately began stabilizing the wounded trooper while the two flight engineers provided covering fire.

Within two minutes, the PJs had the patient onboard and the two aircraft lifted off and reversed their route to Howard, this time depositing their human cargo at the Joint Casualty Collection Point. No sooner had they completed the turnover, when they were tasked to repeat their first mission by escorting the same 14-aircraft special operation assault package back to Colon to hit another suspected Noriega hideout. Once again, surprise and luck were on the side of the force and, although peppered with small arms fire, the assault, search and extraction were accomplished without any American casualties. During the first 12 hours of *Just Cause*, the two rescue crews flew six-combat sorties and logged more than 10 hours of flight time.

The special operations *Pave Hawk* rescue crews and aircraft were not the only helicopter crews that served as medical angels. Midday on D-Day a USAF Special Operations MH-53J *Pave Low* crew scrambled to conduct an emergency MEDEVAC of several infantry casualties at Rio Hato, 55 miles west of Howard. Upon reaching the airfield, the crew found the area littered with parachutes and debris from the initial Ranger-PDF engagements. Unable to land at the predesignated spot, the crew quickly located and set the giant helicopter down on an alternate landing zone. As the litters bearing the wounded were being loaded, the crew was advised that one of the soldiers was in critical condition. He had several bullet wounds, including a sucking chest wound. According to the field medic, the infantryman was fading fast.

In order to save time, the crew elected to fly a direct route to Howard rather than the safer, but more circuitous, over water route. Five minutes into the flight, the aircraft, which was several thousand pounds over maximum gross weight, began to develop a vertical bounce. The crew was forced to reduce speed to keep the vibrations to a minimum. Immediately upon depositing the wounded soldiers, the aircrew was again dispatched on another emergency MEDEVAC mission. This time the mission was to pick up 82nd Airborne Division casualties at the Torrijos/Tocumen airport.

While the injured troopers (none of whom were "Immediates") were being loaded onboard at Torrijos, the MH-53 crew was advised the 82nd had lost radio contact with a Ranger team which was under fire approximately 15 miles further west near Fort Cimarron. Could the *Pave Low* aircraft attempt to locate and extract the Ranger team? The answer was yes. Upon reaching the Ranger's last known location, the aircrew scoured the area, but although the dense jungle foliage kept them from being able to visually locate the Rangers, they were able to establish radio contact.

The Rangers advised the aircrew that they were engaged in a running firefight and were not yet ready to be extracted. During the radio communication, the helicopter came under hostile ground fire, taking a harmless hit through the cargo ramp. Unable to pinpoint the exact location of the hostile fire or the Rangers, the aircrew did not return fire. Due to low fuel and concern for the onboard wounded, the aircrew was forced to withdraw from the area after coordinating a follow-on extraction of the Rangers by another helicopter. Twenty minutes later, all of the 82nd injured were delivered safely to the casualty reception point at Howard.

Early in the afternoon of D-Day, during a two hour period, a flight of two Special Operations Rescue MH-60G, *Pave Hawk* helicopters managed to extract twenty-two 82nd Airborne paratroopers, including one WIA and one KIA, from an unsecured position in the San Miguelito-Tinajitas area. As the MH-60G *Pave Hawks* approached the area, which was covered with tall elephant grass, they coordinated with the American ground troops for an authentication signal of white smoke to be followed by the waving of an orange panel.

As the MH-60Gs closed with the area, they observed an Army UH-60 *Blackhawk* medical evacuation aircraft on the ground in a landing area north of the intended pickup zone. Believing the Army helicopter had successfully accomplished the pickup, the USAF flight began to depart the area when they spotted the prearranged white signal smoke coming from a nearby, but different, position. As they turned back and were approaching the location of the smoke canister, they observed a soldier come out of the brush waving an orange streamer about 100 yards north of the smoke. The lead aircraft continued its approach and landed near the soldier with the orange banner. He was wounded and quickly hustled aboard. He told them he had been left to guard the body of a buddy who had been killed by a mortar round and had subsequently been wounded himself. Just at this time, the ground fire became intense and the aircrew was forced to leave the landing zone without recovering the KIA.

The *Pave Hawk* flight returned to Howard, and dropped off the wounded soldier. Almost immediately, the crew of the Army UH-60, which had also returned to the JCCP, told the USAF crews that they attempted to make the pickup, but were forced to leave when they started taking rounds in the crew cabin. Due to the ferocity of the fire and rapidity of their departure, the Army crew chief who had exited the helicopter to aid the pinned-down paratroopers was left behind. The UH-60 crew asked the USAF flight to return to the area and attempt the recovery of the crew chief and another soldier who had been shot in the head. The *Pave Hawk* crews launched immediately and returned to the lethal location. They elected to make their approaches as single ships with one aircraft providing top cover with their onboard M-60 machine guns.

Once on the ground, the situation changed drastically. In addition to the crew chief and the single wounded man, the balance of the 82nd ground force, some 20 strong, requested immediate evacuation. The first *Pave Hawk* ended up loading on eight soldiers in addition to the soldier with the head wound from a sniper. This left 12 soldiers and the UH-60 crew chief, who had since been shot in the back. The first *Pave Hawk* took off and assumed a protective top cover position while the second UH-60 rescue bird made a quick-in tactical approach, picked up the wounded crew chief and eight more soldiers and leaving the remaining four soldiers dug in on the sides of a small streambed.

Both aircraft headed for the nearest secure U.S. facility, Fort Clayton. After rapidly depositing the 16 troopers, the *Pave Hawk* crews took off immediately and headed back to the landing area for the third time. Realizing that they were really pressing their luck, the lead aircraft commander chose to employ his former gunship experience. He provided very aggressive top cover to the second aircraft which would make the final four-man pickup. The flight lead maneuvered his aircraft to maximize the fire of his gunners on the suspected PDF locations, while the second *Pave Hawk* ducked in and quickly recovered the remaining soldiers. The two aircraft then made the return flight to Clayton. They traded the last four 82nd soldiers for the wounded crew chief and sniper victim, and headed for the JCCP at Howard. Regrettably, the sniper victim with the head injury died enroute to Howard.

Shortly after sunset on D-Day, two other *Pave Hawks* were tasked to extract a six-man Ranger reconnaissance and surveillance (R&S) team from the hills north of Panama City. The flight departed Howard on NVGs and proceeded, low-level navigating over mountainous terrain with countless uncharted hazards, including a string of 300-foot tall tension power lines. Under cover of zero moon illumination, the flight followed its plan to have the lead aircraft feign an approach into the landing zone to provide top cover to the second aircraft. Despite constant small arms fire from the surrounding ridgelines in all quadrants, the second *Pave Hawk* made a perfect NVG tactical landing on the designated spot. Once on the ground the aircrew found that the Ranger force consisted of two R&S teams, for a total of 12 troopers to be extracted.

Loading the first team and taking off quickly, number two helicopter assumed the protective fire support role while the lead *Pave Hawk* made his approach and quickly boarded the second half of the Ranger team. The flight crews jinked the aircraft as they exited the area to increase the difficulty of the PDF gunners getting a steady shot. The tactic was successful and all 12 of the Rangers were delivered safely to Howard. As soon as the Rangers had been unloaded, the flight was immediately tasked with another mission to provide armed escort and medical evacuation assistance to 82nd Airborne Division casualties at La Joya Airport outside of Panama City. The local Panamanian guard element was still contesting U.S. control of this small airfield which was suspected of being a narcotics transfer site.

Upon reaching the area, the *Pave Hawk* flight was unable to make radio contact with the American ground forces and diverted to an aerial refueling track to top off their tanks. The lead ship refueled without difficulty and then assumed an observation position, waiting for the second *Pave Hawk* to refuel. The refueling probe on the second helicopter experienced a malfunction when the pilot attempted to "seat" it in the extended drogue of the HC-130 tanker. The helicopter probe started to leak, spraying fluid across the windshield of the helicopter, causing an abrupt disconnection that, in turn, damaged the probe. The first *Pave Hawk* watching the mishap immediately contacted number two and assumed a lead position. Conscious of the low fuel state and limited visibility of number two, number one led his crippled teammate directly back to Howard.

Once the damaged aircraft was safely on the ground, the lead *Pave Hawk* teamed up with a replacement MH-60 and headed back to La Joya. After making radio contact with the ground forces, the reconstituted flight proceeded to the still contested airfield, knowing that the wounded 82nd troopers were still in need of immediate evacuation. As the lead ship assumed the top cover role, the second ship landed and quickly loaded two litter-borne casualties, then took off and reversed roles with its teammate. The second ship also picked up two wounded soldiers. The two aircraft quickly delivered the injured, but living, cargo to the JCCP without further mishap.

Beginning with the arrival of the second MAC C-141 *Starlifter* into San Antonio, the nature of the injuries began to change. In addition to the small arms and shrapnel damage from PDF mortars and RPGs, dozens of those injured in the second and third wave had major bone fractures. The senior orthopedic specialist, with more than twenty years of surgical experience and a qualified military parachutist himself, was stunned by the severity of the fractures. The situation included the worst array of fractures he had seen in his medical career. He classified the situation as "an absolute orthopedic nightmare... with not only broken bones, but severe damage to nerves and blood vessels as well." The combination made it far more difficult for the surgeons than the normal bone fracture.

During the course of the following week at Wilford Hall, 168 operations were conducted. Most of these were part of a series performed on the same individuals. All 168 operations were performed on a total of 40 soldiers. The longest single operation took six hours. The surgeons usually repaired the nerve and blood vessel damage in the first operation, and for the most part ignored the broken bones at this point, which are of a lower priority on the "must have" treatment scale. A broken bone is already damaged and is not going to get worse. Whereas, a ruptured blood vessel or severed nerve must be treated immediately, as their "health" has a dramatic impact on the proper functioning of the rest of the human system.

Another reason for the series of operations on a patient was the concern for internal contamination. One essential dictum of medicine is that all combat wounds must be considered contaminated and should not be permanently closed after the first operation. In addition to the series of operations on the most damaged, other patients with gunshot and shrapnel injuries, as well as those with fractures, were brought back two and three times to the surgical area. These subsequent visits were to have their injuries cleaned and dressed in a procedure known as repeat debridement (the removal of dead tissue), which speeds the healing process.

Before the week was out, all of the 252 wounded had been treated at one of the two San Antonio Medical Centers.

Because more Panamanians than Americans were injured and killed during *Just Cause*, Panamanian medical heroes were also evident. Two Panama Canal Commission (PCC) Services Division employees, and a PCC Motor Transportation Division (MTD) driver performed a selfless and heroic act – assisting another PCC employee who was severely injured by gunfire in the minutes prior to H-Hour.

Shortly after midnight on D-Day, tow boat engineer Pablo Robinson, operations clerk Jose Loreto, and an MTD driver, Jacinto Long, heard a plea for help over the PCC vehicle radio network. The call was from PCC driver Jose Miniel, who had been shot and was calling for help from his vehicle on pier 18 in Balboa.

Hearing Miniel's weak and desperate voice over the radio, Robinson and Long decided to go to the aid of the wounded man, while Lorento remained at the dispatch office in Diablo and maintained radio contact with both Miniel and the two volunteers.

Within minutes Robinson and Long found Miniel and transferred the injured driver to their vehicle. They did not believe that they had enough room to safely turn the car around at pier 18 given the darkened conditions. They were also concerned about exposing the vehicle, themselves, and the bleeding man to the possibility of rifle or machine gun fire if they tried to turn around in the middle of a nearby intersection. They elected to drive the return route in reverse gear. They were successful in doing this.

Meanwhile, Loreto, who had remained behind to monitor the radio, had prepared a place for the wounded man to rest. As soon as the injured man was positioned, Loreto began applying first aid in an attempt to stop the flow of blood from three gunshot wounds. It was quickly obvious that immediate medical assistance was required. Loreto got back on the radio and called the nearby Corozal Fire Station and requested a team of paramedics and an ambulance be dispatched. Within minutes, a team of Panamanian paramedics was on the scene, administered to the injured man, and transported him to Gorgas Hospital where he received surgical assistance and survived his brush with indirect combat.

The fighting had subsided by the morning of the 21st, and some medical resources were shifted from Fort Clayton to the Empire Range EPW camp and the refugee center at Balboa High School. The latter were to care for the increasing workload of injured Panamanians at the site. Twenty-eight Panamanian civilian casualties were the first transported from Balboa High School to Gorgas Army Hospital that morning. Later in the morning, the JTF-Surgeon reported that SOUTHCOM had found enough medical supplies in PDF warehouses to support 5,000 refugees.

On the 22nd, the 41st Area Support Group received a massive request for female hygiene supplies for the refugee camp. The battalion also received a request from the 193rd Infantry Brigade for ambulance services to move several American WIA and one KIA. Alpha company also dispatched ambulances to transport eight WIA from Albrook Air Force Base to Fort Clayton.

During the morning of the 23rd, a platoon from the 4/6th Infantry Battalion (Mechanized) requested an ambulance at the Comandancia to recover a civilian KIA. Later that day, a doctor from the 142nd Medical Battalion evaluated 15 EPW psychiatric patients, who had been released from a Panamanian mental hospital. A few hours later American soldiers retrieved additional PDF medical supplies from the former PDF Engineer compound and delivered it to the refugee camp.

On Christmas Day, three general purpose medium tents and 50 cots were set up at the Albrook EPW camp as a mini-hospital to formalize and provide sustaining medical support to that camp. Four of the interned EPWs were suffering from gun shot wounds and were evacuated from Albrook Air Force Station EPW point to Gorgas Army Hospital.

During Operation *Just Cause*, SOUTHCOM Medical personnel treated nearly 4,000 patients and inspected 144,627 pounds of food, conducted water and bacteriological test at 17 sites, and satisfied 600 requests for medical supplies.

Although all the U.S. medical vehicles and helicopter carried the international medical symbol, at least three medical evacuation helicopters took ground fire during the course of the first three days.

Additionally, two of the main Panamanian hospitals, Santo Tomas and Caja Seguro Social (CSS), were found to be storage sites for PDF weapons. Santo Tomas was also used to harbor PDF soldiers that were questionably wounded. The Americans later learned that a senior Panamanian doctor, who was Chief of the Dignity Battalions, was seen organizing elements of the DIGBATS within the grounds of Santo Tomas during the evening of D-Day.

Helicopter door gunner's view of Madden Dam. Photo courtesy U.S. Army Center for Military History.

CHAPTER EIGHTEEN
LOGISTICS AND COMMUNICATIONS

THE INVISIBLE UNDERPINNINGS

Several hours before the beginning of December 20, 1989, the 193rd Support Battalion of the 41st Area Support Group (the senior Army support organization) began actively supporting the more than 26,000 U.S. forces to be committed to Operation *Just Cause*. Eventually, a total of 1,200 logistics personnel were committed to supporting the operation. This support took many forms and involved a wide spectrum of skills and specialties.

During the final pre-H-Hour period, soldiers of Alpha Company (Transportation) were busy transporting approximately 250 infantry soldiers to their offensive kick-off positions. Many of the trucks and their drivers remained with the infantry for several days. In more than a few instances, the drivers returned enemy fire alongside "their" infantry.

At 12:30 AM on D-Day, just a few minutes before H-Hour, the support battalion reported helicopter hot refuel points at Vernado and Empire Range were 100 percent operational. Less than 45 minutes into the American operation, the refueling site at Empire Range was the subject of a PDF mortar attack, as was part of Fort Clayton two and a half hours later. Alpha company established and operated these large-scale hot refuel points, pumping approximately 110,000 gallons in the first eight days. On D+4, the company set up a forward supply point at Rio Hato to support the expanding sweep and security operations which dominated that area of operations for the better part of three weeks.

Meanwhile, the 193rd Support Battalion's 1097th Transportation Company (Medium Boat) was busy conducting combat and combat service support missions on the Atlantic (Colon) side and in the Canal itself. Shortly before H-Hour, the LCM company transported elements of 82nd Airborne Division in the first amphibious assault of the operation. The LCMs moved the paratroopers to Renacer Prison at Gamboa, where the waterborne forces were part of the force that overran the PDF prison. Two days later, the LCMs landed troops at the wharves of Colon. By December 31st, the LCM company had transported 2,442 American troops and 848 PDF EPWs, plus 738 short tons of cargo including multiple truck loads of captured PDF arms and munitions.

At H-Hour, the battalion strength stood at 69 percent of its authorized allowance. This was acceptable during a normal peacetime schedule of 1-1.5 shifts a day, but was totally inadequate to meet the 24-hour tempo that accompanies any combat operation. The shortfall was made up by augmenting the battalion with support personnel from a range of diverse organizations. This included India Co, 159th Aviation Regiment; 8th Ordnance Company, 513 Maintenance Company; HHC 7th DISCOM, 364th S&S Company; 612th, 403rd, 408th, 546th, and 126th Transportation

Companies from active duty units; and the HHC 419th Combat Aviation Group from the National Guard.

In total, 88 soldiers from these various units were thrust into the dynamic and demanding support machine. Their assistance was invaluable, their role equally important, and their performance equivalent to that of the battalion regulars and the thousands of unseen support personnel in both Army and Air Force units in the CONUS and Panama. The battalion also received equipment augmentation. This came in the form of 6,000-pound forklifts from Company A and 5-ton cargo trucks from 142nd Medical Battalion.

Multiple logistics decisions and communications actions had been required prior to the start of military operations. In the hours preceding H-Hour, the 41st Area Support Group had set up a Support Operation Center (SOC) to serve as the focal point for logistics requirements. Early in the planning cycle it had been decided to use Luzon Field (an athletic field on Fort Clayton) as the staging area for the aerial resupply of water and fuel tanks, two critical combat consumables. Vehicles and aircraft will not operate without fuel and soldiers cannot function long without water.

By mid-morning of D-Day, due to the magnitude of the distribution requirements, it was decided to transform the fuel and water staging site into a full-blown logistics distribution point. Specific staging areas for each class of supply, particularly, fuel, ammunition, food, and water, was established. Three thousand cases of Meals Ready to Eat (MREs) were immediately pre-positioned. Battalion personnel assembled and filled all available fuel and water blivets (portable, military storage tanks). By mid day, Luzon Field was the hub of an Army Logistics Distribution System for both helicopter and truck movement.

Other logistics requirements included requests for cots, tents, body armor, ammunition, water, wrecker support, drivers with vehicles, fuel support, ammunition transfer point (ATP) support, transportation, explosive ordnance detachment (EOD) support, barrier materials, portable latrines, refugee and EPW support. As they were received the requirements were entered in a relational database by unit and type of support required (equipment, personnel, service, etc.). This enabled the battalion to track the more than 100 immediate requisitions processed each day.

Echo Company, the aviation maintenance support unit, began the operation at 70 percent of its authorized military strength, and although not augmented, was deeply involved in keeping the U.S. Army helicopters flying (largely through cannibalization due to an extensive backlog of parts orders). In addition, the unit repaired several damaged PDF helicopters. At 8:00 PM on the 21st, the aviation repair unit began the job of assessing and repairing 12 PDF/PAF aircraft captured during the American assault at Tocumen the day before. The repair unit brought all the aircraft to operational status within a few days, making them available to transport the new Panamanian civil government to the more distant provinces.

Another small but critical logistics element, the Memorial (Mortuary) Services unit moved to Albrook Air Station which had been chosen as the main location for the processing of Panamanian fatalities. While preparing to depart the motor pool, the convoy received PDF/DIGBAT gunfire from the nearby jungle. The enemy fire was returned and quickly suppressed. Within minutes the convoy departed for Albrook. Immediately upon arrival, a temporary cemetery was established and graves prepared. The next day, casualties began to arrive and kept coming for the following 10 days. The memorial services branch provided full funeral services to include embalming, reconstruction, as well as joint Graves Registration. The Graves Registration services included body preparation, identification, and temporary burial-disinternment, and was accomplished in conjunction with U.S. Air Force and Panama counterparts.

A large percentage of the U.S. Army's Panamanian civilian work force reported for duty on December 21, disregarding their personal safety and the inconveniences of road blocks and security searches. Many stayed at work through D+5 sleeping on cots and makeshift beds, eating MREs alongside their American military counterparts. One example of this was the staff at the Army laundry facility. In spite of sniper fire enroute to and near the facility, laundry workers, both Panamanians and Americans, came to work. Laundry service was resumed on day two of the conflict, and the staff began providing one-day service to the field units.

On the 22nd, the Army commissary at Corozal opened with a skeleton staff. The scene outside reflected the uncertainty of the situation. There were mostly wives, standing in line to purchase essentials. Each individual was allowed only two bags of groceries. They were brought to the commissary and taken back to their housing area on a guarded bus.

On December 24th, the American Command had established a "no questions asked, weapons for cash" program. The program involved Panamanians turning in weapons to the American forces for a set dollar amount, depending on the type of weapon. The program was extremely successful in removing weapons from the streets and closets of the average Panamanian. Nearly 9,000 weapons were turned in during the program while a far larger number were uncovered in PDF arms rooms, warehouses and cache sites.

Beginning at 7:00 PM on December 28th, the ammunition supply point (ASP) received the first truckload of captured arms and ammunition. The flow continued to arrive throughout the night. The final total was 21 truckloads of munitions and weapons. The volume was more than initially expected, and the ASP had to request an additional 250 shipping pallets to properly ship the captured material to the disposal site.

Although reports of clandestine shipments of arms into Panama had been numerous during the previous three years, no one was ready for the magnitude of the arms that were finally found. The volume exceeded the warehouses of arms stocks uncovered in Grenada in 1983 and the earlier enormous illegal Cuban arms shipments to dissidents in Chile. The caches discovered in Chile were enough to arm more than 5,000 men. The Grenada total was enough to equip 10,000. The final total found in Panama included enough weapons to equip five 10,000-man infantry divisions, or more than 60,000 guerrillas.

Most of the weapons found in the warehouses and cache sites were new weapons stored in the original wooden shipping crates, many of which carried Chinese markings declaring the contents to be engineering equipment.

The 565th Ordnance Detachment (ammunition) operated the major in-country ammunition supply points, issuing more than 450 short tons (ST) of munitions. The 565th also had the chore of receiving the multiple truckloads of captured ammunition and weapons that had to be sorted, counted, and inspected for safety and utility. The 565th was not the only EOD unit at work. In addition to the USAF and USN EOD in-country teams, a composite Army Detachment deployed with XVIII Airborne Corp forces. The Fort Bragg 12-man detachment (from the 36th EOD) was augmented by eight personnel from Fort Rucker, Alabama prior to deployment. Once in-country, the combined force was divided into ten 2-man teams. The teams conducted 150 EOD missions

THE MANY FORMS OF COMMUNICATION

The diversity shown within the combat and combat support operations was mirrored in the many facets of communication that were employed. Some, the formal means, were planned for; others were extemporaneous. This section presents a look at the diverse range of communications capabilities employed.

From the initial development of the *Elaborate Maze* mission statement in the spring of 1988 and through the subsequent variations of the Concept of Operations (CONOPS), it was apparent that regardless of the nature of the actual situation or the option to be executed, good communication was absolutely essential if chaos and confusion, as well as the loss of lives, were to be kept to a minimum.

Recognizing the nearly inevitable PDF-US confrontation, the SOUTHCOM Director of Communications (J-6), Colonel Jorge Torres Cartagena, an experienced veteran of contingency planning and JTF operations, quietly set out to improve and convert the existing communications structure, which had not been designed, manned, or trained to support combat operations, into one that could. One of the first strategic improvements was the installation of a state-of-the-art secure telephone system to link the garrison locations of all the SOUTHCOM units. The next major undertaking was the development, coordination, refinement, and publication of a Joint Communications Plan (JCP) which laid out the overall communications structure. The JCP also laid out system capabilities and liabilities, and assigned specific responsibilities to units within the theater signal community.

This was followed by preparation of the operationally oriented Joint Communications Electronics Operating Instruction (JCEOI). The JCEOI focused on the contingency plan(s) and the forces to be involved. It provided implementation guidance and assigned specific frequencies and call-signs to the operational forces. It was first prepared in April 1988 and updated whenever a new force was added or missions reassigned.

In June 1989, the in-country 1109th Signal Brigade was restructured so it would be able to operate in deployable elements, and support the most demanding of the contingency possibilities. This early restructuring and training provided the essential field capability, and laid the ground-work for virtually uninterrupted communications service between the key command and control nodes during the actual operation.

In early September, Colonel Cartagena, acting in his dual capacities as the SOUTHCOM J-6, and the Signal Brigade Commander, sensed the situation was taking on more dangerous overtones. He directed the revision of the normal day-to-day procedures to bring the communications structure in line with the expanded scope of operations and the introduction of the XVIII Corps. During the next six weeks, the communications infrastructure in Panama was unobtrusively transformed to support the demands and stress of combat operations and civilian concerns.

While participating in a series of low-profile exercises, communications personnel drew weapons and combat gear from centralized storage facilities in small amounts and repositioned it at key communications and assembly sites. During the same time, all the Class B and Class C unsecured telephones were electronically preprogrammed to be switched to internal installation use only, "on command." This precaution was set up to eliminate off-post telephone calls during the last hours prior to H-Hour. It also substantially reduced the possibility of overloading the automated switching center.

As prescribed in the SOUTHCOM Joint Communications Plan (JCP), a Joint Communications Control Center (JCCC) was created and exercised many times in the fall of 1989. Beginning in October, signal planners from the XVIII Airborne Corps began a major effort to review and update the Joint Communications Plan and the supporting Joint Signal Operation Instruction (JSOI). The JSOI was used by all the tactical units involved in the operation. It contained the operating procedures and instructions that, for the most part, were non-changing. It was supplemented by the JCEOI, which contains all the frequencies, call-signs, and code words found in the individual service and unit standard Signal Operating Instructions (SOI). This was the common telephone book and was revised periodically.

A small cadre of signal planners formed the nucleus of the corps communications effort. In mid-October, the corps signal team flew to Panama to coordinate the tactical aspects of the plan, and the draft JSOI with SOUTHCOM, the 193rd Infantry Brigade (TF Bayonet) and the 1109th Signal Brigade.

After extensive coordination with all Army and XVIII Airborne Corps units at Fort Bragg, the 7th Infantry Division at Fort Ord, and Army Forces in Panama, the JSOI was coordinated with the three Air Force commands (MAC, TAC, and SAC), plus JTF-Panama and the Marine command in Panama, as well as the operational components and staff of the Special Operations Task Force. The third draft was approved by all commands before the end of October. It was published and distributed under tight security constraints. The procedures outlined in the JSOI were tested and validated in November and early December as different elements and aspects of the overall operation were exercised and rehearsed.

With General Noriega's announcement on December 15th that a state of war existed between Panama and the United States, an increase in communications volume and use of virtually all types of media (except tactical links) was noticeable within the communications community.

In the days leading up to H-Hour, communications specialists at the U.S. SOUTHCOM Telecommunications Message Center (TCC) located in the Quarry Heights tunnel complex (only a few yards) from Command's Operation, Reconnaissance, and Intelligence Centers), processed an ever increasing volume of time-sensitive messages. The majority of the messages dealt directly with ongoing political and military preparations. They were continuously fed to the three information centers across the hall as well as to the Command section on a 24-hour basis. Security and timeliness were paramount.

The level of use and urgency increased again within hours after Lieutenant Paz was killed and word of the young Navy couple's interrogation and harassment was learned. Another plateau was reached within hours of the American Presidential decision to execute *Blue Spoon*. The command Crisis Action Team (CAT) and operational planning staffs throughout the isthmus began running down their pre-execution checklist. At 11:30 PM on the night of December 19th, all the class B and C telephones were cut over to internal installation use only.

With the initiation of the operation, the volume of communications traffic again increased and it became even more urgent to insure 100 percent telecommunications service to and from the field commanders. This was not an easy task; electrical power and air-conditioning in the tunnel was interrupted for several hours shortly after the operation began. Temperatures in the Telecommunications Center quickly exceeded 95 degrees and remained high well into midday, but both equipment and the communications specialists continued to operate at near peak efficiency.

JOINT COMMUNICATIONS CONTROL CENTER (JCCC) ACTIVATION

Communications planning also included quietly activating the JCCC prior to H-Hour to ensure the optimum use of existing information resources (telecommunications, automation, records management, print media, and visual information). The JCCC was activated during the afternoon of December 19th, and operated 24 hours a day throughout the operation. The Center was manned by a team of communications personnel from all of the service staffs and key communication organizations. This included personnel from SOUTHCOM J-6, (the Communications Directorate), the Air Force Communications Group, the Navy signal staff, the Army component headquarters and the 1109th Signal Brigade. The team's skill and experience base covered all the information and communication disciplines resident in the U.S. military services.

The JCCC evolved quickly to be the principal focal point for all non-tactical communications support. It coordinated the installation of new systems and the redistribution of existing systems. This included not only voice communications (secure and non-secure), but all other communications media such as facsimiles and personal computers

JOINT OVERSEAS SWITCHING SYSTEM (JOSS) TELEPHONE CENTRAL

As expected, the conversion of B and C telephone service from full isthmus and community-wide dialing to dialing only within the immediate installation greatly increased the number of external calls to be handled manually by the Joint Overseas Switching System (JOSS) switchboard. To adequately prepare for the increased requirements, additional operators had been called in during the afternoon of the 19th. Five civilian operators responded. This volunteer cadre was augmented on D+1 by three soldiers from the 154th Signal Battalion. The three soldiers received only one hour of instruction on switchboard operations before being committed. During a typical peacetime week, the JOSS normally handled 15,000 calls. During *Just Cause*, that number was exceeded in the first 48 hours. The eight-person team provided full switchboard operations throughout the first week of the operation without any relief. The operators caught some rest between shifts in a nearby room that was converted into a mini-barracks.

The JOSS switchboard became an important information focal point, handling not only local, commercial, and military AUTOVON network calls, but also providing information and directory assistance. Many stateside calls were received from concerned parents of deployed soldiers, as well as the normal volume of family emergency medical calls.

A bilingual operator was assigned to handle all the incoming spot reports from Panamanians on arms caches, DIGBAT activities, and Noriega sightings. This was a valuable adjunct to the Intelligence Hotline. In addition to taking the information, JOSS personnel plotted the location of meaningful reports and suspicious activities. The attached Signal Security Section relayed the tactical information to the JTF SOUTH Joint Operations Center (JOC) for action.

LONG HAUL COMMUNICATIONS AUGMENTED

The need for additional long haul communications links to CONUS was evident prior to the operation and had been considered in the planning. Reliable and stable communications were particularly urgent to ensure the survivability of the new Panamanian government. In order to fulfill this need, the National Communications System (NCS), a confederation of U.S. national agencies, was tasked to deploy a suite of emergency communications equipment. The NCS had been chartered in 1963 by President Kennedy to provide communications during regional or national emergencies. It had done so repeatedly in the intervening years.

This particular communications package was redeployed from Alaska, where it had been providing auxiliary communications in the wake of the recent volcanic activity. Puerto Rico had earlier received NCS emergency support in the form of the same package when parts of the island were completely cut off from local or long distance telephone service due to damage from Hurricane Hugo.

The package consisted of a mobile satellite earth station and an electronic telephone switch board system. It had the capability to handle both military and commercial long-distance calls to and from the United States. Approximately 15,000 customers, widely dispersed in or near Panama City had access to long haul telephone service through the NCS package.

HOTLINE REPORTING

During the tense days that followed, many U.S. and Panamanian civilians contributed their professional and personal expertise to support the ongoing operation. Some were pressed into service; others volunteered. Many performed jobs other than their normal ones. Many assisted in unique ways.

One way people were able to help was relaying information and observations on PDF movements and activities. Early on D-Day, the U.S. Army South Chief of Intelligence at Fort Clayton established an information hotline to handle calls reporting suspicious activities. Bilingual U.S. citizens with security clearances and an intimate knowledge of the streets, neighborhoods, and landmarks of the Republic of Panama were used to man this critical function. These hotline operators worked 12-18 hour shifts during the first few days.

During the first day and night, many callers were very excited and under emotional stress. They had to be calmed down before information could be taken. The hotline attendants tried to follow an orderly data flow, first asking the callers their names and addresses, and then the location, time, and type of activities reported, and finally asking whether the caller was willing to assist U.S. forces in pinpointing the location. Initially, many of the Panamanian callers declined to provide their name, or provide on-scene assistance, as they were afraid of PDF reprisals. However, as the days elapsed, these fears lessened and the callers became more willing to help.

Within three days, the locations of arms caches and PDF holdouts became the mainstream of the reporting. Reports of Noriega sightings (and alleged hideouts) contributed to the continuing flood. The volume rose sharply when the Department of State announced there was a $1 million reward for information leading to the capture of General Noriega.

The Department of State announcement prompted a flood of calls, with alleged sightings scattered throughout the city, and in fact, throughout the country. Correlation and sorting out of these reports, most of which were recirculated street rumors and speculation, was a time-consuming and tedious task for the intelligence analysts. The reports also resulted in a number of fruitless raids on suspected Noriega hideouts by the special operations quick-reaction chase teams.

SUPPORTING THE NEW PRESIDENCY

The American signal community's direct involvement in the rebuilding of the new Panama government began on December 21st. The Endara government had selected the Legislative Palace as the location for the presidential offices. Reliable communications for the new President and his small group were among the first critical needs. Security was another. Initially, American forces provided both. American communications personnel were tasked to ensure the new government could communicate throughout Panama and the international community.

Electrical power had been cut off at the Panamanian telephone Dial Central Office (DCO) when a DIGBAT-initiated fire swept through the building on D-Day. The DCO had been the focal point for telephone service to the Legislative Palace (as well as most of the downtown area). On D+1, the 154th Signal Battalion was tasked to restore power to the DCO and secure the surrounding area. The communicator-soldiers cordoned off the streets in the immediate vicinity with five-ton trucks, erected sand bagged guard positions, and posted armed guards.

While the area was being secured, a combined American-Panamanian technical team composed of personnel from the 154th Signal Battalion, 536th Engineer Battalion, and Panama's Instituto Nacional de

Telecomunicaciones (INTEL) worked together in the unsettled and lethal environment to restore power to the damaged facility. The team had the system back on line by early evening, D+2 (the 22nd). It took an additional 24 hours, plus the installation of a l00kw generator, before the facility was fully operational as its battery bank, which provided continuity in service, had been almost completely drained.

The next critical communications need was expressed by the SOUTHCOM Civil Affairs (CA) team that was supporting the office of the new Panamanian Presidency. The CA team had an urgent need for a secure communications link between the Legislative Palace and SOUTHCOM headquarters. The signal battalion responded by deploying a suite of secure multi-channel equipment, and attempted to incorporate the Civil Affairs team into the Tactical Multi-channel Network and the Single Channel High Command Net. The results were not the best. Three STU-III's secure phones were also installed; however, the poor quality of older inner city Panamanian telephone lines could not support the use of the STU-IIIs in the secure mode. To overcome this short fall, the SOUTHCOM J-6 tasked the U.S. Air Force Southern Air Division at Howard to provide a mobile capability to meet the secure link need.

The USAF 1078th Communications Group, which maintained and operated the SOUTHCOM Commander's mobile contingency communication vehicle (CCV), was tasked to reposition the system and activate its circuits at the Legislative Palace. Shortly before first light the following morning, the 24th, the USAF communicators relocated the vehicle. The system was brought on-line within a half-hour of arrival and the CCV operators began providing secure communications between the palace, JTF SOUTH at Albrook, and SOUTHCOM at Quarry Heights.

At midday, weapons fire from an unidentified sniper confirmed that a rocket or machine gun attack could easily be launched against the legislative complex from any number of the nearby taller buildings. At 1:30 PM, orders were received to tear down and move the Presidential offices to a safer location. The more securable Foreign Ministry complex was chosen as the new site. The move was accomplished without incident and both the multi-channel and single channel communications links were reestablished within 15 minutes of arrival. This included secure telephone service from the American Civil Affairs team's new office to SOUTHCOM headquarters.

The relocation required the American communicators to again request the assistance of Panamanian INTEL telephone personnel to reestablish the Presidential telephone lines at the new location. INTEL agreed to furnish a work crew as long as it was provided an armed escort. The escort was provided and the INTEL crew arrived without incident. The INTEL team transferred the phone service in a matter of hours, substantially improving the quality of the lines in the process. This allowed the American communicators to establish a secure STU-III telephone network, freeing up some of the mobile tactical equipment for other uses.

A week later, on New Year's Eve, the President of Panama and his staff moved their offices for a third time. This time the move, made at night, took them to the Presidential Palace. At the request of the signal battalion, INTEL personnel were again called to assist. The American signal commander also ordered the installation of three portable satellite telephone terminals (from the National Communication System package) to insure the Panamanian president had fast and reliable communications access to virtually any country in the world.

On January 3rd, direct American military communications support to the new government came to an end with a reestablished Panamanian communications structure assuming the responsibility.

A myriad of other forms of communication were pressed into use during the operation. These ranged from the telephone, office fax, Ham radio operators, secure phones and secure fax, frequency modulation (FM) radio and tactical satellite (TacSat) communications. Printing presses, newspapers, wanted posters, safe conduct passes and maps were also used as communication vehicles.

HAM RADIOS SQUAWK

Panamanian and U.S. amateur radio operators throughout the country created their own local and international network that provided another vital information channel. The HAMs relayed information about suspicious activities, passed along health and welfare messages, and maintained contact with other HAM operators throughout Panama. Many of these stations operated 24 hours a day, and were responsible for providing safeguard warnings to entire neighborhoods. The warnings alerted listeners to the movements of roving bands of looters, and DIGBAT paramilitary personnel by exchanging information. One station operated by a husband and wife team received calls from locations throughout the country. The team operated nonstop for three days and nights. They continued to receive calls and relay the information to American authorities well into January.

OFFICE FAX TO THE RESCUE

When SOUTHCOM imposed travel restrictions on all non-tactical movement at the start of combat operations, an alternative to the normal courier and distribution system was needed. There were volumes of text, list, charts and visual aids that had to be moved between the various information centers. The unsecured facsimile network provided one alternative.

Because of the increased demand for this capability by the operating forces, other U.S. Federal agencies, and the new Panama Government, many DOD fax machines were relocated from their normal office locations and redistributed to sites where they were used to satisfy unclassified but critical information transfer requirements.

SECURE FAX

Secure fax machines proved equally vital. Only a few weeks before, U.S. Army South had initiated a routine procurement action for 22 secure fax machines. Shortly after the *Just Cause* warning order was received, the headquarters sent a message to the Department of the Army requesting immediate help to expedite the procurement. The DA staff contacted the manufacturer, a civilian electronic firm, and within two days a technical representative from the manufacturer arrived in Panama with a total of 30 machines. Fourteen of these were installed and operating within 36 hours. The newly delivered machines provided the secure communications network needed and substantially improved the timely transmission of classified and sensitive material in the capital city. It also provided a secure mode of communications for the American forces in the Colon area. The manufacturer's technician was one of the American civilians taken hostage at the Marriott hotel by a PDF UESAT team a few minutes before H-Hour.

SECURE PHONES

Working in tandem with the secure fax was a network of relocatable secure phones. When *Just Cause* began, SOUTHCOM had approximately 1,200 Secure Terminal Units (STU-IIIs) installed and 110 additional units on hand. By the third day of the operation, approximately 90 of the 110 reserve units had been installed. In addition, 80 more units were received from the United States – 30 from Fort Ord, California and 50 from Lexington, Kentucky. These additional terminals were used to support the communications needs of the second and third phase units.

STU-IIIs were also used by the American personnel who were supporting the new Panamanian government to communicate with U.S. federal agencies back in the United States. Other STU-III units were used at interrogation/debriefing stations, providing a secure intelligence reporting network. By the end of the operation, a total of 1,350 STU-IIIs were in use.

TACSAT'S COME OF AGE

Despite the general availability of the in-place telephone system, single channel tactical satellite radio terminals (TACSATs) played an instrumental part in the overall communications infrastructure. Although TACSATs had been used successfully within the joint contingency and special operations communities during the preceding ten years, *Just Cause* was the first time TACSATs were used widely in conventional force operations.

TACSAT radios were used extensively for command nets throughout the JTF SOUTH theater, including the urban sprawl of downtown Panama City and the outlying mountain regions. The nets provided a secure means of command and control for the widely dispersed and mobile units.

The TACSAT Network provided senior commanders the ability to instantly redirect or reinforce operational forces anywhere within the area of operation. At the high point of the operation, more than ten separate TACSAT nets with more than 50 terminals were active.

FOX-MIKE, OLD RELIABLE

Technology, however, still had not replaced the need for a line of sight (LOS) tactical FM (Frequency Modulation) radio. Fox Mike radios continued to be the primary means of communications for commanders at brigade level and lower. To overcome the effects of terrain and distance, retransmission sites were established throughout Panama City and the Canal area.

Although some Fort Bragg and U.S. Army South forces had the new multi-channel SINCGARS radios, the single channel mode was used extensively to insure interoperability with units equipped with the older single-channel ANC/VRC-12 series radios. This was the first use of the SINCGARS in a combat operation since its development in 1986. The FM radio family provided secure communications from the proverbial fox hole to the JTF SOUTH Joint Operations Center (JOC). Virtually every radio network down to platoon level was secured using the VINSON series secure devices.

PRESSES KEPT ROLLING

Anticipating the need for printing support, the wheels were put in motion the afternoon of December 19th. A print crew was requested to remain at the printing plant after normal duty hours on the pretext of putting out a special edition of the *Tropic Times* newspaper. The print plant chief selected seven civilians and three soldiers as his crisis response cadre.

Soon after combat began, the crew realized there would be more to their after hours duty than originally anticipated. Based on advice from the soldiers of the nearby COMSEC (Communications Security) Logistics Support Unit, the print crew took actions to preclude drawing attention to the work site and its after hours operation. They blacked out the windows and relocated their vehicles well away from the building. The atmosphere became tense during the early phases of the operation when the transportation motor pool – only two blocks away – came under PDF mortar fire.

During the first seven days of the operation, the press crew produced increasing quantities of printed items to meet the expanding variety of demands. This included forms needed to process refugees, detainees and prisoners of war, as well as compensation posters and "Cash for Weapons" notices. Other print jobs included receipt forms, travel passes, surrender leaflets, reward notices, plus newspapers and a variety of directories. Other items of critical need were wanted posters, identification cards and additional copies of the classified JCEOI.

The largest single request was for 500,000 Safe Conduct Passes ordered by the U.S. Army South's Civil Military Operations (CMO) section. The print crew managed to produce the first 200,000 passes by dawn. The remaining 300,000 were completed by early afternoon, and the seven civilians (American and Panamanian) who had worked around the clock finally got to go home and get some rest.

The text of the dual language Safe Conduct Pass is presented below.

PASAPORTE A LA LIBERTAD

> ESTE PASAPORTE ES PARA EL USO DE MIEMBROS DE LA F.F.D.D., BATALLON DE LA DIGNIDAD Y LA CODEPADI. SI SEPRESENTA ESTE BOLETO DE LOS ESTADOS UNIDOS, LE GARANTIZAMOS SU SEGURIDAD, ACCESO FACILIDADES MEDICAS, COMIDA, Y UN LUGAR DE DESCANSO Y RECUPERACION. RECUERDEN; NO HAY QUE SUFRIR MAS.
>
> GENERAL MARC A. CISNEROS
> COMANDANTE DE TROPAS DEL EJERCITO SUR

SAFE CONDUCT PASS

> THIS PASS IS FOR USE BY PDF, DIGNITY BATTALION, AND CODEPADI MEMBERS. THE BEARER OF THIS PASS, UPON PRESENTING IT TO ANY U.S. MILITARY MEMBER, WILL BE GUARANTEED SAFE PASSAGE TO U.S. FACILITIES THAT WILL PROVIDE MEDICAL ATTENTION, FOOD, AND SHELTER. SURRENDER; WHY SUFFER ANY MORE.
>
> GENERAL MARC A. CISNEROS
> Commanding General, U.S. ARMY South

Approximately 4,000 members of the PDF and the Dignity Battalions used these Safe Conduct Passes to turn themselves in to U.S. authorities.

PUBLIC INFORMATION CAMPAIGN

Thirty hours into the operation, early on the morning of December 21st, a sergeant from the 4th Psychological Operations Group (PSYOP GRP), stationed at Fort Bragg, arrived at the print shop requesting support for a public information campaign to be launched the next day. Other personnel from the PSYOP group arrived a few hours later and began preparing bilingual editions of two newspapers called *PersPectivas* and *Nueva*

Republica. The two papers were distributed to the residents of Panama City free of charge. For the first three days of *Just Cause*, these newspapers provided the local population with their only source of printed information. A total of six morning and evening editions were printed and distributed throughout the Panama City area.

In addition to the two bilingual papers, the local SOUTHCOM newspaper, the *Tropic Times*, also was printed and distributed without interruption throughout the operation except for D-Day. As the only source of English printed news for the U.S. military and civilian readership, the daily edition of the *Times* was in great demand. Prior to *Just Cause*, the normal print run was 30,000 copies. During the second and third days of the operation (D+1 and D+2) almost 100,000 copies were printed. 60,000 copies were run for the remaining December editions. By January 5, 1990, the print run had returned to the normal quantity of 30,000.

MAPS, A UNIVERSAL COMMUNICATIONS MEDIA

Maps were another communications media that played a crucial role in the operation. During the initial stages of planning, the need for up-to-date maps was clear at all levels of command; however, the volume that eventually would be required was not. Maps, in all shapes and forms, scales and presentations were required. This included aeronautical charts for aerial route planning, and tactical topographic maps for ground force maneuvering. The maps most in demand were those showing the dense urban environment of Panama City, Colon, and their surrounding areas. Panama City maps, in particular, were in constant demand. Every unit and element charged with security and patrolling needed multiple copies. The special operations "Noriega" chase teams and their helicopter crews needed them. The infantry squads of the 82nd Airborne and the 7th Infantry Divisions needed them. Newly arriving MPs needed a complete selection to familiarize themselves with the city environment.

Three days into the operation, a request for 2,500 copies of a Panama City map was received by the officer responsible for maintaining the U.S. Army South's map depot. All the depot's stocks had been largely depleted by the heavy demand of the previous days, and a reprint was needed. The print plant was queried; could they produce the needed copies in time? In addition to being already saturated with print requirements of equal priority, the plant did not have the color scan capability to make new print plates, nor could its limited 3-color press handle the multi-color requirement of the detailed 6-color city map.

The Defense Mapping Agency's (DMA) Latin American Theater Support Center, located at Albrook, was contacted. It had also processed numerous requests from the Air Force, Navy, Marine, Joint staffs, and other government agencies and their on-hand stocks were also critically low. However, once apprised of the need, the DMA Commander authorized the use of protected war reserve stocks, and delivered the 2,500 copies within two hours.

MEDIA SUPPORT

As with any major operation, significant problems arose from the increased communications requirements and the lack of long-distance commercial connectivity outside and within the Republic of Panama. Compounding the problem, INTEL (the Panamanian telephone company) had been largely shut down during the first ten days of the operation, substantially reducing access to commercial international telephone lines.

While the commercial capability had decreased, (it had not been exceedingly robust to begin with), the demand increased substantially. The extensive media focus created additional demands. At H-Hour, approximately 35 media personnel, representing most major international news organizations, were in country. An additional 16 media personnel were mobilized as part of the DOD media pool and flown to Panama during the early hours of the operation. Within eight hours after the operation began, more than 400 additional press representatives from American newspapers and TV stations arrived in Panama to cover the operation. All of them required commercial line access to do their job and many demanded U.S. authorities provide the service.

The SOUTHCOM Quarry Heights Officers Club was commandeered and transformed into a media center. Seven telephone lines were dedicated for media use. Two lines were used for satellite uplinks, one line was dedicated to sending still photos, and four lines were used for fax machines. The media was provided daily operational briefings on the situation at the center (the former Officers Club) as well as administrative support and transportation to points of recent fighting. However their freedom of movement was very limited, particularly during the first two days, due to the ongoing nature of combat and the general unrest. This did not sit well with the action hungry media and the travel restrictions drew criticism from some.

By D+3, the situation was compounded with the arrival of an additional 400 press representatives from such countries as Britain, Italy, Germany, Australia, Japan, Venezuela and Colombia. Each desired telephone connection to their parent country. This demand far exceeded the existing capabilities of the center. Seven more lines were taken from nearby SOUTHCOM buildings and family quarters and transferred to the center. These lines were connected to three additional satellite uplinks, one each for fax, voice and data entry operations.

By the first of the year (day twelve of the operation), the media population had grown to more than 1,000 as press personnel from around the world continued to converge on Panama. More than 800 of these journalists, photographers and technicians officially registered with the SOUTHCOM Public Affairs office.

JTF SOUTH DEACTIVATED

During the course of the first 24 days of operation, (the XVIII Corps/ JTF SOUTH Command tenure), JTF SOUTH issued 42 Frag-Orders (Fragmentary Orders) messages, essentially two a day. One predominantly contained mission assignments and changes in status and was transmitted early in the morning. The midnight (end-of-the-day) edition focused on summarizing the events, directives and operational results of the preceding 24-hour period and included the planning and execution intentions for the next day(s). This latter message served both as an immediate historical baseline and as a single point of reference for the subordinate unit operations staff. It allowed them the opportunity to review their assignments and obligations as well as gain a broader appreciation of other aspects of the ongoing operation.

In addition to guarding against potential hostilities by dissident Panamanian factions, SOUTHCOM and JTF-Panama (primarily U.S. Army South and the 7th ID) were faced with rebuilding the nation and promoting confidence in the newly installed civilian government. Operation *Promote Liberty* was the vehicle chosen to assist the new government in the endeavor.

At 6:00 PM on January 11, 1990, JTF SOUTH was deactivated. Control of all remaining U.S. forces reverted to JTF-PANAMA, commanded by Major General Cavezza (CG 7th ID). General Cavezza assumed responsibility for the overall military operation (and the running of the JOC/TOC).

The transition from JTF SOUTH (XVIII CORPS) to JTF PANAMA (7th ID and the 193rd) went smoothly. Ten days earlier, as operations had begun to shift from combat to combat follow-up, and then to security and then to the restoration of civil order, the 7th ID staff, looking ahead to the inevitable transition, began visiting the JOC/TOC. It coordinated with and queried its XVIII Corps functional counterparts and the other members of the JOC/TOC team as to "how things were done" and "what had been done and what still had to be done." Similarly, General Cavezza, began taking a greater interest in events outside of the existing 7th Division-Task Force Atlantic Area of Responsibility and was fully prepared when the handoff took place.

After General Cavezza became COMJTF, he continued to rely on General Cisneros for advice and assistance in virtually all matters. This reliance was both a recognition of General Cisneros knowledge and his ability to work with the full strata of Panamanian society. It also reflected General Cavezza's awareness that upon his departure and return to the United States responsibility for JTF Panama would revert to General Cisneros who would have to pick up the pieces and carry on the long term effort of rehabilitation and reconstruction of Panamanian - U.S. relations. A reflection of this soldier to soldier respect and sense of equality was the purposeful habit of General Cavezza to always enter and leave a room or a meeting with General Cisneros by his side.

M-113 Armored Personel Carrier on guard duty in Panama City. Photo courtesy U.S. Army Center for Military History.

CHAPTER NINETEEN
THE BEGINNING OF RECONSTRUCTION

Less than eight hours after H-Hour, as U.S. combat forces were still working to secure all the initial objectives, JCS issued an order activating Operation *Promote Liberty* (the Blind Logic Civil Affairs phase of *Blue Spoon-Just Cause*).

Even before the final version of the CINC's Blind Logic had been sent to JCS for formal approval, General Thurman directed Brigadier General Gann, the SOUTHCOM director of CA, planning to move to the Legislative Assembly building, set up as the Civil Military Operations Task Force (CMOTF). Its mission was to assist the new government, which at that time consisted of only three people – one president and two vice-presidents. At 10:00, on December 20th, the majority of the SOUTHCOM J-5 staff displaced to the Panamanian Legislative Assembly building, leaving a small rear element in the tunnel at Quarry Heights.

At the same time, General Thurman told the American Chargé d'Affaires, John Bushnell, that General Gann and his Civil-Military Operations Task Force (CMOTF) worked for Bushnell. Thurman's instructions to Gann were clear and broad, provide Bushnell what he needed to assist the newly inaugurated Panamanian government as well as such additional support that might be required. Within days, this "additional support" would be considerable given the fact that Bushnell's nominal embassy staff of 45 numbered just over a dozen on December 20th and very few of them were senior personnel. State recognized the shortfall and, with DOD support, sent three POLADs (political advisers) to assist the Chargé. They were led by Deputy Undersecretary of State for Interamerican Affairs, Michael Kozak, who had previous experience with Panama dating back to the negotiation of the Panama Canal Treaty. The other two POLADS were a U.S. Information Agency officer, who had worked closely with the former Undersecretary of State for Interamerican Affairs and the former political officer in the Embassy who had forged close links with Endara, Arias Calderon and Ford when they constituted the opposition. The three State Department officers arrived in Panama in the afternoon of D-day, and immediately joined the Embassy country team. Two additional State Department officers followed shortly thereafter and were attached directly to General Gann's SOUTHCOM (CMOTF) team.

Immediate needs included housing the refugees from Chorrillo, reestablishing law and order, and beginning economic recovery. The first task was undertaken immediately. Regrettably for the victims of the mass looting that occurred in Panama City on D-Day and D+1, the second objective, establishment of civil law and order, had to wait almost thirty hours. The restoration had to wait until all the major combat objectives were fully secure before any sizeable portion of the American forces could be transitioned to a "police-security" role. The third task, economic recovery was beyond the role, mission, authority and capability of DOD and SOUTHCOM. This was the function of the new Panamanian government and several of the civilian agencies of the United States government.

The Army Civil Affairs (CA) specialists who developed the *Blind Logic-Promote Liberty* plan had been able to make only limited preparations in the preceding months for a variety of reasons. Three in particular constrained the effectiveness of the Civil Affairs-*Blind Logic* planners.

First, the American Ambassador to Panama had been withdrawn in May (seven months earlier), in the wake of the Noriega-Del Valle confrontation. Almost simultaneously, the American Embassy staff had been reduced, leaving only a skeleton crew. In essence, the U.S. political machinery in Panama was nonfunctional.

Second, DOD policy restricted direct working level coordination with the Department of State on military contingency planning without the approval of the National Security Council (NSC). Due to the sensitivity of the Latin American countries (regarding Panamanian sovereignty), the NSC directed that U.S. military contingency planning not be coordinated with the State Department below the NSC level.

Third, the Civil Affairs specialists charged with developing *Blind Logic* were, for the most part, civilian reservists (as is ninety percent of the DOD CA strength) on short two-three week tours of duty from Reserve CA units in the States.

With these restrictions in place, the core CA planners had focused on those actions which the military had the capability to do and which would have to be done in any contingency situation that potentially involved large numbers of civilians. These actions included the basics of feeding, housing, screening, protecting, and identifying refugees and displaced persons, and providing essential emergency medical care.

The planners established the framework for meeting these needs, and identified the actions to be taken and the military units that would be responsible for accomplishing the actions. The *Blind Logic* planners had anticipated that full-up Civil Affairs reserve units would be activated during the pre-H-Hour execution countdown, and these units would be organized into a Civil-Military Operations Task Force (CMO-TF) which would assume responsibility for CMO operations, including the operation of any civilian refugee camps. For a combination of operational security and domestic political considerations, it was decided not to activate the reserve units but to call-up individual volunteer reservists instead. On D-Day the call went out to individual reservists. More than 2,000 CA personnel volunteered.

On D-Day, Major General Marc Cisneros, concerned about the growing CMO challenge, ordered his Deputy Chief of Staff for Logistics (DCSLOG) to take whatever he needed from the USARSO staff and prepare to set up an support operation to help the Panamanians get back on their feet. The DCSLOG gathered a group that included a logistician, a CA person, and a communicator, plus several others, in USARSO headquarters to assess the situation and await the identification of requirements.

The CMOTF by itself did not have the resources to assist President Endara, Arias Calderon, and Ford in establishing a Panamanian police force. By D+1 the decision had been made to build a new security force from the remnants of the PDF. The decision was taken after consultations that included the three Panamanian officials, General Thurman, Charge' Bushnell, Generals Stiner, Cisneros and Gann, and Colonel Pryor. As a result of these discussions, General Cisneros, based on advice from Colonel Al Cornell, the former U.S. Defense Attaché to Panama who knew most of the officers of the former PDF, recommended Colonel Roberto Armijo to be the commander of the "new" Panama Public Force. President Endara approved the recommendation.

On December 21st, JCS formally ordered the execution of *Blind Logic* in response to General Thurman's message (plan) submitted the previous day. JCS approved the entire plan, with the notable exception of the involuntary call-up of the Reserve CA units. JCS approved the use of individual Reserve CA volunteers instead of unit mobilizations and this with one very critical caveat. The JCS stipulation was that the 25-person core team was approved for active duty tours of no less than 139 days. This played havoc with the planning of the 361st Brigade which had teams geared to deploy for 31 days because most of the reserve personnel, particularly enlisted personnel and junior grade officers, could not afford to leave their civilian jobs for more than 30 days. Of the pre-selected reservists, only three ended up in the initial cadre.

General Cisneros selected the former National Transportation Directorate building (DNTT) on the Panamanian side of Albrook Air Force Station as the headquarters of the Public Force and the screening site for all candidates. Colonel Cornell accompanied Armijo there while General Cisneros sent his Deputy Commander for Security Assistance and told his DCSLOG to set up a U.S. office to support the Public Force. That office became known as the U.S. Forces Liaison Group (USFLG). It was staffed largely with qualified Spanish-speaking Army Foreign Area Officers (FAOS) and others with similar training and education from both the Active and Reserve Components. Its formal mission was to establish the Public Force, see to its initial equipping and training, and assist it in deploying in Panama City, Colon, and the cities and towns of the interior.

The USFLG established the Public Force, oversaw its division into components (Air Service, Maritime Service, and National Police), its disaggregation by the detachment of the investigative arm, the immigration service, the Presidential Guard, the Port Police, and the planned detachment of the prison guards. It coordinated the equipping and starting up of the prison system, and the outfitting and arming of the police.

The USFLG soon began to coordinate other types of activities, most of which related to public security, among JTF SOUTH, COMCMOTF,

CMOTF, the Panamanian Ministry of Government and Justice (under Vice President Ricardo Arias Calderon), the U.S. Embassy, and the last new organization, the Judicial Liaison Group (JLG). The JLG was organized under General Cisneros' direction by the USARSO civilian international lawyer and filled a gap that had not been contemplated by *Blind Logic* planners. The Judicial Liaison Group's mission was to get the Panamanian court system functioning again. This entailed liaison with two separate Panamanian entities, each independent of the Executive: the Courts and the Attorney General.

The JLG coordinated the opening of the night court system to include the participation of prosecutors from the Attorney General's office. It assisted in the reconstitution of the rest of the judicial system and generally acted as liaison between the Panamanian government and U.S. forces on legal and judicial matters. The JLG was successful because it had the expertise of the USARSO international lawyer who had represented SOUTHCOM and USARSO before the Panamanian courts and was extremely knowledgeable of the Panamanian legal system.

On December 22nd, the CMOTF (SCJ5) and the two DOS POLAD augmentees relocated to the Foreign Ministry building from the Legislative Assembly when the Panamanian Presidential offices relocated due to security concerns. Subsequently, President Endara would attempt to occupy the Presidential Palace and General Gann would go with him but the CMO Task Force staff would stay at the Foreign Ministry until January 1st when they returned to Quarry Heights.

The looting and chaos stopped by the 23rd or 24th when sufficient U.S. forces were brought into the city and established a visible presence that discouraged unlawful activity and enforced the curfew that had been declared by President Endara. Most of these forces were infantry from USARSO's 193d Infantry Brigade augmented by MPs. However, the 193d commander was anxious to relieve his troops of a "police and security" mission for which they had not been trained.

To extricate the infantry, three conditions had to be met. First, the new Public Force had to field enough policemen to undertake joint patrols with U.S. MPs. This was accomplished fairly rapidly. Second, before the infantry could leave there had to be a means to deal with the cases of petty criminals and curfew violators. This meant that the night court system had to be operating. Third, there had to be somewhere to put those convicted by the night courts, which meant that the police jails and the city prison had to be operating. But the looters had stripped the jails and the prison of anything that could be taken.

These requirements involved the combined efforts of the CMOTF, the USFLG, and the JLG assisted by CMOTF and CATF and personal encouragement of the commander of the 193d. The result was that the new Panamanian National Police (PNP) officers did go on joint patrols with U.S. forces, night courts did begin to function, and police jails and the prison were made operational with equipment liberated from captured stocks and with the assistance of USARSO's post engineers.

On January 1st, the second group of CA Reservists arrived, some 114 strong expecting to be organized into the three zone task forces - Panama City, Colon, and David. Conditions were not what had been anticipated during the planning and the decision was made to operate one CA Task Force (CATF).

On January 2nd, there were three separate echelons involved with the conduct of Civil Military Affairs – the SOUTHCOM CMOTF, in overall control, which commanded the CATF. Under the command of JTF SOUTH were two other organizations with CMO responsibilities as well as the combat units (augmented by elements of the 96th CA Battalion) which also were responsible for some CMO. Throughout this period, General Hartzog came to the conclusion that a single and more permanent organization for the restoration of Panama was needed. He concluded that the function to be provided was "support." With that he identified the new organization as the "United States Military Support Group" (USMSG) which was created from elements of the earlier organizations.

INTERAGENCY COORDINATION

Meanwhile, the Embassy was reconstituting its staff. A temporary duty senior political officer had arrived in late December and the Political Counselor was finally able to return on January 1. Soon, a new U.S. Ambassador, Deane Hinton, with long experience in Latin America, was appointed and arrived from Costa Rica. As permanent members of the Embassy staff returned to Panama, the three temporary POLADS returned to normal duties in the United States.

The new diplomatic mission personnel initially questioned the extensive military involvement in supporting each of the Panamanian government ministries as they were being reestablished. The DOS personnel looked askance on the situation as not totally "proper," but quickly came to realize that the military had put into place a civil assistance plan and made it work while their Department had no plan or real capability to do all that was required. One Department of State official expressed their perspective in the following manner: "While we thought that some of this closeness to the Panamanian civil government, or at least the reawakening Panamanian civil government, was not appropriate, we also realized that an incredible number of things which needed to be done in the government weren't going to get done any other way. No one else was going to do them."

By the middle of January, Panama did have a government and most public services were restored. The PDF had been broken into its component parts, elements had been detached and reorganized, and there were Panamanian policemen on the street working with U.S. MPs. The Public Force also had a new commander, newly-promoted Colonel Eduardo

Herrera Hassan, whose predecessor had been discovered to have been too tainted with Noriega's corruption to survive in the position.

CA TROOPERS AT H-HOUR

At H-Hour, active duty Civil Affairs troopers jumped with the Rangers into Torrijos/Tocumen. One team accompanied the Ranger force charged with clearing the PDF infantry and Air Force barracks, while another team accompanied the Ranger company responsible for clearing the terminal complex. In both situations, the CA teams aided in the surrender of PDF personnel through their Spanish language skills, and set up the initial collection and screening points for PDF prisoners and civilian detainees. Other CA soldiers were part of the follow-on wave of Rangers that landed at Rio Hato at H+46 minutes. Their mission was similar and included controlling all Panamanian civilians in and around the airhead and ensuring they would not interfere with, or be harmed by, the ongoing ground combat operations.

INITIAL HUMANITARIAN ASSISTANCE

The most pressing need in the immediate aftermath of the H-Hour fighting in Panama City was assistance to the displaced and homeless population of the Barrio Chorrillo. The planners had not anticipated the destruction of an entire neighborhood, but it became apparent by dawn on D-Day that the number of displaced persons was going to exceed the planning estimates. Burned out of their homes, thousands of Panamanians walked the ten blocks to the Balboa High School area where they had received American medical and food assistance during previous natural disasters.

The American support forces had begun creating a temporary refugee camp and POW detention area on the Balboa High School grounds during the early hours of *Just Cause*. The work involved converting the school athletic stadium and the nearby Panamanian athletic fields into holding areas, and the establishment of a food distribution point and a medical treatment facility.

A major portion of the initial effort was the erection of a tent city. More than 4,000 Panamanians lost their homes in the Chorrillo fire and most swarmed to the American relief camp. The number of personnel using the camp facilities continued to grow in the two days after the initial American assaults as looting and erratic firefights persisted in the downtown area.

By D+1, 250 Civil Affairs personnel, drawn from both active and reserve units, were working at the camp. They were involved in a host of chores including handing out meals, diapers, toothpaste and bedding as well as instructing Panamanians in the art of setting up a tent, and the use and sanitation of "Port-a-Potties." One hundred of the Civil Affairs specialist came from the 96th CA Battalion at Fort Bragg, and another 150 from two reserve units, the 361st CA Brigade and the 426th CA Company. The 150 reservists were culled from more than 2,000 volunteers in units throughout CONUS. In making the selections, preference went to the skills most in demand. This translated to public health and safety officials, construction engineers, public works and service administrators, transportation specialists and civilian law enforcement officials.

A computer registration database was set up, and the camp residents were issued registration cards that allowed them to come and go in a somewhat orderly and controlled manner. The most critical problems were medical care, personal sanitation, and the identification and location of friends and family. By D+2, additional food distribution and medical treatment points were being set up at other locations throughout the city.

Within days, Sergio Galvez, a Panamanian who had won the post of District "Mayor" in the aborted May elections (but, along with the other winners, had been denied the office by the PRD/PDF nullification of the election) was sworn in by President Guillermo Endara. Galvez quickly took charge of Panamanian activities at the camp and working with the American commander and the civil affairs personnel, he organized a camp staff, i.e., a management and coordination committee composed of other camp members. The committee created six sub-organizations that assumed responsibility for administering the essential functions of the camp. Within a few days, the chaos and clutter of the first 48 hours was transformed into a well-organized mini-city with its own infirmary, pharmacy, kitchen, and washing facilities. During the first six days (December 20-25) more than 20,000 people passed through the camp.

The camp also became an informal, but effective, focal point for the collection of information about former members of the PDF and DIGBATS. This occurred not only because the camp was a center of Panamanian civilian activity, but also because it was a major point of American and Panamanian cooperation. It was one of only a few American points of contact that had a published telephone number. Additional telephone lines and Spanish-speaking soldiers were added to its telephone center to handle the influx of telephone calls.

Meanwhile, the Army Corps of Engineers was busy coordinating the conversion of a nearby former PDF/PAF aircraft hangar on the Panamanian side of Albrook into a temporary housing facility. The hangar floor was sectioned off and divided into sets of family-style living cubicles. A representative of the Federal Disaster Assistance Office established the construction standards and arranged for the construction material, while Air Force combat engineer personnel did the actual construction. Panamanian workmen who were among the residents of the tent complex were also employed in the construction effort. Although simple and small, the 500 cubicles did provide better shelter and living conditions than the camp/school ground tents. The formal move from the tent city to the hangar housing occurred in mid-January, and involved the relocation of 2,500 Panamanian civilians. Within a week, the Panamanian Red Cross assumed administration of the complex. The total number of personnel that were residents of the original camp at Balboa and the hangar complex at Albrook at one time or another exceeded 11,000.

Less than a mile and a half away, in the burned-out El Chorrillo barrio, American-Panamanian demolition crews, under contract to the Corps of Engineers, were busy leveling and clearing the burned-out areas. This included the total dismantling of the Comandancia and its surrounding support complex. Part of the activities involved assessing the degree of structural damages to the nearby buildings that had sustained damage. This included the 15-story apartment building adjacent to the Comandancia. Other actions included the drafting of an urban redevelopment plan for the area. The survey teams and urban planners determined the number and square footage of both public and private structures damaged and destroyed, and identified historical, religious, cultural buildings and the former business establishments in the devastated district. The information and assessments was subsequently turned over to the Embassy and the U.S. Agency for International Development (U.S. AID) for use in providing follow-on assistance.

COUNTRY WIDE CHALLENGE

The humanitarian assistance challenge was not localized to El Chorrillo or Panama City. By the third day of the operation, CA teams were spread throughout the country. The biggest challenge was to get food and medicine to the outlying neighborhoods and country villages. Initially, the teams traveled with MPs or infantry security patrols. They used loudspeakers to recruit volunteers to help distribute food stocks from captured PDF warehouses and the relief shipments. There was no shortage of volunteers once it was learned the volunteers would be "paid" for their efforts with part of the food stocks. In addition, the CA staff contacted the leaders of the local charities and service organizations such as the Rotary, the Lions, the Kiwanis, and various church groups, and enlisted their help to ensure the food went to the locations most in need and was distributed equitably. In every town and village that the CA teams visited, one of the first actions was to seek out and contact the local civilian leader and have him appoint new police, fire, and water officials.

By the January 1st, humanitarian assistance totaled nearly 540 tons of supplies ranging from food and medical assistance to clothes, blankets and lumber. One of the great travesties of the Noriega/PDF regime was the lack of medical supplies at the local hospitals. More than 150,000 pounds of medical supplies were furnished from U.S. resources before a large PDF warehouse, fully stocked with medical supplies, was found less than 12 blocks from the under-stocked Panamanian hospitals.

Responsibility for the Panamanian Public Health System, which included 60 health facilities, had been split between two ministries. The Ministry of Social Services was directly funded by taxes, and had the responsibility for operating the major hospitals with an emphasis on two major hospitals in Panama City. The Ministry of Health was operated under a separate program, and had responsibility for the rural and neighborhood clinics. Its funding had been erratic with a resulting lower level of capability. Coordination and cooperation between the two ministries had been poor. The American teams attempted to bridge the gap by showing the Minister of Social Services the poor condition of hospitals outside of Panama City, and the inadequacy of the rural facilities. Permanent improvement had to be left to the new Panamanian government, although a more equitable sharing of food and medical supplies was accomplished immediately.

RESUMPTION OF CIVIL AVIATION

On D-Day through D+3, Torrijos Airport was still a major arrival point for follow-on American forces and their sustaining logistics tail. However, by D+4 Tocumen began accepting humanitarian flights, and by the December 30th, three airlines had resumed regularly scheduled flights. More than 5,000 civilians from 12 different countries were evacuated in the initial 5 days of normalcy.

One of the small stories that was part of this movement fabric involved an Air Force intelligence officer, who was given the task to get nine Soviet officials out of Panama and back to Nicaragua. The officer, a captain was a member of the SOUTHCOM Intelligence Directorate and the SOUTHCOM CAT because he was the only one in the CAT who spoke both Russian and Spanish. The task turned into was an all-day affair, involving working with both the 18th Airborne Corps MPs and the American Consulate. It concluded with a graceful exit of the Russians and a taped interview by Peter Arnett and Steve Jaco of CNN. However, the story didn't run. It was overshadowed by the surrender of General Noriega.

American civilian affairs personnel served as airport managers, engineer staff, immigration and customs officials, and labor "boss" for the 154 Panamanian civilians hired to clean up the terminal. USAF air traffic control and logistics personnel handled flight operations and cargo unloading during this period as a continuation of their combat efforts of D-Day through D+3. A civil affairs medical team, working with Panamanian medical personnel, reestablished a neighborhood health clinic in the nearby village of Tocumen to relieve the pressure of Panamanian civilians visiting the American military clinic that had been set up in the airport lobby.

On December 26th, a six-man contingent of U.S. Army Military Customs Inspectors were assigned to assist in the processing of military and commercial aircraft arriving and departing Tocumen International Airport . During the December 26th to January 13th time period, the inspectors provided 24-hour-a-day operations, checking passports and visas, inspecting passenger baggage, military cargo, and all persons attempting to depart Panama through the airport. On D+9, some of the former Panamanian Customs Inspectors and Immigration Officers were rehired by the new

Panamanian Government. They worked with the U.S. inspectors and gradually resumed full control of the clearance process on behalf of the new Panamanian government.

As of January 13th, Military Customs Inspectors and civil immigration officers, augmented by Panamanian Customs Inspectors had cleared 265 aircraft, 1,059 aircrew members, 14,468 passengers, and 689 American troops. Together they examined 35,100 pieces of baggage, 194 pieces of rolling stock, and 227 pallets of cargo. The majority of the military customs inspectors left the airport on January 18, 1990, when customs responsibilities were returned to Panama officials.

During December and January, departing passengers were ticketed at locations away from the airport. They were then transported by bus to an American checkpoint at the airport perimeter for security screening, and then on to Panamanian customs and immigration officials at the terminal for normal pre-boarding processing. At the American security point, the departees were screened against a joint black and gray list prepared by U.S. and Panamanian authorities. The list included a range of questionable individuals from a variety of countries including Panama, Nicaragua, Cuba and Libya. During the course of the screening, about 100 people were detained and denied immediate departure. Detention was usually the result of finding unauthorized items such as weapons, drugs or extensive quantities of cash in their luggage or on their person.

By mid-January the number of commercial flights had risen to 10 per day. By the third week in January, the U.S. Air Force Security Police (SP) detachment (a 44-person security police flight and a five person command and control element), which had been managing the security operations at the air terminal since D+2, was screening 1,500 passengers and 25 international flights a day. The SPs used specially-trained dogs to check luggage for drugs and explosives as well as employing a high resolution X-ray machine on loan from Pan American Airlines. A replacement Panamanian airport security force had been undergoing training by the USAF team with the assistance of a Federal Aviation Administration (FAA) security specialist since late December.

Within days of reaching the 25 flights a day plateau, the USAF Security Police Commander officially turned over control of the civil terminal and the commercial ramp to the new 60-man Panamanian Airport Security force. Another group of 100 Panamanian police had also been trained by the USAF SPs to assume airfield perimeter control responsibilities. This Panamanian force relieved elements of the U.S. 7th Infantry Division of that duty. The 7th ID personnel had assumed the responsibility from the 82nd Airborne Division at D+2, who had previously assumed it from the Rangers at mid-morning on D-Day.

JUSTICE AND CORRECTIONS SYSTEM

The greater challenge for both the new Panamanian government and the U.S. diplomatic and military staff was to institutionalize democracy in Panama. On December 18th, two days before *Just Cause* began, Major General Cisneros had directed the preparation of a small cell that would be the focal point for rebuilding the Panamanian Police Force. Six specialists composed the original group, known as the U.S. Forces Liaison Group. General Cisneros met with the team on the 19th of December and explained the directive and its purpose. Conceptual planning began immediately following the meeting.

On D+1, the fledgling Panamanian national government requested the assignment of American military personnel to act as advisors to each of the functional ministries. As a consequence of this request, the original planning cell was renamed and expanded on December 22nd. Military Support Group (MSG) - Panama was the new designation and was officially designated as a joint headquarters under JTF-Panama. The mission of the MSG was to control and coordinate all civil affairs, PSYOP, intelligence, logistics, communications, Military Police, and engineering efforts that were in direct support of the new government.

Within a week the MSG gave way to, and was incorporated into, a larger and broader missioned Civil Military Operations Task Force (CMOTF). The CMOTF was created to handle the full range of support required to meet the needs of the new situation. Most of the Americans assigned to the task force were volunteer government or municipal specialists from the civil affairs reserve community. Next to the immediate need for refugee relief, the reestablishment of law and order was the primary CA missions. As the CA personnel arrived, they were assigned to the Civil Military Operations Task Force. The task force was structured into functional teams to support the Ministries of Finance, Public Works, Health, and Justice as well as the office of the President and an Embassy Coordination Team.

Of particular importance was the administration of the justice system. Based on this need, the CMOTF commander organized a three-team public security effort. The teams focused on judicial liaison, law enforcement, and the administration of the correction facilities. The teams were staffed by CA specialists including judges, police officers, correction officials, and lawyers. The judicial team's first mission involved review of the records of the more than 5,000 Panamanians detained by American forces. The detainees included former members of the PDF and the paramilitary DIGBATs as well as criminals and street looters. Working with Panamanian officials, the review was completed and most of the detainees were released by January 20, 1990. The judicial team also assisted the Panamanians in getting the court system back in operation during the same period.

Meanwhile, the correction team assessed the major Panamanian prisons throughout the country. Several of the facilities had been the target of the American combat forces. Their mission had been to search for and free imprisoned opponents of the former regime. In some cases the damages inflicted during the American assaults were substantial and repairs were needed to make them serviceable again. In other cases, the original facilities were in such poor condition that they warranted total rehabilitation. The correction team made the assessments, organized the repairs, coordinated the care of the inmates, and assisted in the hiring and screening of the guard force.

The third team focused its effort on restructuring the law enforcement apparatus. An initial and essential step in this process was the development of a new civil-oriented police force supportive of, and responsive to, the democratically elected civil government. Given that many former PDF members would constitute a significant percentage of the new public security force, Fuerzas Publicas de Panama-FPP, a relapse to the old ways of petty graft and corruption was a danger.

U.S. forces initially assisted in vetting the police candidates; however, the ultimate responsibility rested with the Panamanian civil authorities. The first task was to identify candidates who were still loyal to Noriega, who had a history of committing abuses, or had been involved in questionable or illegal activities. The new government took this responsibility seriously. When it was discovered that the first head of the new Public Security Force had a million dollars in his personal bank account, he was immediately relieved of duty by the Panamanian authorities and detained until an investigation could be conducted to determine the source and legitimacy of the money. Other former PDF members were subsequently removed as well.

By the end of January, more than 400 candidates had been screened, vetted, and received training for the new Panamanian Police organization. All of the candidates received a specifically constructed course on basic police ethics and procedures that emphasized protection rather than the intimidation of the civilian population. Two of the new police elements were the Rural Area Police Element (RAPEL) and the Metropolitan Police Liaison Element (MAPLE). The American trainers maintained liaison teams with the two elements to observe and report the progress of the new police officers. The information was provided to the International Criminal Investigative Training Assistance Program (ICITAP), which had the charter to train the police. Normally U.S. military forces are prohibited from training foreign civilian police. This is a provision of the U.S. Foreign Assistance Act of 1961, Sections 660 and 534. However, in Panama, U.S. military personnel, primarily Military Police and Special Forces personnel, were specifically authorized to participate and conduct assistance programs such as combined patrols, precinct house administration, as well as monitoring and reporting adherence to training standards.

In the first six months of 1990, U.S. military police routinely accompanied the new Panamanian police officers on their patrols in the cities. In the interior rural provinces, U.S. Special Forces reservists were assigned to assist the CA civil law enforcement personnel in the development of the new security forces. Many of these SF reservists were policemen in their civilian occupation.

INFRASTRUCTURE ASSESSMENT TEAMS

Civil affairs personnel also participated in area assessments to determine the type and extent of other assistance that was needed. Working with Panamanian counterparts, American teams assessed roads, local power stations, utilities, schools, churches, and water and medical facilities. As the assessments were assembled and amalgamated, they were ranked in importance. Due to the limited amount of military funding available, only a small percentage of the recommendations were immediately implemented. Most of the larger budget items were passed on to the U.S. and Panamanian civil agencies for consideration and action. However, DOD and SOUTHCOM continued to assist the government and people of Panama through a host of nation-building projects. These projects generally fell into one of two major categories: field engineering and medical assistance.

ENGINEER PROJECTS

Engineering assistance projects began early in 1990, and included upgrading roads, repairing bridges, refurbishing schools, health clinics, and other public facilities, drilling wells, and constructing or repairing sewage and water supply systems. The majority of such facilities had deteriorated because of a lack of adequate long term maintenance, not as a result of any U.S. military action.

From April to June 1990, under the auspices of Exercise *Fuertes Caminos-Panama '90* (Spanish for "strong roads"), the U.S. Army South's 536th Engineer Battalion and United States-based engineer units (U.S. Army National Guard, Air National Guard and Air Force engineer units) assisted the Panamanian Ministries of Public Works, Education, and Health in completing 75 projects. These included refurbishing 46 schools, three hospitals, and 14 bridges, as well as repairing 500 kilometers of roads, a seawall, and five public buildings in eight of Panama's nine provinces.

From July to December 1990, under Exercise *Cosecha Amistad '90* (Spanish for "Harvest Friendship") the 536th Engineer Battalion completed another 44 projects, including 19 schools, seven health clinics, 13 wells, 23 kilometers of road, a foot bridge in Darien province, and the San Blas Archipelago. Also completed was the installation of a major sewer system in the province of Las Tablas begun earlier under *Fuertes Caminos*.

From January through August 1991, approximately 5,000 Army and Air National Guard and Air Force engineers deployed to Panama in ten 2-week rotations to participate in a follow-on combined engineer exercise. *Fuertes*

Caminos '91, as the deployment was called, was conducted throughout Panama by two task forces. This seven-month effort involved 144 projects and included repairs to 75 kilometers of roads, 13 schools, clinics and other public facilities, and drilling 14 wells.

During October through November 1991, 150 U.S. soldiers rebuilt three schools and two health clinics in the districts of San Miguelito and Tocumen in Panama Province. Soldiers from the Missouri Army National Guard teamed with soldiers of U.S. Army South's 536th Engineer Battalion and employees of Panama's Ministry of Education to form three 50-man teams. As Task Force 203, the three teams repaired the Guillermo Patterson, Republic of India and Caimitillo Centro schools. Meanwhile, employees of the Ministry of Health joined other American soldiers to repair the San Isidro and Las Mananitas health clinics.

From January through June 1992, approximately 6,000 U.S. Army Guard and Army Reserve soldiers, and Air Force Reservists participated in a combined-joint exercise with several Panamanian Ministries. The American personnel deployed to Panama in ten 2-week rotations for their annual training, and worked with members of the Panamanian Ministries of Public Works, Health, Education and the Water Works Institute.

Together, the U.S. military engineer units, Panamanian government employees, and community volunteers repaired 104 kilometers of roads, 50 schools, 24 medical clinics, and installed 169 water pumps in the provinces of Herrera, Los Santos, Cocle, Panama, Veraguas and the San Blas Archipelago.

MEDICAL ASSISTANCE

During the first weeks of *Promote Liberty*, U.S. forces identified locations long neglected and in desperate need of medical attention. A list of these locations was compiled, and provided to the United States Southern Command Surgeon's Office and the Military Support Group. The 142nd Medical Battalion was tasked to conduct a series of Medical Readiness Training Exercises (MRTEs) at the most crucial locations. During the first 40 days following *Just Cause*, the battalion conducted four major MRTEs, providing medical and dental assistance to more than 4,000 Panamanian civilians in the western provinces.

During the first seven months of assistance, while the engineers were rebuilding vertical and horizontal structures, U.S. military and Panamanian medical teams were providing health care to children, adults, and domesticated animals in remote areas of the country. The teams provided health services to more than 46,000 medical patients and 24,000 dental patients plus veterinary services to 22,000 livestock. Medical treatment included vaccinations, medical exams, and gynecological services for women. Dentists offered prophylactic treatment, fillings, and extractions. Veterinary services included vaccination and deworming. Additionally, a preventive medicine team trained local residents on the importance and benefits of practicing environmental, home and personal preventive medicine.

In conjunction with the Panamanian Ministry of Health, a sustaining medical support concept was developed in April. The major objective in this effort undertaken at the request of the Panamanian Ministry of Health was to demonstrate to the Panamanian people that their government truly cared for them. The effort evolved into Panamanian-American medical assistance teams of 30 to 40 Panamanian health care providers and approximately 20 American medical soldiers.

In the early stages of Operation *Promote Liberty*, more than $2.1 million worth of medical supplies and food were distributed in Panama. Under another humanitarian aid program, the U.S. military in 1990 donated more than $6.7 million in medical supplies and pharmaceuticals. This aid package was arranged through the Department of Defense with the U.S. Army Medical Material Agency in Maryland serving as the purchasing agent and Gorgas Army Community Hospital in Panama serving as the transfer agent.

During 1990, personnel from the Panama-based 830th Air Division (U.S. Air Forces Panama), worked with the Ministry of Health, other Panamanian officials, and community leaders to control the spread of dengue fever by cleaning up mosquito breeding areas in Panama City and nearby areas. More than 1,000 abandoned cars, which were being used as nesting areas for the *aedes aegypti* mosquito (which transmits dengue fever) were removed and destroyed. After 1990, other assistance programs, both engineering and medical, continued to be conducted by SOUTHCOM largely through the use of reserve and national guard units and teams from the United States on their annual two-week active duty tours.

View of Modelo Prison after the Comandancia was leveled. The Modelo prison itself was torn down in the fall of 1996 by the Panamanian government after being condemned as inhumane and unhealthy. Photo courtesy of the author.

New apartment units that replaced those burned during the assault on the Comandancia. Photo courtesy of the author.

CHAPTER TWENTY
AFTERMATH AND HERITAGE

Operation *Just Cause* neutralized the PDF, and unseated the Noriega regime. It began the restoration of democracy. It made possible the installation of those who had actually won the May 1989 elections and eliminated the threats to the U.S. community in Panama.

From the perspective of human cost, the United States paid the least, while the residents of Barrio Chorrillo paid the most. Panamanian deaths (PDF/ DIGBAT/civilian) were confirmed at 272 of which 50 bodies were unidentified. A year later, Panamanian authorities still listed between 75-80 as missing. Subtracting the 50 unidentified bodies from the higher missing figure (80) and adding those 30 to the confirmed count of 272, the total Panamanian deaths during the ten-day period of *Just Cause* numbered 302. This figure included all known Panamanian deaths that occurred during the period including those of normal causes and unrelated accidents.

American military fatalities numbered less than thirty, with non-fatal casualties approximating 300. However, one or two car bomb attacks on American garrison or housing areas, the successful use of a RPGs against American buses, trucks or helicopters, or a mortar attack on the Howard ramp or the Torrijos/Tocumen parking areas could have drastically changed the American figures.

From a political perspective, as indicated by polls taken in January 1990 and later, 89 percent of Panamanians viewed the American military action as a liberation operation. Operation *Just Cause* ushered in a new spirit of cooperation between the two governments which has been manifested by:

- U.S. assistance in rebuilding Panama's economy, including the lifting of the economic sanctions imposed in 1988 and approval of a $420 million aid package.

- Wide acceptance by Panamanians of the follow-on Operation *Promote Liberty* which consisted of nation-building and humanitarian assistance projects throughout the country. The projects were conducted with the concurrence, and many with the participation, of the Panamanian government and included repairing roads, bridges, schools, health clinics, and water and sewage systems, many of which had been neglected for years.

- New emerging working relationships on Canal and treaty issues were achieved. These were reflected by the confirmation in 1990 of the first Panamanian as Administrator of the Panama Canal Commission, and the appointment of four new Panamanians to the Commission's board of directors, replacing the previous Panamanian members. The new era also noted the absence of confrontation in the bi-national joint committee meetings that had been evident throughout most the 18 months preceding the execution of *Just Cause*.

The first formal meeting of the restructured joint committee in twenty-two months was held October 10, 1990 (the last previous meeting was held in December 1988). It was hailed by all committee members as a major manifestation of the new positive relationship between the two countries. With the abolishment of the PDF, all Panamanians on the joint committee were civilians, with the Panamanian co-chairman being the director of the Panamanian Executive Directorate for Treaty Affairs (under the Ministry of Foreign Relations). Another change was the expansion of the joint committee's responsibilities to encompass the activities formerly performed by the combined military board that had been abolished by the mutual consent of both governments.

The U.S. commitment to democracy and Panamanian civil control was clearly demonstrated by the United States' prompt response to President Endara's request for U.S. assistance in putting down a military coup attempt in December 1990. The coup was led by Eduardo Herrera Hassan, a former member of the PDF and recently appointed head of the new Public Security Force. In November, Herrera had been placed under house arrest for engaging in some questionable activities. Herrera and a number of his ex-PDF supporters broke their confinement on December 4th, and declared their opposition to the civil government. The Panamanian President characterized Herrera's actions as a threat to Panama's emerging democracy and requested immediate American assistance.

The American response was quick in coming. The Commander of SOUTHCOM was authorized to support the Panamanian government with military force, as appropriate, to restore order. Approximately 500 American military personnel, working under the Joint Task Force Panama organization and in conjunction with the Panamanian National Police succeeded in recapturing Herrera and his associates one day after they had broken confinement.

THE U.S. MILITARY DRAW DOWN

The U.S. Southern Command has continued to implement the Panama Canal Treaties by carrying out or overseeing U.S. treaty obligations, including planning for the total withdrawal of the U.S. military presence from Panama by December 31, 1999. The long-range planning which began in 1986 has evolved into a preliminary Treaty Implementation Plan (TIP). The preliminary TIP was developed by the Joint Chiefs of Staff in conjunction with Headquarters, U.S. Southern Command, and its service components, and the Office of the Secretary of Defense.

The TIP is a blueprint for an orderly phased withdrawal from Panama of the U.S. military presence by the end of 1999. The plan, originally announced publicly in December 1988, laid out a timetable for the withdrawal of U.S. military personnel and the turnover of 10 major U.S. military installations (as well as a number of other military facilities and areas in the Panama Canal Area).

The Office of the Joint Chiefs of Staff oversees treaty implementation issues through a working group chaired by its Joint Staff representative. The United States Southern Command's Treaty Implementation Division is the command's interface with the Joint Chiefs of Staff, the Office of the Secretary of Defense, the U.S. Embassy in Panama, the government of Panama and the DOD Executive Agent for the TIP, the Department of the Army.

In 1990, and in keeping with continued treaty goals, the U.S. forces resumed turning over facilities to Panama that were no longer deemed necessary by the U.S. forces, although there were no treaty-specified requirements to do so before 1999.

Beginning in 1991, SOUTHCOM conducted tours of U.S. military facilities (February 1991 on the Pacific side and June 1991 on the Atlantic side) for Panamanian officials. These officials included President Endara and his two Vice Presidents to give them an idea of the magnitude of U.S. military installations, facilities and areas to be transferred to Panama.

In January 1993, the United States Department of Defense announced that (in accordance with the Panama Canal treaty implementation) the number of U.S. military personnel assigned to Panama was to be reduced to approximately 6,000 by the end of 1995. In 1995, DOD announced that the SOUTHCOM headquarters would depart Panama in 1998. The official move took place on schedule with the SOUTHCOM headquarters taking up residence in Miami, Florida in the summer of 1998. The gradual draw down of the U.S. Army South and the relocation of the U.S. Army South headquarters to Fort Buchanan in Puerto Rico took place in early 1999. In the latter part of 1998, the residual American military presence was slowly being consolidated at the Howard-Kobbe-Rodman reservation pending the final turnover late 1999.

EPILOGUE
A MILITARY ASSESSMENT OF JUST CAUSE

Operation *Just Cause* set a number of records. It was the largest American use of strategic airlift assets to introduce tactical forces directly into combat since World War II. It was among the most complex and multi-faceted combat contingency operations undertaken by U.S. forces in the previous 30 years. It was also the single largest joint force, combined arms combat operation conducted at night since the Soviets invaded Czechoslovakia in August 1968.

Several new American weapons systems received their baptism of fire during Operation *Just Cause*, and then went on to receive public accolades in the deserts of the Arabian Peninsula in Operation *Desert Shield/Desert Storm* (Sep 1990-Feb 1991). These systems included the *Apache* helicopters, the Hellfire missile, and the F-117 fighter as well as a number of radios and night vision items. The F-117 and the AH-64 *Apache* ushered in a true night time, precision strike capability, that had been waiting in the wings for the previous three years. By the same token, *Just Cause* also confirmed the need and value of developing and fielding a follow-on to the Vietnam-vintage *Sheridan* reconnaissance vehicles.

From a joint command and control perspective, *Just Cause* was the first major execution of an integrated joint force structure involving both conventional and special operations forces. Other integrated force structures and contingency campaigns had been planned and prepared in the preceding five years, but Operation *Just Cause* was the field test. The advanced planning and cultural cross-fertilization of the two communities paid major dividends.

Taken against the quick reaction planning requirements of Grenada in 1983, the planning for *Just Cause*, although cyclical (and not without some organizational conflict), was a substantial improvement and provided a benchmark for integrated planning and focused execution. *Just Cause* planners sought to define the mission requirements, match the available forces against a specific mix of political and military objectives, and then maximize the capabilities of the forces. This was largely done within a framework for joint force command and control structure.

Coupled with these factors were the construction of an integrated communications architecture, and the refinement of many joint operating procedures. Interservice communication interoperability problems, which had plagued many operations in the past, were largely eliminated in *Just Cause*. A very viable combat medical support structure was proven with the resultant low fatality rate once a wounded serviceman was put into the system.

Just Cause was a major turning point – recognition – for both SOF and conventional forces. After years of "working the issue" in a variety of forums and circumstances, and despite differing personalities influencing the ebb and flow of cooperation, a steady measure of progress had been made. *Just Cause* was a reflection and consummation of the value of the cooperation and teamwork that had accrued over the previous three to five years. Mutual understanding and cooperation was evident in both planning and execution. The benefits of mutual support in many areas such as communication, airlift, fire and medical support finally came to the fore. They were proven to be highly effective, and created a major building block to the cooperative success of *Desert Storm* that was to follow a little over a year later.

The operation highlighted two areas that warranted better planning, preparation and follow-through. The most obvious was Civil Affairs, i.e. the preparation for the return to civil order, the protection of property, and the handling of the civilian population, particularly the displaced population of Chorrillo. This is a crucial aspect of any military campaign. It is even more crucial when the political objective is aimed at replacing one government structure with another, and supporting the development of a democratic alternative.

The other, equally critical, is of perpetual concern ,but rarely adequately addressed. This is the vulnerability of the force (and the mission) when the force lacks the means to obtain reliable information on the adversary and the operating environment. This was evident by the more than a half-dozen "dry-holes" the SOF chase teams assaulted in their quest to capture General Noriega. The majority of these attempts were initiated in response to untested HUMINT reporting, most of which was rumor and speculation. Any one or several of these reports could have led the force into a disastrous trap, which could have cost numerous American lives.

In the case of civil affairs and humanitarian assistance, a massive commitment of resources after the combat phase can often offset earlier planning shortfalls. However, this type of after-the-fact remedy (either a last minute rent-a-spy effort or the issue of a reward bounty) cannot be used to offset the force vulnerability (or loss of life) incurred when military, political or humanitarian action is based on unreliable and potentially deceptive information. This vulnerability can be, and is best offset by, detailed intelligence analysis conducted by highly experienced analysts, not the blind acceptance of the philosophy that "more" (reporting) is the solution.

Little did many of the American participants, or our national leadership, know that less than fourteen months later many of them would be involved in the liberation of another nation half way around the world. The lessons of a clear mission, solid planning and joint cooperation were to be proven again in the deserts of Iraq, Kuwait and Saudi Arabia, and the weapons that were baptized in Panama were among the "marvels" of *Desert Shield/Storm.*

In the final analysis, the greatest accomplishment of *Just Cause* was humanitarian and moral. It was the gift of opportunity that the men and women of the U.S. Armed Forces gave to the Panamanian people. It was a gift of joy in the present and hope for the future. As more than one young American said of their reception by the Panamanians, "It was like what we had seen in the pictures of the liberation of Paris; we were welcomed by the people as friends."

RESPONSIBILITIES

Under the terms of the Neutrality Treaty, Panama and the United States have agreed to provide for the permanent neutrality of the Canal, including guaranteeing nondiscriminatory access for merchant and naval vessels of all nations. In addition, U.S. and Panamanian warships are entitled to expeditious passage through the Canal at all times. U.S. freedom of action to maintain the Canal's neutrality is not limited by the treaty. Panama and the United States are committed by the treaty to jointly study the feasibility of a sea-level canal, and, if they agree that such a canal is necessary, to negotiate terms for its construction. In addition, the United States will have the right throughout the term of the treaty to build a third lane of locks to increase the ability of the existing Canal to handle larger ships, principally the new generation of super tankers and outsized container ships.

POSSIBILITIES

Given its national responsibility beyond 1999, a reconstituted Panamanian military would be larger and stronger than the PDF of 1989 and the Panamanian government no less likely to follow an American lead than in 1989. Considering the growing influence of several Asian countries in the economic fiber of Panama (and Canal expansion), any new Panamanian military structure could be a mixture of Chinese military training and philosophy with much of the ground forces weaponry being of Chinese, French or Polish origin. Regardless of the source of training and readiness, the Panamanian force of 2006 and beyond would pose a greater challenge than the PDF of December 1989.

FINAL ASSESSMENT

Could it be done again? It is well documented that the reduction of American forces that has been ongoing since 1994, although offset to some degree by technology, has left the United States with a substantially diminished military strength. Without a reversal of this downward trend, it would be impossible for the United States to field a force equivalent to that assembled for *Desert Storm* (500,000 U.S.) and equally impossible to rerun Operation *Just Cause* with similar forces and effectiveness. The fact that after December 31, 1999 the U.S. will not have the in-place manpower, communications and logistic infrastructure in Panama that contributed to the success of *Just Cause* reinforces that conclusion. It would be a whole new ballgame if the U.S. were required to take unilateral action to protect the Panama Canal in the future.

LIST OF ILLUSTRATIONS

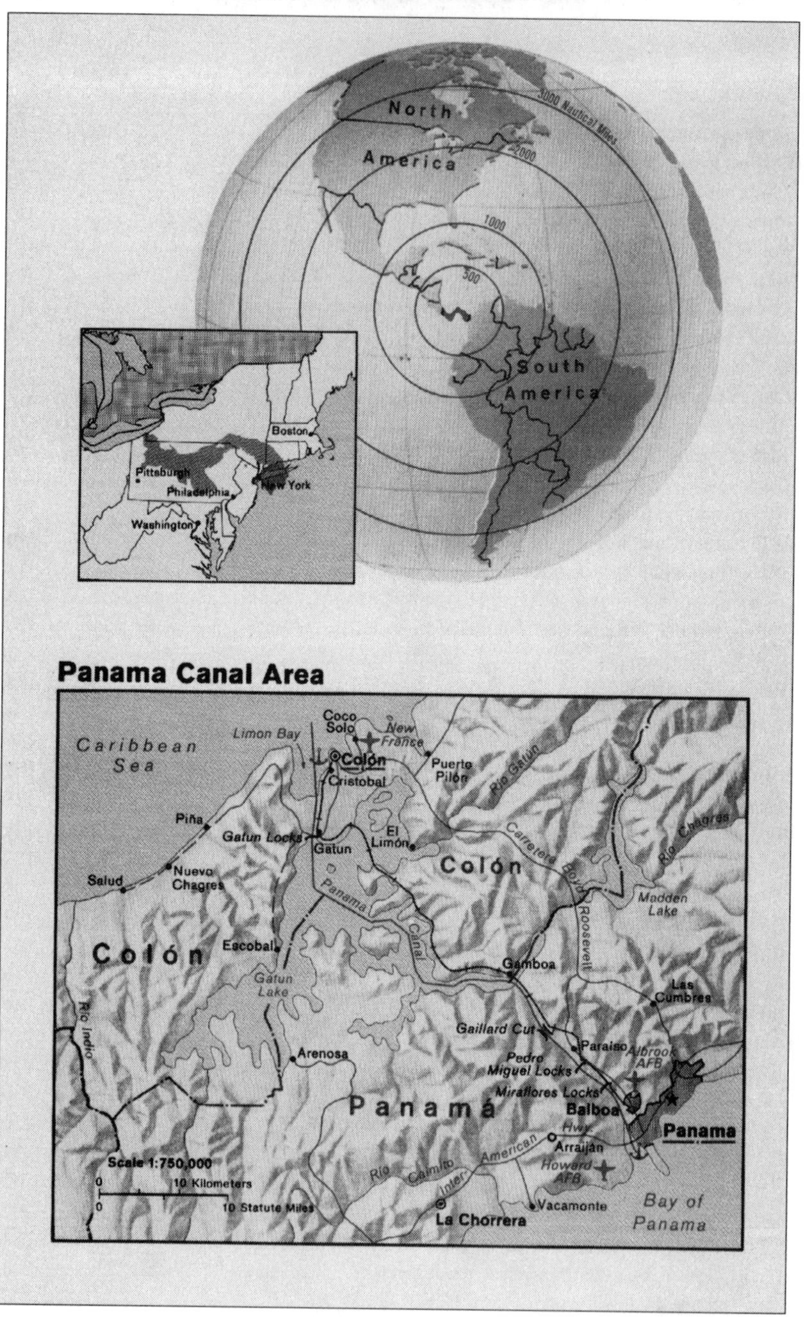

Country Overview

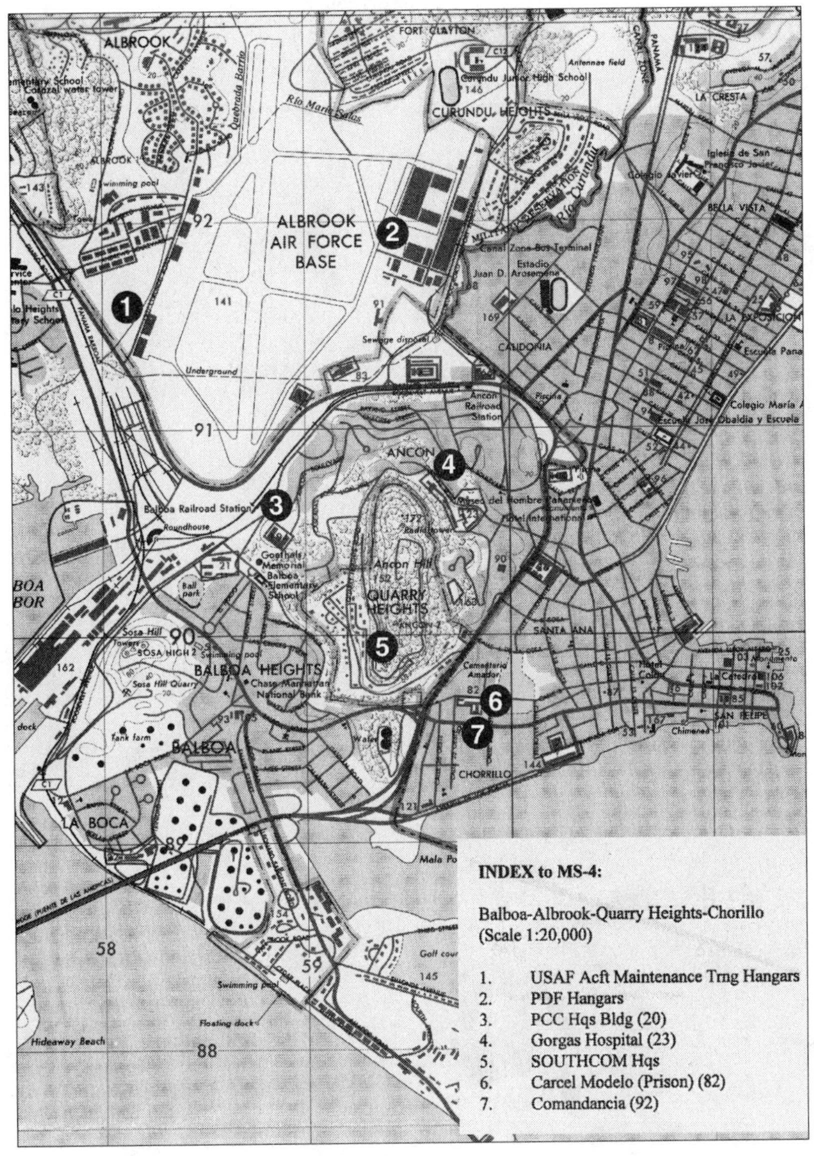

Balboa-Albrook-Quarry Heights-Chorillo (Scale 1:20,000)

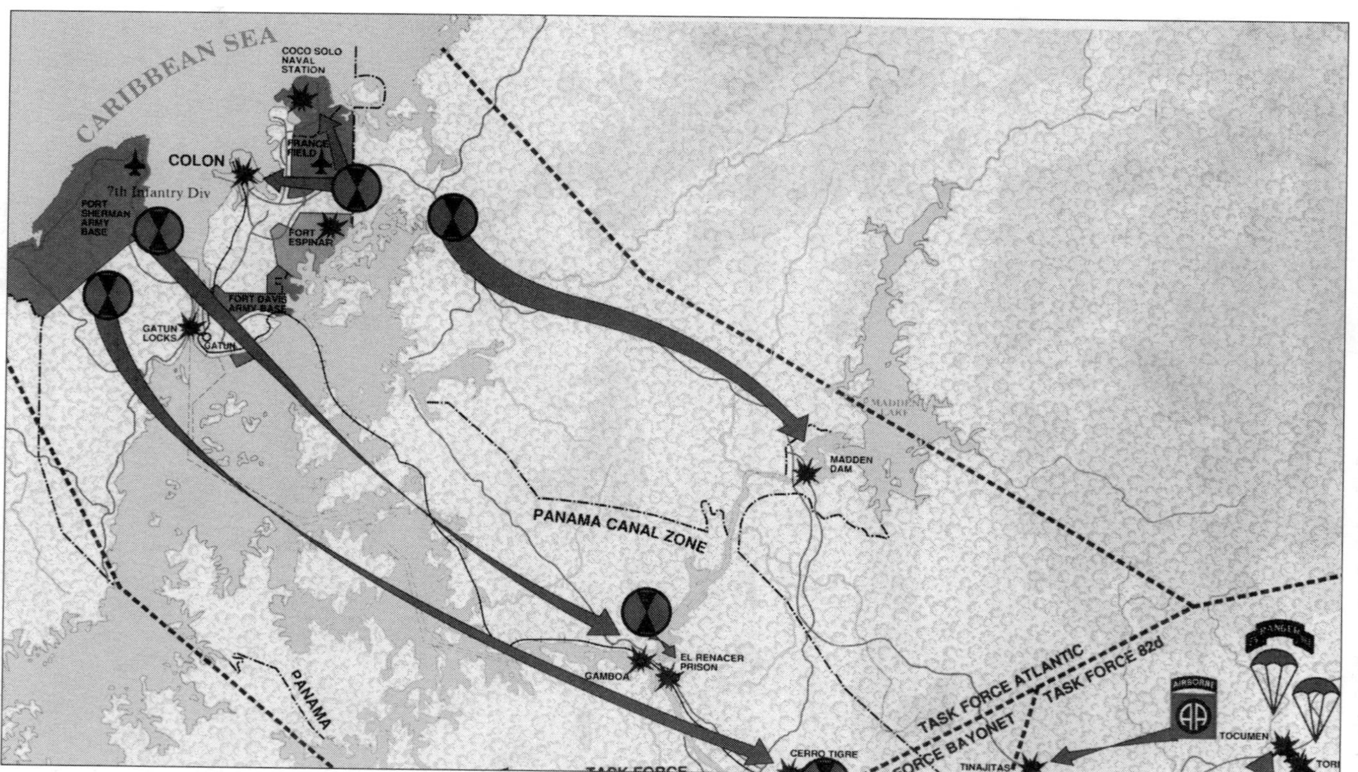

Operations in and around Colon (Atlantic). Map courtesy U.S. Army Institute of Military History.

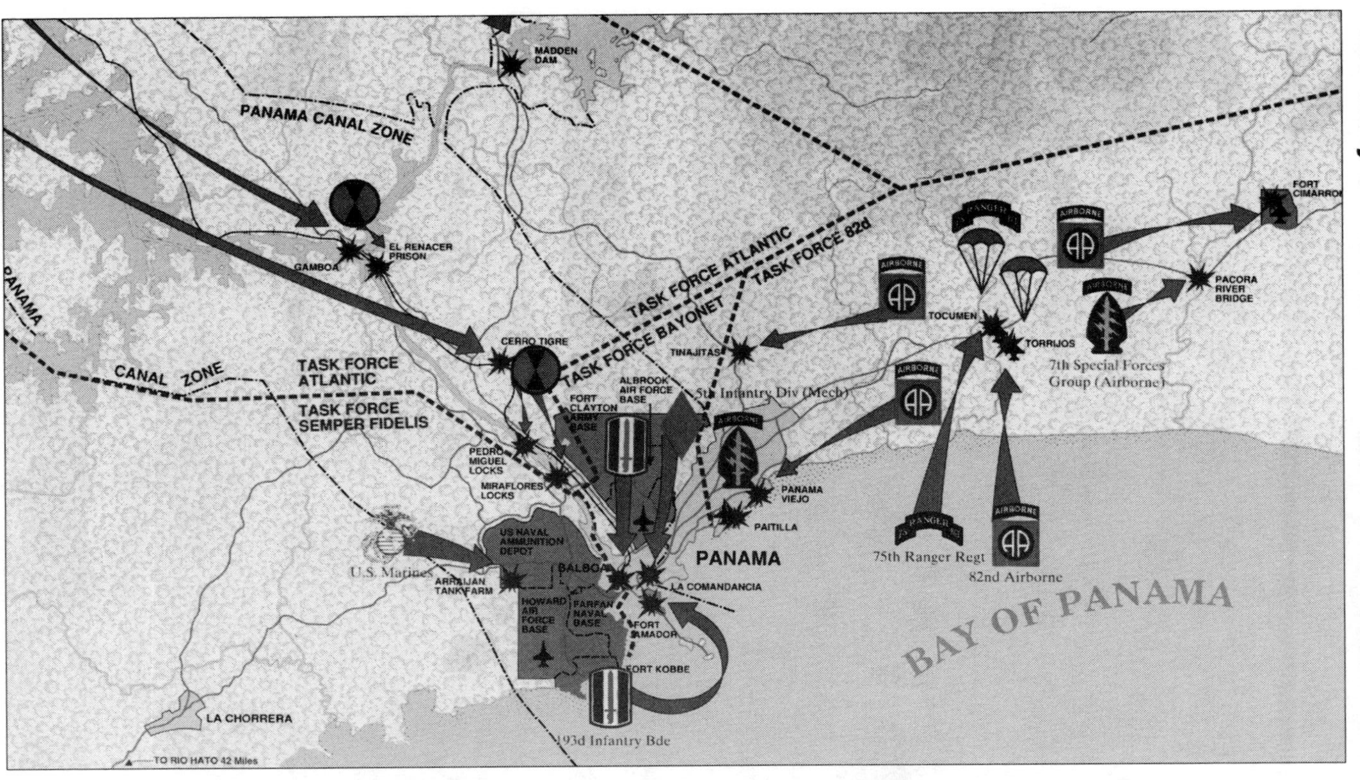

Operations in and around Panama City (Pacific). Map courtesy U.S. Army Institute of Military History.

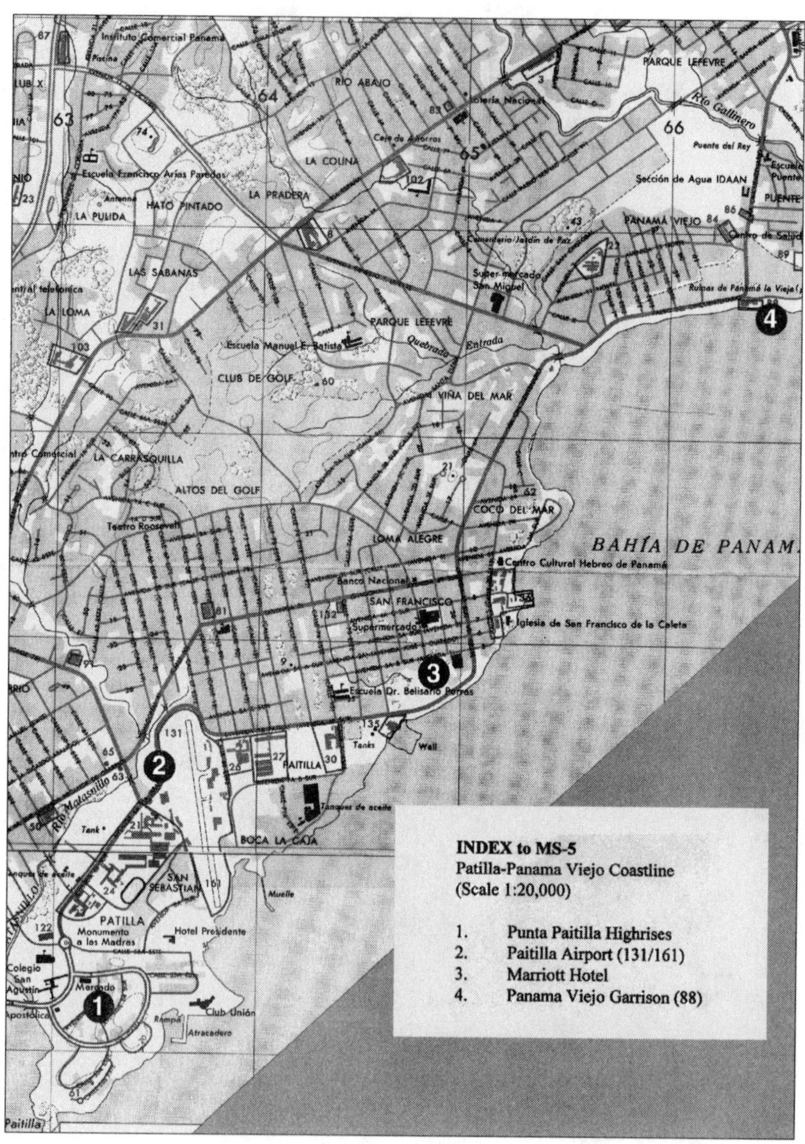

Paitilla-Panama Viejo Coast line (Scale 1:20,000)

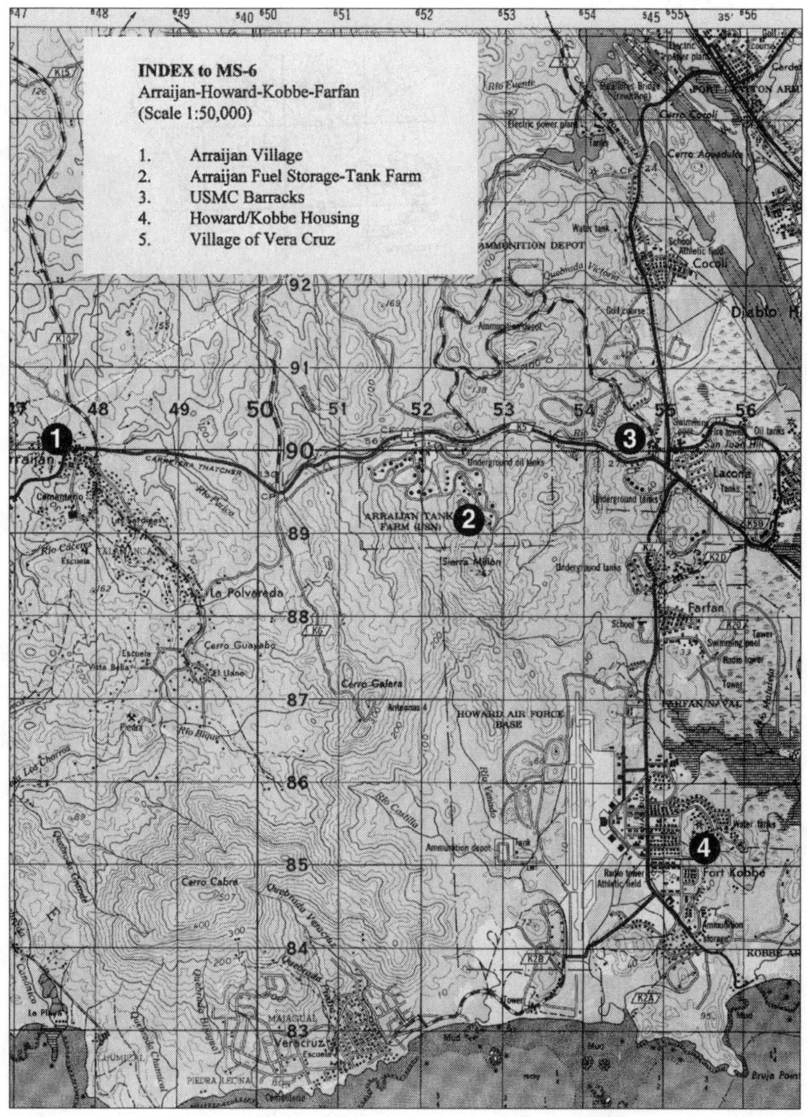

Arraijan-Howard-Kobbe-Farfan Overview (Scale 1:50,000)

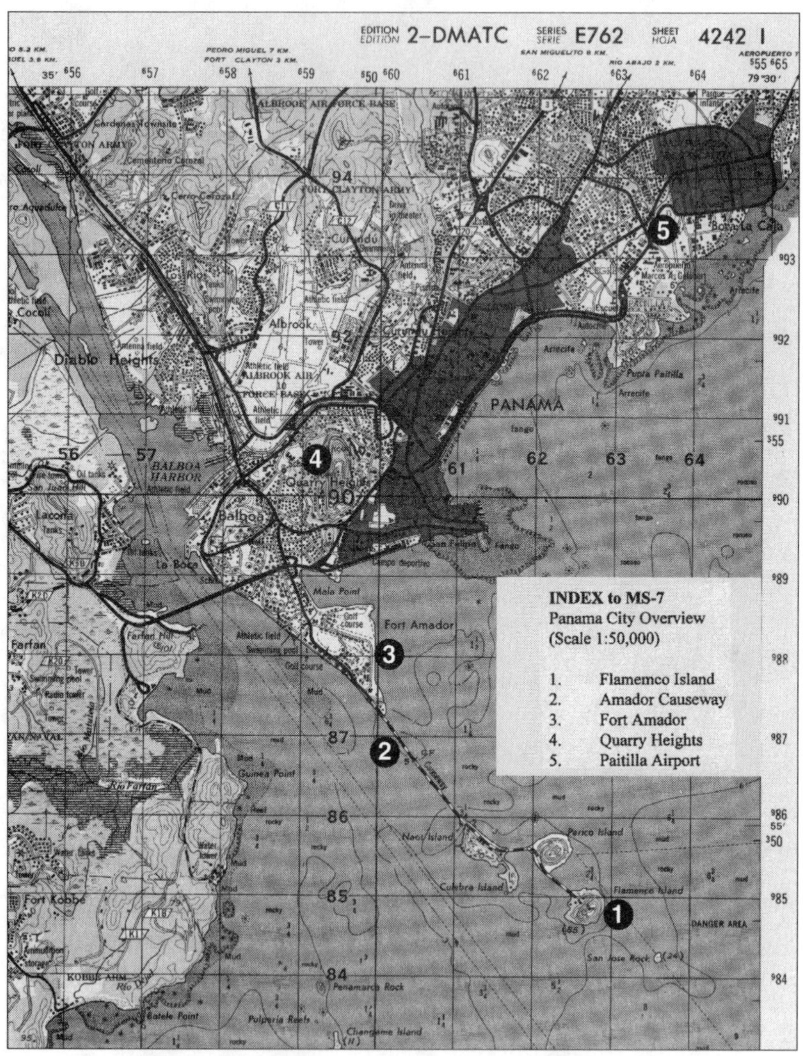

Panama City Overview (Scale 1:50,000)

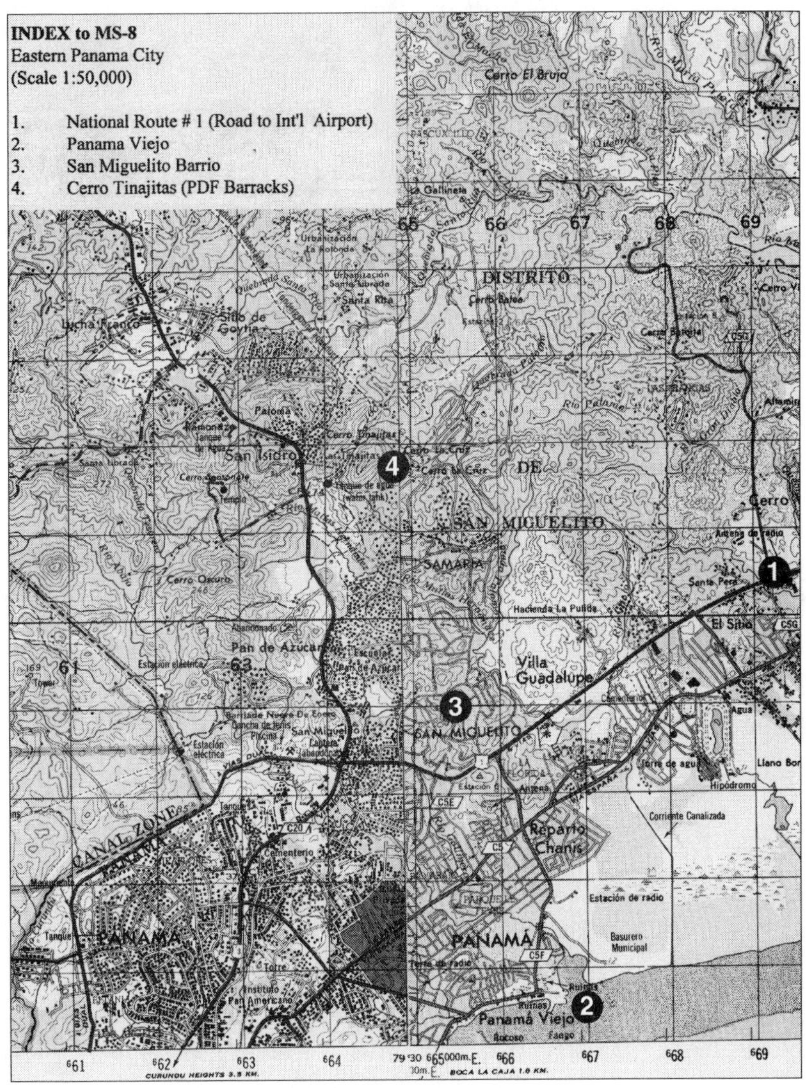

Eastern segment of Panama City (Panama Viejo) (Scale 1:50,000)

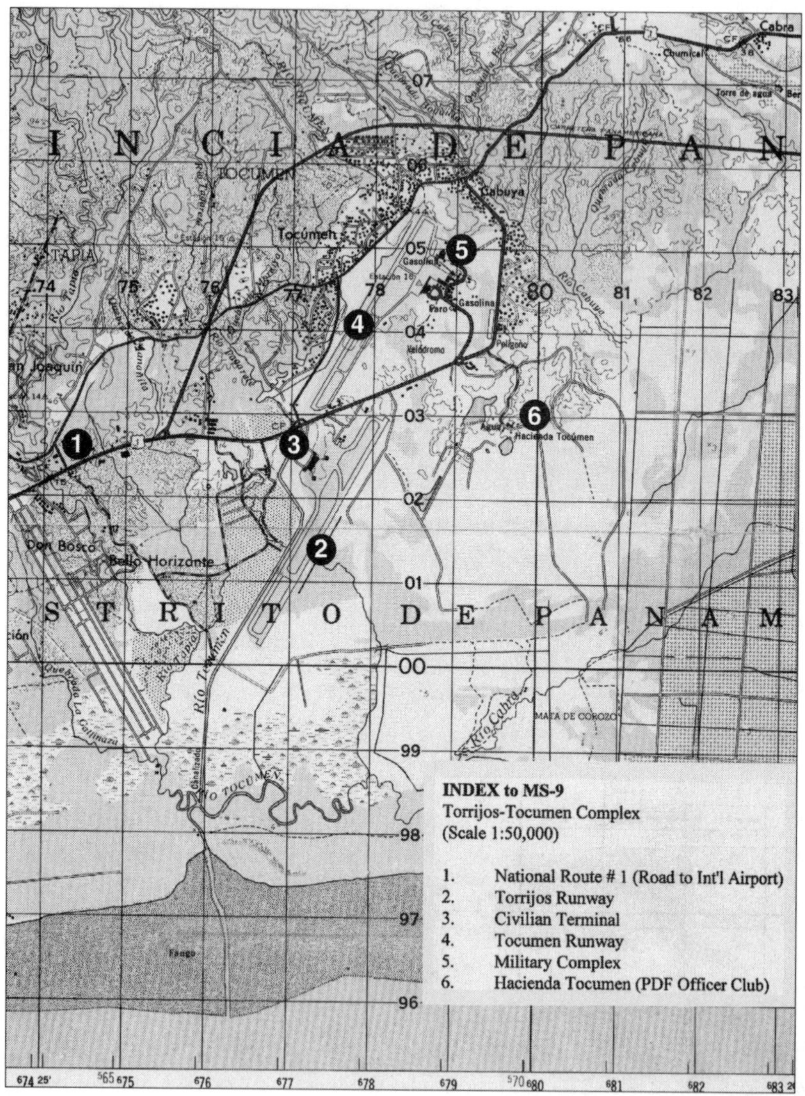

Torrijos/Tocumen Airport/Airfield Complex (Scale 1:50,000)

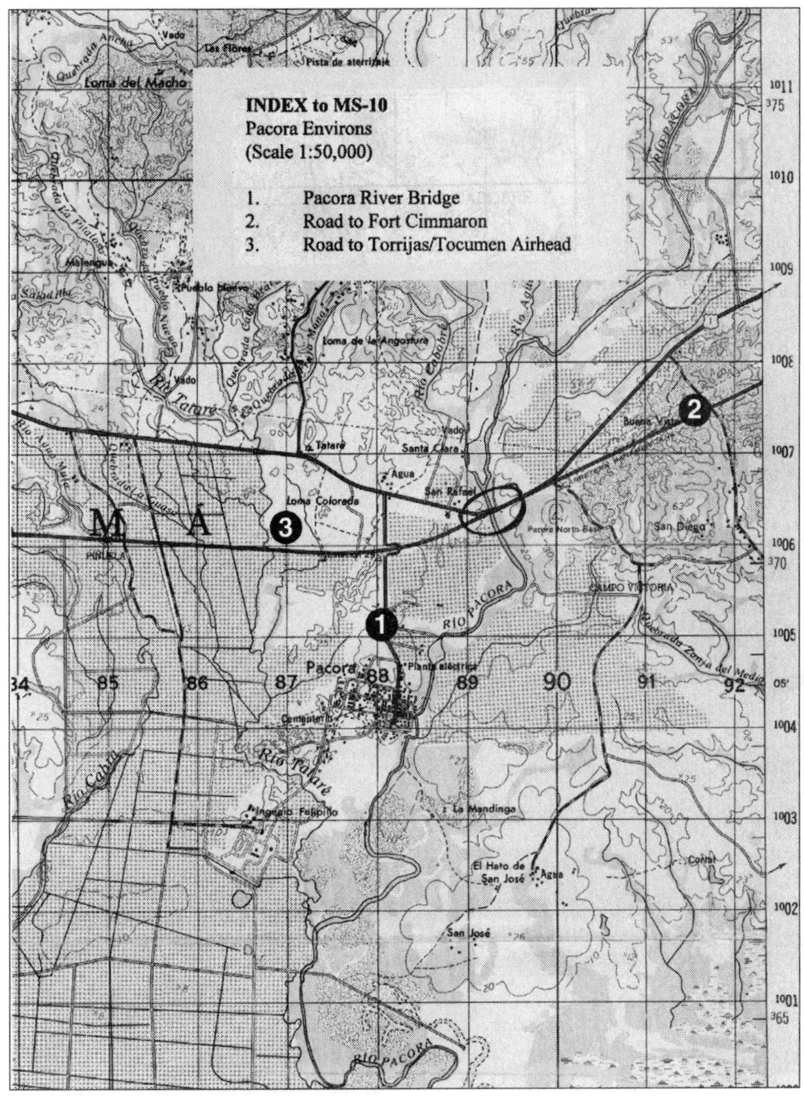

Pacora River Bridge (East of Torrijos) (Scale 1:50,000)

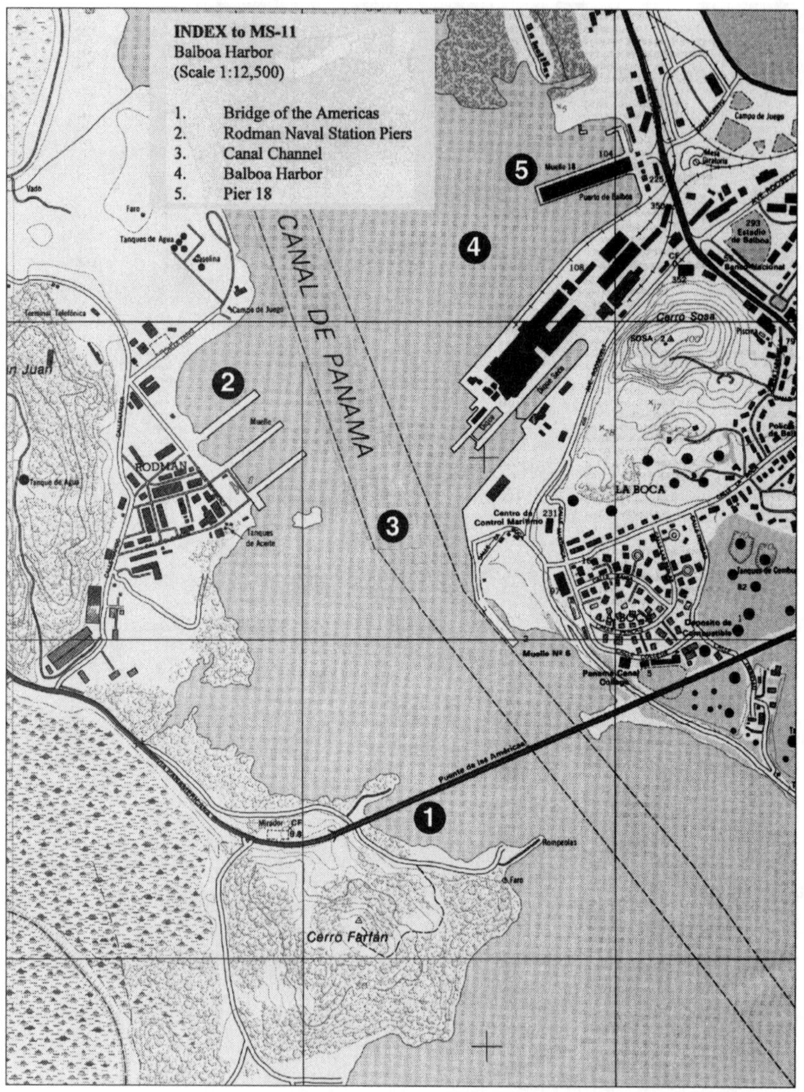

Rodman NS/Balboa Harbor (Scale 1:12,500)

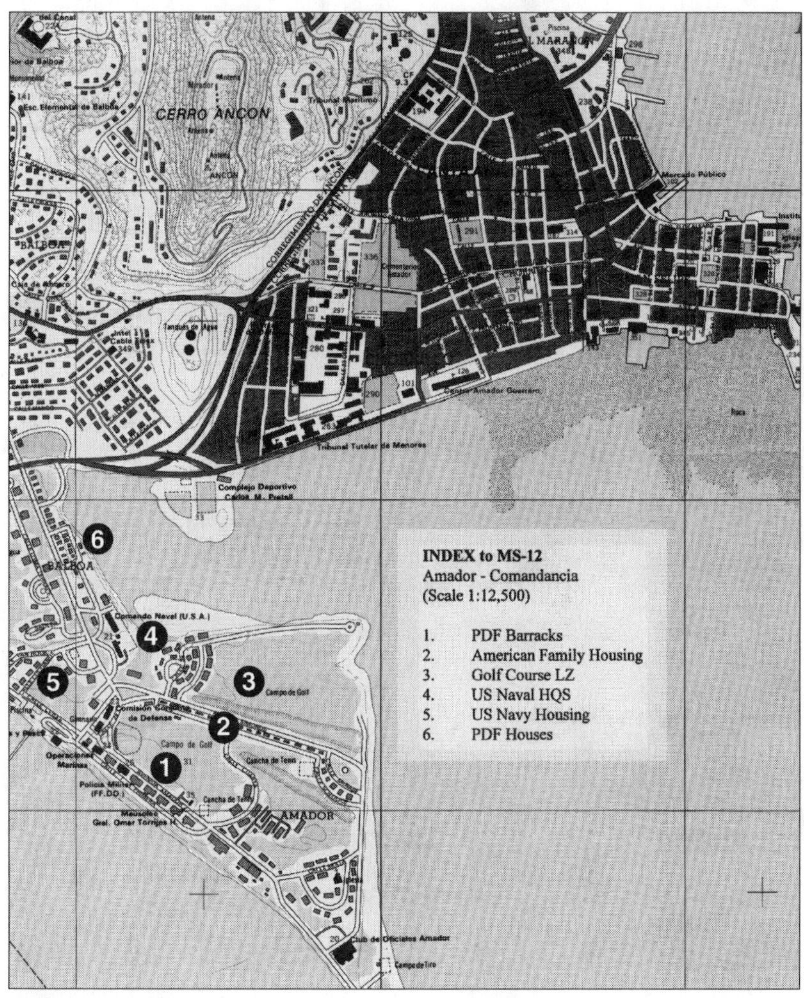

Fort Amador – Comandancia (Scale 1:12,500)

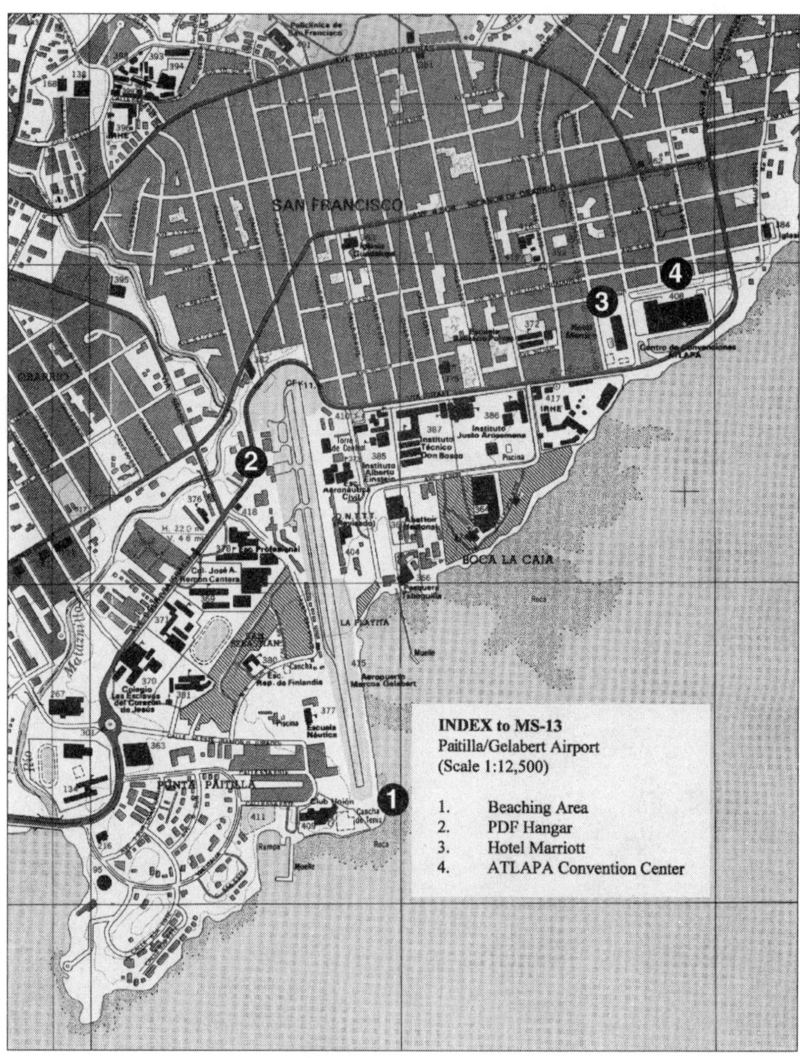

Paitilla/Gelabert Airport (Scale 1:12,500)

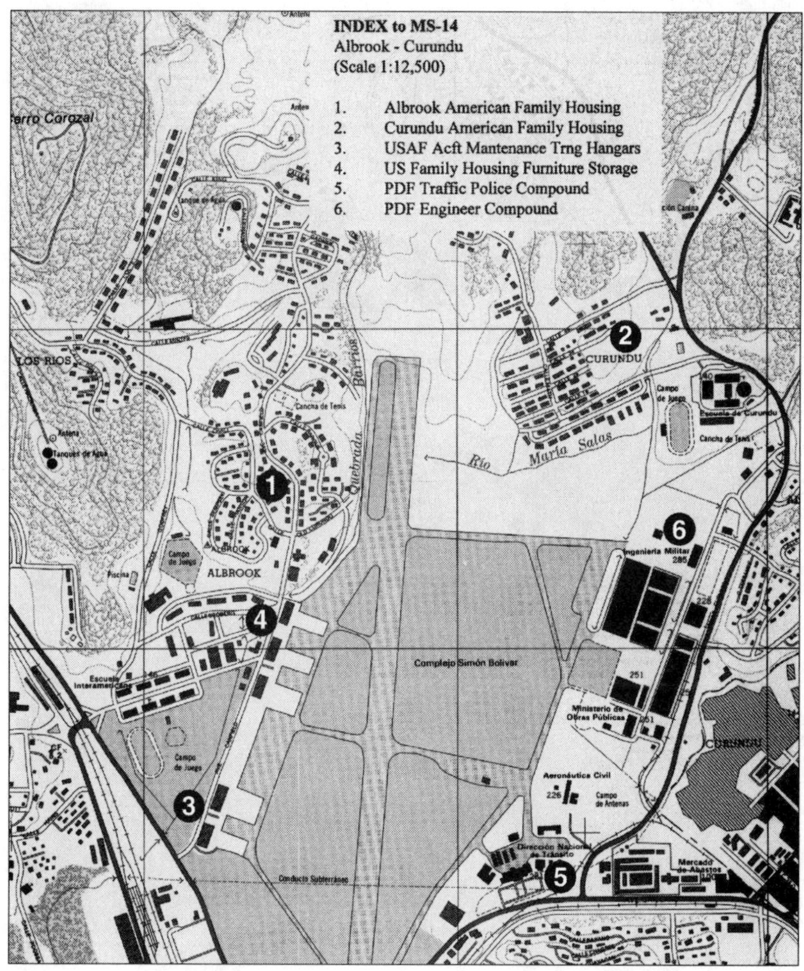

Albrook Runway/Curundu Housing (Scale 1:12,500)

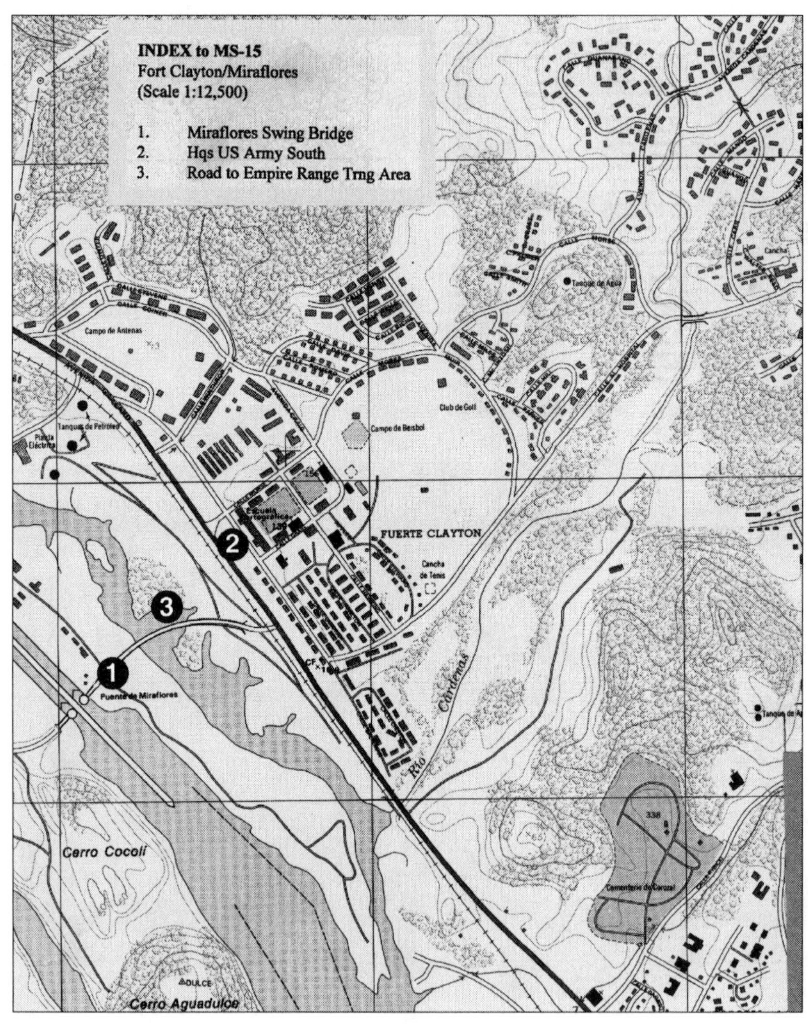

Fort Clayton/Miraflores Swing Bridge (Scale 1:12,500)

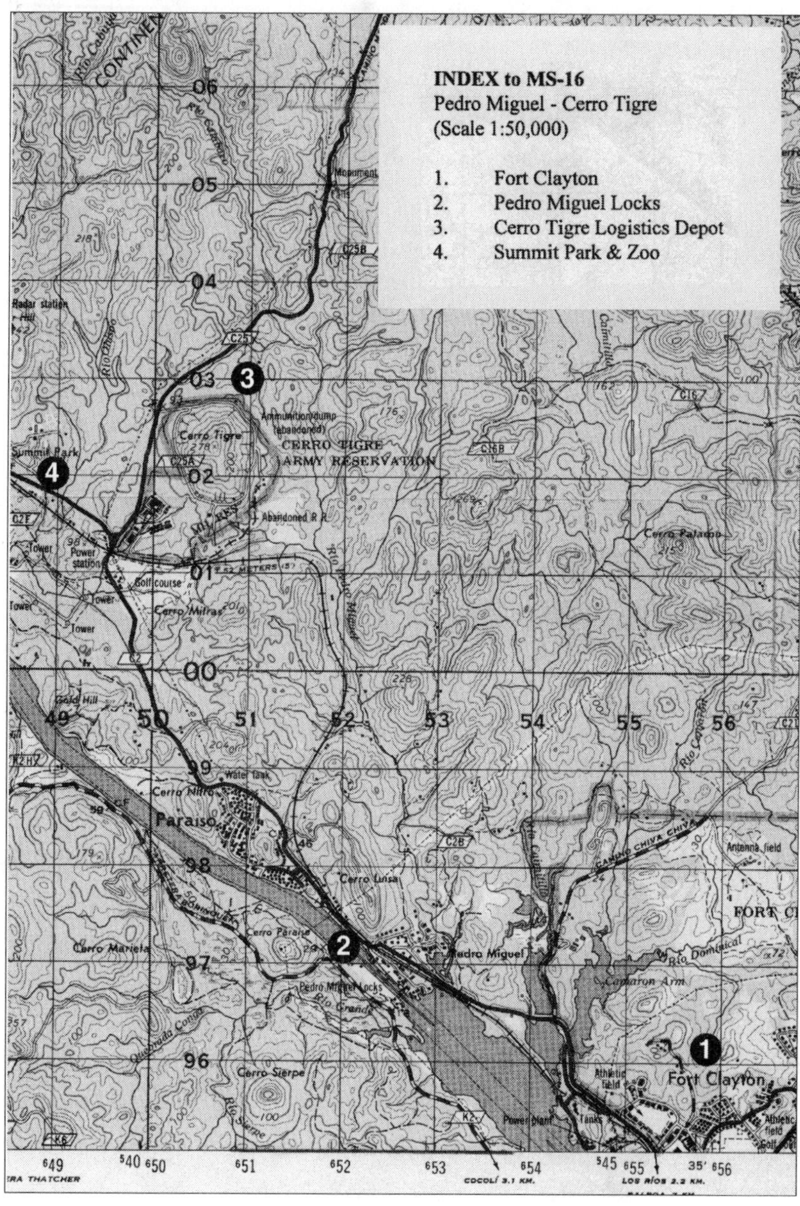

Pedro Miguel Lock & Cerro Tigre Logistics Ctr (Scale 1:50,000)

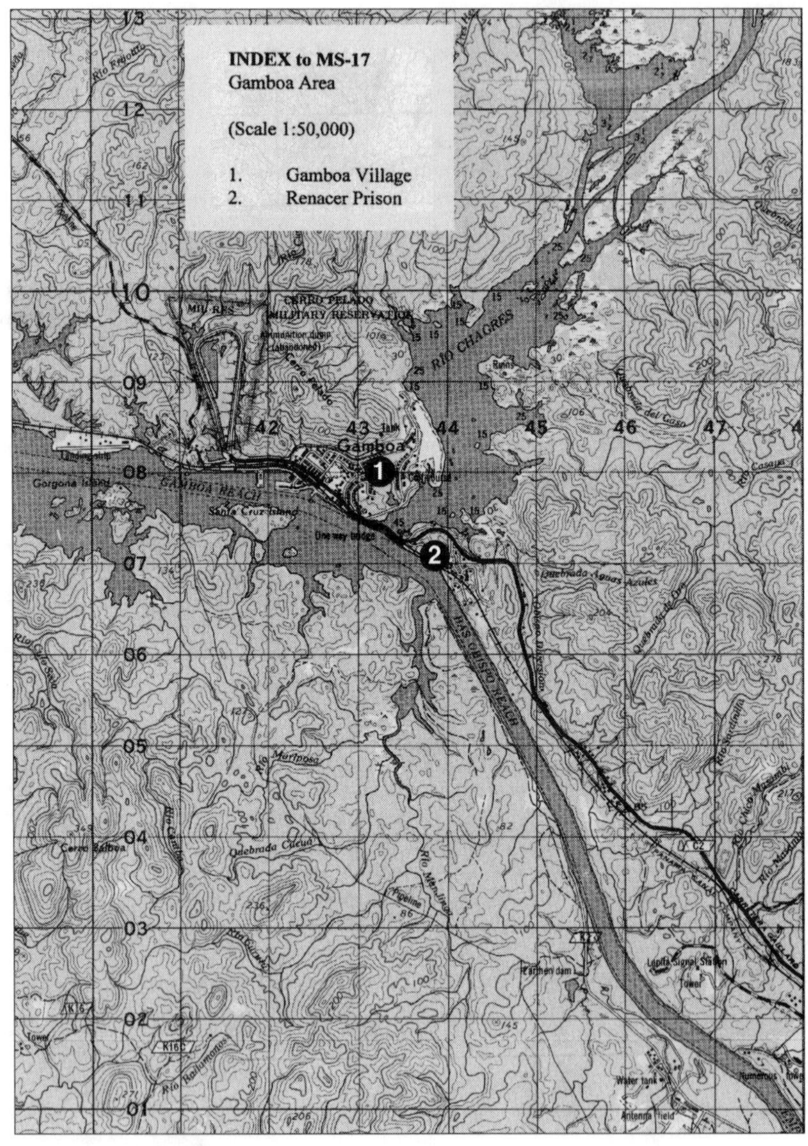

Gamboa Area (Renacer Prision) (Scale 1:50,000)

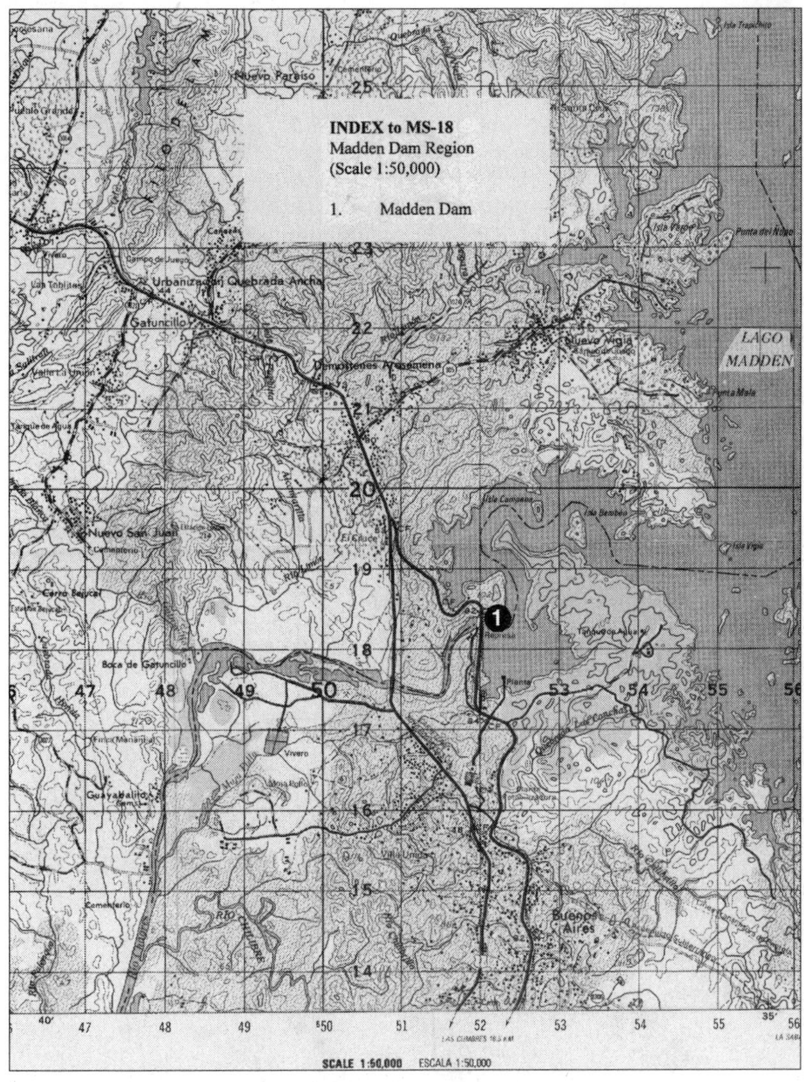

Madden Dam Region (Scale 1:50,000)

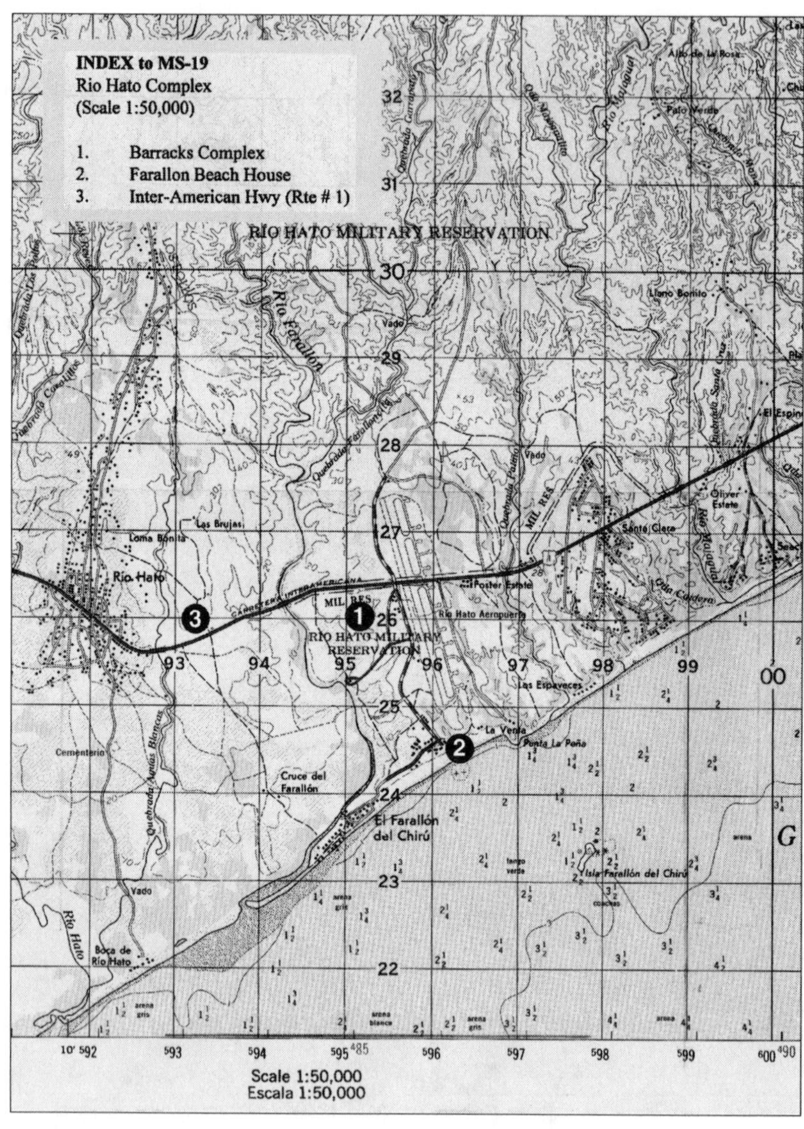

Rio Hato Military Reservation (Scale 1:50,000)

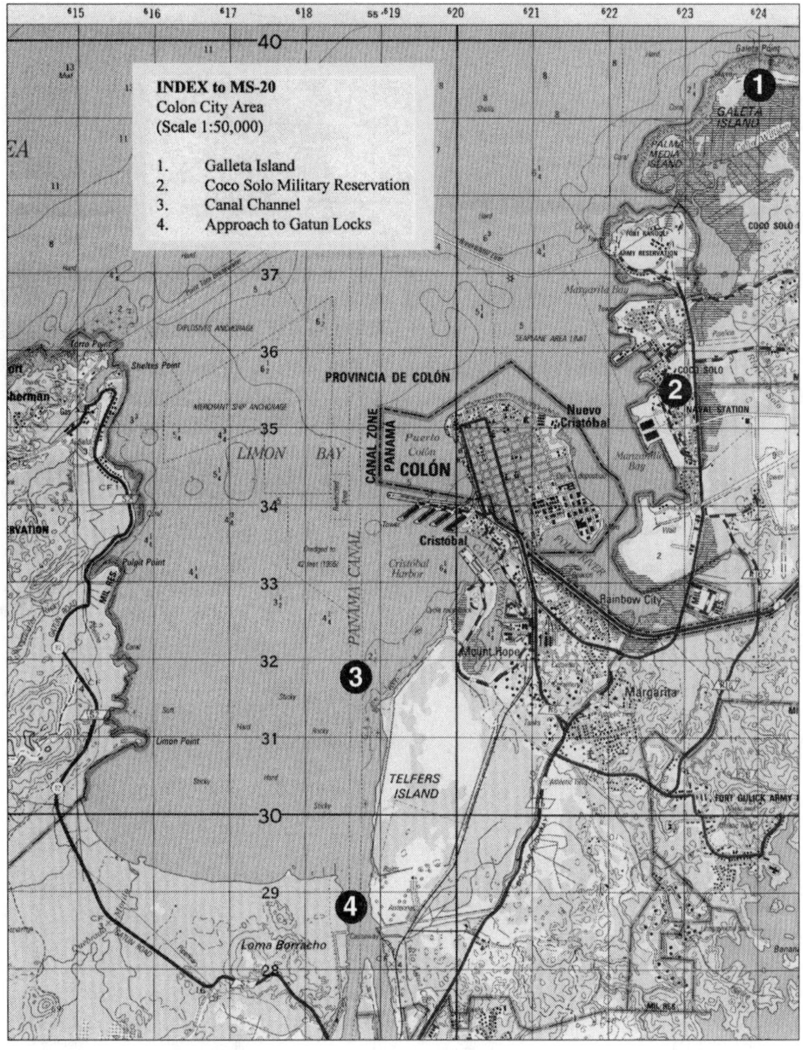

Colon Area Overview (Scale 1:50,000)

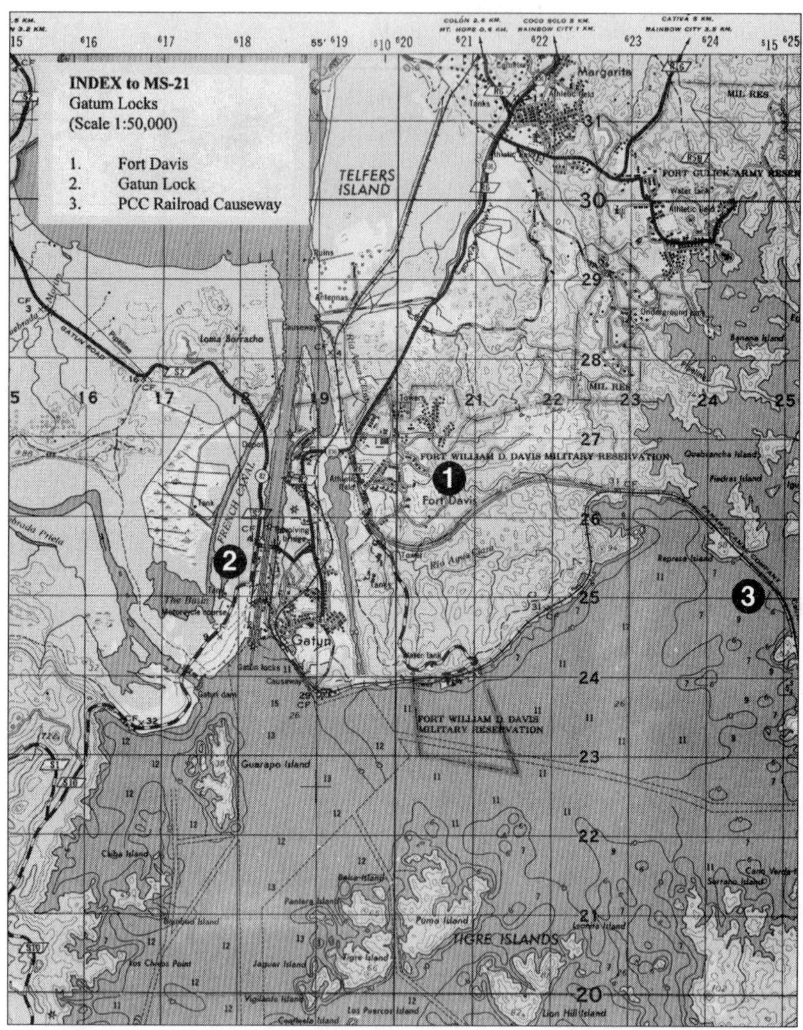

Gatun locks (Vicinity Colon) (Scale 1:50,000)

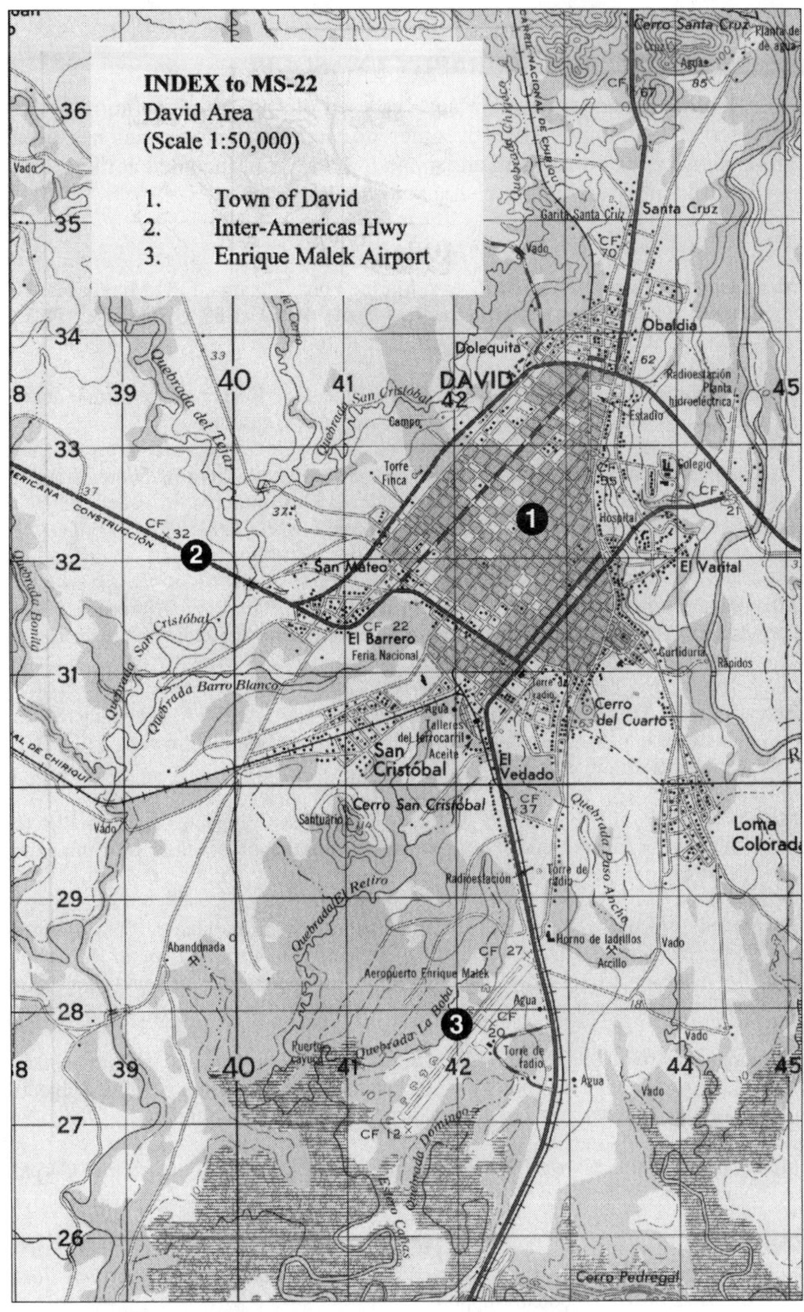

Town of David (Scale 1:50,000)

BIBLIOGRAPHY AND SOURCES

This list presents the main sources used during the preparation of the manuscript. To simplify use by other researchers, the material has been grouped by type of document and a notation has been included at the end of entries to identify the nature or focus of the material.

MEMORANDUMS

Memorandum: *First Impression Report*, Marine Force Panama, FPO Miami, Fla, 10 January 1990 (pages 1-2) with (pages 4-9) of OPORD 5-89, GHOSTBUSTERS /JUST CAUSE After Action Report.

Memorandum: *Panama Query Information*: undated: Response to media query regarding Marine participation in Operation *Just Cause.*

Memorandum from Commander, HHC, 1st Battalion (Airborne), 508th Infantry (Captain John H. Hort) to Commander 193rd Infantry Brigade, Subject: *Narrative Description of Events Surrounding HHC/1-508th INF During Operation Just Cause.*

Memorandum from Commander, Company C, 1st Battalion (Airborne) 508th Infantry (Captain Timothy J. Flynn) to Commander 1-508th IN (A), Subject: *Just Cause Information Request.*

Extracts from After Action Report 1-508th INF BN (ABN) A Company 587th Infantry (Jaguars), B Company 587th INF (Jungle Cats), C Company 587th INF (Combat Operations).

Memorandum from Commanders of Bravo and Delta Companies 3-504th PIR to Executive Officer 3-504th concerning the seizure of Madden Dam and the Cerro Tigre Logistics Center.

Memorandum from Commander 1/75th Rangers to Commander, 75th Ranger Regiment, dated 6 December 1990. Subject: *Summary of Ground Action at Torrijos/Tocumen (TT2) Ground action in Panama during Operation Just Cause* (20-21 Dec).

Memorandum from 193rd Support Battalion, Fort Clayton, Panama, to Commander, 41st Area Support Group, Corozal, Panama, dated 8 January 1990, Subject: *Executive Summary for Operation Just Cause* (Logistics Support).

Memorandum For Record: *JCEOI Operation Just Cause*, XVIII Airborne Corps, November 1991.

Memorandum from U.S.CINCSOUTH/SG (Surgeon General), dated 3 January 1990, to: JTFSOUTH/SG, Subject: *Comments Concerning Operation Just Cause* (2 pages) (Medical Support).

Memorandum For SOUTHCOM PAO, from SOUTHCOM J-3, dated 7 December 1990, Subject: *Just Cause Objectives* (2 pages).

Memorandum for: Commander in Chief, U.S. Southern Command, from Commanding General XVIII Airborne Corps, Subject: *Joint Task Force South* AFTER ACTION REPORT, *Operation Just Cause*, (JULLS FORMAT), dated 19 March 1990 (131 pages).

BRIEFINGS

1/228th Aviation, *Highlights of Operation Just Cause*, (Summary of Army Helicopter Operations conducted by Task Force Aviation which included 1/228th AVN, and Aviation Task Forces Hawk and Wolf) (17 pages).

7th Infantry Division (L) & Fort Ord, *Operation Just Cause*, (Summary of 7th Infantry Division involvement) (33 pages).

U.S. Southern Command, *Command Briefing on Operation Just Cause*, (102 pages).

75th Ranger Regiment, *Operation Just Cause* Briefing (25 pages).

12th Air Force (U.S.SOUTHAF), AIR FORCE CONTRIBUTIONS TO *Operation Just Cause*, (36 pages).

Commander, 1st Special Operations Wing, Press Conference Statement, January 10, 1990 (2 pages).

DOD NEWS BRIEFING, Secretary of Defense Dick Cheney & General Colin Powell, Chairman JCS, At the Pentagon Wednesday, December 20, 1989 - 7:45 AM - Office of the Assistant Secretary of Defense (Public Affairs) (10 pages).

DOD NEWS BRIEFING, by Lt. General T.W. Kelley, U.S.A, Director of Operations, Joint Staff, Thursday, December 20, - 4:40 PM (11 pages).

FACT SHEETS

U.S. Army Military District of Washington, FS-PO5, Casualties from Operation "JUST CAUSE" Panama (undated).

United States Southern Command: *Command History* (Revised 1987) (August 1992).

U.S. Southern Command: *Operation Just Cause; One Year Later* (Panamanian Fatalities and Common Graves) 14 December 1990 (Rev. 3 Jan 91).

U.S. Southern Command: *Panama Canal Treaties of 1977*, Rev. 27 Jan 92.

U.S. Southern Command: *U.S. Military Installations in Panama*, March 1992.

U.S. Southern Command: *Profile of the United States Southern Command*, 24 March 1992.

U.S. Southern Command: Panama Today: *U.S. Southern Command's Operation Promote Liberty*, 22 July 1992 (Rev.).

NEWS RELEASE: Public Affairs Office, Hqs U.S. Southern Command, Quarry Heights, Panama, SCPA 89-12-7 : (17 December 1989) *U.S. Military Officer killed by Panama Defense Soldiers Last Night in Panama City.*

NEWS RELEASE: Public Affairs Office, Hqs U.S. Southern Command, Quarry Heights, Panama, SCPA 93-01-1: *Details of Panama Canal Treaty Implementation Plan Announced.*

SPECIAL PUBLICATIONS

Pamphlet: *Quarry Heights*, Hqs U.S. Southern Command (History of the Site 1908-1984).

Supplement to Annual Command History, Fiscal Year 1990 (300 pages), U.S. Army South, *Operation Just Cause/Promote Liberty* (Details of in country U.S. Army South contributions).

Draft, Chapter XVI, *Operation Just Cause/Promote Liberty*, undated (History of JC from perspective of U.S. Army SOUTH, 142nd Medical Battalion, 193rd Infantry).

Staff Ride: *Operation Just Cause, Task Force Bayonet*, 20 December Panama, March 1991.

Operation Just Cause: Honoring Task Force Regulars (Military Operations), 5th Infantry Division Review, 9 February 1990, *Washington Times* (21 pages).

Historical Summary of Operation Just Cause, 17 December 1989 - 12 January 1990, Headquarters 82nd Airborne Division.

Information Management Bulletin No.7, April 1990, a publication of the U.S. Army South (U.S. ARSO/SOIM), Fort Clayton, Panama (32 pages) (Communications).

Bulletin No. 90-9, Oct 90, *Operation Just Cause Lesson Learned*, Volume I. Soldiers and Leadership, Center for Army Lessons Learned, U.S. Army Combined Arms Command, Fort Leavenworth, Kansas.

Operation Just Cause: The Warriors, Compiled by Department of the Army Observation Team Chief, Colonel Frank Akers, Washington Times(Initial unedited field compilation - January 1990) includes non-Army actions & events such as initial Marine security operations and the U.S. Navy SEAL mission in Balboa Harbor (total of 13 actions told in tabs A-M).

Soldiers in Panama: Stories of Operation Just Cause - Center for Army Lessons Learned (CALL), Fort Leavenworth, Kansas - DA JUST CAUSE Observation Team, Chief Colonel Frank Akers, Edited version of *The Warriors* (less

Marine/SEAL events). Edited for publication by Army Office of Chief of Public Affairs (1990 - 28 pages).

Draft White Paper, submitted for security review prior to publication, o/a March/April 1992, PLANNING, *Operation Just Cause*, December 1989, Dr. Lawrance A. Yates, Combat Studies Institute, U.S. Army Command and General Staff College (12 pages).

(Student) Study Project-US Army War College Class 1992 - Lt. Colonel Douglas I. Smith, Army, Aviation in *Operation Just Cause*, Carlisle Barracks, PA 17013-5050.

Research Report, Strategic Studies Institute, U.S. Army War College. Carlisle Barracks, Pa.

The Fog of Peace: Planning and Executing the Restoration of Panama, (Chapter 3) John T. Fishel, April 15, 1992.

Operation Just Cause (Panama) - Joint History Office, Office of the Chairman of the Joint Chiefs of Staff - January 1990 (Ronald H. Cole) Library of Congress F1567.C64-1995.

JUST CAUSE: Marine Operations in Panama 1988-1990 - History and Museum Division, Headquarters USMC, Washington DC (Lt. Col. Nicholas E. Reynolds, USMCR 1996).

CONGRESSIONAL PROCEEDINGS

Statement of General Fred F. Woerner, Commander in Chief, U.S. Southern Command to the Senate Appropriations Committee, Defense Subcommittee, 13 April 1989 (21-22).

Joint Hearings before the Committee on Intelligence United States Senate, 101st Congress, First Session, October 1 and 17; December 22 1989 (1989 EVENTS IN PANAMA) (S.HRG 101-881), GPO Washington 1990 326-371 (160 pages).

Joint Hearings before the U.S. Senate Committee on Armed Services, Tuesday, May 22, 1990 (Nomination of Lt. Gen. Carl W. Stiner, U.S.A, to be General and Commander in Chief, U.S. Special Operations Command), GPO Washington, 1990 (pages 245-293).

Statement of Major General Hugh L. Cox, USAF, Deputy Commander in Chief, U.S. Special Operations, Command before the House Armed Services Committee (HASC), Sub-Committee, chaired by Representative Earl Hutto (D-FL), (March-April 1990), GPO Washington DC (pages 244- 279).

ORAL HISTORY INTERVIEWS

General Frederick F. Woener, Jr., U.S. Army, conducted by Lt. Colonel Ila Mettee McCutchon, USA, Project 1992-2, Vol. II, Carlisle Barracks, PA 17013-5008.

CONFRONTATION ZONE

Series conducted by: Dr. Lawrance Yates, U.S. Army Combat Studies Institute, Dr. Robert K. Wright, Jr., U.S. Army Center of Military History (Major Robert K. Wright, USA, XVIII Airborne Corps Historian).

Lt. General Carl W. Stiner, Commanding General, XVIII Airborne Corps/COMJTF SOUTH.

Major General William A. Roosma, Deputy Commanding General, XVIII Airborne Corps.

Major General James H. Johnson, Jr., Commanding General, 82nd Airborne Division.

Colonel Thomas H. Needham, G-3 XVIII Airborne Corps (J3JTFSOUTH).

Lt. Colonel Lynn D. Moore, Commanding Officer, 3rd Battalion, 504th Infantry.

Lt. General Carmen Cavezza, Commanding General, 7th Infantry Division (L)

Major General William M. Matz, Jr. Assistant Division Command, 7th Inf. Div. (L).

Colonel Michael G. Snell, Commander, 193rd Infantry Brigade.

Major Butch Muse, Operation Officer, 1st Bn, 228th Aviation Brigade.

PERIODICALS

The following list of periodicals is presented in two versions. The first, *ALPHA* version, presents the material alphabetically by author. The second, *BRAVO* version, groups the material by periodical and presents it in chronological order by publication date.

ALPHA VERSION

PERIODICALS - LISTED ALPHABETICALLY BY AUTHOR

Angelle, Lt. Col. Alexander, "U.S. Armed Forces Public Affairs: Roles in Low-Intensity Conflict," *Military Review* (January 1990): 50-56.

"The Architect of 'JUST CAUSE,' Lt. Gen. Carl Stiner, explains his Panama plan," (Interview), *DOD Early Bird* (from the *Army Times*), (March ?, 1990): B4-B8.

Armeli, Lt. Col. Thomas, "Lightfighter Communications in *Operation Just Cause*," *Army Communicator* (Winter/Spring 1990): 48-52.

"Army helicopter review," *Army* (August 1990): 23-24.

"Army Light Infantry Weapons in Panama: A Foreign Profile," *Army* (Feb. 1990): 12-13.

Baker, Caleb, "Army aims for highly mobile forces," *Army Times* (Jan. 15, 1990): 25.

Bennett, LTC William C.,"JUST CAUSE and the Principles of War," *Military Review* (March 1991): 2.

Bird, Julie, "After Panama - MAC in for the Long Haul," *Air Force Times* (January 15, 1990): 14-15, 68.

Blocher, Bob, "Panama, Training Becomes Reality" (154th Signal Battalion)," *Soldiers.*

Branigan, William, "Rebel Base on Border Blown Up After Three-Week Battle," *Washington Post* (June 26, 1987): 13-14.

Brock, David, "Washington's Long Tolerance Turns into day of Reckoning," *Insight* (January, 1990): 26-28.

Canan, James W., "To Command, You Must Control," *Air Force Magazine* (July 1990): 40-41.

Cantelou, Captain Campbell, "Jumping into a 'JUST CAUSE'," *Army Communicator* (Winter/Spring 1990): 6-11.

"Civil Affairs in *Operation Just Cause*," *Special Warfare* (Winter 1991): 28–37

"Combat Planning Dominates Panama's Communications," *Signal* (March 1990): 95.

"Defense Forum: Laurel to SAC, and Volunteerism Lives," *Armed Forces Journal International* (April 1990): 8.

"Diario Libre de Panama, 20 De Deciembre De 1989: Documentos Para LaHistoria," *La Prensa*, printed as special supplement to the *Miami Herald.*

Donnelly, Tom, "Precision and Professionalism Mark Invasion," *Army Times* (January 15, 1990): 11, 14.

Donnelly, Tom, "With so many weapons…," *Army Times* (January 8, 1990): 7.

Douglas, Col. William A., "Panama, JUST CAUSE Demonstrates Teamwork," *Commando* (January 26, 1990): 2.

DuDney, Robert S., "Low Intensity, High Priority," *Air Force Magazine* (June 1990): 30-34.

Eggers, Maj. Gen. Thomas E., "Today's Air Commandos: Air Force Special Operations Command," *Military Review* (June 1991): 14-21.

Excerpts from Pentagon Briefing, *DOD Early Bird* (from the *Washington Post*) (December 21, 1989): A2-A4.

Feldman, Linda, "U.S. Rethinks Plan to Oust Noriega," *Christian Science Monitor*

(August 28, 1989): 7.

Fulgham, David, "AF Special Ops Gunships Go into Action," *Air Force Times* (January 15, 1990): 60.

Fulgham, David, "Two Stealth Fighters Lead Attack," *Air Force Times* (January 15, 1990): 14-16.

"General Meyers (Dir DISA) Describes Panama Efforts," *Signal* (April 1990): 85.

Geraci, AIC Joe, "Commander (CINCSOC) Welcomes Troops Home," *Commando* (January 19, 1990): 1.

Geraci, AIC Joe, " JUST CAUSE not without Bitter Moments,"*Commando* (January 19, 1990): 1.

Ginovsky, John, "A-7s Took Hostile Fire in Air-Support Mission," *Air Force Times* (January 15, 1990): 15.

Ginovsky, John, "Three Hundred-Plus Airlift Mission Flown," *Air Force Times* (January 15, 1990): 60.

Hamilton, Martha M., "Canal Closing Underscores U.S. Concern," *DOD Early Bird* (from the *Washington Post)*, (December 21,1989): A5, A6.

Hughes, David, "Night Airdrop In Panama Surprises Noriega's Forces," *Aviation Week & Space Technology* (January 1, 1990) 30-31.

Hughes, David, "Night Invasion of Panama Required Special Operations Aircraft, Training," *Aviation Week & Space Technology* (February 19, 1990): 61-62.

"In the Line of Duty," *Army Times* (January 8, 1990): 12, 14, 16.

Jenks, Sgt. Robert, "*Operation Just Cause*: Marines Participate in Combat Against Panamanian Defense Forces," *Continental Marine* (March 1990): 4-5.

Johnson, General H.T., " 'Airlift for the Next 'JUST CAUSE', " *Air Force Magazine* (June 1990): 42-46.

Kingston, Jack A., "U.S. Military Support Group - Panama," *SO/LIC News Letter*, 2, no. 1: 3.

Lavigne, Sgt. Barbara, "Chickens Join Brave Men in Panama," *Commando* (January 19, 1990): 3.

Longo, James, and Elizabeth Donovan, "Panamanians welcome Marines," *Navy Times* (January 8, 1990) 6, 8.

Manegold, C. S. , "A Standoff in Panama," *Newsweek* (January 8, 1990): 28-30.

Maraniss, David, "*UPRIGHT and DIGNIFIED*, San Antonio Military Doctors Conduct

Largest Operation Since Vietnam," *Washington Post* (Dec. 22, '89): A17-A18.

Maraniss, David, "The Wounds of War," *Washington Post* (January 9, 1990, the Health Section,): 12-15.

"Marines in Panama," *Marine Corps Gazette* (February 1990): 4.

McClintock, John M., "Ex-troops Consider Attack on Noriega, Sources Say," *Baltimore Sun* (August 28, 1989): 4.

Miles, Donna, "Panama - A Real-Life Mission Helping Real-Life People," *Soldiers* (April 1990): 6-9.

Morrocco, John D., "F-117A Fighter Used in Combat for First Time in Panama," *Aviation Week & Space Technology* (January 1, 1990): 32-33.

"On the Line," (photo essay), *Air Force Times* (January 8, 1990): 8.

Nelson, Soraya S., "Wounded recall Panama action," *Army Times* (Jan. 8, 1990): 16.

"Panama: *Operation Just Cause*, Part I," *DOD Early Bird* (Special Edition), (Feb. 1990), (Compilation of 66 news articles dating 18 Dec. '89 - 27 Jan. '90.)

"Panama: *Operation Just Cause*, Part II." *DOD Early Bird* (Special Edition), (February 1990), (Compilation of 72 print media editorials dating from 21 December 1989 through 14 January 1990.)

"Panama says U.S. is Planning to Invade," *Washington Times* (August 28, 1989): 10.

"Panama Works to Restore Civil Aviation Operations," *Aviation Week & Space Technology* (January 1, 1990): 33.

"Panamanians Work to Restore Airline, Airport Services," *Aviation Week & Space Technology* (January 29, 1990):70-71.

Parker, Hayden, "Operation Just Cause," *Balance* (March/April 1990): 14-21.

Preston, Julia, "Contras Shoot Down Nicaraguan Helicopters, Lose Border Airstrip," *Washington Post* (June 26, 1987): 13-14.

Rhodes, Jeffrey P., "Special Operations Live," *Air Force Magazine* (June 1990): 36-41.

Ropelewski, Robert R., "Planning, Precision, and Surprise Led to Panama Successes," *Armed Forces Journal International* (February 1990): 25-32.

Roth, Margaret, "Nothing is easy for the families...," *Army Times* (Jan. 8, 1990): 8, 16.

Roth, Margaret, "Panama: an attack plan for the future," *Army Times* (January 8, 1990): 10, 15.

Scarborough, Rowan, "Controversial Night Goggles Hailed in Panama Offensive,"

Washington Times, January 15, 1990): 5, 10.
Scicchitano, J. Paul, "On Patrol: Panama," *Army Times* (January 8, 1990): 6-8, 18.

Schilling, Captain (P) Anthony M., "Force Protection: Military Police Experience in Panama," *Military Review* (March 1991): 19.

Sheehan, Daniel M., "AFA/AEF REPORT: Association Jointness," *Air Force Magazine* (June 1990): 100.

Sheehan, Daniel M., "Total Force Showcase," *Air Force Magazine* (September 1990): 96, 99.

Simpson, Ross W., "Reconnaissance in Force: Marine LAV Crews in Panama Combat Role," *Amphibious Warfare Review* (Summer 1990): 72-78.

"Sowing Dragon's Teeth," *Time*, (January 1, 1990): 24-27.

Steele, Dennis, "*Operation Just Cause*," *Army* (February 1990): 34-44.

Stiner, General Carl W., "The Strategic Employment of Special Operations Forces," *Military Review* (June 1991): 2-13.

"'Surgical Firepower' Trashed Noriega Post, Hurlburt Field, Fla.," *Washington Times* (January 11, 1990): 6.

"Tactical C4I: On Noriega's Tracks," *Signal* (April 1990): 20.

"Target Noriega: The Invasion of Panama," *Newsweek* (January 1, 1990): 12-27.

Text of President Bush's Address, *DOD Early Bird* (from the *Washington Post*) (December 21, 1989): A-1.

Transcript of President Bush's Press Conference, *DOD Early Bird* (from the *Washington Post*) (December 22, 1989): A1-A3.

"The Tunner Award," *Air Force Magazine* (September 1990): 80, 83.

"These are the FACs, on the Ground and in the Air," *Airman* (April 1990): 10-19.

Tropic Times, Daily Newspaper of the U.S. Southern Command, published in Panama primarily for the American military community. Compiled from a range of news wire services and other print media. (All editions from June 12, 1987 through February 2, 1990.)

"U.S. Army Special Operations Command (Airborne)," *The Drop* (Feb. 1990): 20.

"U.S. Reported Airlifting Troops to Panama Base," *Washington Post* (20 December 1989): A1, A32.

Vuono, General Carl E., "Panama 'Validated' Six Imperatives Shaping Today's

Army," *Army*, (February 1990): 11-12.
Waller, Douglas, "Inside the Invasion," *Newsweek* (June 25, 1990): 28-31.

Wenzel, Tracey, "Special-Ops Credited with Noriega Pursuit," (Interview with General Lindsay, Commander, U.S. Special Operations Command), *Northwest Florida Daily News* (January 12, 1990): 1A, 8A.

"When to get out of Panama," *U.S. News & World Report* (Jan. 8, 1990): 20-23.

Witt, Ann J., "MEDIC," *Defense* (September 1989): 688-89, 693.

Yates, Dr. Lawrance A., "Joint Task Force Panama, JUST CAUSE - Before and After," *Military Review* (October, 1991): 58-71.

PERIODICALS

As previously stated, this listing is presented in two versions. The *ALPHA* version, presented above, lists the material alphabetically by author. The *BRAVO* version, which follows, groups the material by periodical and presents it in chronological order by publication date.

BRAVO VERSION

PERIODICALS - LISTED CHRONOLOGICALLY BY DATE PUBLISHED

WASHINGTON POST, 26 June 1987, *Contras Shoot Down Nicaraguan Helicopters, Lose Border Airstrip*, Julia Preston, (Pages 13-14).

WASHINGTON POST, 26 June 1987, *Rebel Base on Border Blown Up After Three-Week Battle*, William Branigan, (Pages 13-14).

CHRISTIAN SCIENCE MONITOR, *U.S. Rethinks Plan to Oust Noriega*, Linda Feldman, August 28, 1989, (Page 7).

WASHINGTON TIMES, *Panama says U.S. is planning to invade*, (AP), August 28, 1989, (Page 10).

BALTIMORE SUN, *Ex-troops consider attack on Noriega, sources say*, John M. McClintock, August 28, 1989, (Page 4).

WASHINGTON POST, 20 December 1989, *U.S. Reported Airlifting Troops to Panama Base* (Reuter) (Pages A1, A32).

TROPIC TIMES, Daily Newspaper of the U.S. Southern Command, published in Panama primarily for the American military community. Compiled from a range of news wire services and other print media. (*All editions from June 12, 1987 through February 2, 1990*).

Special Edition: DOD Early Bird - CURRENT NEWS, Feb. 1990, No. 1827, *Panama: OPERATION Just Cause, PART 1.* (Compilation of 66 Newspaper articles dating from 18 December 1989 through 27 January 1990).

Special Edition: DOD Early Bird - CURRENT NEWS, February 1990, No. 1828, *Panama; Operation Just Cause PART II.* (Compilation of 72 Print Media Editorials dating from 21 December 1989 through 14 January 1990).

DOD NEWS BRIEFING, Secretary of Defense Dick Cheney & General Colin Powell, Chairman JCS, at the Pentagon Wednesday, Dec. 20, 1989 - 7:45 AM -Office of the Assistant Secretary of Defense (Public Affairs) (10 Pages).

DOD NEWS BRIEFING, by Lt. General T.W. Kelley, U.S.A, Director of Operations, Joint Staff, Thursday (Wednesday), December 20, - 4:40 PM (11 Pages).

DOD Early Bird - CURRENT NEWS - SUPPLEMENT: Thursday, December 21, 1989, *NEWS OPINION*:
- Article: *Washington Post*, December 21, 1989, TEXT OF PRESIDENT BUSH's ADDRESS (Page A-1) (AP).
- Article: *Washington Post*, December 21, 1989, EXCERPTS FROM PENTAGON BRIEFING (Pages A2-A4).
- Article: *Washington Post*, December 21, 1989, Canal Closing Underscores U.S. Concern, Martha M. Hamilton, (Pages A5-A6).

DOD Early Bird - CURRENT NEWS - SUPPLEMENT: Friday, December 22, 1989, NEWS OPINION:
- Article: *Washington Post*, December 22, 1989 TRANSCRIPT OF PRESIDENT BUSH's PRESS CONFERENCE. (Pages A1- A3) (AP).
- Article: *Washington Post*, December 22, 1989, "UPRIGHT and DIGNIFIED" San Antonio Military doctors Conduct Largest Operation, Since Vietnam., David Maraniss. (Pages A17-A18).

DOD Early Bird: CURRENT NEWS: SUPPLEMENT: Tuesday, March 6, 1990, *ARMY TIMES*, March 12, 1990, The Architect of "JUST CAUSE", Lt. Gen. Carl Stiner, explains his Panama plan. Interview - Pages B4-B8).

WASHINGTON POST HEALTH, January 9, 1990, *The WOUNDS OF WAR*, David Maraniss. (Pages 12-15).

WASHINGTON TIMES, 11 January 1990, *'Surgical firepower' trashed Noriega post*, Hurlburt Field, Fla (AP), (Page 6).

NORTHWEST FLORIDA DAILY NEWS, 12 January 1990, *Special Ops Credited with Noriega pursuit*, Tracey Wenzel, Pages 1A, 8A (Interview with General Lindsay, Commander, U.S. Special Operations Command).

WASHINGTON TIMES, 15 January 1990, Article: *Controversial night goggles hailed in Panama offensive, Rowan Scarborough* (Pages 5, 10).

INSIGHT, January 1990, WORLD - PANAMA, *Washington's Long Tolerance Turns into day of Reckoning*, David Brock, (Pages 26-28).

The Story of the 1989 U.S. Intervention into Panama

Amphibious WARFARE REVIEW, Summer 1990, Feature: *RECONNAISSANCE IN FORCE (Marine LAV Crews in Panama Combat role)*, Ross W. Simpson, (Pages 72-78).

CONTINENTAL MARINE, March 1990, Camp Lejeune, PAO: *Operation Just Cause: Marines participate in combat against Panamanian Defense Forces*, Sgt Robert Jenks, (Pages 4-5).

MARINE CORPS GAZETTE, February 1990: NEWS: *Marines in Panama*, (Page 4).

NAVY TIMES, 8 January 1990: *Panamanians welcome Marines*, James Longo & Elizabeth Donovan. (Pages 6, 8).

U/I Marine publication, Panama: *MARINES: TRAINING AND PATIENCE PAY OFF*, CWO-3 C.W. Rowe.

ARMY TIMES, January 8, 1990:

- On Patrol: Panama, (Stories) J.Paul Scicchitano, (Pages 6-8, 18).
- With so many weapons..., Tom Donnelly, (Page 7).
- Nothing is easy for the families..., Margaret Roth, (Pages 8, 16).
- Panama: an attack plan for the future, Margaret Roth, (Pages 10, 15).
- In the line of duty, (Biographies of 18 Army fatalities) (Pages 12, 14, 16).
- Wounded recall Panama action, Soraya S. Nelson, (Page 16).

ARMY Magazine, August 1990, (Pages 23-24), Army helicopter review (Sic).

ARMY Magazine, February 1990:

- Front & Center, General Carl E. Vuono: *Panama 'Validated' 6 Imperatives Shaping Today's Army*, (ECL) (Pages 11-12).
- *Army Light Infantry Weapons In Panama*: A Foreign Profile, (ECL), (Pages 12-13).
- *Operation Just Cause*, Dennis Steele, (Pages 34-44).

ARMY TIMES, January 15, 1990:

- Precision and Professionalism mark invasion, Tom Donnelly, (pp. 11, 14).
- Army aims for highly mobile forces, Caleb Baker, (Page 25).

AIR FORCE TIMES, January 8, 1990, Special Report: Air Force Over Panama:

- Photo Essay: *On the Line* (Page 8).
- *The Air Force Role in Panama.*
- *2 Stealth fighters lead attack, David Fulgham*, (Pages 14-16).
- *A-7s took hostile fire in air-support mission, John Ginovsky* (Page 15).
- *300-plus airlift mission flown, John Ginovsky* (Page 60).
- *AF special ops gunships go into action, David Fulghum*, (Page 60).

AIR FORCE TIMES, January 15, 1990, COVER STORY: *After Panama - MAC in for the long haul*, Julie Bird, (Pages 14-15 & 68).

AIR FORCE MAGAZINE, publication of the Air Force Association (AFA), Mar.

'90, *Aerospace World*, J.P. Rhodes, Aeronautics Editor (Summary of Aviation activities by USAF Commands by aircraft type & Army - AH-64 Apaches).

AIR FORCE MAGAZINE, publication of the Air Force Assoc. (AFA), June 1990:
- AFA/AEF REPORT: *Association Jointness*, Daniel M. Sheehan (Page 100).
- *Airlift for the Next Just Cause*, General H.T. Johnson, USAF (Pages 42-46).
- *Special Operations Live*, Jeffrey P. Rhodes, (Pages 36-41).
- *Low Intensity - High Priority*, Robert S. DuDney, (Pages 30-34).

AIR FORCE MAGAZINE, publication of the Air Force Association (AFA), July 1990, *To Command, You must Control*, James W. Canan, (Pages 40-41).

AIR FORCE Magazine, publication of the Air Force Association (AFA), Sept. 1990:
- *The Tunner Award* (Pages 80, 83) (AC-130 Support).
- *Total Force Showcase*, Daniel M. Sheehan (Pages 96, 99).

AIRMAN, internal information publication of the USAF, April 1990, *These are the FACs, on the Ground and in the Air*. (Pages 10-19) (Story of TAC Tactical Air Control Teams).

ARMED FORCES JOURNAL INTERNATIONAL, April 1990, Defense Forum: *Laurel to SAC, and Volunteerism Lives* (Air Force Reserve Crews) (Page 8).

ARMED FORCES JOURNAL INTERNATIONAL, February 1990, *Planning, Precision, and Surprise Led to Panama Successes*, Robert R. Ropelewski, (Pages 25-32).

AVIATION WEEK & SPACE TECHNOLOGY, January 1, 1990, Panama Invasion:
Night airdrop in Panama surprises Noriega's forces, David Hughes, (Page 30-31).
F-117A fighter Used in Combat For First Time in Panama, John D. Morrocco, (Page 32-33).
Panama Works to restore Civil Aviation Operations, (Page 33).

AVIATION WEEK & SPACE TECHNOLOGY, January 29, 1990, *Panamanians work to restore Airline, Airport Services*, David Hughes (Page 70-71).

AVIATION WEEK & SPACE TECHNOLOGY, February 19, 1990, *Night Invasion of Panama Required Special Operations Aircraft*, Training, David Hughes, (Page 61-62).

BALANCE, Periodic Publication, March/April 1990, Article: *Operation Just Cause*, Hayden Parker, (Pages 14-21) (Medical Support).

DEFENSE, September 1989, Article "*MEDIC*", Ann J. Witt, (Pages 688, 689, 693).

COMMANDO,... Weekly Base Paper, 1st USAF Special Operations Wing, Hurlburt Field, Florida, January 19, 1990:

- Article: *Commander (CINCSOC) Welcomes Troops Home*, AIC Joe Geraci, (Page 1).
- Article: *JUST CAUSE not without bitter moments*, AIC Joe Geraci, (p. 1).
- Article: *Chickens join brave men in Panama*, Sgt Barbara Lavigne, (p. 3

COMMANDO,... Weekly Base Paper, 1st USAF Special Operations Wing, Hurlburt Field, Florida, January 26, 1990.
- Article: Panama, *JUST CAUSE demonstrates teamwork*, Col. William A. Douglas (p. 2).

The DROP, (18th Airborne Corps Publication), Feb. 1990: Page 20, Article & Sidebar; *U.S. Army Special Operations Command (Airborne) (SOF Oper.)*.

LA PRENSA, (In Spanish), Diario Libre de Panama, 20 De Diciembre De 1989: *Documentos Para La Historia*. (Printed as special supplement to *Miami Herald*).

MILITARY REVIEW, Journal of the U.S. Army, January 1990:
- Article: U.S. Armed Forces PUBLIC AFFAIRS, *Roles in Low Intensity Conflict*, Lt Col. Alexander Angelle (Pages 50-56).

MILITARY REVIEW, Journal of U.S. Army, March 1991- JUST CAUSE:
- Article: JUST CAUSE and the Principles of War, LTC William C. Bennett, U.S.A (Page 2) (Force Planning).
- Article: Force Protection: Military Police Experience in Panama, Captain (P) Anthony M. Schilling. U.S.A (p. 19) (Military Police Operations).

MILITARY REVIEW, Journal of U.S. Army, October 1991:
- Article: Joint Task Force Panama, JUST CAUSE - Before and After. Dr. Lawrance A. Yates, Combat Studies Institute, U.S. Army Command and General Staff College, (Pages 58-71)

MILITARY REVIEW, Journal of the U.S. Army, June 1991:
- Article: The Strategic Employment of Special Operations Forces, General Carl W. Stiner, U.S. Army, (Pages 2-13).
- Article: Today's Air Commandos: Air Force Special Operations Command, Major General Thomas E. Eggers, USAF, (Pages 14-21).

Draft White Paper, submitted for security review prior to publication, o/a March/April 1992, *PLANNING, Operation Just Cause, December 1989*, Dr. Lawrance A. Yates, Combat Studies Institute, U.S. Army Command and General Staff College (12 Pages).

ARMY COMMUNICATOR, Publication of the U.S. Army Signal Corps, Fort Gordon GA., PB 11-90-1 Winter/Spring 1990 Volume 15 Number 1:
- Article: *Jumping into a "JUST CAUSE"*, Capt. C. Cantelou, (pp. 6-11).
- Article: *Lightfighter communications in Operation Just Cause*, Lt. Col. T. Armeli, (Pages 48-52).

SIGNAL, Publication of AFCEA, Mar. 1990, *Combat Planning Dominates Panama's Communications*, (Page 95) (Communications planning with a joint perspective).

SIGNAL, Publication of AFCEA, April 1990, *Tactical C4I: On Noriega's Tracks*, (Page 20).

SIGNAL, Publication of AFCEA, April 1990, *General Meyers (Dir DISA) Describes Panama efforts, Industry Forecast* (Page 85).

SOLDIERS, U.S. Army Publication,... Article: *Panama, Training Becomes Reality (154th Signal Battalion)*, Special Bob Blocher, PAO office U.S. Army South, Fort Clayton, Panama. (Communications Support).

SOLDIERS, U.S. Army Publication, April 1990, Article: *Panama - A Real Life Mission Helping real-Life People*, Donna Miles, (Pages 6-9).

SO/LIC News Letter, Volume 2, Number 2, Page 3, PROFILE IN PROFESSIONALISM: Article; *U.S. Military Support Group - Panama*, by Jack A. Kingston.

SPECIAL WARFARE, Winter 1991, a Publication of the U.S. Army Special Warfare Center, Fort Bragg NC. Article: *Civil Affairs in Operation Just Cause* (Pages 28-37 plus background from pages 5, 9, 20, & 24).

TIME, January 1, 1990, *Sowing Dragon's Teeth*, (Page 24-27).

NEWSWEEK, Jan. 1, 1990, *Target Noriega: The Invasion of Panama* (Pages 12-27).

NEWSWEEK, Jan. 8, 1990, *A Standoff in Panama*, C.S. Manegold, (Pages 28-30).

U.S. NEWS & WORLD REPORT, Jan. 8. 1990, *When to get out of Panama* (pp. 20-23).

NEWSWEEK: June 25, 1990, *Inside the Invasion*, Douglas Waller, (Pages 28-31).

BOOKS

TIME-LIFE Books, The New Face of War Series, SKY SOLDIERS Volume, Chapter 5 Combat Jump into Panama, (Pages 126-153) Focus: Review of Airborne Operations by 82nd ABD.

TIME-LIFE Books, The New Face of War Series, COMMANDO OPERATIONS Volume, Chapter 4 - An Auspicious Comeback in Panama, (Pages 111-153) Focus: Review of Special Operations

JUST CAUSE: (THE REAL STORY OF AMERICA'S HIGH-TECH INVASION OF PANAMA), Malcolm McConnell, St Martin's Press, 1991, New York. Focus: The operational sequence of events of 19/20 Dec. 1989 from a participant's view.

OPERATION JUST CAUSE: (THE STORMING OF PANAMA), Thomas Donnelly, Margaret Roth, Caleb Baker, Lexington Books, (Macmillan, Inc.), 1991, New York, NY. Focus: Presents events from a Washington high level Army perspective beginning in August/October 1989 then moves into tactical details of operations 20/21 December 1989.

The Story of the 1989 U.S. Intervention into Panama

OPERATION JUST CAUSE: (Panama, December 1989), A Soldier's Eyewitness Account), 1st Lieutenant Clarence E. Briggs III, U.S.A, Stackpole Books, Harrisburg, PA. Focus: Operations of 82nd ABD Battalion in vicinity of Colon.

THE COMMANDERS, (Chapter 12), Bob Woodward, Simon & Schuster, 1991, New York (Pages 132-145) (Focuses on the higher level, inside the beltway, political perspective of events leading to Operation).

PANAMA: (The Whole Story), Kevin Buckley, Simon & Schuster, 1991, New York (295 Pages). Focus: Compiled beginning in 1987 captures flavor of the political-economic events in Panama that formed the basis for unrest in Panama.

THE BATTLE FOR PANAMA: Inside *Operation Just Cause*, Edward Flanagan, Brassey, 1993, Mc Lean VA. (251 Pages) Focus: Compiled from an Army - XVIII Airborne Corps Perspective, puts major emphasis on events after October 1989, includes good picture of Ranger operations at Rio Hato.

AMERICA'S PRISONER: The Memoirs of Manuel Noriega, Manuel Noriega and Peter Eisner, Random House, 1997, New York (293 Pages) Focus: A relatively objective but slightly slanted defense of Manuel Noriega, seeded with an indictment of American senior officials in the Bush administration and their objectives, maneuvers and perceived motives.

MAPS, GRAPHIC AND PHOTO SOURCES

Pamphlet: *Maps of the U.S. Military Installations in Panama*, an Army Community Service Publication, Corozal, Panama.

Pamphlet: *The Panama Canal*, a pictorial map, Panama Canal Commission, Director of Public Affairs, Panama.

Joint Operations Graphic (JOG) Scale 1:250,000, DMA Series 1501, Sheets NC 17-11, NC 17-12, NC 17-15, NC 17-16 (Map Information 1968).

Panama City Graphic Scale 1:20,000 DMA Series E965X Panama, Sheet 1 and Sheet 2 (Map information date 1974).

Panama (City Area), Scale 1:50,000 DMA Series E 762x Sheets 4242 I, 4243 II, 4343 III (1977).

Pina Training Area (Colon Area) Scale 1:50,000 DMAHTC Composite of Sheets 4134 I, 4244 III, 4243 IV, 4143 II, 4243 III, Compiled in 1964, Updated 1977, reprinted 2/90.

Empire Area Scale 1:50,000 DMA Composite Sheets 4242I and 4243 II (undated circa 1964-77).

Alcalde Diaz, Scale 1:50,000 (Cerro Tigre/Gamboa/Tinajitas) DMS Series E762x Sheets 4243 II and 4243 III (1977).

Pedregal, Scale 1:50,000 (Torrijos/Tocumen) DMA Sheets 4343 III (1968/84/88).

Panama City Graphic, Scale 1:12,500, printed as DMA Series E962 Edition 1, (1984), compiled by Panamanian Instituto Geographic Nacional "Tommy Guardia" IGNTG (Sheets 1, 2, 3, 4 & 5 - 1984).

DMA Limited Edition (Red Light Readable) Composite Planning Graphic, Series of composite strip and locale maps printed front & back on single sheet. Frontside: Upper Half - Gamboa to Panama City, Lower Half - Panama Canal to Atlantic Scale 1:50,000. Backside: Scale 1:12,500, Panama City and Vicinity.

OPERATION Just Cause, Composite Pictorial Map Graphic (U.S. ARMY Center for Military History - CMH 70-33).

Panama Composite Country Graphic - CIA Series 50427 (545665) July 1981.

Land and Waters of the Panama Canal Treaty Scale 1:250,000 CIA Series 801067 (543418) Oct 81.

VIDEO SOURCES

Videotape reflecting Psychological Operations conducted during JUST CAUSE, under cover of Memorandum from Executive Officer, 4th PSYOP Group, Subject: JUST CAUSE, dated 2 July 1990.

AC-130 LLTV/INFRARED Video Footage, Compiled by USAF 1st Special Operations Wing with verbal summary of Battle Damage Assessment.

PHOTOGRAPHY SOURCES

Private collection of Master Sergeant Edgar E. Castro, USAF Security Police, Howard AFB., RP (December 1989-January 1990).

Private collection of Robert R. Ropelewiski, (Staff member *Armed Forces Journal*), (December 1989-January 1990).

Private collection of author (1985-1992).

GLOSSARY OF TERMS AND ABBREVIATIONS

NCA - *National Command Authorities* - The national level leadership responsible for the development, approval and execution of national security policy. The NCA consists of the President, the Secretary of State, and the Secretary of Defense. The employment of United States military forces is typically proposed by either the Secretary of State or the Secretary of Defense, with military advice provided by the Chairman of the Joint Chiefs of Staff. The President is the approving authority. Based on a Presidential approval or directive, the Secretary of Defense approves the release of the execution order (typically an electronic message) and the Chairman of the JCS communicates the order.

JCS - *Joint Chiefs of Staff* - The formal title of the chiefs of the four military services when they are operating in their joint-corporate role as the senior United States military deliberation body. The members of the JCS are the Chiefs of Staff of the Army and the Air Force, the Chief of Naval Operations and the Commandant of the Marine Corps and the Chairman of this corporate body, the senior American military officer on active duty.

CJCS - *Chairman of the Joint Chiefs of Staff* - The formal title of the Presidentially selected senior military officer of the United States Armed Forces. The CJCS, the designated military advisor to the President, in partnership with the Secretary of Defense, the Secretary of State and the President constitute the National Command Authorities (NCA). Within this context of civilian control, all major force deployments outside of the United States are authorized by the Secretary of Defense and communicated by the Chairman to the Unified Commands and Military Services through the JCS Staff, formally titled Office of the Joint Chiefs of Staff.

OJCS - *Office of the Joint Chiefs of Staff* (also referred to as the *Joint Staff*) - This group of officers, enlisted personnel and civilians develop policy, review plans, monitor resources and coordinate action in support of and between the Joint Commands and the Military Service staffs. The Joint Staff is organized along traditional staff functions - J1 Personnel, J3 Operations, J4 Logistics, J5 Plans, J6 Communications, etc., with the exception that the Defense Intelligence Agency acts as the J2 and provides intelligence support.

Unified Command - Term applied to a joint theater-level, i.e., geographic command, or a national level joint functional command of the United States Armed Forces. There are five Unified Theater Commands - European, Pacific, Atlantic, Southern (Latin America), and Central Command (Southwest Asia/Middle East). In addition, there are four national-level joint Commands - the Transportation Command, the Strategic Command, the Space Command, and the Special Operations Command. Each is composed of combat and support elements from two or more of the Military Services (Departments) - Army, Navy, Air Force, and Marine Corps. These entities are referred to as "component commands or service component commands."functional command.

United States Southern Command (SOUTHCOM) - This command, headquartered at Quarry Heights just outside of Panama City until 1998, is responsible for guaranteeing the security of the Panama Canal. In addition, it is responsible for managing and coordinating American military assistance and training programs throughout Latin America, and pursuing other political and military policies and objectives as defined by the National Command Authorities and the Joint Chiefs of Staff. As a unified force Commander, the Commander of SOUTHCOM has the authority to create a joint task force (JTF) or a joint special operations task force (JSOTF) to meet specific requirements within the Command's area of responsibility.

Joint Task Force//Joint Special Operations Task Force - Typically, a Joint (or special operations) Task Force is created from within the service forces assigned to the command. These service forces are referred to as component forces. The SOUTHCOM components included U.S. Army South (USARSOUTH), 12th Air Force (USAF SOUTH) and Naval Forces South (NAVSOUTH). In addition, SOUTHCOM, as the other unified theater commands (e.g., Pacific, Europe, etc.), have a small special operations joint staff that can provide the nucleus of a Joint Special Operations Task Force (JSOTF). This staff is known as Special Operation Command South (SOCSOUTH) and had only one service component permanently assigned – the 3rd Battalion of the 7th Special Force Group. Other special operations forces required for a JSOTF would be provided by the United States Special Operations Command (USSOCOM).

Special Operations Forces (SOF) - An umbrella term used to identify a segment of the United States military force structure, regardless of military service, which has been designated, trained and equipped to carry out a range of missions not normally assigned to the conventional forces. The Army, Navy and Air Force have forces trained, equipped and designated as special operations forces. Special operations forces include Army Special Forces personnel, Army Ranger and helicopter units, Navy SEALs and Special Boat Units, Air Force Special Operations transports (C-130s) and Special Tactics Squadrons as well as Army and Air Force Psychological and Civil Affairs units. As of the late 1980s, virtually all special operations forces were assigned to the United States Special Operation Command that was activated in 1987.

Contingency Forces - A general term typically applied to military forces not "owned" by a specific unified command. Certain of these forces may be "earmarked" and trained to operate in specific theater of operations or may be a quick reaction "fire brigade" that can be employed almost anywhere in support of any Unified Command or JTF or JSOTF as the mission, availability and skills dictate. Examples include the XVIII Airborne Corps, or an afloat Marine Air-Ground Task Force.

ABBREVIATIONS

AA	Anti-Aircraft
ABCCC	Airborne Command, Control, Communications
ASP	Ammunition Supply Point
ATP	Ammunition Transfer Point
ATV	All-Terrain Vehicle
CA	Civil Affairs
CCP	Casualty Collection Point
CCV	Contingency Communications Vehicle
CMO	Civil Military Operations
CMOTF	Civil Military Operations Task Force
CRRC	Combat Ready Raiding Craft
DENI	Department of National Investigations
DNTT	Department of Transportation in Panama
DRB	Division Ready Brigade
DZ	Drop Zone
EDRE	Emergency Deployment Readiness Exercise
EPW	Enemy Prisoner of War
EW	Electronic Warfare
FAC	Forward Air Controllers
FAP	Panamanian Air Force
FARP	Forward Arming and Refueling Point
FAST	Fleet Anti-Terrorist Security Team
HMMWV	High-Mobility, Multipurpose Wheeled Vehicle
JCCC	Joint Communications Control Center
JCCP	Joint Casualty Collection Point
JCEOI	Joint Communications Electronic Operating Instructions
JCS	Joint Chiefs of Staff
JSOC	Joint Special Operations Command
JSOTF	Joint Special Operations Task Force
JTF	Joint Task Force
LAI	Light Amphibious Infantry
LAV	Light Assault Vehicle
LCM	Landing Craft Medium
LZ	Landing Zone
MAC	Military Airlift Command
MOUT	Military Operations in Urban Terrain
MRTE	Medical Readiness Training Exercises
NAVSO	U.S. Navy South (also abreviated as USNAVSOUTH)
NAVSOUTH	U.S. Navy South (also abreviated as USNAVSO)
NCA	National Command Authorities
NCS	National Communications System
NEO	Noncombatant Evacuation Operation

OP	Observation Post
PCC	Panama Canal Commission
PSYOP	Psychological Operations
PSYOP HB	Psychological Operations Handheld Broadcast
RAPEL	Rural Area Police Element
RATV	Rescue All Terrain Vehicle
ROE	Rules of Engagement
RPG	Rocket Propelled Grenade
USAFSO	U.S. Air Force South
USAFSOUTH	U.S. Air Force South
USARSO	U.S. Army South
USARSOUTH	U.S. Army South
USNAVSOUTH	U.S. Naval Forces South (also abbreviatiated as NAVSO)
USSOUTHCOM	U.S. Southern Command
SOF	Special Operations Forces
SOUTHCOM	Southern Command
STS	Special Tactics Squadron
TACSAT	Tactical Satellite
TCC	Tele-Communications Center
TCP	Tactical Control Point
TF	Task Force
TOC	Tactical Operations Center

View from Quarry Heights of new Panamanian housing in Chorillo Barrio with Panama Bay in background. Photo courtesy of the author.

INDEX

ABOUT THE AUTHOR

The author served 32 years in the United States Armed Forces, beginning with five years in the enlisted ranks and retiring in 1988 at the rank of Colonel. Half of his career (16 years) was spent in joint (multi-service) assignments giving him an exceptional perspective. His joint tours (MACV 67/68, NATO 68-71, U.S. Readiness Command 76-79, OJCS 79-82, and U.S. Southern Command 86-87) were as varied as his Air Force service assignments, which included tours in USAFE, SAC, TAC and MAC.

The inspiration for this work was his long-term association with many of the force elements from all services that were involved in Operation *Just Cause*. His specific association with events in Central America and Panama in the 1980s added to this background. His last two active assignments, Director of Intelligence Operations, U.S. Southern Command, and Director of Intelligence, USAF Special Operations Command, provided him with an intimate and continuing knowledge of Panama and the evolution of Operation *Just Cause*.

This is his second major work. The first, published under the title *Crippled Eagle* (Narwhal Press, 1998), was an historical perspective of the evolution of U.S. Special Operations Forces from 1976 to 1996. It documented the decline in capabilities that contributed to the abort of the Iranian rescue mission in April 1980, provided details of the Iranian rescue effort and the subsequent tremendous rebuilding of U.S. special operations capabilities that came about as a result of Desert One. Without that rebirth Operation *Just Cause* and the subsequent Liberation of Kuwait (Operation *Desert Storm*) would have been substantially different and much more difficult.

Colonel Lenahan is currently working on a book about Francis Marion's partisan forces and their role in defeating the British forces in South Carolina in the last throes of the American Revolution. The lair of the elusive "Swamp Fox" has recently been rediscovered as well as some of his personal correspondence.